Women, States, and Nationalism

D0179378

In the post-Cold War era, nationalism has emerged as a major force in global politics. From Europe to Asia, and Africa to North America, women are central to the politics of nationalism, albeit in contradictory ways: as phantasmagorical, sexualized or maternal symbols that embody national identities and boundaries; as active participants in nationalist movements; and as victims of sexualized violence undertaken in defence of nationalist identities and boundaries. Yet, much contemporary scholarship persists in ignoring the significance of the gendered dimensions of nationalist politics.

Women, States, and Nationalism counters this attitude and examines the many and contradictory ways in which women negotiate their places in "the nation." The volume includes theoretical essays that explore the multiple ways in which the very concept of "nation" is based upon notions of family, sexuality, and gender power that are often overlooked or downplayed by "male-stream" scholarship. It gathers together an outstanding panel of feminist scholars and area studies specialists, who, through a series of focused case studies, analyze diverse issues which include:

- Gender and sectarian conflict in Northern Ireland
- The paradox of Israeli women soldiers
- Women, civic duty, and the military in the USA
- The Hindu Right in India
- Power, agency, and representation in Zimbabwe
- Political identity and heterosexism

This timely volume is a highly valuable resource for students and scholars of Nationalism, International Studies, and Women's Studies.

Sita Ranchod-Nilsson is Assistant Professor and Director of the International Studies Program at Denison University, Ohio, USA. She has published widely on women and politics in Zimbabwe.

Mary Ann Tétreault is Professor of Political Science at Iowa State University, USA. She has written and edited many books, including *Women and Revolution in Africa, Asia, and the New World*.

Women, States, and Nationalism

At home in the nation?

Edited by
Sita Ranchod-Nilsson
and Mary Ann Tétreault

London and New York

First published 2000 by Routledge
11 New Fetter Lane, London EC4P 4EE

Simultaneously published in the USA and Canada
by Routledge
29 West 35th Street, New York, NY 10001

Routledge is an imprint of the Taylor & Francis Group

Typeset in Baskerville by Florence Production Ltd,
Stoodleigh, Devon
Printed and bound in Great Britain by
TJ International Ltd., Padstow, Cornwall

British Library Cataloguing in Publication Data
A catalogue record for this book is available from the British Library

Library of Congress Cataloging in Publication Data
Women, states, and nationalism: at home in the nation?/
edited by Sita Ranchod-Nilsson and Mary Ann Tétreault.
    p.   cm.
  Includes bibliographical references and index.
  ISBN 0–415–22172–2   ISBN 0–415–22173–0 (pb)
  1. Women in politics.   2. Nationalism and feminism.   3. Women
in politics—Case studies.   4. Nationalism and feminism—Case
studies.   I. Ranchod-Nilsson, Sita, 1961–   II. Tétreault,
Mary Ann, 1942–
HQ1236.W6425 2000
305.42–dc21   99–088061

Contents

Plates

Contributors

Suresht R. Bald is a Professor of Politics at Willamette University, Oregon. She is the Author of *Novelists and Political Consciousness: Literary Expression of Indian Nationalism 1919–1947*, and has published extensively on the South Asian diaspora in Britain. Currently she is engaged in two projects: the discourse of weaving and the erasure of women in the Indian national narrative, and the place of gender in the "new" cultural politics in India.

Geeta Chowdhry is Associate Professor of Political Science at Northern Arizona University, Flagstaff, Arizona. Her research and teaching interests focus on Third World development, gender and development, international political economy (trade, environment, and structural adjustment), Comparative Politics, and South Asia. She is the author of many articles on gender and development. She is currently completing a manuscript entitled *Engendering Development? International Financial Institutions, the State and Women in the Third World.* She is also co-editing a volume entitled *Power in a Post-colonial World: Race, Gender and Class in International Relations.*

Zillah Eisenstein is Professor of Politics at Ithaca College and a feminist author and activist. Some of her most recent books are *The Color of Gender* (Univ. of California 1994), *Hatreds* (Routledge 1996), and *Global Obscenities* (NYU PRESS 1998). Presently she is completing a book, *Feminism from the Breast.*

Edna Levy received her Doctorate in Political Science from the University of California at Irvine in 1998. She has lived in Israel for six years and recently relocated to upstate New York, where she is Director of the Rochester Kollel, a center for Jewish learning.

Mary K. Meyer is Associate Professor of Political Science at Eckerd College, where she teaches courses relating to international relations, US foreign policy, inter-American relations, and women and politics. She co-edited *Gender Politics in Global Governance* (Rowman and Littlefield 1999), and has published articles on Latin American diplomacy in the

Central American peace processes and on the Inter-American commission of Women. Her current research focuses on gender politics in the
Northern Ireland peace process.

Haya al-Mughni earned her Ph.D. in Sociology from the University of
Exeter in Great Britain in 1990. She has since worked in various research
institutions in Kuwait as an independent researcher and consultant. Her
research interests, focusing on Kuwait, include gender and citizenship,
women's groups, social movements and social policy. She has published
numerous articles and contributed to a number of books on these
subjects. She is the author of *Women in Kuwait: The Politics of Gender*
(London: Saqi Books 1993).

V. Spike Peterson is Associate Professor of Political Science with
appointments in Women's Studies, Comparative Cultural and Literary
Studies, and International Studies at the University of Arizona. She is
the editor of *Gendered States: Feminist (Re)Visions of International Relations
Theory* (1992); and co-author (with Anne Sisson Runyan) of *Global Gender
Issues* (1999, 2nd edition). She has published numerous articles and chapters on feminist theory, gender and international relations. Peterson is
currently working on a book-length project, tentatively titled *Beyond
Sovereign Subjects: Rewriting (Global) Political Economy as Reproductive, Productive
and Virtual (Foucauldian) Economies*.

Linda Racioppi is Associate Professor of International Relations at James
Madison College, Michigan State University. She is the author of *Soviet
Policy towards South Asia since 1970*, co-author of *Women's Activism in
Contemporary Russia* (Temple University Press 1997), and articles on social
movements, gender, nationalism, Russian foreign policy and arms trans-
fers. Katherine O'Sullivan See and Linda Racioppi are currently
completing a book on gender and ethno-nationalism in Northern
Ireland.

Sita Ranchod-Nilsson is Assistant Professor in and Director of the
International Studies Program at Denison University in Granville, Ohio.
She has written numerous articles on women and politics in Zimbabwe.
She is currently working on a book manuscript entitled *Forward with
Our Cooking Sticks!: Gender, Liberation and Constructing the Nation in Zimbabwe*.
Her current research explores the impact of transnational organizations
on women's organizations in sub-Saharan Africa.

Katherine O'Sullivan See is Professor of Social Relations at James
Madison College, Michigan State University. She is the author of *First
World Nationalisms: Ethnic and Class Politics in Northern Ireland and Quebec*
(University of Chicago Press 1986), co-author of *Women's Activism in
Contemporary Russia* (Temple University Press 1997), and numerous
articles on nationalism, gender, social movements, social policy, and

race and ethnicity. Katherine O'Sullivan See and Linda Racioppi are currently completing a book on gender and ethno-nationalism in Northern Ireland.

Cheryl Logan Sparks received her Ph.D. in Political Science in 1996 from the University of North Carolina at Chapel Hill and previously taught political science and history at the Ohio State University and North Carolina State University. She now works with the Center for Democracy and Governance at the United States Agency for International Development, where she supervises the Center's internet and is also a member of the Women and Politics team. Her work has appeared in the *American Political Science Review*.

Mary Ann Tétreault is a Professor of Political Science at Iowa State University where she teaches courses on gender, international political economy, and Middle East politics. She is the author of four books dealing with international energy regimes and Middle East politics, including *Stories of Democracy: Politics and Society in Contemporary Kuwait*. She also has edited five volumes of essays on gender issues and international political economy.

1 Gender and nationalism

Moving beyond fragmented conversations

Sita Ranchod-Nilsson
and Mary Ann Tétreault

It is, by now, no great revelation that the post-Cold War world has seen a resurgence of nationalisms. The collapse of old political frameworks and the reconfiguration of global economic power have been accompanied by an impulse to redefine, (re)assert, and reconfigure meanings of the nation on multiple levels. Many of these definitions and metaphors are both gendered and sexual. In the former Yugoslavia, for example, the expression of what Zillah Eisenstein refers to as "new-old" national identities occurred in the context of mass rape (Eisenstein 1996; see also Allen 1996; Mia Bloom 1998; MacKinnon 1994). Meanwhile, in sub-Saharan Africa, the rush to characterize conflict in Rwanda in terms of "primordial ethnic identities" obscured both the economic underpinnings of the genocide and the sexualized violence that targeted women on both sides of the much-publicized Hutu–Tutsi ethnic divide (Block 1994). In the United States, too, the culture wars to determine contemporary meanings of "the nation" are being fought on the terrain of women's bodies and life circumstances. The national discourse on such issues as immigration, health care, and welfare reform is charting new national boundaries along the fault lines of gender, race, ethnicity, sexuality, and class (Eisenstein 1994; Fraser and Gordon 1994; Naples 1997).

In each of these cases, and in many others occurring elsewhere in the world, the centrality of gender to resurgent nationalist forces and discourses continues to be striking. The connections in nationalist movements between assertions of national identity and violence against women – sexualized violence as well as structural or economic violence – also is striking. These events have prompted extensive conversations among feminist scholars. The "new" cases did not seem to fit our understandings of nationalism, either those reflected in masculinist literatures which give scant attention to gender (e.g. Kaplan 1993; Moynihan 1993), or those recounted in some of the growing feminist literatures on nationalist movements and gendered discourses on "the nation" (e.g. see the chapters in Yuval-Davis and Anthias 1989).

In February 1995, we convened two panels at the annual meeting of the International Studies Association (ISA) in Chicago. The panels were designed to bring together feminist scholars who are writing about the multiple gender dimensions of resurgent nationalisms and those engaged in rethinking the gender dimensions of earlier nationalist movements in light of recent developments. Eight women from political science, history, and sociology presented papers that addressed gender and nationalism in a variety of contexts. Their contributions ranged from examinations of theoretical dilemmas to case studies highlighting women's involvement in nationalist movements and the centrality of gender to meanings of the nation in a variety of contemporary and historical settings. The comments of the discussants, historian Jane Parpart and political scientist Gita Chowdhry, along with the conversation among panelists and audience participants, were unusual in their continuity and coherence, and there was broad agreement on several points.

What emerged first from the conversation was a sense of frustration over the lack of engagement between "masculinist" writings on nationalism and recent feminist work. For, as Geoff Eley and Ronald Suny acknowledge, "we . . . need to consider the gendered dimensions and meanings of nationalist discourse more seriously, for this remains an astonishing absence in most of the scholarly literature, whether general or particular" (Eley and Suny 1996: 27). Language proved to be especially problematic in this conversation. To cast as "mainstream" or "orthodox" writings on nationalism by (mostly) white, male scholars who give scant attention either to women as actors within nationalist movements or to the gendered meanings inherent in ideologies of "the nation" is at once to relegate feminist scholarship on nationalism to the margins, privileging or reifying male domination within the realm of scholarly production, and also to accord undeserved primacy to analyses that are partial in a single distinctive way. Whereas feminist scholars attending the panels felt that they had actively engaged this masculinist literature – not only to criticize the neglect of women and gender concerns but also to challenge accepted meanings of basic conceptual categories such as "family," "nation," and "state" – there was little evidence that most of the men writing about nationalism had reciprocated (for notable exceptions, see Mosse 1985; Parker *et al.* 1992a; Sells 1996; Theweleit 1987). These oversights are particularly glaring in circumstances where women's active involvement in nationalist movements and nation-building practices has been well publicized, and the imagery of sexualized violence against women, such as in the genocidal rape campaigns in Bosnia and Rwanda, is impossible to ignore.

Second, despite the significant body of research produced by feminist scholars, a similar truncation of inquiry also can be seen in many feminist treatments of nationalism. This occurs in two ways. First, feminist scholarship on the role of women in nationalist movements challenges ideas about the location, form, and focus of nationalist politics through systematic empirical analyses (e.g. Geiger 1987; O'Barr 1976; Tétreault 1994). Other scholars tend to concentrate on theory, drawing attention to ways in which "the nation" is premised on particular gender identities and meanings (e.g. Hunt 1984; Mayhall 1993; Parker *et al.* 1992a; Taylor 1998; True 1993; Warner 1982; Yuval-Davis and Anthias 1989). Both types of studies of women's involvement in particular nationalist movements invariably reveal the shortcomings of these movements' commitments to women (Kruks *et al.* 1989; Seidman 1993; Tétreault 1994). Reading these accounts is depressing. The conclusion we come away with is that women do not reap long-term benefits as a result of their involvement in nation-building efforts. But there has to be more to the story: what issues and concerns motivate women's engagement in nationalist movements? Where do women express their political interests once their movements no longer are receptive to new demands? In what ways do culturally based meanings of the nation continue to be shaped by women's desires and needs, as well as those of men, once well-defined and bounded movements merge into the more amorphous processes of producing and reproducing culture?

A second pattern of truncated inquiry results when feminist scholarship on nationalism concentrates too much on whether nationalist movements are or are not feminist (e.g. West 1997). These analyses stop too soon, before they can engage fully with linkages between nationalist movements and other manifestations of political action and change. Having found evidence of gender hierarchies and the systems of dominance they underpin, their authors rarely go beyond their initial findings to examine class, caste, and other dimensions that cut across the categories defined primarily by gender and ethnicity. We discuss this problem in greater detail, with regard to not only feminist scholars but also others, in what follows below.

Finally, there was an overall sense of intellectual excitement generated by these conversations. The global resurgence of nationalism in all its forms, seen in light of recent feminist scholarship on identity, political movements, and the state, challenges us to push past ideological and disciplinary barriers and broaden the scope of scholarly work on nationalism. No serious scholar writing about nationalism today can ignore or marginalize the gender dimensions of nations – the theoretical insights and empirical evidence generated by feminist scholarship are too overwhelming. At the same time, to the extent that feminist scholarship is narrowly focused on analyses of gender representations and/or meanings, and engages in arguments about whether nationalist movements are "feminist" enough, the results are equally incomplete and unsatisfying. The conclusion of the panel was that our efforts must be directed toward broadening the ideological and substantive scope of feminist scholarship to deal with the very real material consequences of nationalist constructions for women's lives globally. While there is much to gain from undertaking scholarly work in the context of supportive communities that share both intellectual interests and an ethical perspective (such as the Feminist Theory and Gender Studies section of the ISA), the conversations sparked by these panels disclosed a strong desire to move beyond the comfortable confines of this intimate circle and take our work into a larger intellectual universe.

Feminist scholarship on nationalism

Much of the contemporary scholarship on nationalism focuses on the construction of identity and the conceptualization of social categories. Arguably, no contemporary body of work has done as much to question assumptions about social categories and reveal the complexities of identity construction as feminist scholarship. "The multiplicity, fluidity, contextual, and contested qualities of identities that studies of gender have highlighted have undermined any notion of a single all-embracing primary identity to which all others must be subordinated at all times and costs" (Eley and Suny 1996: 10). Feminist scholarship on nationalism challenges traditional assumptions, based on public–private dichotomies, about both the form and the location of politics (Gaitskell and Unterhalter 1989; Geiger 1987; Lazreg 1994; Longva 1997; Šiklová 2000; Tétreault 1993a). Feminist scholarship also has revealed multiple meanings of "the nation" – in terms of membership, boundaries, and origin myths – and the ways in which these meanings are permeated with notions of masculinity and femininity (see Elshtain 1992; Enloe 1993). Given the global and historical scope of this literature, as well as its conceptual insights, it is nothing short of startling that several recent works on nationalism give little more than token acknowledgement of these contributions (this view is echoed by Calhoun 1997; Eley and Suny 1996).

There is a large case study literature within feminist scholarship on women's involvement in nationalist movements. This work contained numerous insights about the social roots and political significance of nationalism. For example, women's active involvement in nationalist movements throughout the former colonial world raised questions about their status as citizens in the broader projects of modernizing states (Jayawardena 1986; Tétreault, 1994; Van Allen 1974), the location of politics in the so-called "public" sphere (Enloe 1993; Geiger 1990; Ranchod-Nilsson 1992a), and the gender dimensions of state power (Kruks *et al.* 1989). As we noted above, other feminist frameworks examined how women's issues or concerns are incorporated into nationalist movements and state politics, asking whether women are "used" by nationalist movements during periods of mobilization and political struggle only to be discarded or pushed to the margins during later periods of state consolidation (Park 1994; Stacey 1983; Tétreault 1994). However, ending simply by posing the dilemmas that arise from considering gender and nation in this way foreclosed promising routes of inquiry, including explorations of a more complex theorizing of the state that would move from women's participation in nationalist movements to address the gender dimensions of citizenship, sovereignty, and state power (e.g. Manicom 1992). For example, while arguments about the centrality of gender often are supported by evidence of the ways in which the family is the dominant trope in nationalist myths and ideologies, the nation-as-kinship model seldom is expanded far enough to include the many different kinds of kinship relations that impose obligations and also confer entitlements on various members of kin/national communities. Suad Joseph (2000) analyzes female citizens' entitlement claims as rooted in analogous entitlements by women occupying various kinship positions, not only in the narrow sense of kinship as blood relationship but also as claims made by women who assert quasi-kin relationships as the basis of these entitlements. A similar construction of claims underlay the "children of the people" strategy employed by members of the National Liberation Front (NLF) during the American war phase of the Vietnamese anti-colonial conflict. NLF guerrillas scattered throughout South Vietnamese villages referred to themselves and behaved as though they were the children of families in these communities. Their acts of filial obligation evoked protective responses by the villagers they lived with that shielded the guerrillas from government forces (Fitzgerald 1972). Other anti-colonial liberation movements such as the Zimbabwe African National Liberation Army also employed this strategy (Kriger 1992; Ranchod-Nilsson 1992b).

These examples show that nationality and citizenship are far more complex and internally differentiated concepts than they usually are represented as being. Although scholars often sketch "nation" and "state" as respectively horizontal and vertical social structures, this shorthand elides both the verticality of kin and nation and the egalitarian ethic of the modern state. The first embodies many unequal relationships – some of which, such as husband/wife, are templates for feminist criticism of family structure and family ideology. The second ignores the successes, however limited, of movements asserting republican equality as the basis on which excluded social groups press for equal protection under constitutionally mediated law. Consequently, the analytical utility of "nation" and "state" tends to be both limited and inconsistent (for an exception see Stevens 1999).

Feminist scholarship also has focused on the gender dimensions of cultural constructions of "the nation." This work looks at the social construction and shifting nature of gender identities and meanings, revealing multiple ways in which women are implicated in nationalist struggles that transcend particular social movements. In other words, the boundaries of "the nation" are always in flux as "insiders" and "outsiders" grapple for political power in ways that are not entirely reducible to the actions of organized movements. Here numerous works reveal ways in which idealized images and real bodies of women serve as national boundaries. As biological and social reproducers, women's bodies are claimed for the nation and, as a result, often become battlegrounds in nationalist conflicts (Eisenstein 1994; McClintock 1993; Tétreault 1997a; Yuval-Davis and Anthias 1989). Because women are biological reproducers of national collectivities, the conditions under which, when, how many, and whose children women will bear are questions of national importance (to men) and matters of civic duty or outright oppression (to women) (Dresser 1998; Peterson 1994; Tétreault 1997a, 1997b; Yuval-Davis and Anthias 1989). Additionally, as mothers with primary responsibility for rearing children, women are the producers and transmitters of national culture (Gaitskell and Unterhalter 1989). Through restrictions on sexual and marital relations, women reproduce the boundaries of national groups and acculturate their children to function within them (Manzo 1996; Yuval-Davis and Anthias 1989). Finally, as figurative representations of the nation, women "symbolically define the limits of national difference and power between men" (McClintock 1993: 2). These works shifted scholarly attention from questions about the form and location of women's participation in nationalist movements to the gender dimensions of broader conceptual categories such as "nation," "state," and "citizenship."

Feminist literature examines ways in which ideas about masculinity and femininity are intrinsic to constructions of the meaning of "the nation." It also draws attention to the dynamics of gendered and racialized self–other dichotomies within nationalist movements and, more broadly, in discourses on national identity (see the chapters in Parker *et al.* 1992a; also Mosse 1985). However, it leaves us with a dilemma as we struggle to come to terms with women's active involvement in national identity construction, whether in the context of social movements seeking political power or in more diffuse discourses redefining national identities. The shift from a focus on women's activism within nationalist social movements to the gendered representations of symbols intrinsic to projects of national construction can too easily obscure women's political activism, and also the diversity of nationalist projects in which women are engaged (see Ranchod-Nilsson in this volume).

Recognizing the diversity of feminist scholarship on nationalism we are poised to confront several challenging issues. The first is to acknowledge the diversity of nationalist projects, which range from organized national liberation movements to multiple and competing discourses about national identity, and to recognize that women, like men, can be found on all sides of these projects. One of the reasons that nationalism continues to thrive despite numerous predictions that it would not survive the spread of transnational capitalism may lie in the diverse organizational contexts that can serve the purposes of defining and defending the boundaries of "the nation." These contexts shift over time and can include organized political movements challenging, consolidating, or defending state power. In this volume chapters by Suresht Bald on Indian nationalism in the 1940s, Geeta Chowdhry on the communal nationalism of the Bharitya Janata Party (BJP) in contemporary Indian politics, Mary K. Meyer on competing nationalisms in Northern Ireland, Mary Ann Tétreault and Haya al-Mughni on Kuwaiti nationalism before and after the 1990 Iraqi invasion, and Sita Ranchod-Nilsson on the changing representations of the "good nationalist woman" in Zimbabwe all explore the gender dimensions of nationalism in the context of organized political movements. Comparisons among these cases reveal general similarities in the ways in which women serve as idealized symbols for the nation at very different moments of defining insider/outsider status. However, comparisons also reveal important differences in the ways in which representations of women shape opportunities for women's activism within nationalism movements. The military plays a key role not only in defending the nation-state, but also in arbitrating criteria for membership (citizenship) in the nation. Edna Levy's chapter on women in the Israeli military reveals multiple ways in which the category of "soldier" is differentiated, and unequal, in gendered ways. Cheryl Logan Sparks's chapter on the military and citizenship in the United States argues that not only military service, but also the vulnerability associated with dying for one's country, are key criteria of equal citizenship. Nationalism can reflect sectarian or secular interests. Cultural approaches to nationalism also point out the importance of sites of ideological production such as the family, the media, and the educational system in defining "the nation" and determining its membership.

The chameleon quality of nationalism means that it can be couched in multiple and, at times, competing organizational forms and this confounds any attempt at glib generalization or universalizing pronouncements. The idealized, often sexualized, representations of women that permeate nationalist discourse in its variety of contexts – or as Zillah Eisenstein writes "fantasmatic femaleness – shape locations and possibilities for women's activism."

Because of this gender-related plasticity, we need to address the ways in which nationalist projects are historically and culturally embedded. While it may be true that all nations are gendered, we must be alert to the specific gender meanings invoked at particular times and places and the ways in which these meanings change over time. In other words, we must resist theorizing the gender dimensions of national identities in terms of concepts that are static or artificially universal: there is no single "woman's view" of the nation; there is no unambiguous "woman's side" in nationalist conflicts. We also must make every effort to treat nationalism and nationalist movements similarly and together with other aspects of domestic politics. Such a strategy is integral to going beyond the "women are used" argument to evaluate what nationalist movements do *for* women as well as what they might do *to* them.

Finally we are challenged to explore representation and participation as focal points of studies of nationalism and nationalist movements. As Joan Connelly (1994) notes with regard to national identity among ancient Greeks, women were represented and participated in political life in ways that were regarded by themselves and others as essential to the survival of their communities even though their roles and behaviors differed sharply from those of men (see also Elshtain 1992). A well-integrated conceptualization of the politics of nationalist movements avoids reductionist analysis and encourages recognition of different types of nationalism in historically and culturally specific contexts. It also helps us to avoid "primordial" conceptualizations of the nation that create both ideological dynamics and social-political processes that play out in similar ways regardless of time and context. Perhaps your nationalism and mine are not the same things at all. Our exploration of varieties of nationalism should go beyond the simple dichotomy between civic nationalism and ethno-nationalism to see just what else might be there.

Themes and variations

The chapters in this collection touch on themes familiar in feminist writings on nationalism and also in writings on nationalism that do not address gender issues directly. We did not ask the authors to conform to any analytical template or theoretical framework on gender or nationalism when they prepared their chapters. Nevertheless several themes emerge from the contributions. These include the ways in which categories of self-versus-other are used to construct power relationships along a variety of parallel and intersecting axes, the ways in which sovereignty implies relations of domination and subordination at the level of the state and also within households and communities, the variety of organizational forms encompassed by nationalism, and the importance of vulnerability as text and subtext of discourses on citizenship. To be sure, all of these issues have been incorporated in feminist analysis and the rich feminist literature that explores gendered constructions of power. Here we argue that gendered analyses of nationalism(s) have important implications for these broader issues and that, by setting our sights on them, we not only can establish frameworks for intellectual engagement but also transform our practical understanding of nationalism in useful ways.

Self–other dichotomies

Geeta Chowdhry's chapter on contemporary Indian politics employs sets of socially defined contrasts between various self-versus-other categorizations whose analytical utility was demonstrated in Simone de Beauvoir's (1952/1974) classic work, *The Second Sex*. Since then, many "second wave" feminist analyses of gender have incorporated examinations of dualism modeled on the self–other dichotomy. As Beauvoir described it, sexual dimorphism was a template for constituting women as "other" creatures. It emphasized not simply women's physical differences from men, but also the psychological differences brought about through socialization during which women internalized men's judgments about the inferiority and otherness of women in the process of their own identity-formation. Feminist theorists from very different intellectual and disciplinary perspectives – examples include Dorothy Dinnerstein (1976), Gayle Rubin (1975), and

Nancy Chodorow (1978) – examined in equally innovative ways sexual and gender dimorphism as both rationale and pattern for constructing many different "takes" on male domination. These and other analysts, such as Judith Butler (1990) and Trinh Minh-ha (1989), charted multiple social consequences of the various self–other dualisms embedded in particular political economies and cultural systems.

Gender dualism also has been useful in explaining forms of domination that incorporate dualism along other dimensions. For example, in the same year that Chodorow's *The Reproduction of Mothering* was published, Edward Said (1978) produced his classic work analyzing the cultural apparatus of western domination of the Muslim [Middle] East. This book, *Orientalism*, is equally classical as an example of male scholarship that completely ignores the work of feminists: Beauvoir's deconstruction of gender could have been but was not used as a roadmap to guide the deconstructions of other dominance systems such as the orientalism that Said describes. In his more recent work – one example is *Culture and Imperialism* (1994) – Said does incorporate insights from feminist scholars such as Leila Ahmed (1992), whose work is exemplary in untangling the independent contribution of gender as a tool of imperial manipulation and control.

In *Culture and Imperialism*, Said offers a compelling and multilayered comparison between two novels depicting "hearts of darkness," one by Joseph Conrad and the other by Jane Austen. This comparison enriches our understanding of imperialism as a process that constructs and is reinforced by the role of gender in structuring and experiencing power. Said's examination of these two hearts of darkness illuminates the intimate as well as the public dimensions of imperialism. We are most familiar with the public dimensions which encompass such things as military conquest, colonization, and the capture of economic resources (e.g. Wolf 1982). We are less familiar with the connections between these activities and the structures and processes underpinning them which normally are hidden within the private sphere. These include the consequences of primogeniture on the life chances of younger sons – those most often involved in imperial adventures; the need to provide dowries if daughters are to marry – a major preoccupation in novels of manners such as Austen's; and, even more fundamentally, the reproduction of attitudes and techniques of domination in such institutions as the English public school (see also Gay 1995; Greven 1992).

Said's openness to the possibilities of what Gayle Rubin (1975) calls "sex-gender systems" as lenses through which to view political economies rarely has been emulated by analysts of nationalism. As you read the three theoretical chapters that make up the next section of this volume, you will find that, for the most part, studies of nationalism tend to be framed in one of two ways. On the one hand, many theoretical explorations and case studies of nationalism can be described as "gender deficient." In this approach sex, sexuality, and gender are absent both as concepts and as variables. On the other hand, while most feminist scholarship on nation-alism does consider gendered participation in nationalist movements and the gendered meanings and representations inherent in the construction of nations, too often in these analyses women simply replace men as the standpoint for viewing the same set of phenomena. Yet women's perspec-tives on nationalism and other public-sphere preoccupations are con-strained by the limited arena from which most women engage them, that is, from the confines of households. This is the rationale for some of the unwillingness of masculinist scholars to incorporate gender in their analyses: they assume that whatever improvement in explanation that would result is likely to be trivial. However, men's perspectives also are limited. Overwhelmed by the vast expanses of politics in the public arena of the state, scholars studying nationalism from this perspective exclusively rarely look for its echoes – *and origins* – within the private confines of domestic space (an exception can be found in Taylor 1998). This intel-lectual dichotomy – where gender either is absent or else is the principal focus of analysis – misses exciting possibilities suggested by Ahmed's and Said's multiply framed considerations of gender and gender politics as guiding only one of several interrelated strategies for achieving imperial domination.

Linda Racioppi and Katherine O'Sullivan See's chapter in this volume tries to bridge this gap in a close analysis of a set of major works on nationalism all of which can be described as "gender deficient." While some of it mentions sex or gender, all of it stops well short of fully exploring how gendered participation and meanings shape nations and nationalist movements. This chapter identifies important issues that remain unex-plored and the consequences of omitting a serious analysis of gender. V. Spike Peterson's chapter charts new ground. It moves beyond the exam-ination of gender as a symbolic and material marker of difference to consider the impact of gender ideologies about sexuality in the structuring of state and nation. Peterson invites us to consider a range of consequences that flow from embedding heterosexism in national imagery in political and social institutions. Zillah Eisenstein's chapter considers sex as a tool of domination, drawing a novel and provocative portrait of the nation as predator, batterer, and stalker. Sita Ranchod-Nilsson's chapter on Zimbabwe shows how gender, sex, and sexuality constitute a language of contestation in conflicts over who shall define and dominate a nation in the process of imagining itself into existence.

However, despite their shortcomings, approaches that omit gender also have much to say about nationalism. Perhaps surprisingly, given their different ideological starting points and ranges of substantive concerns, they usually describe nationalism in substantially similar terms as analyses that concentrate on gender at the expense of equally important concepts such as race and class. Even so, it is our contention here that, like Said's examination of orientalism, however path-breaking they are in other ways, both approaches are self-limiting because they stop before they reach points of mutual engagement. In the absence of conceptual and methodological integration, neither can go far enough to explore the ways in which the intimate worlds in which attitudes and techniques of domination are devised and transmitted shape, and are shaped by, broader social and political processes. Among the results in masculinist writing is that nationalism is reduced to ethno-nationalism, a primordial identity conferred by culture and history (Connor 1994 – others writing from this perspective include Kaplan 1993; Moynihan 1993; Smith 1991a). Without any consideration of the structures and practices reproducing social identity, ethno-nationalism remains a curiously ahistorical concept that, however compellingly described, remains resistant to rational analysis.

To begin to get around this problem, we might first want to differentiate among nationalisms. With respect to those who omit gender from their frameworks – for example, Benedict Anderson (1991), Liah Greenfeld (1992), and Ernest Gellner (1983) – an explicitly historical analytical framework helps to concentrate attention on mechanisms of group identification and their political manifestation in national and international politics. All three writers represent nationalism as a product of modernization associated with increasing egalitarianism, mass literacy, and national systems of technical education, and describe how these ingredients create perceptions among large and disparate populations that they share a single national identity. Yet, in the process of tracing the historical development of national identities, these authors leave us with little to connect to contemporary nationalist movements, most of which appear to be hierarchical, violent, recurrent, and exclusionary rather than egalitarian, evolutionary, persistent, and inclusive. The superficiality of their analyses of how other population variables, such as class, also influence the acquisition and expression of national identity, adds to the extent of the "heart of darkness" that lies at the center of all our understandings of nationalism.

Similarly, feminist analyses often begin and end with the gendered nature of the state as a set of policies, practices, and institutions (Jayawardena 1986; McClintock 1993; Ranchod-Nilsson 1997). They highlight ways in which gender differences are "naturalized" as codes guiding processes of constructing and reconstructing nations, but overlook or underplay women's active involvement in nationalist movements that even the least perceptive could not help but judge as anti-woman. Claudia Koonz's (1987) excellent study of female Nazi leaders exposes the pervasiveness of essentializing assumptions about gender and gender coding that prevents some feminist writers from penetrating any further into nationalism's heart of darkness than their non-feminist peers. Simona Sharoni's (1995) highly nuanced parallel study of gender in Israeli and Palestinian nationalism shows how activists are equally likely to be guided by essentialist assumptions, not only about their antagonists, but also about themselves.

Sovereignty

One goal of this volume is to connect the development of national-identity nationalism, also called state-centered nationalism and civic nationalism, to the ethno-nationalist forms likely to incorporate explicitly gendered dominance systems. An interesting way to see this is to begin from a distinction made by Peter Taylor (1998) that frames "state" and "household" as historically old constructions of space, and "nation" and "home" as relatively modern constructions of place. In her comments on the panel at which Taylor's paper was presented, Tétreault noted that state and household are, to use the current idiom, multicultural spaces. Each includes inhabitants who can be differentiated by blood, origin, and status. In contrast, the inhabitants of nations and homes are (or are imagined to be) related to one another, sharing a common origin and a similar "membership" status. Consequently, these are monocultural sites. The combination of state and nation in the modern nation-state thus embodies a contradiction in that the exclusiveness of the monocultural nation exists in tension with the inclusiveness of the imagined multicultural state. Taylor speculates that there are parallels in the evolution of the home-household and the nation-state. One source of those parallels may well be found along the axis corresponding to the degree of inclusion compatible with state ideas and family forms, structures that are mutually constituted. The chapter by Mary Ann Tétreault and Haya al-Mughni includes a consideration of this issue in the construction of Kuwaiti nationalism.

Taylor's (1998) argument suggests to us that sovereignty is another – and related – theme that infuses studies of nationalism, one that allows us to link up the public and private ways in which nationalist politics gets played out. Sovereignty is most commonly understood as "autonomy" or "self-determination," the self-definition of a political unit and its recognition by others as an autonomous entity. Robert Jackson (1990) calls this "negative sovereignty," a concept that refers to juridical equality among the members of the international community of states that makes each one's internal affairs forbidden territory to the others (Jackson 1990: 27; see also Rosenberg 1990). The other dimension of sovereignty is legitimacy, the authority of the state to control its resources, including its population, by any available means including violence. Here it is useful to employ John Ruggie's (1986) conception of sovereignty as analogous to private property. Just as the sovereign "owns" his or her territory and all the resources it contains, the head-of-household "owns" the home and all the resources – including spouse, children, and servants – that it contains (see also Pateman 1989).

Taylor's (1998) comparison of nation-state and home-household and Ruggie's (1986) comparison of sovereignty to private property both were prefigured in what is perhaps the first fable recounting the development of sovereignty as one of the foundations of modern politics, Jean-Jacques

Rousseau's *Two Discourses on Inequality*. In the *Discourses*, Rousseau explains the genesis of social inequality as the result of private property. To do this, he contrasts what he advertises as "the" state of nature – egalitarian and idyllic – to hierarchical "civilization." But Rousseau does this in the same way that the book of Genesis tells the story of the creation of human beings, in two parallel stories one of which treats men and women equally and the other which privileges men (Rosenberg and Bloom 1990). In Rousseau's gender-egalitarian version, both women and men live atomistic – and autonomous – lives. They have no property and no fixed abode. They subsist on what they find by hunting and gathering and they reproduce as the result of chance encounters. The only social relationships are between mothers and infants and, on both sides, these relationships are instrumental rather than affective. When a child is old enough to fend for itself – Rousseau, whose practical experience as a parent was limited by choice, thought this would be at about 5 years of age – the child goes off on its own to become another human atom.

The discovery of agriculture provides an interlude between the state of nature populated by human atoms and the hierarchical modern civilization that Rousseau disdains. Susan Moller Okin (1979) finds in this interlude a different representation of the state of nature, one that unfolds with no explanation or transition. In this second state of nature, natural men are transformed into corporate executives, heads of atomistic households populated by women and children. Independent women roaming an unbounded space vanish; women-as-property appear as subjects of the tiny kingdoms headed by sovereign men.

The first version of Rousseau's state of nature really is a model of a socially egalitarian world. No person has property, rank, or entitlements and all that separates one from another is her or his skill at survival. Equality disappears in the second, patriarchal, state of nature. The transition to property ownership does indeed introduce inequality but, unacknowledged by Rousseau, inequality first emerges during the transition between the state of nature populated by atomistic individuals and the state of nature populated by sovereign household corporations in which men own women (Okin 1979).

Rousseau's fable of sovereignty, which concludes with a critique of the societies and politics of the nascent nation-states of early modern Europe, is a sharp contrast to the historical picture we have of the heteronomy of ancient and medieval states. Those multicultural spaces featured multiple, overlapping, and variously constructed patterns of membership and belonging – not only family but also city, sect, shire, occupation, voluntary association, and others (Habermas 1991; Ruggie 1986; Springborg 1986). Ruggie tells us that, during the medieval period, political "units viewed themselves as municipal embodiments of a universal community," and the development of sovereignty as a norm of the incipient nation-state system actually truncated complex and varied patterns of identities and rights along with a conception of universal values based on the teachings of the Roman Catholic Church (Ruggie 1986: 143). The cosy heteronomy of the medieval period gave way to the harsh dichotomies of sovereignty, with its consolidation of a worldview based on the division of the self from the other – the self divided from everything and everyone else. The notion shapes not only relations between sovereign states, but also sovereign (patriarchal) households and, as we have seen, other dichotomies envisioned as systems of dominance. Suresht Bald's chapter on early twentieth century India looks at the mobilization of "private" resources by one premodern but aspiring nation-state. Mary K. Meyer's chapter shows how long and at what cost a duel between two opposing state ideas, one a caricature of masculinist sovereignty and the other a relic shaped from memories of an idealized pre-modern past, can continue to battle over which will guide the imagination of Northern Ireland.

Vulnerability

Vulnerability is a primary constitutive element of sovereignty, and also is an unstated criterion of citizenship. Taking a materialist view of state sovereignty as protective of populations and resources located within bounded territories, and patriarchal autonomy as protective of dependents and private property located within households, the state ruler and the household head are imagined as self-regarding individuals struggling against similarly situated actors in a system characterized by "self-help" – unregulated competition. Each individual is subject to anticipated predation by one or more peers and routinely engages in such predation. Sovereigns and household heads each are defined in terms of their rights, although such egalitarian atomism may be mediated by contracts governing the organization and operation of alliances, businesses, and other forms of voluntary association among themselves.

In consequence of the greater individual freedom offered by modern cosmologies, all sovereign actors are vulnerable to threats from non-obligated agents as free as themselves. Security – both national and individual – is conceived as a function of privatization and the ability to create a protected space for the members of the domestic community – that is, for citizens/family members. This conceptualization of security demands that those sharing the sovereign's space – whether citizens or household members – submit to the sovereign's authority (Tétreault 1998a). Thus, the sovereign's dependents are obligated to obey in return for the sovereign's protection; they submit in return for the reduction in their overall vulnerability. Edna Levy's chapter looks at some of the consequences of such a social contract on Israeli women and the Israeli state.

Several of the chapters in this volume illustrate the poetics of sovereignty and vulnerability as characteristics of the nation-state written in specifically gendered and sexualized terms. A particularly interesting

example is Cheryl Logan Sparks's chapter. It considers effects and incon-
sistencies in juridically mandated equality applied to male and female
citizens occupying positions of vulnerability made unequal by differences
in gender, sexuality, and technology. Inconsistences in gendered imagining
of the nation intensified following the advent of nuclear weapons with
their capacity to ignore the frontiers and border guards of even the largest
and best endowed nation-states. Masculinist poets of the nation subsequently found themselves writing from a feminine, if not a feminist, point
of view. Thus defense intellectuals speak of "impregnability," "penetration," and "violation," and measure the capacity to repel or retaliate in
such openly sexual terms that Helen Caldicott (1986) castigated their activities as "missile envy" (see also Cohn 1989).

The chapters by Eisenstein, Ranchod-Nilsson, Meyer, and Levy illustrate in detail how the poetics of nationalism are infused with gendered
and sexualized images, not only the reassuring image of mothers of the
nation, but also terrifying images of seduction and rape: ruined women,
ravaged landscapes. The nation-state is so permeated by these gendered
and sexualized meanings that control of female citizens becomes synonymous with self-defense in the minds of many ardent nationalists. Women
are both battleground and prey of attackers at the same time that they
are glorified as producers and symbols of the nation (e.g. Guy 1991; Kesič
1994; Mernissi 1992; Tétreault 1997a; Theweleit 1987).

Vulnerability of individuals also may be connected to women and to
notions of citizenship through psychological linkages between sex and death.
William Thompson (1981), for example, sees sexuality – a property of
women – and sexual reproduction – a consequence of sex and sexuality –
as responsible for human mortality and thus connected to death in the
minds of men (see also Brown 1994; we recall that a French euphemism (!)
for orgasm is "the little death"). Klaus Theweleit's (1987) examination
of the writings of members of the German Freikorps offers supporting evidence of this connection, finding repeated narrative and linguistic links
between women's bodies and fears about personal and national vulnerability. Taking a different perspective in her recent and highly innovative inves-
tigation of the causes of war, Barbara Ehrenreich (1997) deconstructs its
sacramental quality, which she believes is embedded in the primal experiences of human beings who evolved for millennia as the prey of other
animals.

Ehrenreich's theory is ambitious and provocative. She imagines war and
the defense of the group as autonomous from gender, class, nation, and
the other axes of division among human beings that conventionally are
seen as determinants of differential patterns of behavior. Ehrenreich (1997:
232) argues rather that war is a self-replicating pattern of behavior which,
once adopted, spreads among all human groups through the proliferation
of structural constraints – a phenomenon that economists call "convergence." A similar analysis can be made regarding the structural alterations

initiated by capitalism, alterations that ensure its replication through the systematic destruction of other forms of social organization designed to meet human needs (Polanyi 1944). Yet some forms of these self-replicating systems do change. As Ehrenreich notes, we no longer sacrifice small children – mostly little girls (see Connolly 1994) – as initial attempts to propitiate the forces of destruction. However, we do continue to send adolescent boys and young men to kill one another in defense of the state. Either way, full citizenship is linked to physical vulnerability, the risk of death. Those who are not vulnerable in the context of national defense are subordinate citizens, subject to the obligations but not recipients of the full benefits of membership in sovereign states and sovereign households (see also Elshtain 1992; and the chapters by Levy and Sparks in this volume). These provocative analyses invite investigations of repetitive constructions of self–other dichotomies as subliminal triggers of violence against the enemy–other, a strategy that is justified morally and practically as reducing vulnerability (a different example is implied by Goldhagen 1996). As the original model of human difference, sexual dimorphism is a paradigm of self–other relationships in multiple realms, including the realm of the nation.

The connection between gender and sex and sexualized images of the nation-state also reflects the fundamental reality of women's corporeal and cultural roles in reproducing the next generation. As a result, the notion of "republican motherhood" is not a simple image but a concept embedded in a complex of vulnerabilities. It represents an ideology seeking to limit material vulnerability by the post-conflict relegation of women to the private sphere of childbearing and rearing to compensate for population losses from war or revolution. At the same time, as the examples of Kuwait and Zimbabwe emphasize, it also reflects an effort to assuage psychological anxieties about vulnerability by recreating or reinforcing body boundaries for men and nations. Both elements ensure that the pattern of gender difference and hierarchy based on that difference is replicated in subsequent generations to prepare them to defend the national "self" against the alien "other."

Vulnerability also is addressed by appealing to sacred power and claiming divine authority. Just as Protestantism was a constitutive element of nation-state formation, religion continues to be an instrument of modern nationalist movements (Manzo 1996; Moynihan 1993; Sells 1996; Anthony Smith 1991a), and is itself a primary ideological and institutional force for creating, maintaining, and providing cosmic justifications for a wide variety of sex-gender systems. There is a sense in which revivalist religious movements and ethno-nationalist movements are strongly parallel in their impulses, a phenomenon highlighted in Meyer's chapter on Northern Ireland. Both types of movements seek to de-emphasize if not de-legitimize diversity within the community, and also to redefine and strengthen the boundaries separating the community from outsiders – its enemies. Like nationalism, fundamentalist ideology is highly gendered and organizes much of its defense of the internal community around its control of women, who are simultaneously elevated as virtuous paragons and vilified as sources of evil and chaos (e.g. Haeri 1993; Hardacre 1993; Hawley, 1994 – compare to Sells 1996; Theweleit 1987). In addition to Meyer's, chapters by Bald, Chowdhry, and Tétreault and al-Mughni in this volume also analyze the role of religion in modern nationalist discourses and practices involving gender, and reveal the mutual support and legitimization contributed by militantly religious and militantly nationalist organizations and institutions to one another's projects.

Moving forward

The chapters in this collection begin and end with a focus on the gendered dimensions and meanings of nationalism through a variety of disciplinary and theoretical frameworks. This diverse application of feminist perspectives on nationalism engages masculinist literatures that fail to address gender adequately, if at all, in their examinations of the subject. Some of the contributors to this volume also are critical of what they see as overly narrow feminist approaches to the study of nationalism. The chapters as a whole constitute a multidimensional and multivariate treatment of this theoretically and empirically complex subject, drawing from extensive literatures and bases in fieldwork not only to reveal where we are in the study of nationalism but also to mark out directions in which we need to proceed.

Because no package of theoretical guidelines or substantive issues guided the authors, each grappled with the subject in an arena defined primarily by her previous work and her substantive concerns. Each sought ways to understand how gender shapes the meaning of "the nation" and to determine how women's relationships to nationalist movements reflect their capacities as persons as well as their identities as women. One-by-one and in their entirety, these chapters suggest fruitful avenues for additional theoretical and empirical exploration as they bring important issues raised by feminist analysis to bear on the contemporary study of nationalism.

2 Engendering nation and national identity

Linda Racioppi
and Katherine O'Sullivan See

Let it burst! Whatever will, whatever must!
I must know my birth, no matter how common
it may be – I must see my origins face-to-face.
She perhaps, she with her woman's pride
may well be mortified by my birth,
but I, I count myself the son of Chance,
the great goddess, giver of all good things –
I'll never see myself disgraced. She is my mother!
And the moons have marked me out, my blood-brothers,
one moon on the wane, the next moon great with power.
That is my blood, my nature – I will never betray it,
never fail to search and learn my birth!

(Sophocles, *Oedipus the King*)[1]

The eminent scholar of nationalism, Anthony Smith, begins one of his major works on national identity (1991a) with a discussion of Oedipus the King.[2] Sophocles' tale of Oedipus is pre-national, yet, as Smith and other scholars have noted, it remains one of the most profound myths on the problem of identity and therefore a compelling narrative for thinking about the complexity of national identity. The words, "That is my blood, my nature – I will never betray it, never fail to search and learn my birth!" speak to us not only of the agony and hope of identity not yet discovered but also of the power of ancestry and social ties to determine that identity. In the process of Oedipus' search, he (and we) learn that identity is multiple and socially constructed, and that often its sources are unknown by the individual. Despite its premodern origins, the myth of Oedipus reflects what for many scholars is at the core of modern national identity, the myth of blood and belonging.[3]

From Oedipus' promise to discover the murderer who brought plague upon Thebes to his self-inflicted blinding and exile, the play is a search for identity, a search that makes Oedipus, like all of us, human. Oedipus begins with a clear and coherent identity: Greek, conqueror-king, hero, husband, father. The plea of the Thebans to help end the crisis besieging their city and the subsequent challenge from Tiresias to find the true murderer of Laius leads Oedipus on an exploration of his own identity and to the discovery that he is not who he thought he was. Tiresias' words echo with foreboding:

> A stranger you may think, who lives among you,
> he soon will be revealed a native Theban
> but he will take no joy in the revelation.
> Blind who now has eyes, beggar who is now rich,
> he will grope his way toward a foreign soil,
> a stick tapping before him step by step.
>
> Revealed at last, brother and father both
> to the children he embraces, to his mother
> son and husband both – he sowed the loins
> his father sowed, he spilled his father's blood![4]

For Oedipus, all of the facets of identity that he thought constituted his "true nature" are revealed to be false. He was instead Theban (yet, destroyer of Thebes), murderer of his father, incestuous son, slave, whom Tiresias foretold. Smith argues that the Oedipal myth "reveals the way in which the self is composed of multiple identities and roles – familial, territorial, class, religious, ethnic and gender" (Smith 1991a: 4). As important, we would argue that the Oedipus myth illuminates that we cannot escape these multiple forces as they shape our identity – the new Oedipus was constituted within the same categories of identity as the old Oedipus.

Although these categories are interactive, they do not form identity in equal and similar ways for Oedipus, nor at all times for all peoples. "I must know my birth, no matter how common it may be – I must see my origins face to face . . . I'll never see myself disgraced." Oedipus is prepared to confront and live with the fact that he may be a commoner; what he fears most is that he may be an incestuous son and murderer of his father. (Indeed, he moved away from Polybus and Merope [the people he believed to be his parents] in order to avoid the prophecy.) To explore the story of Oedipus is to be struck by the overwhelming ways in which sexuality and gender are at the core not only of this Sophoclean tragedy but also of all searches for identity. What does it mean to be a "good" son, husband and father? Could Oedipus be a "good" king and be an incestuous son?

> I'd never have come to this,
> my father's murderer – never been branded
> mother's husband, all men see me now! Now,
> loathed by the gods, son of the mother I defiled
> coupling in my father's bed, spawning lives in the loins
> that spawned my wretched life. What grief can crown this grief?
> It's mine alone, my destiny – I am Oedipus![5]

For Oedipus, the painful, personal knowledge of what he has done, of who he is, is compounded by its social and cultural/religious consequences: "all men see me now"; he is "loathed by the gods." His fate is not merely personal: it affects his children and their futures, his country, and their relationship to the gods. The connections between personal identity and collective identity are intense.

Anthony Smith uses the Oedipal myth in his own work on nationalism to illustrate the complexity of individual and collective identity; this myth illuminates the multiple forces that make a self; and it underscores the ways in which all identity is socially constituted. As Smith puts it, "the question of identity, collective as well as individual, broods over the action. 'I will know who I am.' The discovery of the self is the play's motor and the action's inner meaning" (1991a: 3). He suggests that it is difficult to separate "I will know who I am" from "We will know who we are"; that such a search requires understanding the multiple dimensions of the self and that the self is always connected to some collectivity. Only as Oedipus comes to know who he is as son, husband and father, can he come to know who he must be as citizen and ruler.

Anthony Smith is not alone among the scholars of nationalism who appreciate the multiplicity of identity that shapes the political identity of "the nation." But in employing the Oedipus myth, Smith explicitly directs our attention to those aspects of identity which are at the center of the self: sexuality and gender. How can we connect this central insight to the "mainstream" literature on nations, nationalism and national identity, much of which has taken a macro-level, gender-neutral approach?[6] Eric Hobsbawm (1990) in *Nations and Nationalism since 1780* has identified versions of this methodological problem for the study of nationalism: how individual sense of self and individual experiences are connected to the development of collective national identity, and how diversity can be recognized within the purported homogeneity and unity of the "nation." How can we respond to this methodological challenge through gendered analysis? And what are the theoretical implications of a gendered analysis for the study of nations and nationalism?

The problem of nationalism and gender

From the genocidal conflicts in Rwanda to persistent rivalries in Eastern and Southern Africa, to ethno-religious strife in the Indian sub-continent and ethno-nationalist claims in Eastern Europe and the former Soviet Union, the persistence of nationalist conflict has commanded global attention and reinvigorated the scholarship on nationalism. From rape as the symbol of conquered terrain to invocations that women must reproduce the nation, gender is a key dimension of many of these conflicts and it is clear from their political appeals that nationalists take gender seriously. Even a cursory examination of the conflict in Bosnia (where rape was used as an instrument of ethnic cleansing) or of the nationalist rhetoric of Zhirinovsky (which appeals to traditional Russian notions of masculinity and femininity) makes the centrality of gender to nationalism seem obvious. Yet, the "mainstream" scholarship on nationalism has not taken up the gendered aspects of nationalism in more than a tangential way.

Nonetheless, the literature is rich with insight, teaching us about the extraordinary range of nationalism. Scholars have examined the powerful philosophical roots and ideological manifestations of nationalism (e.g. Gellner 1983; Kedourie 1993; Kohn 1967). They have analyzed psychological dimensions of ethnocentrism, racism, and nationalism (e.g. Adorno *et al.* 1950; Allport 1954; William Bloom 1990; Doob 1964; Horowitz 1985), and they have probed the ethnic origins of nations (e.g. Armstrong 1982; Connor 1994; Smith 1981). They have also explored the influences of economic development, state-building, and political elites (e.g. Anderson 1991; Brass 1991; Deutsch 1966; Geertz 1963; Greenfeld 1992; Hechter 1975; Hobsbawm 1990; Horowitz 1985; Harry Johnson 1965; Mayall 1990; Nairn 1977; See 1986; Seton-Watson 1977; Smith 1981, 1986; Tilly 1975; Young 1976). Still others have focused primarily on the cultural dimensions of nationalism (e.g. Anderson 1991; Bhabha 1990; Chatterjee 1993a; Hutchinson 1987; Mosse 1985). Within the disciplines of sociology and political science, substantial numbers of scholars have concentrated on understanding ethnic conflict and violent forms of nationalist struggle (e.g. Esman 1977; Gurr 1994; Horowitz 1985; Lijphart 1975). Given the wide range of approaches and issues addressed in the "mainstream" literatures on nationalism, it is not surprising that scholars are not in accord about its range and manifestations: for some, nationalism constitutes something approximating profound patriotism and citizenship (e.g. Barber 1984; Greenfeld 1992; Kohn 1967; Lipset 1967); for others, nationalism constitutes the promotion of the culture of an ethnic group or politicization of ethnic identity (e.g. Connor 1994; Horowitz 1985; Hutchinson 1987; Moynihan 1993; Said 1994; Smith 1991a; Taylor 1992). Despite the rich debates and theoretical insights that have been provoked by this literature, for the most part, nations, nationalism, and nationalist movements have been treated as non-gendered phenomena.

In contrast to this "mainstream" blindness to gender, feminist literature has begun to address the glaring absence of gendered analyses of nationalism. Scholars are examining the important roles that women play in nationalist movements, are critically analyzing the ways in which nationalist ideologies construct womanhood and manhood, are examining sexuality, reproduction and family processes in "bounding" the nation, are critiquing the ethno-nationalist assumptions in feminist theory and research, and are exploring the complex bundling of racial, ethnic and gender identities (e.g. Collins 1992a; Minh-ha 1989; Moghadam 1994a; Mohanty *et al.* 1991; Mosse 1985; Rowbotham 1993; Spelman 1988; Yuval-Davis 1997). Related to this, an important scholarship is developing that examines the gendered aspects of state-building (e.g. Yuval-Davis and Anthias 1989; Gordon 1990; MacKinnon 1989; Pateman 1988a; Peterson 1992a; Skoçpol 1992) and the connection between nationalism, militarism and gender (e.g. Enloe 1983, 1993; Tickner 1992). Even a cursory review of this scholarship should convince us of the centrality of gender to the phenomenon of nationalism and the need to "engender" the "mainstream" literature on nationalism. This chapter is an initial step in bridging the gap between "mainstream" and feminist approaches through deconstruction of the contours of some of the "mainstream" literature, what it has focused on, what it has failed to examine, what we can learn from it despite its "gender neutrality," and how this literature might be enriched by consideration of gender.

In this chapter, we take up the feminist and "Hobsbawmian" challenges through interrogating some key works in the "mainstream" literature. We ask of each of these works: how does it understand the power of the nation as source of identity, discursive practice and basis for social mobilization; how would attention to gender enrich this work's study of nations and national identity? As we have suggested above, the "mainstream" literature is wide-ranging. We examine several very different approaches, selecting four of the most influential and frequently cited works: Anthony Smith's *National Identity*, Eric Hobsbawm's *Nations and Nationalisms since 1870*, Benedict Anderson's *Imagined Communities*, and Donald Horowitz's *Ethnic Groups in Conflict*. The intellectual ambitiousness of each of these works is impressive: they seek, from different theoretical perspectives and levels of analysis, to explain the origins and development of national identity and the many forms of nationalism. Smith, Hobsbawm, and Anderson offer compelling explanations of why and how nations became central both to the search for identity and to political mobilization in the modern era. Horowitz focuses on decolonization in the twentieth century and shows how state structures and political party systems interact with ethno-kinship ties to forge ethno-national politics and identities. Each of these works provides insights into the development of nations and national identity and sheds light on how to think about the relationship between individual and national identities. Together they suggest different questions we might pose for understanding the gender dynamics of nationalism.

Deconstructing the "mainstream"

Anthony Smith, author of at least ten major works on nationalism (1971, 1973, 1976, 1979, 1981, 1983, 1986, 1991a, 1994, 1997) and one of the most important scholars of this subject, writes,

> National identity does in fact today exert a more potent and durable influence than other collective cultural identities; and . . . for the

reasons I have enumerated – the need for collective immortality and
dignity, the power of ethno-history, the role of new class structures
and the domination of inter-state systems in the modern world – this
type of collective identity is likely to continue to command humanity's
allegiances for a long time to come, even when other larger-scale but
looser forms of collective identity emerge alongside national ones.

(Smith 1991a: 175–176)

Although he identifies five categories that compose social identity (ethnicity,
religion, class, space, and gender), Smith argues that the vitality of the nation
is rooted in the singular power of the ethnic community. He argues that class,
space, and gender are less potent bases for social identity and mobilization.
Social class binds people on the basis of economic interest and generates conflict which reinforces class identity but, according to Smith, it is infrequently
"the stuff of stable collective identities," because classes are often territorially
dispersed, and economic interests fluctuate and fragment (1991a: 5–6). The
category of space or territory is also important, and we frequently refer to
peoples according to their territory of origin. But there is little historical
evidence of sustained territorially based mobilization; and spatially based
interests can be attenuated through localization, fragmentation, and competition for level of territorial significance. As Smith puts it, "regions are
geographically difficult to define; their centers are often multiple and their
boundaries ragged" (1991a: 4). In contrast to class and space, Smith recognizes that gender is an important, universal and pervasive category of identity that "stands at the origins of other difference(s) and subordinations"
(1991a: 4). Despite its significance, gender, for Smith, is the category of social
identity which is least likely to produce collective mobilization, because
"geographically separated, divided by class and ethnically fragmented,
gender cleavages must ally themselves to other, more cohesive identities if
they are to inspire collective consciousness and action" (1991a: 4).

Smith finds that religion forms a more compelling base for the development of national identity, because it provides an interpretation of the
meaning of life and death, values, beliefs, traditions and rituals which
can create communal experience and collective identity (1991a: 6–7). It
also provides a "supra-empirical reality" for believers (1991a: 6). Religious
communities often coincide with or give rise to ethnic identities. Indeed,
Smith argues that "for the greater part of human history, the twin circles
of religion and ethnicity have been very close, if not identical" (1991a: 7).
While religion provides believers with a collective proper name and possibly
a sense of solidarity, common culture and historical memory, it is not the
same thing as ethnicity. Ethnic communities must also share a myth of
common ancestry and an association with a specific homeland.

Most important it is myths of common ancestry not any fact of ancestry
(which is often difficult to ascertain) that are crucial. It is fictive descent

> and putative ancestry that matter for the sense of ethnic identity. . . .
> A linkage between family and nation reappears in nationalist mytho-
> logies and testifies to the continuing centrality of this attribute of
> ethnicity. . . . The sense of "whence we came" is central to the defi-
> nition of "who we are".
>
> (Smith 1991a: 22)

Religious identity often coincides with ethnic identity but these are not
coterminous. Religion can divide ethnic groups into conflicting belief
communities or it can unite believers across ethnic boundaries.

   Although each of these categories contributes distinctive features of social
identity, Smith (1991a: 24) appreciates that they overlap in complex ways
and argues that individuals can possess simultaneous loyalties at different
intensities. His argument is not incompatible, then, with the feminist scholarship on nationalism which emphasizes the ways in which national
identities are socially constructed and overlap with other dimensions of
self (Collins 1992a; Minh-ha 1989; Moghadam 1994a; Spelman 1988).
Although Smith is attentive to the complex interplay and multiple leveling
of identities, culture, history, territory, class, religion and ethnicity, ethnicity
in particular is a core identity from which nationalism develops.

   In his work, Smith identifies three waves of nationalism. He roots the
first wave of nationalism in the highly discontinuous effects of the transition from feudalism to capitalism, the concomitant transformation of
military and administrative methods of control and the replacement
of ecclesiastical authority with secular states (1971: 231–236; 1981: 74–85;
1986: 129–152). Nationalism was formed in these contexts in two ways:
a "western" state-to-nation route: through common citizenship (legal identity, shared rights, duties and relevant documents) which worked "only in
a context of implicitly shared meanings and values, with common myths
and symbols" (1986: 136) (e.g. England, France, and the United States);
and an "eastern" ethnic nation-to-state route, in which elites mobilized
the educated strata by appeals to customary and linguistic ties to demand
rights to autonomy from large empires (1986: 133–176; 1991a: 123–124)
(e.g. Japan, Russia). He examines the two subsequent waves of nationalism in the European colonies and post-colonial states of Asia, Africa and
the Caribbean and since the 1960s, in the "revival of ethno-nationalism"
in separatist movements in western Europe and North America. He argues
that ethnically based nationalism is more prevalent and more powerful
than civic nationalism, precisely because it provides a sense of collective
immortality and dignity to which political elites can appeal.

   The approach in *National Identity* is on the macro level: the work is concerned with large historical forces and movements that shape international
relations. It focuses largely on nationalist mobilization revolving around
or directed at the state and political autonomy (even when the ultimate
claims are not for an independent state). How might this approach be

enriched by attention to gender? To understand "civic" nationalism, for example, it should be recognized that the identity of citizen was rooted in gender. How did women belong to the nation? In the "eastern" form of nationalism, the political elites and ideologists identified as the architects of the nation were men. How did women participate, if at all, in the "making" of ethno-national identity? How were men and women constituted within the ancestral myths, national images and culture? But who are the political elites? How did women participate in ethno-national movements? To bring gender in at the macro level would mean that the analysis must move beyond narrowly defined political forces and public spheres. Otherwise, we have a theory about homogenized ethnic-humankind. Smith does appreciate the need to pinpoint the root of collective identity. He argues that

> We need to reconstitute the notion of collective cultural identity itself in its historical subjective and symbolic terms. Collective cultural identity refers not to a uniformity of elements over generations but to a sense of continuity on the part of successive generations of a given cultural unit of population, to shared memories of earlier events and periods in the history of that unit, and to notions entertained by each generation about the collective destiny of that unit and its culture.
>
> (1991a: 25)

These crucial insights stress the complexity of understanding historical subjectivity. Whose historical subjectivity is being reconstituted? What shapes a sense of continuity on the part of successive generations? How is it articulated to appeal to men and women? Who constructs shared memory? How is collective destiny defined? Smith identifies the family as central to the creation of the nation. It is through myths of common ancestry that the nation draws its boundaries, and the nation becomes "superfamily." As Smith states,

> [T]he metaphor of family is indispensable to nationalism. The nation is depicted as one great family, the members as brothers and sisters of the motherland or fatherland, speaking their mother tongue . . . [T]he family of the nation overrides and replaces the individual's family but evokes similarly strong loyalties and vivid attachments. Even where local allegiances are tolerated and real families given their due, the language and symbolism of the nation asserts its priority and, through the state and citizenship, exerts its legal and bureaucratic pressures on the family, using similar kinship metaphors to justify itself.
>
> (1991a: 79)

Smith's analysis suggests some crucial questions for gendering the nation. Can the family be theorized as more than a metaphor in relation to the nation? How and by whom are family boundaries constructed? In what ways are myths of common descent and familial ties created and maintained? There is an irony here: if ethnic identity and ethnic group formation are rooted in notions of descent and familiality, then gender is necessarily at their heart. In Smith's own words, "If not immutable, gender classifications are universal and pervasive. They also stand at the origins of other differences and subordinations. We are in many subtle ways defined by our gender as are many of our opportunities and rewards in life" (1991a: 4). Rich in historical scope and analytic power, *National Identity* illuminates the processes of nation formation and the multiple components of individual and collective identity, but does not pursue its crucial insight about the centrality of gender.

Though dramatically different from Smith in his analysis of nations and national identity, Eric Hobsbawm also uses an historical and macro approach to assess and interpret nationalist movements. In *Nations and Nationalism since 1780: Programme, Myth, Reality*, Hobsbawm (1990) promises to pay close attention to national identity as a collective and yet individual phenomenon and therefore to remedy the distorting focus on elites and "public politics" prevalent in much of the literature. This echoes the emphasis of much feminist scholarship on the ways an exclusive emphasis on elites obscures the important roles of women and minorities in shaping history and on the ways in which the public and private spheres are deeply interrelated. Hobsbawm critiques analyses which look at nationalism from the top down ("modernization from above") but admits that the "view from below, i.e. the nation as seen not by governments and the spokesmen and activists of nationalist (or non-nationalist) movements, but by the ordinary persons who are the objects of their action and propaganda, is exceedingly difficult to discover" (1990: 11). Like Smith, Hobsbawm appreciates that national identity is composed of multiple components:

> Men and women did not choose collective identification as they choose shoes, knowing that one could only put on one pair at a time. They had, and still have, several attachments and loyalties simultaneously, including nationality, and are simultaneously concerned with various aspects of life, any of which may at any one time be foremost in their minds, as occasion suggests. For long periods of time these different attachments would not make incompatible demands on a person, so that a man might have no problem about feeling himself to be the son of an Irishman, the husband of a German woman, a member of the mining community, a worker, a supporter of Barnsley Football Club, a Liberal, a Primitive Methodist, a patriotic Englishman, possibly a Republican, and a supporter of the British empire. It was only when one of these loyalties conflicted directly with another or others that a problem of choosing between them arose.
>
> (1990: 123–124)

Echoing Smith and much of the feminist literature, Hobsbawm also argues that "we cannot assume that for most people national identification – when it exists – excludes or is always even superior to, the remainder of the set of identifications which constitute the social being. In fact, it is always combined with identifications of another kind, even when it is felt to be superior to them" (1992: 11).

Hobsbawm first describes the invention of nationalism as a product of intellectual and political claims about sovereignty asserted by eighteenth century state builders who invented symbols of nationality as a way of mobilizing support. They were able to mobilize people on the bases of such claims, because they built on what Hobsbawm calls the "grassroots of nationality," aspects of identity that are "supralocal forms of popular identification which go beyond those circumscribing the actual spaces in which people passed most of their lives" (1990: 46). He traces a range of "protonational" symbols (e.g. language, ritual, iconography) before conceding that it is very difficult to detect what the masses of people believed or how firmly protonational they may have been (1990: 79). The subsequent analysis skirts the "grassroots of nationality" and national identity. Instead we learn of the political bonds and rhetoric used by "select groups more directly linked to states and institutions and . . . capable of generalization, extension and popularization" (1990: 46–47). Nations and national identity appear as forms of politicized consciousness; and "the consciousness of belonging or having belonged to a lasting political entity" is the "most decisive factor" in proto-nationalism (1990: 73) and renders twentieth century national identity as politically manipulated consciousness. Hobsbawm goes so far as to argue that the political importance of contemporary ethno-nationalism will fade under the forces of a globalized economy and supranationalist institutions. Nationalism in the world today "is at most a complicating factor or a catalyst for other developments" (1990: 191).

Unlike some of the literature on nationalism, *Nations and Nationalism* does not distinguish between civic and ethnic nationalism, between nations and nation-states, and between patriotism and nationalism. It does not explore the ways in which overlapping identities of class, citizenship and religion might interact with and support each other; nor does it question whether the range of possible overlaps may be more circumscribed or expanded for certain sectors of the population than for others. Most obviously, gender is never mentioned, and the impression is left that either women and men experience national identity similarly, given similarities of class background, etc. (or less generously, that women are simply irrelevant to the study of nationalism). Nonetheless, in his recognition of the importance and empirical difficulty of analyzing the "view from below," Hobsbawm points to a key dilemma in studying nationalism as gendered, since that "view from below" is often undocumented or obscured in the historical record. Moreover, if Hobsbawm is right, that nationalism does not have the kind of tenacity that Smith depicts and that the "ordinary persons" are more likely to respond to other calls to identity politics, it seems especially important to take up his call to study the complex sets of identifications that he claims sometimes do and ultimately will override national identity – including gender.

Benedict Anderson's *Imagined Communities: Reflections on the Origin and Spread of Nationalism* (1991) might seem more hospitable to considerations of gender, given its emphasis on the cultural/ideological constitution of the nation. And indeed, feminist scholars have paid substantial attention to the symbolic and cultural construction of nations and nationalisms as gendered (Koonz 1987; Parker *et al.* 1992a; Sommer 1991; Yuval-Davis 1997). The socially constructed nature of the nation is emphasized in Anderson's conceptualization of the nation as "an imagined political community – and imagined as both inherently limited and sovereign" (Anderson, 1991: 6). For Anderson, the nation

> is imagined as a community, because, regardless of the actual inequality and exploitation that may prevail in each, the nation is always conceived as a deep, horizontal comradeship. Ultimately it is this fraternity that makes it possible over the past two centuries, for so many millions of people, not so much to kill, as willingly to die for such limited imaginings.
>
> These deaths bring us abruptly face to face with the central problem posed by nationalism: what makes the shrunken imaginings of recent history (scarcely more than two centuries) generate such colossal sacrifices? I believe that the beginnings of an answer lie in the cultural roots of nationalism.
>
> (Anderson 1991: 7)

The notion of the nation as an imagined community echoes Smith's depiction of the nation as mythic creation. This is an inviting approach – to examine the cultural roots of nationalism suggests a careful look at how symbolic boundaries are developed, invoked, and reinforced. And, in the remainder of *Imagined Communities*, Anderson seeks to explain how the decomposition of feudal cultural systems (the religious community and the dynastic realm) combined with the forces of modernization (secular time, the printing press, shipping and railways, the spread of vernacular language, and capitalism) to make the nation such a potent imagined community, capable of commanding *men's* total allegiance. Why did the nation become such a psychologically powerful construct?

> The century of the Enlightenment of rationalist secularism, brought with it its own modern darkness. With the ebbing of religious belief, the suffering which belief in part composed did not disappear. Disintegration of paradise: nothing makes fatality more arbitrary.

Absurdity of salvation: nothing makes another style of continuity more arbitrary. What then was required was a secular transformation of fatality into continuity, contingency into meaning. . . . Few things were (are) better suited to this end than the idea of a nation. If nation-states are widely conceded to be "new" and "historical," the nations to which they give political expression always loom out of an immemorial past, and still more important glide into a limitless future. It is the magic of nationalism to turn chance into destiny.

(Anderson 1991: 11)

Anderson argues that nations are imagined as a way of dealing with the disruption of traditional, continuous time by the processes of modernization. "Awareness of being imbedded in secular, serial time, with all its implications of continuity, yet of 'forgetting' the experience of this continuity – product of the ruptures of the late eighteenth century – engenders the need for a narrative of 'identity'" (1991: 205). This narrative, for Anderson, is structured by death (by martyrdom, assassination, war, holocaust) remembered as "our own" moments that move us toward our national destiny. Nationalism, then, is a product of the need for and imagining of immortality.[7]

The notion of the nation as imagined community has provided a powerful metaphor for scholars interested in the cultural roots of nationalism. His work has paved the way for important studies that interrogate the symbolic and discursive dimensions of the national project, especially among scholars of literature and cultural studies. Yet, some pressing questions are provoked by Anderson's analysis. If the "nation" is imagined as a "deep, horizontal comradeship," a "fraternity" ready to die for one another, how do men and how can women belong to the national "fraternity?" In what ways is the imagined community of the nation gendered? Who imagines the nation? When and how do women participate in this imagining? How are nations portrayed over time? What symbols evoke "national" loyalties? As Nira Yuval-Davis and Floya Anthias (1989: 7) have pointed out, "Very often (women) constitute the actual symbolic figuration" (of the nation); they are "signifiers of ethnic/national differences." How do men and women respond to such gendered "figuration" and "signifiers?" Do national symbols make particular presentations about patriots and heroes, and about masculinity and femininity?

A second set of questions emerges from Anderson's analysis of the impact of modernization, especially technology, on cultural formations. For example, given the emphasis on print technology and literacy as essential for nation-building and the diffusion of national myths, how were print media disseminated and consumed; to whom and by whom were they disseminated? What do differential literacy rates mean? Did the nation mean something different to women and men of lower and upper classes in the eighteenth and nineteenth centuries? A final set of questions is raised by Anderson's analysis of how the nation fulfills the search for transcendent meaning for its members. Who are the new "priests" who purvey the nation as transcendent? Do men and women respond to the transcendency myths in different ways? If, as *Imagined Communities* suggests, the "nation" fuses the past and the future, how do other forms and practices of communal transcendence (e.g. the family, sexual behaviors, reproduction) connect to the "nation?"

Donald Horowitz's *magnum opus, Ethnic Groups in Conflict* (1985), begins the difficult theoretical work of exploring this last question. Horowitz points out that "the meaningfulness of ethnic identity derives from its birth connection – it came first – or from acceptance by an ethnic group as if born into it. In this key respect (the primacy of birth), ethnicity and kinship are alike" (1985: 56–57). Of course, ethnicity as extended kinship may be partially "imagined"; it may be fictive, but "the idea . . . of common ancestry makes it possible for ethnic groups to think in terms of family resemblances – traits held in common, on a supposedly genetic basis, or cultural features acquired in early childhood – and to bring into play for a much wider circle those concepts of mutual obligation and antipathy to outsiders that are applicable to family relations" (1985: 57).

How do we move from family to ethnicity as a basis for group loyalty? For Horowitz, it is a consequence of the process of political and economic development, particularly the experiences of colonialism (and capitalism). *Ethnic Groups in Conflict* seeks to understand the failure of civic nation-building in Asia, Africa and the Caribbean, and what he finds is the primacy of ethnic ties in social relations. Under the impact of the colonial administrative state in all these areas, "the network of transactions grew in scale out of all proportion to the reach of preexisting sentiments of community. With migration, trade, and a central bureaucratic structure, among other things, it became necessary to establish social relations far beyond the village or locality" (1985: 76). There were two possibilities for the construction of these new social relations: the development of so-called civic nationalism or the extension of already existing familial ties through the ethnic group. Horowitz acknowledges that social, political, and economic interests may also be served by ethnic affiliation. Ethnic ties are powerful then, because they can appeal to both interest and affect.

Horowitz focuses much of his work on the ways in which colonialism and the post-colonial state structured ethnic boundaries out of kinship networks and how those boundaries and state policies helped produce and then exacerbated inter-ethnic rivalries.[8] Although *Ethnic Groups in Conflict* is largely centered on concerns with the state, one of the most compelling aspects of Horowitz's work is his theoretical focus on the psychological dimensions of ethnic identification.[9] Drawing from the work of experimental social psychology, Horowitz argues that belonging to a group produces a positive identification with the group and the desire to improve the group's position *vis à vis* other groups.[10] This powerful identification seems to persist even in the face of clear material disadvantage to the group member. Identification with ethnicity is a particularly powerful basis for group affiliation. Ethnicity is kin to familial ties. These "affiliations . . . are putatively ascriptive and therefore difficult or impossible to change" (1985: 147). Individuals receive multiple psychological rewards for ethnic group membership. And the "emotive quality of the competition for group worth" is more acute for ethnic groups than for other types of groups in part because ethnic groups compete over long periods of time in many spheres (1985: 147).

Here, we have a partial answer to the question of why ethnic identification is so powerful. Family ties are considered more powerful than other collective interests or "imagined community." The transference of kin loyalty to ethnic and national loyalty is not only politically necessary for the building of nationalism, it is also emotionally satisfying for individuals.[11] *Ethnic Groups in Conflict* invites us to explore the process by which ethnic loyalties are transferred from kin groups or the possibility that these new loyalties are imposed upon individuals as a consequence of power relations within kin. Obviously, gender is a key factor here: rules about who is kin, about who will marry whom, norms about the scope of familial loyalty, about how one is socialized to group identity, and cultural rituals and rites of belonging are all gendered. What are the internal group dynamics that generate particular understandings of identity and that help formulate what the psychological rewards of group membership will be? Do women and men get the same psychological rewards from ethnic group membership?[12] These are all gendered phenomena left unexamined by Horowitz. This inattention to gender, however, should not obscure the brilliance of Donald Horowitz's attempt to link micro and macro levels, to think systematically about the relationship between kinship, ethnic and state structures and processes.[13] In fact, his recognition of the need to bridge the gap between family, ethnic group, and state recalls for us the fundamental feminist insight about the political dimensions of "personal" life and the deep interrelationship between the "public" and "private" spheres. Indeed, the growing feminist scholarship on the gendered dynamics of family and the state may provide a base for answering some of the questions suggested by Horowitz's work.

Despite their different approaches, theoretical frameworks, and contributions to the study of nationalism, all four of these works share a gender neutral approach. We have delineated the ways in which such gender neutrality eclipses important questions and limits our understanding of the complex dynamics of ethno-nationalism; however, we have also tried to suggest the important insights that can be derived from these works.

Conclusion

> When did we become "a people"? When did we stop being one? Or
> are we in the process of becoming one? What do these questions have
> to do with our intimate relations with each other and with others?
>
> (Said 1986, cited in Bhabha 1990: 7)

If we are to comprehend the phenomenon of ethno-nationalism, it is
absolutely essential that we think more systematically about how national
identities develop, about the forces that make them so powerful, about the
ways in which they affect our social relations and personal identities. The
authors whom we have examined in this chapter have been particularly
concerned with some of Said's questions. For all, becoming a people is
rooted in the development of myths of ancestry, kinship, and group history.
We become a nation out of the processes of modernization in a specific
socio-historical context. We become a nation under the influence of intellectual and political elites, of shifting group interests, and ideas of
nationality. We learn from these authors greater precision about "the
processes of becoming a people." From Anderson, we learn to appreciate
the ways in which technology shapes the presentation of images and the
production of narratives of heritage and therefore makes possible the imagining of this form of communal identity. Hobsbawm reminds us that
nationalism and national memory are neither given nor immutable; they
require popular support and must draw from popular experience and ideas
to have any power. That support and those experiences and ideas will
change over time and by local context. Indeed, they will have an end.
Horowitz reminds us that the potency of nationalism and its myths lies in
its resemblance to kinship, in the psychological needs met by extended
kinship bonds and in the structural relations between family and state.
Smith reminds us above all of the significance of ethnicity and its partic-
ularism; he emphasizes that a focus on any single dimension of ethno-
national identity will distort our understanding of nationalism. Together,
these authors exemplify a "mainstream" literature which may recognize
the importance of "our intimate relations" to national identity but has not
explored how our "intimate relations" engender that identity.

Let us return, briefly, to the Oedipus story, a story of human intimacy,
identity, and political crisis. As a mythic figure, what makes Oedipus who
he is are his military triumphs and his sexual relationship: he is the
conqueror of Thebes and the husband of Jocasta. His personal and social
identities had everything to do with his intimate relationship. Oedipus was
taken back by the myths, stories, and familial ties that preceded him: he
rediscovered his identity only in the context of that past. Similarly, nations
rediscover and create their identities out of their mythical pasts and imagined community. The historical myths and the imagined communities are
deeply gendered; the processes by which myths are constructed and

purveyed tell us something about gender relations in any particular nation. They present normative images of what it means to be a male or female member of the nation, and they will therefore affect members of the nation differently. The Oedipus myth is pre-national, yet it prompts us to recognize that the development of national identity, like all forms of identity formation, is itself a gendered process. Although the four works we have examined here suggest different and insightful ways to think about the development of national identity and the nation, our reading of them has prodded us to be mindful of the ways in which nations and narrations about the nation privilege particular forms of identity and social relations, and subordinate others. Silence about gender excludes many questions which are essential for understanding national identity and the dynamics of nationalism. How is the nation created? By whom? What does it mean for women or men to be Theban/Irish/Russian/Yoruba? How does the nation circumscribe their personal identities? How is gender, as one of the multiple aspects of identity constituted within the nation, and how does it constitute the nation? What are the relations of domination and subordination *within* nations that help support the national identity? How do nations and nationalists privilege particular forms of masculinity and femininity and subordinate others? What are the differences between *groups* of men or women within the nation (e.g. class, sexual orientation, religion)? Which aspects of identities are subordinated and why? If Homi Bhabha is right that "Nations, like narrations, lose their origins in the myths of time and only fully realize their horizons in the mind's eye" (1990: 306), then we need to think carefully about whose mind's eye we are looking into and why.

Notes

1 In Sophocles (1982) *Three Theban Plays*. Trans. Robert Fagles. New York: Viking Penguin, p. 224. All quotations from Sophocles are from the Fagles edition.

2 We should note that Smith cites from the Watling translation of Sophocles' play.

3 The phrase "blood and belonging" has been used by Michael Ignatieff (1994) in the title of his book on nationalism.

4 Sophocles (1982: 185).

5 Sophocles (1982: 242).

6 We use the term "mainstream" to refer to those social science approaches and methods which have dominated the study of nationalism, as evident by inclusion in anthologies, core journals in the social science disciplines and citation in published work. We appreciate that the contrast we make between "mainstream" and feminist literature is problematic: we do not assume that feminist literature cannot be part of the "mainstream" of social science. And we recognize that some feminist work on nationalism has been included recently in anthologies and journals. Thus far, however, its impact on the field has been limited, in large part, as we show in this chapter, because feminist approaches invite a re-conceptualization of the study of nationalism.

7 Anderson's argument is reminiscent of that of Harold Isaacs (1976), who argued that ethnicity is powerful precisely because it provides humans with a sense of self-esteem – belonging to a group that is positively valued – and of immortality.

8 Horowitz also discusses ways in which the state might be ordered within the legacy of colonialism, but that analysis is not germane to the purpose of this chapter.

9 William Bloom (1990) has also used psychological theories to try to explain the power of nationalism; however, his work does not distinguish between types of nationalism.

10 Experiments in inter-group discrimination by Michael Billig and Henri Tajfel, for example, have proved the willingness of group members to sacrifice individual gain for comparative advantage of the group (Horowitz 1985: 143–147).

11 Ethnic conflicts are intense, because to challenge an ethnic boundary in this context is to threaten the self.

12 Indeed, most of the psychological literature from which Horowitz draws his theory is based on experiments done with men.

13 Unfortunately, it is not for this contribution that Donald Horowitz's work is so frequently cited in the scholarship on ethnic conflict.

3 Writing bodies on the nation for the globe

Zillah Eisenstein

Nationalism in the twenty-first century operates alongside the discourses of globalism and multiculturalism. This chapter is a brief examination of nationalism within its twenty-first century global context.[1] I ask you to see the nation as a complete invention, as completely mythic and unnatural. National identities and geographies shift and change. The idea of nation is a fantasmatic imagining that misrepresents the diversity that exists within the borders it names.

To the extent that I theorize the masculinist aspects of nationalism I risk overgeneralization, almost a kind of essentialist viewing of nation. Although no one viewing grasps the varieties of nationalism, I think I agree with Aijaz Ahmad (1995), that "an essence is *given* to it, in particular situations." So, I may unintentionally homogenize the gender exclusivity of nation in order eventually to divest nationalism of its masculinist borders.

The nation constructs gender, sexuality, and their racial meanings through moments of nation-building, like the gulf war "when the nation becomes a family" (Jeffords and Rabinovitz 1994); or the video beating of Rodney King, when the nation becomes white (Ruth Gilmore in Butler 1993a); or when president Clinton equates securing u.s. borders from haitian refugees with the national security.

The fantasized bodies of a homogenized "womanhood" – maybe a maternalized Barbie doll – are used to mark "the" western nation. Nation-building is already, then, encoded with a series of racialized/ sexualized/engendered silences. The symbolized woman, as mother of us all, psychically attaches the nation to family and nature with their racialized meanings.

Colored bodies are scrutinized in relation to this fantasmatic femaleness as though femaleness were a monolithic construction. This process makes americo-euro women painfully visible to women of color, given the racial power they wield.[2] Yet, these same americo-euro women are made invisible as part of the fantasmatic gender hierarchy of the nation.

Post-cold war politics creates new challenges for masking the racial/ sexual/gender exclusivity of nation-building. On the one hand there are the nationalisms in eastern and central europe which manipulate racial/ethnic identities for the purposes of nation-building as they struggle to establish a place in the new global marketplace. On the other hand, there is the nation-building of the u.s., which requires the redefinition of politics and public life given the necessities of global capital. The u.s. is no longer to think of itself as an economic nation, but rather a site within the transnational economy. In this process, the racialized/sexualized symbolization of the nation and its fantasy structure become recoded.

Salman Rushdie in the *Satanic Verses* says that because we have to live in the world, we have to "make believe" (1988: 469). It is tricky to know who is making believe, and what they are imagining when they do so. Is it that the end of the bi-polar superpower world has instigated a crisis of masculinity, just at the point that we thought the need to strut would be quieted? Are wars and violence today due to a new "manliness" which leaves us with a pure aggression that has no particular name (Enzensberger 1994: 20–21)? Is this what Jacqueline Rose (1993) means when she asks if "war mimics and participates" in the ambivalence towards one's own difference? For her, "the familiar destructiveness of war represents not as is commonly supposed, finality, but uncertainty, a hovering on the edge of what, like death, can never be totally known" (Rose 1993: 16, 17). Meanwhile, I wonder how we might "make believe" without war.

I assume that we will first have to move beyond the need to "other," and beyond the need of nationalism, to be able to move beyond hatreds.

Post-1989 politics and eastern european nationalisms

In the spring of 1989 western journalists and politicians celebrated the revolutions in eastern and central europe as a victory for democracy. Little was made of the fact that they were at best male dominated democracies, and at worst examples of recycled ex-communist paternalist opportunism. By the early 1990s the western discourse shifted; the new democracies were defeated by ethnic nationalist rivalries. Whereas democracy had supposedly replaced communism, now nationalism has displaced democracy. Little is said about the sexualized/gendered constructions of these racialized/ethnic borders.

These new-old nationalisms define the twenty-first century. They have developed during *as well as* in response to the transnational economy that has established a globalized cultural telecommunications system. The rise of these new-old nationalisms is a reaction against former egalitarian communist rhetoric and the promise of new consumer markets. They are also continuations of old racialized hatreds like anti-semitism. Post-cold war nationalisms are then a mix of the old and new: they utilize racialized/engendered hatreds but with a new license given restructuring by the global economy.

This discussion is complicated because nationalism has become a central facet of the "west's" language for looking at "other" post-communist societies. The u.s. criticizes these countries for succumbing to ethnic hatreds. Clinton looks *at* bosnia and complains that it is a hopeless morass. By default the west looks good even though we have our own kind of nation-building and our own racial/ethnic/gender hatreds. Instead of looking elsewhere and seeing ourselves, the u.s. looks elsewhere to caution marginalized groups within the u.s. not to demand too much for themselves. Affirmative action for blacks is called balkanized separatism, and challenged for destabilizing the common ground of the nation as a whole.

But the common ground is shaky. The los angeles rebellion following the verdict in the Rodney King trial revealed enormous rage by people of color toward the racisms within the u.s. Nazi graffiti on subway walls in new york city is a ready reminder of the anti-semitism which flourishes within our own borders. The bombing of abortion clinics and the killing of their doctors constitutes terrorist activity against women "within" the west. The paramilitary militia movement hates the federal government because it supposedly has given away the country to blacks, jews, hispanics, *and* women.

All this mixes up the way we see hate, and difference, and nations, and democracy. Old borders no longer hold: enemies exist inside and outside what were once considered nations. Post-cold war conflicts are not easily cast within the bi-polar framework of communist/anti-communist. Instead, (western) democracy is positioned against a plural set of enemies: islamic fundamentalism, ethnic nationalism, foreign terrorism. As enemies are constructed, so are nations. And, if the enemies are multiple and not simply located outside, it becomes more difficult to project unity. Then fantasy becomes more prominent.

The in(ex)clusivity of the nation

Nations provide an "identity" beyond the self, a sense of belongingness, and connectedness. This space beyond the "private" self is the domain of the "public" nation. The individual, their connection to others, and their sociality, are crucial to the construction of the idea of "nation." Any notion of "we" is in part an "imagined community" (see Anderson 1991). Nationality provides an identity that exists outside the self (Pfaff 1993: 40) at the same time as it constructs a notion of self that is exclusionary of other identities. The notion of likeness *can* be dangerous if it is used to exclude, and silence, and punish. Nazism, south african apartheid, serb nationalism – each provides an identity for some while declaring a non-identity for others.

The nation implies borders and boundaries that bespeak both openings and closings (Edgar Morin in Bennington 1990: 121). A nation requires an inside and an outside – natives and foreigners, immigrants, refugees, and the people coming from the outside. A nation is defined by its unity;

differences and particularities within it challenge its universality. Shared commonness is privileged against diversity, which is problematized as disorderly.

Nationalism articulates a "communal loyalty" which is positioned against loyalties that are seen as subversive to the recognized shared identity (Pfaff 1993: 137). So one person's sense of nation can easily not be someone else's. The idea that all (white) men (not women or people of color) are created equal supposedly binds the nation. It clearly binds some people more than others.

In the u.s. one usually speaks of patriotism rather than nationalism; of a melting pot or mixed society rather than a racial or religious state; of (liberal) pluralism rather than ethnic nationalism; of federalism rather than centralization. U.S. stands for "united" states – unity with its distinct parts. Yet the "unity" reflects a war of conquest against mexico and native americans; the black slave trade and the vicious practice of slavery; its own civil war. The nation utters different narratives for its different inhabitants. Not everyone is a citizen with full access to his or her rights. And yet the discourse of liberal democracy promises the "dream" of the collectivity to everyone.

One's sense of nation shifts according to one's positioning within it or outside of it. When living outside one's "own" country in a first world country one becomes asian, or third world. Third world identity "gives a proper name to a generalized margin" (Spivak 1993: 55). Otherwise, from within their homeland these identities are specified as bengali, korean, japanese, chinese, and so on.

In the two decades of Reagan-Bush-Clintonian-privatization, when individuals are expected to take care of themselves and government has less responsibility for the public welfare, nationalism becomes a curious attempt at publicizing individualism.[3] But the western post-cold war nation is left emptied of its publicness. The self-centered discourse of the privatized state denies the realm of public responsibility or public welfare. As governments are expected to do less for the individual, the very notion of politics, with its publicness, is undermined.

It is not clear for the twenty-first century what will become of nations without publicly minded (however partial) governments. Although a fiction, the modern nation depended on the differentiation between economic (self-interest) and political (public interest) arenas. As global capital challenges the role of nation-states in this process, the construction of a nation devoid of economic borders becomes the new imaginary. Nation-building becomes newly artificial. Rituals, emblems, flags, and anthems must stand-in, for the old, as the nation shifts (Enzensberger 1994: 107). Just remember the yellow-ribbon campaign of the gulf war; or the storybook fantasy remake of Nixon's presidency at his televised funeral.

Racializing the exclusivity of the nation

Serb nationalists specify their racial blood as formative of "the" nation, much like Hitler defined germany by aryan blood. In these cases the specific racial category becomes the statement of the collectivity. Singularity and exclusivity define unity. The nation has no universally inclusive meaning beyond this. Nationalism instead becomes a form of racism, although always set in a particular context: croatian, german, american. Or as Hannah Arendt argued, race becomes a substitute for the nation (Arendt 1951: 185).

Nazis were consistent here: the "decent" jews were zionists because they thought in "national" terms (Arendt 1977: 60). Today the question of israel has become much more complicated: jewish nationalism looks different than it did in 1948, so there are new "victims" to be considered. Non-jews in palestine have their own experience of zionism (Said 1992: xxi, 87).

According to Paul Gilroy, race often coincides with national frontiers; the nation distinguishes itself from immigrants and foreigners (Gilroy 1987: 46). One can assume that global capitalist markets will continue to rename nations and their racialized borders through a multiculturalist twenty-first century vision. The relationship between race and nation develops together but they are not, as David Goldberg (1993) argues, synonymous or fixed in meaning. Instead, "as *concepts*, race and nation are largely empty receptacles ... population groups ... invented, interpreted, and imagined as communities or societies" (Goldberg 1993: 79).

Nationalism, as such, is often disguised. In u.s. post-cold war nationalist rhetoric, racism is not defended by a blood/color exclusivity. Instead it is constructed by a "color-blind" language of democracy. This discourse claims that white males suffer today from reverse discrimination and unfair treatment which favors white women and people of color. White men, who still dominate in public office and the economy, use civil rights legislation to challenge the demands made by people of color and white women to secure the nation for themselves.

The significance of racism in the american psyche must not be lost on the reader. Michele Wallace argues the place of blacks "as central figures in the national imagination" (Dent 1992: 9). The psychic construction of "the" nation is white; built on and out of black slavery. The imaginary remains somewhat sedimented in the black/white divide with a "veneer of fixedness" (Goldberg 1993: 81). This residue threads through new as well as old circumstance. Racist arrangements then change, but also do not.

Democracy when used on behalf of nationalist rhetoric allows racism to flourish. In many of the east european post-communist nations, freedom of speech has allowed hatred – towards jews, roma, and other ethnic minorities – to be spoken openly. When freedom of speech allows a freely spoken hatred, it is hard to distinguish masculinist democracy from ethnic nationalism (Strom 1993: 50).

The rhetoric of nationalism has also been used by marginalized groups like Queer Nation and the Black Panthers in the u.s. to legitimize a liberatory identity of the excluded (Parker *et al.* 1992b: 8). When nation is used by "outsiders" to challenge the "inside" of the nation, these attempts are rejected by established authorities as divisive and separatist, and racist (Marshall 1991: 86).

Cold-war nationalisms positioned the nation for or against communism. The newer ethnic/racist nationalisms use the homogeneity of a racialized "difference" to draw borders where none were before. These post-cold war nationalisms construct nations out of geographical maps that are complicated by changed allegiances (Bennis 1993: 48). These identities emerge even when they are desperately fought against. As one sarajevan, Mikica Babic, angrily and sadly states: "'We never, until the war, thought of ourselves as Muslims. We were Yugoslavs. But when we began to be murdered, because we were Muslims, things changed. The definition of who we are today has been determined by our killers. In a way this means these Serbs have won, no matter what happens in the war.'" (Hedges 1995).

There are new geographical borders formulated in and through these racialized imaginings. Multicultural expressions of difference either destabilize the nation, as in ex-yugoslavia, or become suspect as separatist and divisive to the nation, as in the u.s., *and* have also become an integral part of global capitalism. But these new "nations" are not able to encompass the plural, shifting and multiple identities they confront.

A nation cannot encompass its diverse identities from a homogenized standpoint. Nationalism, imaging unity, then simultaneously creates and excludes difference. As Faisal Fatehali Devji states: in india, the muslim, as opposed to the hindu, appears as a sign of national failure because of the very politics of nationalism itself (Devji 1992: 3, 7). One would need to envision universality differently in order that the nation not be confining and dominating (Snead 1990: 245).

Multiculturalism signifies multiplicity rather than singularity. It is increasingly said that the united states is no longer a nation but a multicultural regime (Kurth 1992: 32; see also Huntington 1993a, 1993b; the responses to Huntington in *Foreign Affairs* 72:4 1993 issue; Porter 1993). This reflects a shift within the discourse of multiculturalism from a vision defined by marginalized groups to a recognized necessity of the new regime. Multiculturalism becomes the language of the monocultural society in the hopes of deradicalizing its original potential to subvert the universality inherent in the meaning of nation.

Post-cold war nationalisms fictionalize ideal ethnic-linguistic homogeneity while they are more readily recognized as plurinational and pluricultural states (Hobsbawm 1990: 185, 187). "Ethnic states leave no room for people with different ethnic identities" (Soros 1993: 15; see also Block 1993; Glenny 1993). They establish this exclusivity along racialized/sexualized lines that collapse into themselves. As Renata Salecl (1992) describes serb nationalism:

if you add an albanian (dirty, fornicating, violent, primitive), and a slovene (antipatriotic, unproductive merchant, profiteering), you get a jew (Salecl 1992: 57; also 1994). This kind of nationalism is a devastating mix of racializing sexuality and engendering race.

Racism always differentiates in order to establish hierarchy.[4] And the hierarchy is also coded through a gendered formulation of family which authenticates the nation. Even the liberatory discourse of black nationalism, which openly decried u.s. racism, utilized an "authoritarian pastoral patriarchy," according to Paul Gilroy (1992). He argues that "an Americo-centric, postnationalist essence of blackness has been constructed through the dubious appeal to family." This appeal images a racial family that is organic and natural (Gilroy 1992). Angela Davis celebrates aspects of black nationalism but also recognizes its misogynist overtones within hip-hop culture (Davis 1992).

A nation always has "a" gender and "a" race although the gender is usually not spoken. Racism is clearly spoken in nazi germany, south african apartheid, and serb nationalism, while gender is encoded (naturalized) through patriarchal familialism. The symbolization of the nation, as the "mother country," em*bodies* the nation as a "woman." "The" imagined female body represents the nation and silences patriarchy simultaneously. So nations are pictorially represented by women, depicted as mothers (reproducers) of the nation. As such, nationalism, as a form of familialism is neutralized and women become the mothers of "the" race. Gender is racialized in the process: muslim women raped by serb nationalists provide ethnic cleansing, and a greater serbia.

Mother russia; the nation as homeland. The language of male privilege (sexism) speaks through the metaphors of love. It embraces the feminine as mother, nurturer, caregiver. It is a symbolic motherhood: women are the mothers of *all* children of the nation. In nationalism the fictive power of motherhood stands against the varied realities of women's experiences in society (Hassim 1993).

Interestingly, though, the nation is sometimes spoken of as "the" fatherland, it also imagines "the" brotherhood of fraternity. This is not the case for "the" mother country, which imagines the nation as a fraternity, *not* as a sisterhood. Nationalism reduces women to their motherhood. Nowhere in the iconography of nations is there space for women *as* sisters, *as* a sisterhood.[5]

The war memorial chosen as the symbol for the reunited germany intended to honor the war dead is a statue of a "mother and son." The statue was criticized by many for "using the image of a suffering mother to promote national unity. Perpetrators and victims are gathered into her lap" (Kinzer 1993). The unity expressed through mother's love and represented through patriarchal imagery is supposed to erase the hatred of nazism and its violations.

Nationalism speaks men, and applauds the fraternal order while imaging women to call forth notions of motherly love. Hatred is not spoken here.

Love and duty are, so women are used as symbols of national identity (Walby 1992). And hate is instead spoken in terms of the racialized identities of men or women. Those who differ from us in color or ethnicity cannot be "our" mother. So one is free to express the fear, the anger, the blame.

Virginia Woolf in *The Three Guineas* wrote that as a woman one has no country (Woolf 1938: 109). Women do not belong to a nation. They instead construct the mythology of nationhood. Anannya Bhattachardee (1992) argues that nation-ness is inextricably linked to the fiction of womanhood. The myth of indian womanness is a signifier of the indian nation. Indian women represent tradition and custom as metaphor for chastity and sanctity. However, live women, rather than mythic ones, can always subvert this representation and the national boundaries constructed by it (Bhattachardee 1992: 20, 30, 31).

Nationalist imaginings and women's bodies

Nations are a blend of fictive imagining and pose the problem of an impossible unity (Bhabha 1994; Chatterjee 1993b; Gellner 1983: 15). Benedict Anderson writes of nationalism as an "imagined political community" which thinks of the nation with love. Nationalism allows a new way of thinking about fraternity, power, and time. The nation appears "interestless" and demands devotion as such (Anderson 1991: 6, 22, 36, 144). Anderson's community is made up of men and their devotion to a "deep, horizontal comradeship," a passionate brotherhood. As such, he thinks nationalism is an identity like kinship, or religion, rather than an ideology like liberalism or fascism (Anderson 1991: 16, 6, 15). He does not recognize that nationalism is an instance of phallocratic construction, with brotherhood, rather than sisterhood at its core. Nor does he recognize racism as part of the historical articulation of the nation (Anderson 1991: 141–154).[6]

Nations are made up of citizens and the fiction here requires that anyone can be of the nation. W. E. B. Dubois clarified early on that the nation echoes and enforces inequity for blacks (DuBois 1969: 51). Citizenship has long been shown, by excluded groups, to exclude them: people of color, white women, and the other "others." Minorities who are excluded by the nation as deviant are positioned against the silent standards of the nation as a whole (Anthias and Yuval-Davis 1992: 22).

This "imagined community" is a fantasy world with women present, but silenced. They are absented from the fraternity which is masculine. They are given no citizen voice, although they often take it. Instead they create the borders for the fraternal order. Geraldine Heng and Janadas Devan (1992: 356) describe this: "women, and all signs of the feminine, are by definition always and already anti-national." Women guard the home and create domesticity against which men construct their fictive manliness (Mosse 1985: 1).

We are presented with what Heng and Devan call "uterine nationalism" which derives "out of the recesses of the womb" (Heng and Devan 1992: 349). Women are the procreators and not the citizens (Slobin 1992: 249). The female/maternalized body becomes the site for *viewing* the nation. It is an imaginary site that is wholly naturalized through the symbolization of the female body. "All nationalisms are gendered" (McClintock 1991: 104). It is the bordered differentiation of women's bodies from men's bodies rather than the bodies themselves that construct the fiction of nations.

Because "the" nation fantasizes women in a homogenized, abstracted familial order, women become a "metaphor" for what they represent, rather than what they are. First world women of the west represent modernity; women of the third world south and east represent tradition. As symbolizations, they become static and unchanging like the constructions of timeless motherhood. Their representation, as the nation, defines them fictively, and reproduces the fiction.

Women lose their "own identity" when used as markers for the nation. Their status stands in for the progress of "the" nation, rather than their own (Collins 1992a: 78–79). They become political signifiers for Judith Butler because of their "phantasmatic investment and phantasmatic promise." As a sign, rather than as a description of "real" women, it "produces the expectation of a unity, a full and final recognition that can never be achieved" (Butler 1993b: 191).

As mother of the nation, woman is invisibly visible as a symbolic fantasy. And the different layerings of invisibility are accorded along racial, economic and sexual lines. A black lesbian reflects this complex invisibility. In contrast, the fantasmatic woman becomes the body of the nation. In the process she is desexualized and "regulated" as the mother of us all. Her maternal body fictionalizes motherhood and the nation simultaneously. She represents safety through the boundaries of her body. She is embraced by the glorification of womanhood. She represents morality itself.

No wonder real, actual women pose a problem for the nation, because much of this fictive symbolization does not resemble life or common sense.[7] Yet, two Barbie dolls are sold every second. In life-size terms, Barbie's body would be 40-18-32; although we all know she is just a doll she is also very real (Quindlen 1994). She represents the symbolic use of women in what Nalini Natarajan (1994), albeit in another context, calls the "erotics of nationalism": the "dream image of women" servicing the "psychic needs of the male subject." Although Barbie is not symbolic of motherhood as a "spectacle" which "cements" and "unifies," she operates to legitimize the fantasy structure which underlies this construction: the homogenized and congealed (hetero)sexuality which sediments and contrasts with motherhood (Natarajan 1994: 79, 83, 85, 88).

Women, as cultural symbols (Moghadam 1994a) and symbolic of particular communities, become the site where tradition is "debated and reformulated" (Mani 1990: 118), and where the nation is "regenerated"

(Chakravarti 1990: 79). The present situation of algerian women reflects the importance of traditionalist patriarchy for religious islamic nationalists. Women are the "symbol" of what the future algeria will become so women who defy their traditional symbolic role – by not wearing the veil, or holding a job outside the home – are subject to grave danger (Bennoune 1994).

Psychic needs and the racialized/gendered nation

Nationalized identity blends real and unreal constructions with a psychic resonance that is imaged in real and made up ways, with no conscious-ness that it is not "perfectly true."[8] Edward Said (1978) elicits a similar understanding when he describes how one's mind designates familiar spaces as "ours" and unfamiliar spaces beyond "ours" as "theirs." The distinctions, often geographical, can be entirely arbitrary (Said 1978: 54).

Said writes of the myth/images that use all material for their own end to displace any other thought. Orientalism, as a myth/image, explains the familiar – europe, the west, us – against the strange – the orient, the east, them. The orient, like nation, is a creation that is "essentially" an idea; a "man-made" idea which has little connection to a "real" orient. Said argues that we endow things with meaning all the time and this is an imaginative, figurative, interpretative process. It even has a quasi-fictional quality. "Imaginative geography and history help the mind to intensify its own sense of itself by dramatizing the distance and difference between what is close to it and what is far away." An imagined geography draws dramatic bound-aries (Said 1978: 312, 43, 5, 55, 73). Nationhood is constructed in and through psychic identities that institutionalize "difference." People live and experience their identity through their bodies; the physical and psychic knowing of their sex, gender, and race. Women are the "boundary subjects" defining this process (Kristeva 1993: 35). And gender according to Nancy Chodorow has an "individual, personal, emotional and fantasy meaning." It is an "intrapsychic experience," that resonates differently according to one's experience and one's unconscious fantasies (Chodorow 1995: 518, 536, 541).

Because gender and nation are always being negotiated femininity is not the same as femaleness; gays can be feminine, or "effeminate." So can muslims and jews. Masculinity is not one and the same with maleness; masculine males are "men," whereas non-masculine males are not-"men." Learning one's gender is no easy or automatic process which explains why moving into adolescence can feel like "emigrating to a foreign culture"; girls must leave home and learn a new language (Hirsch 1994: 75).

Imaginings, which are always part fantasy, are activated through different means. For Julia Kristeva woman is never fully represented as she is because she is unrepresentable, a poetic version of femaleness as mother, uttering incest, or the repressed maternal element. "Woman" reinstates maternal territory for Kristeva (1980: 136–137). Then, the nation becomes the imagined fantasmatic investment (see Mitchell and Rose 1983; Salecl

1994). Women, being not-men, are included inside the nation as "mother." As mother, she can be distanced without being made an outcast (Mosse 1985: 132–134).

Salecl, a slovene feminist, views the traumatic gender fantasy structure which supports ethnic hatred as interlaced with nationalism. To unlearn nationalism is to unlearn the psychic physicality of racialized bodily borders.

South africa, the newest of the post-cold war attempts at democracy, faces the conundrum of a multi-ethnic democratic nationhood. According to Mark Gevisser (1994), a south african journalist, non-racialism has been the guiding principle of the African National Congress (ANC). Zulu ethnic identity politics stands counter to this non-racial democratic vision. And "coloreds" – those of mixed race identity – are weary of a black identity considered more pure than their own racial mix. "To fight apartheid, the ANC chose to erase differences – to espouse a non-racialism that did not address ethnic identity" (Gevisser 1994). Zulus, coloreds and whites, each cling to a racialized/ethnic/blood line identity. It remains to be seen if a multicultural democracy and not a new racial (and male) apartheid can emerge out of this mix. I think it is a bit early to declare that south africa has "the makings of a wobbly but workable, wheeling-and-dealing, pluralist democracy," but we can hope (Charney 1994).

Rey Chow argues that the "west" owns the codes of fantasy. So imaginings will be westernized while also produced locally. The politics of seeing is simultaneously a politics of not seeing. Nationalized identity involves a "positional superiority" (Chow 1991: xiii, 3) of homogenized masculinity produced locally.

According to feminist and ex-yugoslav Zarana Papić, nationalism smashes democracy. For her, in Belgrade there is only the national truth as stated by serb nationalists. Serbian nationalism is so deeply historically and culturally patriarchal it does not have to articulate or accentuate its control over women.

Papić makes clear that serb nationalism requires an aggressive violence that even many men cannot sustain. In the beginning of the bosnian war 20,000–30,000 men left the country so as not to have to fight. She tells the story of one young man who was not so lucky. "In one unit somewhere near Sid some soldiers wanted to desert and go home, but others decided to stay. One unhappy young man of 18 first went to the line of deserters, then changed his mind and went back to the line of those who decided to stay. But he could not stay in that line also. He left both lines, stood for awhile and shot himself" (Papić 1993; see also Papić no date). Psychic hatreds are mobilized in the balkans. Anti-semitic and xenophobic violence is on the rise and neo-nazis continue to gain strength (Schmidt 1993; see also Milosv 1993; Whitney 1993). Slobodan Milošević, formerly a loyal communist party hack, invented serb nationalism to reposition himself for the post-communist transnational economy. Although his real commitment is to his own power, he has been able to re-instigate psychic racialized/gendered hatreds for this purpose, all too easily.

More recently Milošević found that whipping up "pan-serbian fervor" does not serve him well. Instead he paints Radovan Karadzić, leader of the bosnian serbs, as the lunatic of serb aggression and presents himself as reasonable and open to negotiation. Predrag Simić, director of a foreign policy center in Belgrade, says that Milošević was never a nationalist. "He was only a politician surfing on the nationalist wave. That explains how he was able to change course so easily" (Kinzer 1995).

On the other hand, the people of Sarajevo will not leave. "We simply refuse to die – as a city, as a people, as a future . . . if we only had a little more peace and electricity." And fantasies of all sorts die hard as well. As a 6 year old in Sarajevo says: "Who knows, maybe Santa Claus will bring me a leg for the new year. I'd sort of like that, if he can. If he can't, maybe it'll happen another time" (Dizdarevic 1994: 49, 54).

The use of violent nationalism and ethnic cleansing has created thousands of refugees. These refugees have become the new "others" in western europe. England and germany have tightened their borders against them. Once again, one hears that germany is for the germans. And while a revisionist reading of the holocaust is embraced by some, the gulf war has also made germany a world player for the first time since World War II (Schmidt 1993: 215, 217; see also Hockenos 1993; Lewis 1993; United Nations High Commissioner for Refugees 1993).

Against this ethnic disintegration and nationalist fervor is the privileging of the patriarchal family unit. Nationalism demands a moral renewal that is pre-communist: return women to the home (Antic 1992: 178). Women are imagined as mothers and protectors of hearth and family. The psychic connectors between nationalism, racism, and women's lives are continually rejoined. Ethnic nationalisms tell only part of the story. They speak the anger of racism and cover over the intimate relationship which defines the constructs of race/sex and gender.

Masculinist nationalism and war rape

Because nations are symbolized by women, ethnic cleansing directs its fears and desires onto the bodies of women. On the one hand women are idolized and revered; on the other hand they are brutalized, tortured, raped, and often killed. The war rape of ethnic cleansing in bosnia is set on destroying and annihilating the "mother"; if she can no longer comfort or create safety she can no longer defend the nation. Shame her, and her family, and her nation, and they are defeated.

Lydia H. Liu sees rape as an appropriation of the female body by the nation to eroticize women's victimization (1994: 161–162). War rape uses the devastation of women, and their families, to represent the plight of the nation. The ties of homeland and nation are played out in nationalistic fixations about the mother (Reich 1970: 57). And these unconscious fantasies are let loose in times of crisis (Seifert 1994: 65).

Women become the objects of hatred when men play out their psychic fantasies of desire and fear. Women are targets because of who they are, and how war expresses a militarist masculinity. Rape then constructs men's domi*nation*, and women's subordi*nation*.

Ethnic nationalisms are racialized through sexual violation and strip the "imaginary community" of its love. The raping of women in war defiles the nation of which she is a part, while marking nation-ness. When this war rape is described as ethnic hatred, women are given no specificity.

Women's bodies, then, are used, literally and figuratively, in shaping national identities (Mertus 1993). Masculinist nationalism is why rape has been consistently used to exert a kind of "male apartheid" (Castle-Kanerova 1992: 102) in bosnia. Serbian nationalism violates women, bodily. It nationalizes identity along blood lines. It defines legitimacy in terms of birth. It uses old patriarchal familial traditions to elicit the naturalness of the nation as such.

Serb nationalist ethnic cleansing requires the complete annihilation of women's identity. Serb men plant their serb seed in muslim women and supposedly serb children will be born. The fictive purity of this ethnic identity demands the entire negation of the woman's identity. She becomes a hollowed vessel for serbia. Even in nazi germany women played a part in the jew's racial identity. If one were born to a jewish mother and christian father one was considered half-jew; if one's grandmother was a jew one was a quarter-jew. Not so, in serb fantasy.

Ethnic cleansing focuses the violence on blood lines even though it is played out on and through gender (Cigar 1995; Udovicki and Ridgeway 1995). To name only the ethnic hatred is to make gender hatred invisible. It names the gender violence as something different than hatred. It normalizes the violence against women by not naming it. This invisibility of violence towards women sustains it, like in domestic violence, in violence toward women refugees, and so on (Jones 1994; see also Love 1994; Pendo 1994). Or, as Catherine MacKinnon states: "What is done to women is either too specific to women to be seen as human or too generic to human beings to be seen as specific to women" (MacKinnon 1994: 184).

Many bosnian and croatian women's and refugee groups have protested the depiction of mass rape as simply a "weapon of war." They argue that the "genocidal particularity of rape" is very *ethnically* specific to muslim and croatian women in bosnia-herzegovina and croatia. They argue that if this particular aspect of rape is not understood, the specifically genocidal use of rape by serbian soldiers goes unrecognized.[9] For them, this is a different kind of rape. It is nationalist in its origin and a "war crime" (Mertus 1993: 20).[10] Although initially the United Nations (UN) Balkan War Crimes Commission did not conclude that a "systematic rape policy by the serbs had been proved,"[11] judge Richard Goldstone has now included rape as a war crime.

Genocide is the attempt to destroy a people's identity. War rape is sexualized violence which seeks to terrorize, destroy, and humiliate a people through its women. Rape is being used as a tool of ethnic cleansing, but as Rhonda Copelon advises, one does not want to exaggerate the difference between genocidal rape and "normal" rape because it obscures the atrocity of common rape (Copelon 1994: 205).

However, genocidal rape has its own horrors. It takes place in isolated rape camps, with strict orders from above to force either the woman's exile or her death. Rape is repeatedly performed as torture; it is used to forcibly impregnate; it is even used to exterminate. Women in the camps are raped repetitively, some as many as thirty times a day for as much as three consecutive months. They are kept hungry, they are beaten and gang raped, their breasts are cut off, and stomachs split open (Seifert 1994: 65).[12]

The war rape of women is aimed at the destruction of their physical and personal integrity. Inger Agger explains how women's body borders and boundaries are violated to create sexual trauma (Agger 1994: 106). War rape politically uses sexual trauma as shame. One's body is exposed, abused, and violated; and there is no private self left (Agger 1994: 7–8, 21, 106). Rape itself is like war: "a violent invasion into the interior of one's body" (Seifert 1994: 55).

Sexual humiliation and degradation is an integral part of the rape camps. The terror is brutal and deliberate. The "rapes stifle any wish to return" to the "cleansed area" if one survives (Stiglmayer 1994: 85). And the rape and humiliation are not limited to women. In some of the concentration camps men have also been raped, castrated, and forced into brutalized homosexual acts.[13] Less has been reported about the sexual abuse and torture of men because it destabilizes the very notion of gender that is central to nation-building. The homo-erotic and its relation to masculinist fears and desires is kept silenced while the war rapes of women are sensationalized (Borneman 1994).

Rape transcends historical eras and national borders (Borneman 1994: 57). Frantz Fanon (1963) discusses the rape of algerian women by french soldiers: she was raped to dishonor her husband, she was told to tell her husband what was done to her (Fanon 1963: 254–259). Mass rape has been a part of most wars; in serbia it is said to be a war strategy. It is reported that in rwanda's ethnic massacres in 1994 that thousands of women and girls were raped. The scope of the rape "defies imagination – every girl and woman not killed – was raped." The rape was "systematic, arbitrary, planned and used as a weapon of ethnic cleansing to destroy community ties."[14] A 19 year old air force cadet, Elizabeth Saum, in training at a u.s. academy, was required to take a survival course which included a mock rape scenario. Still suffering from side-effects of the humiliation, she says: "I felt so hated and degraded."[15] She has yet to recover from the brutalizing ordeal.

On a visit to belgrade in May 1995 I met with the anti-war activists, "women in black,"[16] who stand every wednesday in the center square to voice their opposition to serb nationalism. I also met with women from the "autonomous women's center against sexual violence." These women have been assisting women who have been victimized by war rape. Many of the raped women – croat, muslim, and serb – try to find abortions and/or a place to stay in belgrade until the dreaded birth.

The feminists I met in belgrade say that the sensationalized reporting of war rape has been used to create nationalist fervor on all sides, more than it has been used to help the traumatized women. They instead intend to use the present focus on war rape to better assist the women who have been violated and brutalized. The tragedy is deep and profound. Many of these raped young girls and women are unable to say anything at all about what has happened to them – some were/are only 14 years old. Some recognized their rapists as their neighbors. Some of the women were serb, raped by muslims and/or croats. Some of the women were muslim, coming to belgrade for abortions. Some of the women are serb/muslim by marriage; others croat/serbs; others muslim/croat. They have been tortured by a war they have not made, nor want. With all the variety of the women I met, I did not meet one woman who was a nationalist of any sort.

Post-cold war politics has decentered the super-power struggles and dispersed warfare and hatred to multiple local sites. At stake are the meanings of racialized/ethnic identity, multiculturalism, and nationalism for global capitalism. Women's bodies, as an imaginary, are central to these negotiations. Gender, however, falls off the international map when the politics of the twenty-first century is theorized.

Economic globalism and local nationalisms mix uneasily. New-old nationalisms exist within a cultural and economic network that is global. Transnational economies require multiracial workers. Whereas economic transnationalization articulates an imaginary of "new world unity," ethnic nationalisms splinter the world into separate identities (Brennan 1990: 46). Woman, as the embodiment of the nation, begins to unravel as an imaginary along with economic borders themselves.

The challenge remains to dislodge the fiction of universality through exclusion and reframe transnational economies into richly diverse cultures. Nations will move beyond psychic fantasies of racial purity and misogynist fraternities. Diversity will still exist but it would simply be outrageous to think that rape and/or torture could ever bring closure to fear or desire. Differences would be so pluralized that they could only create an anarchy of pleasure. Then gender and its multiracial richness could be theorized as part of the liberatory politics of the twenty-first century.

U.S. backlash: us vs. them

Instead of this richness neoconservatives and right-wing republicans in the u.s. have successfully dismantled the civil rights legislation of the 1960s and renamed what remains of it the "new" racism. Insurgent multiculturalism has been painted with this same brush; it is called the "new tribalism" threatening "the" american way of life.[17] An organized back-lash that engulfs much of the u.s. electorate has already begun. California, texas, and florida have all had initiatives seeking to contain the multiple identities within our borders. This initial politics of exclusion targets "illegal aliens" as unworthy foreigners and attempts to exclude them from eligi-bility for social services.[18]

Proposition 187 – also known as "save our state" (s.o.s.) – would elim-inate any form of public welfare, including non-emergency medical care, prenatal clinics, and public schools, for all undocumented immigrants.[19] This initiative if applied nationwide would affect 13 percent of all immi-grants, who make up 1 percent of the u.s. population. Yet it smears all immigrants with the same charges even though immigrants (as a group) actually create more jobs than they fill, and generate more in taxes than they absorb in services.[20]

In response, legal immigrants, feeling stigmatized, are applying for citi-zenship in record numbers.[21] But citizenship will not protect them from the police state developing in the southwest, where no one of color travels freely even within u.s. borders.[22]

However, hysteria is never assuaged by facts. Newt Gingrich articulates a u.s. right-wing nationalism which rivals that of the balkans. Sadly, the privatized visions of selfishness and exclusivity are not limited to republi-cans. Democrats have become "kinder and gentler republicans and Felix Rohatyn, who came to this country at 14, in 1942, and could have just as easily ended up in auschwitz death camp, says he now feels like a polit-ical refugee again."[23]

Crime, unemployment, welfare abuse, illegtimacy – are labeled foreign, and imaged on immigrant bodies of color, or african americans.[24] The language of hate, towards jews, and blacks, and latinos has become more vocalized by reactionary factions in government right alongside corporatist multiculturalism. They critique "dependency" as the effect of an overgen-erous and bloated welfare state. And dependency has been racialized and feminized; while welfare has been completely racialized and sexualized.[25]

As many as 4 million people in the u.s. live in walled communities. They think they are being overtaken by people who are not assimilating; in the southwest "everything's turning Mexican."[26] Given these attitudes it is hard to fathom what Sheldon Hackney, chair of the National Endowment for the Humanities, means when he says we must find a way to express a national identity rather than splintered interests.[27]

Racism splinters. As such, race itself becomes something to overcome, rather than embrace (Giroux 1993). White racism seeks to erase race – which means colored – because whiteness remains intact in the process. Racial harmony then assumes sameness, as whiteness, or sameness to one standard. Similarity, rather than whiteness, defines the image of japan-ese racial homogeneity. The likeness is supposedly responsible for a more "civilized" lifestyle (Fallows 1993: 78; see also Fallows 1989). Recent difficulties in japan with cults and poison gas subway explosions will assuredly lead to a review of this imaginary.

Neocons, like Samuel Huntington, worry that diversity will only further fragment the nation. He is troubled by what he sees as the subversion of individual rights, by group rights; and a color-blind society replaced by color consciousness (Huntington 1993b: 190; 1993a). He praises the politics of assimilation along with the mythic immigrant who only wished to become a part of society. It was a time when "those in charge had confidence in the universal application of their culture."[28] Today the universals have supposedly been displaced by chaos.

White males in particular respond by calling foul play. Clearly, the reactionary responses are not limited to white males, but this is the voice most clearly heard in neocon public/state discourse. Reverse discrimination has become the major focus of this discourse; affirmative action is the culprit. Neocons call for color-blind politics. Multiculturalists respond by asking why color-blindness could not have been the politics of choice when they needed it years ago.[29]

The "imaginary" operating here is that affirmative action has taken away white men's jobs. However, this public imag*ination* is quite different than the actual denial of opportunities for whites.[30] First off, white men still dominate in professional, and managerial jobs. They hold more than 95 percent of them.[31] Second, when white men have lost their jobs, they have lost them to transnational corporate downsizing, not to people of color. The racialized culture of today makes it easy for whites to blame blacks for their problems, while whites accuse blacks for blaming everyone else for their problems.

When all else fails in the blame game, there is always "biology as destiny." Enter Charles Murray and Richard Herrnstein (1994), who argue that blacks' i.q. is fixed by nature and cannot be improved upon. Much of the information cited in *The Bell Curve* is from writers of *Mankind Quarterly*, which is, according to Charles Lane, "a notorious journal of 'racial history' founded by men who believe in the genetic superiority of the white race."[32] Murray uses their data to argue that blacks are intellectually doomed by the "bell curve" to welfare dependency and poverty, and there is not much that the government can do to change this.[33] This argument is then used to justify the privatization of the social welfare state. This neo-racism openly rejects an affirmative action state and recycles old hatreds to do it (Fraser 1995).

The privatization of public services and the cutting of the federal government's budget is a center piece of right-wing reactionary politics. Gingrich's "contract with america" is suppose to return the country to the way it used to be for men like him.[34] He will take it back from blacks, jews, HIV carriers, immigrants, and so on. Never mind that 99,000 people – half of all americans with AIDS – are either homeless or likely to become so. Our privatized state leaves them alone to wander the streets of n.y.c, miami, los angeles, and detroit.[35] "America" becomes a nation defined by those who are able to take care of themselves, like white men used to be able to take of their families.

It is harder for the imaginary to work today because the u.s. is populated by so many more people of color from all over the world than it used to be. It is also harder to homogenize racial difference by the black/white divide. Nevertheless, blackness is made the bedrock signifier of race and racial hatred and african americans stand-in for the multi-race threat.

Blackness, repressed in the mind's-eye, threads through the processes of "othering" which are further pluralized by demographic changes. While u.s. whites partake in practices that they use to distance others; boundaries of self–other are confounded. When the food we eat comes from all over the world; when the transnational economy challenges our conception of nation; when global communication webs make for easy transnational viewing; difference appears everywhere. But the differences and desires are psychically distanced and translated as fear. Then, exclusion rather than inclusion repositions monoculturalism against its multiplicity.

And, the nation lives in fear of the globe.

Notes

1 See my *Hatreds: Sexualized and Racialized Conflicts in the Twenty-First Century* (Eisenstein 1996) for a full accounting of this argument. This chapter is a revised version of Chapters 2 and 3. I do not capitalize the names of countries or racial groups in order to query their seemingly "naturalized" status.

2 I am grateful to Joy James for helping me to clarify this point of differential privilege within the nation.

3 For a full discussion of state privatization see Eisenstein (1994).

4 For an interesting discussion of the continual redefinition of racial and sexual discrimination see Wallerstein (1991: 34).

5 I am indebted to conversations with Rosalind Petchesky for clarification of this point.

6 For critiques of Anderson's treatment of "race and nation" see: Bhabha (1994: 248–250) and Goldberg (1993: 79).

7 I do not mean to make this all too simple. The use of familial symbolisms has been successfully used to mobilize women in the support of the nation. Women in the Ku Klux Klan circulated "racial, religious, and national bigotry." See Blee (1991: 3). For an interesting discussion of the common-sense realities of fictive imagery, see Annie Marie Smith (1994).

8 I am indebted to conversations with Linda Zerilli for clarification of this discussion.

9 Slavenka Drakulic. (1993) "Women Hide Behind a Wall of Silence." *The Nation.* 256: 8: 253–272; Jeri Laber (1993) "Bosnia: Questions about Rape." *New York Review of Books.* March 25: 3–6; Paul Lewis. (1993) "Rape was Weapon of Serbs, U.N. Says." *New York Times.* October 20: A1; Laura Pitter and Alexandra Stiglmayer. (1993) "Will the World Remember? Can the Women Forget?" *Ms. Magazine.* 3: 5: 19–22; Pitter and Stiglmayor. (1993) "Serbia's War Against Bosnia and Croatia." *Off Our Backs.* 23: 5: 4–6. Alan Riding. (1993) "European Inquiry Says Serbs' Forces Have Raped 20,000." *New York Times.* January 9: A1.

10 Also see Pine and Mertus (1993). For a different viewing of the issue of rape in its more generalized statement of gender violence see MacKinnon (1994).

11 "Correction." *New York Times*. October 23, 1993: A1. This was a revision of Paul Lewis. (1993) "Rape Was Weapon of Serbs, U.N. Says." *New York Times*. October 20: A1.

12 Also see Mandy Jacobson's film *War Crimes Against Women* (1996), Bowery Productions, Community Television (tel. no. 212–219–1385).

13 Discussions with John Borneman first alerted me to this reality. Also see Victoria Stegic. (1995) "Des Milliers d'hommes victimes de violences sexuelles dans les camps en ex-Yougoslavie?" *La Presse*. Montreal, March 9: 25.

14 Donatella Lorch. (1995) "Wave of Rape Adds New Horror to Rwanda's Trail of Savagery." *New York Times*. May 15: A1, A6.

15 As discussed in Laura Palmer. (1995) "Her Own Private Tailhook." *New York Times Magazine*. May 28: 22–25.

16 The "women in black" take their name from the israeli women who are anti-war and committed to building bridges with palestinian women.

17 William Honan. (1994) "Unity to be Theme of Town Meetings." *New York Times*. January 16: A22.

18 Larry Rohter. (1994) "Florida Opens New Front in Fight on Immigrant Policy." *New York Times*. February 11: A14. Also see B. Drummond Ayres Jr. (1994) "California Governor Seeking Identification Cards for All." *New York Times*. October 27: A1; Ashley Dunn. (1994) "In California, the Numbers Add Up to Anxiety." *New York Times*. October 30: E3; Joel Kotkin. (1994) "Hotheads in California." *New York Times*. October 27: A29.

19 Elizabeth Kadetsky. (1994) "Bashing Illegals in California." *The Nation*, special issue "The Immigration Wars." 259:12: 416.

20 David Cole. (1994) "Five Myths about Immigration." Ibid: 410.

21 Sam Howe Verhovek. (1995) "Legal Immigrants Seek Citizenship in Record Numbers." *New York Times*. April 2: A1.

22 Leslie Marmon Silko. (1994) "The Border Patrol State." *The Nation*, "The Immigration Wars." 259: 12: 413–14.

23 Felix Rohatyn. (1995) "What Became of My Democrats?" *New York Times*. March 31: A31.

24 Major Garrett. (1995) "Beyond the Contract." *Mother Jones.*, 20: 2: 52–62; David Shipler. (1995) "My Equal Opportunity, Your Free Lunch." *New York Times*. March 5: E1.

25 See the interesting discussion by Fraser and Gordon (1994: 323, 327). Also see Isabel Wilkerson. (1995) "An Intimate Look at Welfare: Women Who've Been There." *New York Times*. February 17: A1.

26 Dale Maharidge. (1994) "Walled Off." *Mother Jones*. 19: 6: 31.

27 Richard Sennett. (1994) "The Identity Myth." *New York Times*. January 30: E17.

28 Andrew Hacker. (1993) "'Diversity' and its Dangers." *New York Review of Books*. 40: October 7: 21.

29 Michael Kinsley. (1995) "The Spoils of Victimhood." *New Yorker*. March 27: 64.

30 Ibid., p. 69.

31 (AP). (1995) "Reverse Discrimination of Whites is Rare, Labor Study Reports." *New York Times*. March 31: A23.

32 Charles Lane. (1994) "The Tainted Sources of 'The Bell Curve'," *New York Review of Books*. 41: December 1: 14.

33 Herbert Gans. (1994) "Letter" to the *New York Times Book Review*. November 13: section 7: 3.

34 Richard Berke. (1994) "Defections Among Men to G.O.P. Helped Insure Rout of Democrats." *New York Times*. November 11: A1.

35 Felicia Lee. (1995) "Cuts Set Off Debate on Helping Homeless with AIDS." *New York Times*. March 21: B1.

4 Sexing political identities/nationalism as heterosexism

V. Spike Peterson

A great deal of analytic work has been done by feminists in different parts of the world on demystifying the state's will to represent itself as disinterested, neutered, and otherwise benign. [note deleted] . . . Much less work has been done, however, on elaborating the processes of heterosexualization at work within the state apparatus and charting the ways in which they are constitutively paradoxical: that is, how hetero-sexuality is at once necessary to the state's ability to constitute and imag-ine itself, while simultaneously marking a site of its own instability.

(Alexander 1997: 65, citing Hart 1994: 8)

Because the logic of the sexual order is so deeply embedded by now in an indescribably wide range of social institutions, and is embedded in the most standard accounts of the world, queer struggles aim not just at toleration or equal status but at challenging those institutions and accounts. The dawning realization that themes of homophobia and heterosexism may be read in almost any document of our culture means that we are only beginning to have an idea of how widespread those institutions and accounts are.

(Warner 1993: xiii)

As the quotation from Jacqui Alexander suggests, feminists have critically analyzed the gendering of the state, and are currently engaged in gendering nationalism. This chapter draws from and shifts the focus of these studies. I first locate nationalism as a subset of political identities and identifica-tion processes, then take (heterosexist) gender identities as an indispensable starting point in the study of political identities. I next turn to early Western state making and its writing technologies to materialize the *normalization* of (hetero)gender binaries in thought (western metaphysics/phallogocentrism) and practice (divisions of power, authority, labor). Finally, I chart five

This chapter was previously published in 1999 in *International Feminist Journal of Politics*, 1: 1.

gender-differentiated dimensions of state-centric nationalism that expose the latter's heterosexist presumptions – and enduring problems.

Locating nationalism

Nationalism is a particular – and particularly potent – manifestation of political identification.[1] Political identities associated with subnational, international or transnational groups take a variety of forms (social movements, religious communities, non-governmental organizations) but typically do not seek a territorially bounded political status. Nationalism then becomes the territorially based *subset* of political identity that takes one of two related forms: state-led (assimilation of all within a state to the state's preferred cultural forms) and state-seeking (mobilization of group identification in pursuit of recognition as an independent state).[2] As Charles Tilly (1992: 709) argues, "state-led nationalism stimulates state-seeking nationalism" as the homogenizing project of the former threatens the viability of non-state identities. To ensure the latter, subgroups seek the sovereignty afforded by state status – and if successful, tend to impose their own homogenizing project.

Analysts have always recognized that nationalism is problematic from the vantage point of conflict between nations: sameness within the state is purchased at the price of institutionalizing difference – and too often, conflict – among states. But nationalism has also been problematic from the vantage point of those within the nation who share least in élite privilege and political representation, especially those whose identity is at odds with the projected image of homogenous national identity.[3] Gregory Gleason (1991: 223–8) clarifies these relationships by identifying three "faces" of nationalism: liberation (the positive association of nationalism with self-determination and democratization), exclusivity (the promotion of group homogeneity and "difference" from "others"), and domination (the negative effects of suppressing difference within the group and/or domination of "outsiders" in the name of the group). Hence, whether construed as "imagining" (Anderson 1991) or "inventing" (Gellner 1983) a national identity, or in terms of privileging a particular "natural" community (Smith 1991b), the promotion of uniformity within the group – by persuasive and coercive means – threatens some more than others, even as differences *between* groups fuel conflict.

Nationalism looms large today, both in embodied politics and political analysis. But it is the conflict *between* (state-centric) nationalist groups that dominates conventional discussions. How nationalism is a subset of political identifications more generally, and how it relates to other identities – within and beyond the nation – are less developed inquiries. To a significant extent, this neglect is due to knowledge regimes that privilege positivist binaries and mono-disciplinary investigations. As one consequence, conventional vantage points yield impoverished and politically suspect accounts of not only nationalism, but of the production and effects of identities/identifications more generally.

56 *V. Spike Peterson*

This is particularly apparent in international relations (IR), the discipline now haunted by nationalist conflicts. Constrained by its positivist and modernist commitments, IR theorists typically assume a Euro-centric model of the agent (subject) as unitary, autonomous, interest-maximizing and rational. IR's realist commitments additionally cast subjects as inherently competitive. So too with states. The latter are understood as the primary (unified, rational, self-interested and competitive) actors in international relations, and a collective political identity is assumed rather than interrogated.[4] Positivist/modernist binaries reign in IR and, as feminists have persuasively argued, these binaries are gendered (e.g. Haraway 1988; Hekman 1990; Lloyd 1984; Peterson 1992b). Through conventional IR lenses, the dichotomy of public–private locates political action in the former but not the latter sphere; the dichotomy of internal–external distinguishes citizens and order within from "others" and anarchy without; and the dichotomy of culture–nature (civilized–primitive, advanced–backward, developed–undeveloped) "naturalizes" global hierarchies of power. Most telling for the study of nationalism, positivist dichotomies that favor instrumental reason and public sphere activities fuel a neglect of emotion, desire, sexuality, culture and – hence – identity and identification processes.

IR's conventional accounts, however, are increasingly challenged by empirical and epistemological transformations. In terms of empirical transformations, post-Cold War nationalisms have forced IR theorists to acknowledge new actors and even new rules (e.g. Ferguson and Mansbach 1996; Krause and Renwick 1996; Lapid and Kratochwill 1996). Similarly, state-centric political identity is no longer the exclusive focus of IR studies. Sub and transnational social movements transgress territorial boundaries in favor of identities based on ecological, race/ethnic, feminist, religious, and other non-state-based commitments. Moreover, the globalization of production and finance undercuts national economic planning, eroding state sovereignty and the political identities it presupposes (e.g. Mittelman 1996; Scholte 1997). And even as supra-national forces alter state power, subnational conflicts expose the illusion of homogeneity promoted in nationalist narratives.

In terms of epistemological transformations, critiques of positivism, modernism, and masculinism have altered our understanding of agents and subjectivity. Challenging conventional models of subjects – and states – as unitary rational actors, contemporary social theory illuminates the multiplicity of subject locations (implying multiple identifications) and their dynamic interaction "within" the "self" *and* in relation to the "self's" environment. That is, identities are socially constructed as on-going processes: they are embedded in and interact with historically specific social contexts composed of intersubjective meaning systems (discourses), material conditions, social practices, and institutional structures. Moreover, feminists argue that conventional models of the agent/subject assume male sex and masculine identity. From a postmodernist feminist perspective, the study of identities must be historical, contextual, and dynamic: asking not only how identities are located in time and space but also how they are (re)produced, resisted, and reconfigured.

Gendering the politics of identity and identification

Identities are politically important because they inform self–other representations, embed subjects in meaning systems and collective agency (W. Bloom 1990), and mobilize purposive, politically significant actions. They are important windows on "reality" because "internal subjective self-change and external objective social change" are inextricable (Bologh 1987: 147). In this sense, identifications "bridge" agency and structure, are multiple and sometimes contradictory, and can be understood as strategies.[5]

Feminists have a number of reasons for attending to political identity and the politics of identification.[6] First, constructions of femininity and masculinity that inform our identification as women and men have pervasive implications for the lives we lead and the world(s) in which we live. Wendy Brown summarizes a decade of feminist philosophy in stating that "there has been no ungendered *human* experience" (Brown 1988: 190). If all experience is gendered, analysis of gender identities is an imperative starting point in the study of political identities and practice. Bound up with constructions of sexuality and desire, the implications of gender extend from the most intimate to the most global social dynamics (e.g. Peterson and Parisi 1998).

Second, to the extent that personal gender identities constitute a "core" sense of "self," they fundamentally condition our self-esteem and psycho-sociological security. This means that challenges to gender ordering may appear to threaten a personal identity in which we are deeply invested (Lorraine 1990). A fear of loss or destabilization may then fuel resistance to deconstruction of gender identities and ideologies, with many – and mostly negative – implications for feminist movement and the production of less hierarchical relations of "difference."

Third, given the significance of gender identities in every domain of human endeavor, feminists have criticized biological explanations that essentialize maleness and femaleness and developed alternative explanations of gender identity formation and its effects (e.g. Fausto-Sterling 1992; Keller 1985; Rubin 1984). Exposing the social construction of binary male and female identities involves a parallel deconstruction of western dichotomies as gendered, culminating in feminist critiques of masculinist science and the development of alternative epistemologies (e.g. Hekman 1990; Alcoff and Potter 1993).

Fourth, feminist studies have established that the identity of the modern subject – in models of human nature, citizenship, the rational actor, the knowing subject, economic man, and political agency – is not gender-neutral but masculine (and typically European and heterosexual). The unacknowledged privileging of élite male experience and perspective – androcentrism – has profoundly structured our conceptual categories and concrete activities. There is now a vast literature exploring the many ways that androcentrism marginalizes women and all that is denigrated by association with "femininity," which includes nature, "effeminate men," and subordinated "others."

Fifth, feminist identity itself is a problem for feminism. If a universal category of "woman" is a necessary condition of feminist movement, then the actual diversity among women contravenes that condition (Mohanty *et al.* 1991). Essentialist characterizations of "woman" and homogenizing effects within feminist movements have been irrevocably disrupted by the realities of "difference." Contemporary feminisms are both challenged and enriched by struggles to address diversity without abandoning solidarities enabled by shared experience and/or shared objectives (Genew and Yeatman 1993; Grewal and Kaplan 1994). That is, differences among women have compelled feminists to take a politics of difference seriously, including a politics of accountability even in the context of postmodernist theorizing.

Finally, identity groups (whether based on race/ethnicity, religion or nationality) that have been most closely associated with (state-centric) political power have also been based on (heterosexist) gender inequality. As members of state-centric groups, women have interests in their group's "success," including the group's acquisition of political power *vis-à-vis* competitors. But, insofar as these groups reproduce gendered hierarchies (social hierarchies linked by denigration of the feminine), identification with and support for them is problematic for feminists and all who seek non-oppressive social relations. Here, the heteropatriarchy of state orders is key.[7]

For all of these reasons, and more, feminists have taken the lead in multidisciplinary and wide-ranging studies of identity, identification processes, and their relationships to power at local, national, and global "levels."

Nationalist politics/heterosexist practice

In spite of its current potency, the analysis of nationalism is notoriously inadequate. Jill Vickers observes that "this difficulty of understanding nationalism as a form of self-identification and of group organization reflects the profound difficulty that male-stream thought, in general, has had in understanding the public manifestations of the process of identity construction" (Vickers 1990: 480). For Vickers, the public–private dichotomy codifies a false separation between the public sphere of reason and power and the private sphere of emotion and social reproduction, where identity construction – which enables group reproduction – presumably takes place.

Group reproduction – both biological and social – is fundamental to nationalist practice, process, and politics. While virtually all feminist treatments of nationalism recognize this fact, they typically take for granted that group reproduction is heterosexist. I refer here to the assumption – institutionalized in state-based orders through legal and ideological codifications and naturalized by reference to the binary of male–female sex difference – that heterosexuality is the only "normal" mode of sexual identity, sexual practice, and social relations. Heterosexism presupposes a binary coding of polarized and hierarchical male/masculine and female/feminine identities (ostensibly based on a dichotomy of biophysical features) and denies all but heterosexual coupling as the basis of sexual intimacy, family life, and group reproduction. And heterosexism is key to nationalism because today's state-centric nationalisms (the focus in this chapter) not only engage in sexist practices that are now well documented by feminists, but also take for granted heterosexist sex/gender identities and forms of group reproduction that underpin sexism but which are not typically interrogated even in feminist critiques.[8] Because a critique of heterosexism is central to this chapter, and relatively undeveloped in treatments of nationalism, I briefly summarize the underlying argumentation before addressing nationalism as heterosexism more directly.

Making states/making sex

Whereas heterosexuality refers to sex/affective relations between people of the "opposite" sex, heterosexism refers to the institutionalization and *normalization* of heterosexuality and the corollary exclusion of non-heterosexual identities and practices.[9] For analytical simplicity, I make reference to interactive dimensions of heterosexism: as conceptual system, gender identities, sex/affective relations, and social institutions. Briefly here, and elsewhere at length, I argue that the conjuncture of heterosexist ideology and practice is inextricable from the centralization of political authority/coercive power that we refer to as state-making.[10] The argument is expanded in the discussion of gendered nationalism that follows.

Heterosexist ideology involves a symbolic order/intersubjective meaning system of hierarchical dichotomies that codify sex as male–female biological difference, gender as masculine–feminine subjectivity, and sexuality as heterosexual–homosexual identification.[11] Heterosexism is "naturalized" through multiple discourses, especially western political theory and religious dogma, and by reification of the (patriarchal) "family" as "pre-political" – as "natural" and non-contractual. The binary of male–female difference is exemplified and well documented in western metaphysics (hence, political theory/practice) but evident in all collective meaning systems where the *hierarchical* dichotomy of gender is foundational to symbolic ordering and discursive practice. This symbolic ordering produces the binary of male–female bodies as well as a binary of masculine–feminine identities.

The conceptual ordering of masculine over feminine is inextricable from political ordering imposed in state-making and reproduced through masculinist discourse (political theory, religious dogma) that legitimizes the state's hierarchical relations. Insofar as (hegemonic) masculinity is constituted as reason, order, and control, masculine domination is reproduced through conceptual systems that privilege male entitlement – to authority, power, property, nature. Central to this ideology is male entitlement to women's sexuality, bodies, and labor.

Heterosexism as sex/affect involves the normalization of exclusively heterosexual desire, intimacy, and family life. Historically, this normalization is inextricable from the state's interest in regulating sexual reproduction, undertaken primarily through controlling women's bodies, policing sexual activities, and instituting the heteropatriarchal family/household as the basic socio-economic unit. This normalization entails constructions of gender identity and hegemonic masculinity as heterosexual, with corollary interests in women's bodies as objects of (male) sexual gratification and the means of ensuring group continuity. In complex – and even contradictory – ways, masculinity as entitlement and control is here linked to heterosexual practice as an expression of power and violence. In short, and as feminists relentlessly document, the hegemonic masculinity constituted by heterosexist practice normalizes the subordination of women and naturalizes rape as an expression of male power against women and "insufficiently masculine" men.

The argument here is that rape is not reducible to but is inextricable from heterosexism. To clarify briefly, the objectification of women and forced penile penetration as an expression of power requires for its intelligibility the polarized identities and objectification of the feminine that is constituted by heterosexist ideology, identities, and practice. In this framing, women/the feminine are passive and denigrated by definition and it is the definitively masculine role of agency and penetration that exemplifies heterosexism, whether the denigrated *object* of that agency is female or male. Hence, male–male rape exemplifies heterosexism's objectification of the feminine even though no females are involved. Stated differently, the willingness/desire to rape is not established by the presence of a (normally flaccid) penis but by the internalization of a masculinist/heterosexist identity that promotes aggressive male penetration as an expression of sexuality, power, and dominance. It is, presumably, the mobilization of some version of such an identity and ideology that renders rape a viable strategy for social control. On this view, heterosexist masculinity is mobilized to sustain gender hierarchy *within* groups (e.g. domestic violence in "private" and the threat/reality of rape in "public") and to enact masculinist violence *between* groups (e.g. castration of "Other" males, forced prostitution, and mass rapes in war).

Heterosexism as a social institution is inexplicable without reference to state-making in two senses: early state-making (as the pre-modern transition from kin-based to centralized political orders) and subsequent state-based orders (modern states and state-centric nationalisms). *Early* state-making (the urban revolution, the emergence of civilization) marks the convergence of centralized power/authority, the exploitation of re/productive labor, and the technology of writing such that, once established, centralized authority was able to turn coercive power to historically novel effect through enhanced systemic control (e.g. Cohen and Service 1978). In the western tradition, this involved "normalizing" definitive dichotomies (public–private, reason–affect, mind–body, culture–nature, civilized–barbarian, masculine–feminine) both materially, in divisions of authority, power, labor, and resources, as well as conceptually, in western metaphysics, language, philosophy, political theory. Not least because early state-making marked the invention of writing, these systemic transformations were codified and that codification (in western philosophy, political theory, and classical texts) has profoundly shaped subsequent theory/practice. These codifications of language/thought are inextricable from the disciplinary regime of hetero-sexist *practice* institutionalized in early state-making.

To recapitulate the argument, I am suggesting that the following are conceptually and structurally linked in early western state-making: the codification of sex/gender binaries (male–female bodies, masculine–feminine gender identities, gendered dichotomies) as foundational symbolic order; the production of oppositional gender identities in service to state-centric heterosexist reproduction and hierarchical relations (patriarchal families/ households; state regulation of reproductive sexual activities); the conceptual *and* material constitution of gendered spheres of social activity (not least, the public–private) that structure hierarchical divisions of authority, power, labor, and resources; and state centralization of authority, power, accumulation, and reproduction ideologically (through heterosexist language, philosophy, religion, political theory) and concretely (through the juridical and coercive powers of the state).

I believe that the development of writing – specific to early state-making – is of singular importance to critical analyses of "power" and, especially, feminist critiques of the gendered symbolic order. Writing made possible economic, political, military, and socio-cultural coordination not possi-ble with the limitations of face-to-face communication. Through the materi-ality – hence durability – of the written word, *masculinist* élites were able to extend their authority and power across time and space, and this authority and power entailed élite conceptions of how the world works and who should be authoritatively in charge. Contemporary critical social theory recognizes that *whose* representations secure authority and sedimentation is an effect of power relations. The invention of writing (in the context of early state-mak-ing and under élite male control) structurally altered power relations by *systemically* enhancing state power – and the voices of state élites. Like all tech-nological revolutions, the development of writing had multiple and complex effects. What I emphasize here is how writing permitted state élites to "fix" or stabilize a historically particular symbolic ordering (and its corollary political ordering) as "given." Not only is a heterosexist symbolic order stabilized (not least, essentializing gendered dichotomies) but also the political *making* of that historically contingent order is erased. In its place, the authority of durable texts "grounds" heterosexism and its gendered binaries as foundational. An important point here is that the "symbolic" power of the early state, though rarely the focus of analysis, is as significant as the "structural" power of the state, which commands most of the critical attention. More accurately stated, the symbolic power of the state is rendered visibly structural through writing technologies. This is particularly important for feminist theory/practice insofar as it permits us to *materialize* (historicize, politicize) the symbolic order of gendered binaries that features prominently in feminist critiques (see note 10).

Because this argumentation is unfamiliar, I attempt to further clarify it by reference to multiple "contracts" that underpin western philosophy and political theory. I am arguing that the "heterosexual contract" (Wittig 1980) naturalizing binary gender identities and heterosexism), the "social contract" (naturalizing centralized political authority, hierarchical social relations, and the transition from "pre-contractual" relations associated with the state of "nature" to contractual relations associated with "culture"), and language codification (the invention of writing, the articulation of western metaphysics as phallogocentric) are historically contingent and mutually constituted processes that constitute what we describe as early state-making. Moreover, this mutuality is not "simply" a *conceptual* linkage (e.g. between symbolic constructions of masculinity, heterosexuality, contract, and stateness) but a historical, empirical, and *structural* linkage that is visible through a genealogical feminist lens on early state-making, its technologies, and its interpretive productions. These linkages are structural in two interactive senses: both as historical-empirical material practices and institutions (the more conventional sense of social structures), and as signifying/meaning systems, knowledge claims, and enduring narratives that produce even as they are produced by material structures. Stated differently, in early state-making the interaction of (gendered) signifying processes and structural dynamics produces both conceptual and political codifications, with particularly powerful and durable effects.

These effects are visible in subsequent modern state-making (and nationalism), which takes the "heterosexual contract" as given (Pateman 1988; Coole 1993). Through the sedimentation of symbolic ordering (reproduced through writing and then printing technologies; paradigmatically, the Bible), masculine dominance and gendered binaries are taken for granted in the context of European state-making, the interstate system it constituted, and the colonial practices it imposed. A now vast feminist literature documents how (hetero)sexist symbols, identities and divisions of authority/power/labor are reproduced and rarely interrogated in modernist narratives. This is not to argue that early and modern states are identically heterosexist, conceptually and/or structurally. It is to emphasize how gender symbols/discourse/dichotomies stabilized through early state-making produced conceptual and structural effects in the modern era, and *that these effects are depoliticized by being taken as "natural."* Whereas the relationship of male to female, patriarchy to matriarchy, and polity to kin-based community was a focus and key contestation of early thought, in the modern period heteropatriarchal discourse is for the most part presupposed. The success of early states marginalized matristic principles, and monotheistic religions displaced female and androgynous deities. Moreover, both state and religious élites appropriated female procreativity: in Athenian political theory, men gave birth to immortal ideas and to the body politic (state); in religious doctrine, men gave birth to order and even to life itself. In spite of other deeply antagonistic commitments, in the modern era emerging state authorities and religious élites spoke in one voice when author(iz)ing heteropatriarchy.

In regard to nationalism, the modern state's juridical and productive power denies male homosocial sexuality in favor of male homosocial politics.[12] In the fraternal state, what men have in common is masculine privilege and entitlement *vis-à-vis* women, which promotes male bonding across age, class and race/ethnic differences within the state/nation. Ideologically (symbolically), the coding of public sphere activities as masculine allows all men to identify with state power/authority. And in practice, militarization as a male rite of passage encourages men to bond politically and militarily as they play out the us/them script of protecting "their own" women and violating the enemy's men/women.

At the same time, differences among men ensure that the privilege of male domination is not homogeneously experienced but differentiated by multiple hierarchies (of age, class, ability, culture, race/ethnicity, and so on). Bonding across these differences must be continuously secured, lest loyalties be redirected. Not least, (male) homosexual desire and practice threatens to redefine fraternity in ways potentially subversive of state-centric interests.

While men are expected to bond politically with other men of the state/ nation, the heterosexist state denies women's homosexual bonding, and the public–private dichotomy denies women's political bonding. Rather, as an effect of patriarchal households and the family wage model, women are linked to the state through their fathers/husbands; women are expected to bond only through and with "their men." Jacqui Alexander (1997) argues that:

> women's sexual agency ... and erotic autonomy have always been troublesome for the state ... pos[ing] a challenge to the ideological anchor of an originary nuclear family, ... which perpetuates the fiction that the family is the cornerstone of society. Erotic autonomy signals danger to the heterosexual family and to the nation.
>
> (Alexander 1997: 64)

Gendering nationalism/nationalism as heterosexism

The remainder of this chapter develops a framework for analyzing gender in nationalist politics. More specifically, I identify five overlapping and interactive ways in which women and men are differently situated in relation to nationalist processes: as biological reproducers of group members; as social reproducers of group members and cultural forms; as signifiers; as embodied agents in nationalist struggles; and as societal members generally.[13] In presenting the five dimensions, I attempt to illuminate how attention to heterosexism deepens our understanding of (patriarchal) group reproduction and hierarchical social relations within and between groups.

Women as heterosexual/biological reproducers of group members

What Vickers (1990: 485) calls the "battle of the cradle" is about regulating under what conditions, when, how many, and whose children women will bear. The forms it takes are historically specific, shaped by socio-religious norms, technological developments, economic pressures, and political priorities. But all groups seeking multi-generational continuity have a stake in biological reproduction. Pro-natalist policies may include restriction of contraceptive knowledge and techniques, denial of access to abortions, and provision of material rewards for bearing children. From Sparta, where a mother "reared her sons to be sacrificed on the alter of civic necessity" (Elshtain 1992: 142) to South Africa, where white women were exhorted to bear "babies for Botha" (McClintock 1991: 110–111), to financial incentives for child-bearing in contemporary France, women have been admonished to fulfill their "duty" to the state/nation by bearing children in the service of group reproduction.

Particularly chilling examples of decrying abortion as treason are quoted in Julie Mostov's discussion of nationalism in the Balkans. She writes

> Croation President Franjo Tudjman blamed the tragedy of the Croation nation on "women, pornography, and abortion." Women who have abortions are "mortal enemies of the nation," . . . Women who have not given birth to at least four children are scolded as "female exhibitionists" who have not fulfilled their "unique sacred duty." [citing Renata Salecl 1992: 59] . . . Hungarian nationalists have also tied abortion to the "death of the nation." Abortion is described as a "national catastrophe." According to one article, "Four million Hungarians . . . had been killed by abortion [during] the liberal abortion policies of the Communists." [citing Susan Gal 1994: 271]

(Mostov 1995: 518–19)

Of course, not all reproduction is equally desirable to state/nation élites: "some breeders and 'breeds' are more acceptable than others" (de Lepervanche 1989: 176). To limit the size of "undesirable" groups, immigration controls, expulsion, sterilization, and even extermination have been – and are being – practiced. Thus, "while 'our' women are to be revered as mothers, all women's bodies must be controlled" (Mostov 1995: 519). Women's bodies become the battleground of men's wars, with rape as a potent weapon. For example, in nationalist conflicts, systematic rape and sexual enslavement not only violate countless women of particular group identities (e.g. Jews in Germany, Muslims in Bosnia) but also sabotage the underpinnings and therefore continuity of their communities. These are not epiphenomena of war or displays of innate male aggression: they are politically driven strategies in the context of group conflict.

The battle of the cradle is also a battle of sexualities and bedrooms. Pro-natalist policies are threatened by non-reproductive sex. Hence, the latter is disciplined by insisting that the bedroom is heterosexual and that a (the?) primary purpose of "family life" is sexual reproduction in the service of élite-driven collective interests. Moreover, as argued above, rape as a weapon of war is unintelligible in the absence of heterosexist ideology and sexual objectification of the "Other." By mobilizing nationalist sentiments, the state promotes homosocial bonding within the group which simultaneously obscures differences among in-group men while it magnifies differences across groups. State/nationalist élites manipulate political homosociality and prevent sexual homosociality and bonding with "different" men. In this regime, women are cast as baby-makers requiring protection to ensure group reproduction while men are encouraged to violate "others" and risk violation themselves to ensure hierarchical relations within and between imagined communities.

Women as social reproducers of group members and cultural forms

What Vickers (1990: 485) labels the "battle of the nursery" is about ensuring that children born are bred in culturally appropriate ways. This may involve the regulation – through religious dogma, legislation, social norms, and coercion – of sexual liaisons so that religious, ethnic, class, and citizenship boundaries are maintained. By enforcing legislation regarding marriage, child custody, and property and citizenship inheritance, the state controls the reproduction of membership claims.

For example, under British nationality laws, until 1948 a British woman was deemed an "alien" if she married a non-British subject and until 1981 she could not pass on her nationality (in her own right) to children born abroad (Klug 1989: 21–2). Roxana Ng (1993) notes the discriminatory effects of "independent class" or "family class" specification of landed immigrant status in Canada. The "family class" category tends to disadvantage married women, who are assumed to be dependent. "Furthermore, once categorized as 'family class' immigrants, these women are ineligible for social assistance and ... programs available to their 'independent class' counterparts and other Canadians" (Ng 1993: 56). In Australia, de Lepervanche (1989) notes that:

> aboriginal people were not even counted in the census until 1967. Some non-European men were allowed to reside in Australia after 1901, but non-European women particularly were usually excluded or, if permitted entry ... the permission depended on satisfactory [evidence of] their husbands' or fathers' capacity to support them.
>
> (de Lepervanche 1989: 167)

Insofar as states assume responsibility for provision of basic needs, claims to citizenship assume life-sustaining importance, determining not only one's obligations but also one's rights – to work, stable residency, legal protections, educational, health and welfare benefits. Hence, the denial of same-sex marriage prevents homosexuals from enjoying the membership privileges available to heterosexual couples. In regard to immigration and citizenship rights, this discrimination works across state/nation borders. But it also works within communities in the form of (heterosexist) family law and homophobic policies.

The battle of the nursery also involves the ideological reproduction of group members. Under heteropatriarchal conditions, women not only bear children but also are expected to rear them. Especially within the family, women are assigned the primary responsibility for inculcating beliefs, behaviors, and loyalties that are culturally appropriate and ensure intergenerational continuity. This cultural transmission includes learning the "mother tongue" – the codified meaning system – as well as the group's identity, symbols, rituals, divisions of labor, and worldviews. Research indicates that from an early age, children are aware of and identify specifically with a "homeland." Robert Coles (1986) studied the "political life of children" on five continents and concluded that everywhere, "nationalism works its way into just about every corner of the mind's life," fostering children's recognition of their nation's flag, music, slogans, history, and who counts as "us" and "them" (Coles 1986: 60, 63, as quoted in Elshtain 1992: 149).

Of course, ideological reproduction implies reproduction of the community's beliefs about sex/gender, race/ethnicity, age, class, religion, and other axes of "difference." Repression of non-heterosexual identities and ideologies reduces their potential to disrupt state-centric hierarchical scripts, either conceptually or structurally. Reproduction of the symbolic order sustains gendered dichotomies and oppositional gender identities, while exclusively heterosexual family life ensures that heterosexual practice and gendered divisions of labor/power/authority are the only apparent options.

Moreover, heterosexist beliefs are inextricable from multiple social hierarchies, as the subordination of "others" is fueled and legitimated by
castigations of them as inappropriately masculine or feminine.

Because of their assigned roles in social reproduction, women are often
stereotyped as "cultural carriers." When minority groups feel threatened,
they may increase the isolation of "their" women from exposure to other
groups or the legislative reach of the state. Tress writes that in Israel,
"Zionist ideology considered women to be the embodiment of the home
front" (Tress 1994: 313). While political transformations might require a
"new Jewish man," the Jewish woman was to remain domesticated. In
Lebanon, competing indigenous groups insisted that marriage, divorce,
adoption, inheritance, and so on, were matters under the exclusive control
of the community rather than subject to central authorities. In cases where
the state promotes a more progressive agenda than patriarchal communities, this kind of agreement among men to "leave each other's women
alone," may be at the expense of women gaining formal rights. If the
private sphere constitutes the "inner sanctum" of group identity and reproduction, nationalist men have an incentive to oppose those who would
either interfere with it or encourage women's movements outside of it
(Kandiyoti 1991b).

Heterosexism demonizes and even criminalizes non-reproductive sex
and denies all but heterosexist families as a basis of group reproduction.
As one consequence, it is extremely difficult for non-heterosexuals to engage
in parenting, even though many desire to do so. At the same time, heterosexist divisions of labor ensure that heterosexual men are expected to
participate in family life, but not as the primary parent or care-giver.
Worldwide, male parenting and care-giving take many forms, but nowhere
are men encouraged (or commanded) to parent and care for dependents
to the same extent and in the same way that women are. Hence, some
men who want to parent are denied this option, and most men who have
the option do not engage it fully.

Of course this leaves women with far too great a burden of responsibility for social reproduction. But it also deeply impoverishes men. One
does not have to be a Freudian or romanticize care-giving to make the
argument that men's systematic exclusion from primary parenting and
care-giving has profound effects – on experience, identity, and worldview.
It locks women and men into patterns that serve both poorly (Johnson
1997). Of particular importance in the present discussion, it circumscribes
too narrowly the forms of bonding that men may experience – with children, dependents, women, and significantly, with other men.

This division of labor powerfully shapes both the early – and psycho-
socially formative – experience of the infant (who interacts primarily with
women) and the "reproductive" years of men and women, whose lives
differ systematically as a result of this division and who reproduce the
division by assuming heterosexist parenting and care-giving roles. In short,

the division of labor that structures social reproduction is a linchpin of heterosexist ideology, identities and practice – and their depoliticized reproduction.

Women as signifiers of (heterosexist) group identities and differences

As biological and social reproducers, it is women's capacities and activities that are "privatized" in the name of heterosexist collectivities. But women also serve as symbolic markers of the nation and of the group's cultural identity. Shared images, symbols, rituals, myths, and a "mother tongue" are essential to the continuity of social groups that are based on abstract bonds between men, understood here as political homosociality. Men appropriate a "familial" model of reproductive ties but their distancing from reproductive activities compels them to privilege "imagined" relations wherein "identity, loyalty and cohesion centre around male bonds to other men" (Vickers 1990: 484). In this context, the symbolic realm is elevated to strategic importance: symbols become what is worth fighting – even dying – for and cultural metaphors become weapons in the war. The metaphors of nation-as-woman and woman-as-nation suggest how women – as bodies and cultural repositories – become the battleground of group struggles.

The personification of nature-as-female transmutes easily to *nation-as-woman*, where the motherland is a woman's body and as such is ever in danger of violation – by "foreign" males/sperm. To defend her frontiers and her honor requires relentless vigilance and the sacrifice of countless citizen-warriors (Elshtain 1992). Nation-as-woman expresses a spatial, embodied femaleness: the land's fecundity, upon which the people depend, must be protected by defending the body/nation's boundaries against invasion and violation.[14] But nation-as-woman is also a temporal metaphor: the rape of the body/nation not only violates frontiers but also disrupts – by planting alien seed or destroying reproductive viability – the maintenance of the community through time. Also implicit in the patriarchal metaphor is a tacit agreement that men who cannot defend their woman/nation against rape have lost their "claim" to that body, that land.

Hence, "rape" becomes a metaphor of national or state humiliation (Pettman 1996: 49).[15] To engender support for its war on Iraq, the United States made frequent reference to the "rape of Kuwait." Regarding India, Amrita Basu (1993) argues that while "the realities of economic and political life" preclude Hindu claims of Muslim domination, the Hindu nationalist party justifies "Hindu violence by pointing to the sexually predatory Muslim male and the vulnerable Hindu woman"; it "has made the raped Hindu woman symbolic of the victimization of the entire Hindu community" (Basu 1993: 28, 29; see also Bacchetta 1993). Here, as in countless other nationalist conflicts, the metaphor of rape triggers deeply gendered feelings and identities, mobilizing fear in most women and aggressor/protector responses in many men.

Heterosexism underpins both the rape and the nation-as-woman metaphor. As suggested above, rape as a social strategy relies upon (and reproduces) rigid binaries of male–female, masculine–feminine, and self–other in which the domination by the first over the second term is "justified" by reference to the latter's threatening or destabilizing potential. Rape "makes sense" as a political-military strategy only under the assumption that men are willing – even eager? – to violate women/the feminine in this way.[16] Similarly, the nation-as-woman trope "works" only if the imagined body/woman is assumed to be (heterosexually) fertile. Imagining the "beloved country" as a female child, a lesbian, a prostitute, or a post-menopausal wise woman generates quite different pictures, which enable quite different understandings of community.

In nationalist rhetoric, the territory/woman is in effect denied agency. Rather, "she" is man's possession, and like other enabling vessels (boats, planes) is valued as a means for achieving male-defined ends: the sovereign/ man drives the ship of state. Thus, the motherland is female but the state and its citizen-warriors are male and must prove (its) their political manhood through conflict: "The state is free that can defend itself, gain the recognition of others, and shore up an acknowledged identity" (Elshtain 1992: 143). In Cynthia Enloe's words: "If a state is a vertical creature of authority, a nation is a horizontal creature of identity" (Enloe 1990: 46). In political theory and practice, this horizontal identity is distinctively *fraternal* (Pateman 1988b), cast here as homosocial politics among men. Excluded intentionally from the public domain, women are not agents in their own right but instruments for the realization of male-defined agendas.

Woman-as-nation signifies the boundaries of group identity, marking its difference from alien "others." Assigned responsibility for reproducing the group through time, women are singled out as "custodians of cultural particularisms" and "the symbolic repository of group identity" (Kandiyoti 1991b: 434, 435). Because symbols of cultural authenticity are jealously guarded, actual women face a variety of pressures to conform to idealized models of behavior. In Jan Jindy Pettman's (1992) words:

> Women's use in symbolically marking the boundary of the group makes them particularly susceptible to control in strategies to maintain and defend the boundaries. Here women's movements and bodies are policed, in terms of their sexuality, fertility, and relations with "others," especially with other men. This suggests why (some) men attach such political significance to women's "outward attire and sexual purity," seeing women as their possessions, as those responsible for the transmission of culture and through it political identity; and also as those most vulnerable to abuse, violation or seduction by "other" men.
>
> (Pettman 1992: 5–6)

In the context of Iran's nationalist movement against "Westoxification," Nayereh Tohidi notes (1994: 127) that a "woman's failure to conform to the traditional norms could be labeled as renunciation of indigenous values and loss of cultural identity. She could be seen as complying with the forces of 'Western imperialists'." Gender issues were also central to political struggles in Afghanistan, which additionally illuminates geopolitical alignments. Valentine Moghadam (1996) observes that the Saur Revolution in 1978 was committed to transforming patriarchal and tribal authority but encountered especially fierce resistance in relation to improving the lives of women, who were denied even literacy. In the civil war that followed, mujahidin forces (supported not least by the United States) unabashedly proclaimed patriarchal power. Although mujahidin factions fought among themselves, "the men all agreed on the question of women. Thus the very first order of the new government [in 1992] was that all women should wear veils" (Moghadam 1994b: 105).

We observe manipulation of gender ideology whenever external intervention is justified by reference to a "civilizing mission" that involves "saving" women from the oppression of their "own" men. As an extensive literature now documents, European colonizers drew upon notions of bourgeois respectability to legitimize their global domination of "others." This respectability relied upon heterosexist as well as racist and classist commitments (especially, Mosse 1985; McClintock 1995). Identities and practices at variance with Victorian codes of feminine respectability and masculine decency were singled out as demonstrating the "backwardness" of indigenous peoples. Lacking respectability, these peoples had no claim to respect and the equality of relations it entails: foreign domination is then not only justified but re-presented as a project of liberation.

As Partha Chatterjee notes in regard to India:

> By assuming a position of sympathy with the unfree and oppressed womanhood of India, the colonial mind was able to transform this figure of the Indian woman into a sign of the inherently oppressive and unfree nature of the entire cultural tradition of a country.
>
> (Chatterjee 1989: 622)

More recently, during the Gulf War the "oppression" of Arab women (veiled, confined, unable to drive cars) was contrasted with the "independence" of United States women (armed, at large, able to drive tanks), thus suggesting a "civilizing" tone to the war against Iraq.[17]

Women as agents and heterosexism as ideology in political identity struggles

In reality, women are not only symbols and their activities extend well beyond the private sphere. In contrast to the stereotype of women as passive and peace-loving, women have throughout history supported and participated in conflicts involving their communities (Jones 1997). They have provided essential support in their servicing roles (feeding, clothing, and nursing combatants), worked in underground movements, passed information and weapons, organized their communities for military action, taken up arms themselves, and occasionally led troops into battle. In short, women must be recognized not only as symbols and victims, but also and significantly, as agents in nationalisms and wars. As both agents and victims (not mutually exclusive categories), women are increasingly visible in processes of political conflict.

As agents, women have slowly but steadily increased their presence in formal and informal political arenas. Always the primary activists at the grassroots level, women are now more visible as these movements themselves acquire visibility. But women's agency in service to heterosexist nationalisms is inherently problematic, as it necessarily entails the reproduction of hierarchical difference, both within and between groups.[18] To be effective, women are drawn toward masculinist strategies, including the denigration of "others." Hence, even as political agency transgresses gender "givens" and may empower particular women, in the context of heterosexism it also reproduces difference and hierarchy. The complexity is captured in Basu's description of "the three most powerful orators of Hindu nationalism":

> At their most benign, [Vijayraje] Scindia, [Uma] Bharati, and [Sadhvi] Rithambara render Muslim women invisible; more often they seek to annihilate Muslim women. Yet all three women have found within Hindu nationalism a vehicle for redressing their experiences of gender inequality and for transgressing sex-typed roles.[19]
>
> (Basu 1993: 31)

As victims, moreover, women have suffered new levels of violence in recent wars. In the first place, in contrast to earlier wars fought with different technologies, women and children have become those most likely to lose their lives in militarized conflicts.[20] More generally, insofar as women are responsible for maintaining homes, families, and their well-being, when societies are militarized, the costs – economic, environmental, emotional – are borne disproportionately by women. Finally, while rape has long been a weapon of war, it has recently been deployed as a weapon of genocide. Here women's bodies *are* the battlefield.

For reasons alluded to earlier, women have historically been denied the homosocial political bonding of public sphere activities. Although this is slowly changing, women rarely appear in combatant or leadership roles and in the top echelons of political power. Because conventional accounts of nationalism and war focus on these activities, it is not surprising that women appear only as "an off-stage chorus to a basically male drama"

(Enloe 1987: 529). Contemporary analysts continue to understand war as a "basically male drama" but they recognize that battlefield action is only the tip of the iceberg. Leadership personalities, gender expectations, popular sentiments, historical animosities, political alignments, diplomatic protocols, media politics, and normative principles are some of the multiple variables upon which battlefield outcomes depend. There is no fixed pattern in how gender shapes the most pertinent variables and their interaction in a specific case. But we can no longer pretend that heterosexist identities and ideology are irrelevant to these practices and the reproduction of identity-driven conflicts.

Historically, and in most countries today, women and homosexuals have been excluded from military service. Recent challenges to this exclusion have exposed how heterosexist premises underpin hegemonic masculinity. As a site of celebrated (because non-sexual) homosocial bonding, the military affords men a unique opportunity to experience intimacy and interdependence with men, in ways that heterosexist identities and divisions of labor otherwise preclude. These points are central to Carol Cohn's (1998) article on "gays in the military," where she brilliantly reveals and analyzes the "chain of signification: military, real man, heterosexual" and how uncloseted homosexuality disrupts this foundational chain (Cohn 1998: 146). Her conclusion captures a variety of points and echoes arguments from this chapter:

> An important attraction of the military to many of its members is a guarantee of heterosexual masculinity. That guarantee is especially important because the military provides a situation of intense bonds between men, a much more homosocial and homoerotically charged environment than most men otherwise have the opportunity to be in. In that the military guarantees their manhood, men are allowed to experience erotic, sexual, and emotional impulses that they would otherwise have to censor in themselves for fear of being seen (by others or themselves) as homosexual and therefore not real men. They are not only escaping a negative – imputations of homosexuality – but gaining a positive, the ability to be with other men in ways that transcend the limitations on male relationships that most men live under in civilian life.
>
> (Cohn 1998: 145)

Women as societal members of heterosexist groups

This category extends our mapping of gender beyond the immediate context of nationalist struggles. It reminds us that women are not homogeneous or typically united, but are multiply located and participate in heterosexist hierarchies that oppress "other" women. Heterosexism insists that women bond not with each other but with men and that women place their childbearing capacity under the control of male-dominated élites, in service to group reproduction through heteropatriarchal family forms and social relations. States structure family forms and policies, but these are also influenced by the beliefs and practices of individuals. At the same time, individuals, families and states shape and are shaped by trans- and supranational dynamics that are also embedded in heterosexist ideology and practice (e.g. Peterson 1996a).

Structural axes of differentiation – race/ethnicity, class, age, ability, sexuality, religion – are intermeshed, such that gender is always racialized and race genderized.[21] Heterosexist practice promotes women's loyalty to male-led (reproductive) groups at the expense of loyalty among women qua women. Located within "different" hierarchical groups, women are differently located in relation to axes of power. The "success" of élite groups typically involves benefits for women within these groups, and in this (limited) sense it is "rational" for women to pursue objectives that often have the additional effect of exacerbating hierarchical relations among groups, and among women. What these insights suggest – and contemporary feminist literature confirms – is that there can be no simple or single "feminist" project. In the words of Alexander and Mohanty (1997: xxii): "There are no fixed prescriptions by which one might determine in advance the specific counterhegemonic histories which will be most useful." How and to what extent feminisms realize their "positive" (transforming social hierarchies linked by denigration of the feminine) rather than their "negative" (enabling some women but leaving hierarchies in place) potential cannot be discerned independent of historically specific contexts.

Hence, allegiance to particular causes may complement, coexist with, or contradict allegiance to other group objectives. How and to what extent feminist and nationalist projects converge depends on contextual specifics. Kumara Jayawardena (1986) found that at the end of the nineteenth and beginning of the twentieth centuries, feminism was compatible with the modernizing dynamic of anti-imperialist national liberation movements in Asia and a number of other colonized countries. In contrast, Val Moghadam examines contemporary movements and concludes that "feminists and nationalists view each other with suspicion, if not hostility, and nationalism is no longer assumed to be a progressive force for change" (1994c: 3). Nationalisms in Eastern Europe and the former Soviet Union exemplify how women's lives/interests are subordinated to the pursuit of nation-building that continues to fuel intergroup conflicts and ensures the reproduction of heterosexism (e.g. Einhorn 1993; Funk and Mueller 1993; Moghadam 1992). In other instances, nationalism has been recast from a secular, modernizing project to one that emphasizes "the nation as an extended family writ large" or "a religious entity" wherein "women become the revered objects of the collective act of redemption, and the role models for the new nationalist, patriarchal family" (Moghadam 1994c: 4). Whether secular or religious, the heterosexist commitments underpinning states and monotheisms ensure that feminist, gay, lesbian, and queer agendas are at best marginalized in today's nationalisms. In all nationalist contexts, women – as symbols and child-bearers – face a variety of pressures to support nationalist objectives even, or especially, when these conflict with feminist objectives.[22]

In short, women are situated differently than men, and differently among themselves, in regard to divisions of power, violence, labor, and resources. Especially important is the paid, underpaid, and unpaid work that women do and how individual women are situated in relation to labor markets and entrepreneurial opportunities. In the context of nationalism, these various locations shape – but do not readily predict! – the allegiance various women, or women in concert, will have toward group identity and objectives. How the tradeoffs are played out may have international consequences. For example, Denmark's initial rejection of the Maastricht Treaty – a "no" vote that threatened to undermine European Community solidarity – was significantly shaped by gender issues. Danish feminists campaigned against the treaty because work and welfare provisions in the Community structure are less progressive than those obtaining already in Denmark (True 1993: 84). Different tradeoffs pertained in the United Kingdom. There, lack of equal opportunity legislation meant that British women had a political interest in seeing their country adopt more progressive Community policies, even though this represented a loss of traditional sovereignty (Walby 1992: 95).

Yet another form of gendered nationalism is discernible in the political economy of migrant workers. Women employed to clean households and tend children reproduce gendered divisions of labor but now often far away from "home," in "other" national contexts. (At the same time, their "independent" lifestyles and economic contributions to family households disrupt traditional gender stereotypes.) Tourism is one of the world's most lucrative enterprises and it too relies upon heterosexist images and ideologies to seduce individuals away from home to "exotic" sites. International patterns in sex tourism and bride markets also are shaped by nationalist stereotypes and histories. In sum, heterosexism and nationalism intersect as employers, pleasure seekers, and bride-buyers deploy nationalist images to distinguish reliable workers, exotic lovers, and beautiful but dutiful wives.

Conclusion

By drawing upon but shifting the focus of feminist studies of nationalism, this chapter has considered heterosexism as historical project and contemporary presumption. I have argued that heterosexism entails the gendered binaries epitomized in western metaphysics but present more generally in codifications based on binary sex difference. The either/or thinking that this imposes fuels hierarchical constructions of difference and social relations of domination. Heterosexist identities produce and are the effect of heterosexist symbols embodied in subject formation, ensuring that there is no "ungendered" identity or experience. Hence, gender is an imperative starting point in the study of identities, identification processes and their multiple effects, and heterosexism is an imperative starting point for critiques of gender (as well as heterosexist, classist, and racist) domination.

Because gender identities are contingent constructions they must be continuously re-created and demonstrated. Heterosexist regimes ensure that the costs of non-compliance are high. Moreover, like all oppositional dichotomies, gender emphasizes either/or difference rather than shared attributes more conducive to solidarity. And *hierarchical* privileging of the masculine – in symbolic and political ordering – puts particular pressure on males to constantly "prove" their manhood, which entails denigrating the feminine, within and beyond the identity group.

Heterosexism as practice involves gendered divisions of activity and entitlement, naturalized by reference to binary sex and its corollary production of masculine and feminine identities and appropriate "roles." Though also a site of potential resistance, the heterosexual family is decisive in these arrangements, exemplifying, naturalizing, and reproducing the heterosexist symbolic order, binary gender identities, and heterosexist practice.

I draw two related conclusions from my research on heterosexism as historical project and contemporary presumption. The first informs studies of political identities and their conflictual effects, as exemplified in nationalism. In fundamental ways (e.g. polarized gender identities, heterosexist families, masculinist ideology, patriarchal power and authority), heterosexist collectivities/societies achieve group coherence and continuity through hierarchical (sex/gender) relations *within* the group. As the binary and corollary inequality that is most naturalized, gender difference is simultaneously invoked to justify *between-group* hierarchies. As a consequence, the gender hierarchy of masculine over feminine and the nationalist domination of insiders over outsiders are doubly linked. That is, nationalism reproduces heterosexist privilege and oppression within the group (at the expense of women and feminized males), regardless of the political identity (race/ethnicity, religion, etc.) by which it differs from other groups. At the same time, nationalism is also gendered in terms of how the *naturalization* of domination between groups (through denigration of the feminine) invokes and reproduces the "foundational" binary of sex difference and depoliticized masculine dominance. In this important sense, feminist and queer critiques of heterosexism are central to *all* critiques of social hierarchy, including those responding to conflicts among local, subnational, national, and transnational identities.

The second conclusion informs debates in critical theory/practice regarding "difference" and how sex/gender is structurally related to "other" axes of oppression (race/ethnicity, nation, class). Shifting our focus from sexism to heterosexism extends feminist theorization of social hierarchies beyond male versus female identity politics and masculine over feminine cultural projects. That is, feminists are better able to theorize domination between as well as within groups. I can only note briefly here how separating gender from, for example, race is a problematic claim. On the one hand, gender, in practice, is inextricable from manifestations of race/ethnicity, religion, class, etc., and a claim suggesting otherwise is both ontologically and politically suspect. On the other hand, I want to distinguish "within group" and "between-group" hierarchies analytically in order to clarify how feminism (as a critique of heterosexism) is differently but significantly relevant to both.[23]

Consider that *within* heterosexist groups, the dominant empirical register of hierarchy/oppression is that of sex difference, generalized to gender. Hence, and conventionally, feminist critique here speaks both to the empirical/material and symbolic/cultural registers of oppression: to the identities and practices of those privileged (men, hegemonic masculinity) and subordinated (women, the feminine) as well as to the ideology that depoliticizes that oppression.

Between heterosexist groups, the dominant empirical register of hierarchy/oppression is that of "group" rather than sex difference, in the sense of race/ethnicity, religious, or class difference as a "group" identification. Feminist critique here assumes a different relevance. It still speaks to the empirical register of oppression but in a circumscribed sense: only insofar as women constitute a proportion of those who are subordinated – *and* those who are privileged. But it continues to speak, I believe indispensably (but not exhaustively), to the symbolic register of conflicts between (heterosexist) identity groups. That is, even though the empirical "mark" of oppression and group conflict is not that of sex difference, the naturalization – read, *depoliticization* – of that oppression is inextricable from heterosexist ideology and its denigration of the feminine.[24] Specifically feminist critique is imperative for deconstructing this – all too effective – naturalization of intergroup conflict, a point which is especially salient to students of IR.

Through conventional – and even many critical – lenses, heterosexism is *not* the most visible or apparently salient aspect of political identities and their potential conflicts. I have argued, however, that its foundational binary is relentlessly productive of hierarchical difference and, especially, the naturalization of hierarchies through denigration of the feminine/Other. Hence, in the context of systemic violence (within and between groups), heterosexism may be the historically constructed "difference" we most need to see – and to deconstruct.

Notes

1 In this chapter I employ the concept of political identity as a way of referring to identification with a particular group – whether that group is bounded by race/ethnicity, kinship, culture, territory, or shared purpose – and actions on behalf of that group as they influence and are influenced by power relations broadly conceived. For elaboration see Peterson (1995a, 1995b, 1996a).

2 As many critical theorists argue, this state-centric definition of nationalism is inadequate. It is especially problematic in the context of today's globalization, changing sovereignties, proliferating actors, deterritorialization and space/time compression. I also emphasize here that generalizations about states, nationalisms, women and men always oversimplify and obscure significant particularities. My focus in this chapter, however, is nationalism understood as state-centric and I indulge such generalizations in order to pursue the less familiar discussion of heterosexism.

3 For an early and compelling account, see Corrigan and Sayer (1985). Of course, recent feminist and other critical interrogations of nationalism address the internal effects of nationalist projects.

4 Jill Steans (1998: 62) writes: "It is perhaps because the nation-state continues to function as the irreducible component of identity that gender, along with class, race or other facets of identity, continues to be rendered invisible in International Relations." Other feminist treatments of identity in IR include Pettman 1996; Sharoni 1995; Tickner 1996; Zalewski and Enloe 1995; Zalewski and Parpart 1998.

5 If social theories bring agency, order and change into intelligible relation, then identifications offer one way of "bridging" agency (subjectivity, identities, micro-level) and order (structure, institutions, macro-level) and change (transformations – of agency and order – as effects of action mobilized by variance in identity salience and shifting identifications).

6 The following six points are adapted from Peterson (1996a).

7 M. Jacqui Alexander credits Lynda Hart (1994) as the originator of the term heteropatriarchy and uses it to "combine the twin processes of heterosexualization and patriarchy" (Alexander 1997: 65). In this chapter, I use heteropatriarchy to refer to sex/gender systems that naturalize masculinist domination and institutionalize/normalize heterosexual family forms and corollary heterosexist identities and practices.

8 While sex and gender feature in feminist work on nationalism, relatively few authors *explicitly* problematize and/or investigate how sex and gender presuppose heterosexism/homophobia. Exceptions include the pioneering analysis of Mosse (1985) and subsequent work on sexualities in the context of nationalisms: e.g. Alexander 1994, 1997; McClintock 1995; Parker *et al.* 1992.

9 To clarify: a critique of heterosexism is no more (or less) an objection to heterosexuality "*per se*" than a critique of sexism is an objection to sex "*per se.*" It is the meaning of "sex" (especially insofar as it reproduces the heterosexist binary) that is problematic; and it is heterosexism's refusal of other expressions of identity, intimacy, and "family" life that is politically objectionable. Discussion of sex/ualities is complicated by the historical contingency and therefore instability of discursive concepts. Contemporary sexualities literature cautions against retrospectively reading, for example, "homosexuality" into history, especially prior to modernist discourse on sexualities in these terms (e.g. Butler 1990; Halperin 1990). Hence, in this chapter my references to heterosexism and sex/gender identities in early state-making (below) should be read as focusing on the regulation of reproductive sexual activities that is a dominant feature of the state-making conjuncture (thus leaving aside expressions of non-reproductive sexual activity). I would argue, however, that this regulation necessarily had effects on non-reproductive expressions of sexuality and is deeply implicated in the instantiation of sex/gender binaries more generally. In this chapter, I use homosexual and non-heterosexual (identities, practices, persons) as terms encompassing lesbian, gay, bisexual, and transgender (transvestite, transsexual) expressions of sexuality.

The relationship between sexism (associated with feminist studies) and heterosexism (associated with queer studies) is complex and contested, not least because the meaning and relationships of key concepts are so contested. This is in part an unavoidable consequence of challenging the binary and essentialist terms that have traditionally demarcated spheres of activities and corollary studies of them. In brief, I intend this work as a contribution to both feminist and queer theories, which seek to deconstruct conventional binaries of sex, gender, and sexuality. Queer theorists quite rightly argue that "the study of sexuality is not coextensive with the study of gender" (Sedgwick 1993: 27) and that acritical reliance on the latter – which characterizes some feminisms – fuels heterosexist bias (Sedgwick 1993: 31). This chapter attempts to deconstruct gender as a binary that is symbolically and structurally inextricable from the heterosexism of states/nations and to argue, by implication, that feminist theory is not coextensive with but cannot be separate from, or indifferent to, queer theory. In this I follow Butler (1994) and Martin (1994) in arguing that critical analyzes of sex and sexualities are inextricable and feminist and queer studies should avoid reproducing any dichotomization of their relationship. Rather, as Butler (1994: 15) suggests, it is conceptually more productive and politically more appropriate "for feminism to offer a critique of gender hierarchy that might be incorporated into a radical theory of sex [gay, lesbian, and queer studies], and for radical sexual theory to challenge and enrich feminism." I return to these issues in the conclusion.

10 My enduring interest in state-making springs from two convictions. First, although the state is a key category in IR, it remains poorly theorized, due to inadequate historical attention and disciplinary blinders. Hence, my own theorization of states draws on research in archeology, anthropology, classical studies, western philosophy, political economy, state theories, and feminist scholarship (for elaboration and citations see Peterson 1988, 1992b, 1997). Second, with other critical postmodernists, I wish to move beyond arguments for postmodernist understanding (necessary in the face of obdurate modernist/ masculinist commitments) to postmodernist theorizing that more readily (though never simply or innocently) informs political practice. Cast as challenges to reigning approaches, the former tend to emphasize the symbolic and cultural (signification, intersubjective meaning systems, language, discourse, representation, interpretation, identities), apparently – but not necessarily intentionally – at the expense of the concrete and structural (material conditions, political economy, institutions, social hierarchies, coercion, direct violence). Rather than this paralyzing (and polemical) polarization, critical postmodernism seeks to illuminate the interaction of signs and structures; that is, to analyze how culture and power, discourse and dominance, identity and political economy are inextricably linked – mutually constituted – in historically specific contexts. I intend my subsequent argumentation to demonstrate that political centralization affords not only a paradigmatic example of this interaction (thereby illustrating the appropriateness and productiveness of a critical postmodern orientation) but also a politically significant example for understanding contemporary power dynamics.

11 In Judith Butler's (1990) words:

> The heterosexualization of desire requires and institutes the production of discrete and asymmetrical oppositions between "feminine" and "masculine," where these are understood as expressive attributes of "male" and "female." The cultural matrix through which gender identity has become intelligible requires that certain kinds of "identities" cannot "exist" – that is, those in

which gender does not follow from sex and those in which the practices of desire do not "follow" from either sex or gender.

(Butler 1990: 17)

See also Bem (1993) for an especially clear and comprehensive discussion linking androcentrism, gender polarization, biological essentialism, and (hetero)sexual inequalities.

12 "Typically represented as a passionate brotherhood, the nation finds itself compelled to distinguish its 'proper' homosociality from more explicitly sexualized male–male relations, a compulsion that requires the identification, isolation, and containment of male homosexuality" (Parker *et al.* 1992b: 6). On homosocial forms of domination in relation to denial of homoerotic bonding, see also Sedgwick (1985, 1990).

13 The five dimensions are drawn from Peterson (1994, 1995b) and are indebted to, but different from, the framework introduced in the singularly important work of Yuval-Davis and Anthias (1989); see also Anthias and Yuval-Davis (1992) and Yuval-Davis (1997).

14 Beverly Allen (1992) notes that the cultural specificity of Italian nationalism is: first, that the gendering of "terrorism" as male insures the gendering of the victim as female, and second, and more importantly as far as Italian cultural specificity is concerned, this gendering of the victim as female insures an "identification" – based on centuries of literary precedents – of that female victim as the Italian nation "herself." (Allen 1992: 166)

15 Significantly, Pettman (1996: 49) notes how the metaphor "also confuses the rape of actual women with the outrage of political attack or defeat, and in the process women's pain and rights are appropriated into a masculinist power politics."

16 The fact that rape is not present in all societies and that many men resist rape practices (even under wartime pressures to commit rape) confirms the *social* construction – not givenness – of this heterosexist objectification of the feminine.

17 The principle of gender equality was not an objective but a pawn in these conflicts: European colonizers oppressed women at home and abroad, and the United States was ostensibly defending Kuwait, where women cannot even vote. Enloe argues that these apparent contradictions make sense if viewed not as strategies of liberation but of justification: legitimating the domination by some men over "other" men and their communities (Enloe 1990: 49).

18 This is not to argue that nationalist struggles are never worth fighting, but that they are implicated in larger and problematic dynamics that must also be contested, and not simply *relegated in importance.*

19 Bacchetta (1993) writes similarly of a militant Hindu woman she refers to as Kamlabehn, who defies stereotypes of passive femininity and decries sexual harassment by Hindu men, while displacing her resentment of this onto Muslim men.

Indeed, by projecting such characteristics onto Muslim men, Kamlabehn is able to discharge emotion that might otherwise accumulate into an impossible and unacceptable rebellion against the macho Hindu men in her environment. Instead, her representation of Muslim men only concretizes her solidarity with Hindu men by rendering even the most offensive of the latter as less offensive than the former. Such an attitude functions to confine Hindu nationalist women within a Hindu community whose boundaries and landscape are determined essentially by Hindu nationalist men.

(Bacchetta 1993: 50)

20 Pettman (1996: 89) writes: "In World War 1, 80 per cent of casualties were soldiers; in World War 2, only 50 per cent. In the Vietnam War some 80 per cent of casualties were civilian, and in current conflicts the estimate is 90 per cent – mainly women and children."

21 I regret that my focus on heterosexism in this chapter has been at the expense of attending to race/ethnicity and class. Analyzing how these "come into exis-tence *in and through* relation to each other" (McClintock 1995: 5) is central to critical theory/practice. In this regard, I especially commend the work of post-colonial feminists more generally, and the following authors in particular: Jacqui Alexander, Ana Alonso, Zillah Eisenstein, Cynthia Enloe, bell hooks, Lily Ling, Anne McClintock, Val Moghadam, Chandra Talpade Mohanty, Roxana Ng, Jindy Pettman, Gayatri Spivak, Ann Stoler, Jacqui True, Brackette Willams, Anna Yeatman, Nira Yuval-Davis.

22 The tremendous variety in nationalist struggles, in women's roles and in women's resistances must be emphasized, but cannot be addressed here.

23 I intend these arguments as a contribution to feminist theory/practice: enabling us to address the embodied "realities" of women's lives (e.g. women as strategic empirical referent) while honoring/invoking gender as an analytical category (e.g. denigration of the feminine as pivotal dynamic within and between groups). As clarified in note 9, I also intend this work as a contribution to queer theory: enabling "a more expansive, mobile mapping of power" (Butler 1994: 21) by situating sex/gender as inextricable from heterosexism. In both instances, I am attempting to deconstruct binary rigidities through a critical genealogy of both historical-empirical processes (e.g. early state-making) and conceptual/symbolic developments (e.g. western metaphysics, political theory). As intimated in note 10, I intend these efforts as a contribution to depolarizing – without "resolving" – the tension between material/structural/modernist and symbolic/discursive/postmodernist orientations.

24 Similarly, even though male–male rape is not apparently heterosexual, the naturalization of expressing domination in this form is inextricable from hetero-sexist ideology and its denigration of the feminine.

5 The politics of Gandhi's "feminism"

Constructing "Sitas" for *Swaraj*

Suresht R. Bald

In 1982–1983, while conducting research for a review article on the women's movement in India, I was struck by what seemed to me then to be a glaring inconsistency in Gandhi's writings and speeches. On the one hand, Gandhi supported and strengthened tradition when he insisted that, because women were "naturally" different from men, they should perform tasks for which nature created them; on the other, he supported the potentially radical belief that one's conscience was the only "voice" one need heed and obey. For example, Gandhi wrote,

> It is not for women to go out and work, as men do. If we send them to the factories who will look after our domestic and social affairs? If women go out to work, our social life will be ruined and moral standards will decline. ... I am convinced that for men and women to go out for work together will mean the fall of both.[1]
>
> (Joshi 1988: 43–44)

Switching roles spelt ruin: "In trying to ride the horse that man rides, she [the woman] brings herself and him [the man] down" (Hingorani 1966: 14). These and other statements by Gandhi underscored what a woman could or could not do. At the same time, however, he also maintained that, "The wife has a perfect right to take her own course, and meekly brave the consequences when she knows herself to be in the right, and when her resistance is for a nobler purpose" (Hingorani 1966: 5). On other occasions when he was not referring to women in particular, Gandhi insisted that "each should regard his own conscience as the authority" (Iyer 1987: 443). At one point he claimed that the "Inner Voice" was the "voice of God" (Iyer 1987: 131). If we accept that one's conscience is the final judge, then social norms and traditions that construct what we tend to consider "natural" lose their significance. A woman becomes a free agent who acts of her own "free" will regardless of the roles assigned her by society and endorsed by Gandhi. For example, if a woman's "conscience" urged her to work outside the home, presumably she could flout social custom and tradition (and Gandhi's injunctions) and do so. In this chapter I suggest that while the above inconsistency may seem glaring if we look at Gandhi's views on women as a coherent ideology *separate* and *independent* from his primary goal of ending British colonialism in India, it vanishes when his ideology of women is treated as *secondary* to his interest in winning independence from the British. When Gandhi's writings and statements on women are examined as a *part of* his political strategy for achieving *Swaraj* (self-rule), one can see how his concerns for women tended to be defined by his perception of whatever was politically most effective; in fact, when viewed in the context of the changing political needs of the nationalist movement, Gandhi's views on women become surprisingly coherent.[2] I argue that Gandhi was not interested in women's liberation *per se* but rather that women's involvement in social and political issues was important to him *because* he considered it crucial for the *success* of his politics of non-violence. Gandhi needed women to promote *khadi* (home-spun); to picket in front of shops selling liquor and foreign cloth; and to raise funds for his campaigns. Always sensitive to the media, he was shrewd enough to know that pictures and accounts of ordinary housewives marching or demonstrating peacefully would have a strong impact on people around the world. These in turn would help the Indian cause.

However, accepting that Gandhi used women as a *means* for achieving political independence does not detract from the fact that his particular brand of politics facilitated women's entry into politics, thus ensuring that they could not be totally ignored in the development politics of independent India. It was *because* his "feminization" of the male idiom of politics made women important actors in the drama of the nationalist movement (they were not only to spin at home but also to picket and demonstrate *outside* the home), that it was necessary for Gandhi to avoid undermining traditionally defined gender roles. Gandhi's commitment to national harmony and consensus dictated that female satyagrahis not disrupt the traditional gender system. Just as in his economics, workers and capitalists were to accept each other's "rightful" place in society, men and women were to accept their "naturally" defined spaces. Indeed, even as he was asking women to picket liquor stores, Gandhi's statements supported the sanctity of the family and the home: he reiterated that a woman's *real* place was the household where she was the "queen." It was his genius that he was able to support women's involvement in the public arena of politics at the same time that he defended their traditional roles as mothers and wives who were expected to work within the confines of the home. I suggest here that Gandhi framed the political discourse that continues to determine the politics of women's rights, duties, and identity in India today.

Gandhi's greatness and status as an icon makes an impartial appraisal of his work difficult. No doubt I bring to my analysis my own feminist consciousness and memories of my feminist mother's discomfort with some of Gandhi's views on women. It has taken me more than a decade to return to Gandhi's writings to examine what I found troublesome; I do so with the benefit of several excellent collections of his writings and statements on women, and his ninety volumes of collected works (hereafter CWMG) that have been published during the interim.[3]

Recent critical readings of Gandhi by feminist scholars have initiated a line of analysis that has provided us with important insights into Gandhi's perceptions of women's role, the assumptions that underlie his notions of women's sexuality, his views on the origin and nature of gender differences, and his explanations for women's subordinate position in British India (see Katrak 1992; Kishwar 1985b; Patel 1988). Except for Patel, each scholar discusses Gandhi's ideology of "woman" and his politics as parallel constructions rather than as elements of the same edifice. It is this that leads them to insights, which though important, remain partial. All agree that Gandhian ideology treats women as subjects or actors. They fault Gandhi, however, for not challenging the patriarchal structures on which Indian society was constructed. Since calling woman a "subject" in a patriarchal society seems contradictory, Katrak and Kishwar suggest that Gandhi's ideology sent ambiguous messages to Indian women. Katrak's (1992) study illustrates how Gandhi's use of tradition actually strengthened patriarchy even as his political mobilization of women provided them with "positive legacies of non-violent ideology – passive resistance, mass demonstration, appeal to the moral aspects of wrong-doers – [which] are currently used to protest dowry murders" (Katrak 1992: 401–402). To Kishwar (1985a), Gandhi's concern for women is a moral one rather than political or economic, that is, she sees him as treating women as moral agents though without claims to political and economic power. Kishwar criticizes Gandhi for explaining women's oppression as an "abstract moral condition" for which both men and women are responsible, and for failing to understand that it was "a social and historical relation, related to production relations" (Kishwar 1985a: 1699). However, she does not explore reasons why Gandhi did not pursue this line of reasoning. She does not ask how the moral and the spiritual fit into Gandhi's politics, or what role morality played in his political strategy.

Patel (1988) calls Gandhi a "political strategist par excellence who attempted to unite different unevenly developed strata" through his essentialist ideology regarding the Indian woman (Patel 1988: 386). Though I agree with her proposition that Gandhi's views on women should be studied and understood within the framework of the nationalist struggle, I question her thesis that Gandhi's objective for the "construction and reconstruction of woman" was to bring the different classes and castes together against imperialism by creating a uniform image of Indian womanhood. Though Patel's rich and illuminating analysis traces the different stages of Gandhi's reconstruction of the Indian (Hindu) woman and explains the role such a reconstruction played in the construction of Indian nationalism, her central point that this was essential because of the class/caste divisions among Indians is not persuasive. While this may have been a consequence of Gandhi's politics, nowhere does he specifically give this as a reason for his stance. Instead he provides us with a number of statements that suggest that his references to Sita, Draupadi, and Damyanti are an attempt to convince the Indians and the world (especially the British) that Indian women were once strong and brave; they were not man's playthings but his "better half," equal to, but different from, men. In Gandhi's judgment, rejection of Hindu ideals of womanhood such as chastity, self-control, and sacrifice had led to women's enslavement and the enslavement of the Indian nation. Perceived thus, his use of the chaste Sita, courageous Damyanti, and fearless Draupadi become as much a means for making Indian women (and men) feel a sense of pride in their heritage, a heritage that had come under severe attack by the British, as to instil a particular code of behavior (*brahmacharya*) that he considered important among his *satyagrahis* if men and women were to participate together in the nationalist struggle. In addition, Sita, Savitri, and Draupadi are heroines who have *always* been accepted and revered by *all* Hindus, so Gandhi's references to them, I submit, were more to articulate his political agenda in a familiar idiom than to construct a common ideal for *all* women. An unfortunate result was that the use of Hindu symbols tended to alienate non-Hindu Indians. So, in some ways, contrary to Patel's assertion, one could argue that Gandhi's particular packaging of his ideals of womanhood actually divided rather than united Indian women.

While Kishwar, Patel, and Katrak extend our understanding of Gandhi's views on female sexuality, they do not ask why Gandhi's views of women's empowerment were limited to the domestic arena, or why it was important for Indian women to live according to the ideals of womanhood represented by the heroines of the Hindu epics "Ramayana" and "Mahabharata." It is the insights contained in Suzanne and Lloyd Rudolph's seminal work on Gandhi's politics (Rudolph and Rudolph 1967, 1983) and the third world and feminist scholarship on colonialism and imperialism (see e.g. Fanon 1963; Mohanty *et al.* 1991) which clarify Gandhi's writings on women and help us to answer some of the puzzling questions raised by his statements.

The Rudolphs say that Gandhi took to heart the British critique that branded Indians as "unfit to rule"; they see his politics as a response to that critique. They and Erik Erikson explain Gandhi's redefinition of courage within the context of the British claim that Indians were "unmanly" and "lacking in courage." For, as the Rudolphs point out, Hindu notions of manliness and courage which treated internal battles of the self as the only worthwhile battles to win, were incomprehensible to the British who were brought up to equate these virtues with the ability to overcome challenges *external* to the self. But there is something else to consider. As the feminists' and third world scholars' works on colonialism and imperialism suggest, one can argue further that it was not just the inability of the British to understand Hindu culture that led them to perceive the Indians as "effeminate" but rather that such an inference is intrinsic to colonialism. Colonialism, a relationship based on power, is akin to a male–female relationship where the colonizer, the "male," feminizes the colonized in order to subjugate, control, and "protect." Gandhi's genius was to question and reject the British version of the meaning of courage and develop instead a strategy that placed "femininity" on its head. He "masculinized" the colonized by redefining "feminine" traits as "manly" or courageous. In doing so, he made the British critique of the Indian irrelevant. To give his claims legitimacy and authenticity, Gandhi drew upon a particular Hindu culture and experience to reconstruct the notion of "courage." He made it clear that, according to Hinduism, violence, or inflicting pain on the "other," is the weapon of the weak, while self-control that enables one to *bear* pain is a sign of courage.

When Gandhi made this "new" kind of courage the basis of his politics of Satyagraha, he elevated what he considered to be women's "natural" traits of endurance, non-violence, and self-sacrifice (Joshi 1988: 222) above the so-called "masculine" virtues of force and physical strength, and made "femaleness" respectable (see also Bald 1986). This meant that those who possessed these traits "naturally," women, now became crucial to the success of his movement for *Swaraj*. But except for the brief period of protest against the partition of Bengal in 1905, Indian women by and large (except for a few upper class/caste westernized women like Sarojini Naidoo) had traditionally stayed out of politics. To get women involved in his politics, Gandhi set out to redefine their place in Indian society. He did it as he had accomplished his redefinition of courage, by selective use of Hindu culture.

Spinning to *Swaraj*

The first time that Gandhi appealed directly to Indian women was in connection with his *swadeshi* (homespun) movement. In a 1919 speech at a women's meeting in Bombay, he said:

> The swadeshi vow, too, cannot be kept fully if women do not help. Men alone will be able to do nothing in the matter. They can have no control over the children; that is the women's sphere. To look after children, to dress them, is the mother's duty and, therefore, it is necessary that women should be fired by the spirit of swadeshi. So long as that does not happen, men will not be in a position to take the vow.
> (Joshi 1988: 23)

In another speech on *swadeshi* at a women's meeting in Nadiad two months later, Gandhi reminded his audience of well-to-do women that imported cloth cost Indians "two rupees a head annually." This loss, which over the one hundred and fifty years of British rule was a considerable amount, he claimed, was responsible for India's poverty and enslavement. Indian women were to help in the effort of reviving India's economy by returning to the *charkha*, the spinning wheel:

> Just as a good family should have a quern, so also it should have a spinning wheel. ... Use swadeshi. Produce swadeshi. ... If all men and women agree, we can see to it that foreign cloth disappears in 11 days. ... If all the women embrace this dharma, be sure our emancipation is near at hand, within 15 days.
>
> (Joshi 1988: 31)

The message was repeated at meetings in different parts of the country. Names of Hindu epic heroines were evoked to emphasize the message and the women's heritage. Gandhi referred to Sita as a "nationalist" who always wore *swadeshi*:

> Sitaji used to wear cloth made in India. In her days not a bit of foreign cloth was imported into India. But the ladies of the present day wanted cloth from France, Japan, and Manchester. To use foreign cloth was impurity. ... Sisters ought to spin at least half an hour everyday.
>
> (Joshi 1988: 125)

To convince women to give up their fine imported silks and cottons he redefined beauty:

> Wearing of foreign cloth makes a woman ugly. There is a touch of the harlot in a woman seeking loveliness by fine dressing. What is our image of Sita and Damyanti, whom we adore? We revere Damyanti who wandered in the forest half-clad, and Sita who suffered vanavasa (exile) for fourteen years. Was Harishchandra's queen, who served as a maid, dressed in fine clothes? ... I am truly handsome, since the clothes I am wearing are made by yarn spun by women and lovingly woven by men.
>
> (Joshi 1988: 63)

To be virtuous and beautiful like the epic heroines, a woman had to wear homespun. Sita and Damyanti, along with Indian women, were recruited to help Gandhi's strategy for gaining independence.

For *swadeshi* to work there needed to be enough homespun cloth for the country's requirements. Since spinning was traditionally a woman's job and weaving a man's job, Gandhi's message for *swadeshi* included urgent demands that women spin at least half an hour a day: "*swaraj* is tied to the strand of yarn. These are the words of Brahma. ... it is the women who are the spinners. Therefore it is women who will play a larger part in the non-violent struggle for *swaraj*.

(Joshi 1988: 216)

Not only was spinning good for the country's struggle for freedom, but also it was good for women's chastity: "swadeshi is not merely a means of protecting India's wealth but it makes for protecting women's honour" (Joshi 1988: 42). The reason for this, explained Gandhi, was that the women "who cannot procure work which may be done at home go out for labour, which they procure at the price of their chastity" (Joshi 1988: 33). For example, he cited the case of women in Umreh who

> added to their little income by winnowing pulses for merchants. They have to go to them to receive and return the pulses and there they have to put up with all sorts of indecent jokes and abuse. . . . It seems to me that a hundred years ago, when millions of our mothers used to spin cotton, such things must not have been happening.
>
> (Joshi 1988: 33)

His advice to the women of Umreh is to earn money by taking up spinning in the privacy of their home.[4] Such a move was to accomplish several ends – further the nationalists' cause, improve women's well being by giving them access to cash, and strengthen gender roles and the family.

It is important to keep in mind that to Gandhi, differences between male and female tasks did not imply superiority of one over the other. In fact, in a 1927 letter to Shardabehn Kotak, although he maintained that "men must do their duty of protecting women," he also stated that "there is the same *atman* (soul) in woman as in man" (Joshi 1988: 157). This made men and women equal.

Women as persuasive picketers

In the case of spinning, Gandhi's political ends and his staunch belief in naturally prescribed gender roles did not come into conflict. However, in 1930, when women wanted to join the men in the Dandi Salt March, he was reluctant to include them. Instead he claimed that he needed them to picket outside shops selling liquor and foreign cloth. Though such work would take the women from the domestic into the public arena, they could do it "even while attending to their domestic duties" (Joshi 1988: 221). The Salt March, on the other hand, would have taken them away from their homes. In addition, the assigning of women to the picketing of shops fit well into Gandhi's overall strategy. The use of women, he believed, would ensure that the picketing would remain non-violent. In 1921, when men were entrusted with this task, their encounters with shopkeepers and the police turned violent and the movement failed (Joshi 1988: 222, 227). Because Gandhi saw picketing as a way of appealing to the "buyers of foreign cloth and [to] the liquor dealers and addicts," he felt that women with their "moral power" could "make a more effective appeal to the heart" (Joshi 1988: 222). "If I go and reason with them, they will quarrel with me as they will with other men. They will not, however, be disrespectful or insulting to any woman. They are not such beasts. . . . As soon as they come in contact with you they will be awakened" (Joshi 1988: 217). Moreover, Gandhi believed that "the Government . . . will not make war upon women" if all the picketers were women. But if the women took "part alongside of men in defense of salt pans," Gandhi was afraid either that they would be assaulted or that their presence would lead the government to refrain from being "provoked," thus blunting the edge of his "aggressive non-violence" (Joshi 1988: 230). If that were to happen, the effectiveness of the Dandi March would be compromised. It was important, therefore, that women *not* participate in the Dandi March. But since the women did not want to be excluded, Gandhi assigned them a different task – picketing shops. To make it more acceptable to the women, he placed the picketing of shops selling foreign cloth and liquor on the same level as the more "exciting" Salt Satyagraha.

Finally, Gandhi realized that a movement "initiated and controlled exclusively by women" had a certain "charm" and was bound to receive press coverage in India and abroad.

> Personally, I am convinced that if we should succeed in these three things [salt satyagraha, picketing of foreign cloth and of liquor shops] swaraj would soon be an accomplished fact, the women would realize their power in no time and, without any effort on our part, the whole world would see how ours was indeed a holy war.
>
> (Joshi 1988: 221)

But the women felt cheated out of "glory" and Gandhi had to convince them that picketing also could be "dangerous." When women complained that "there was no excitement and no adventure in the liquor and foreign-cloth picketing," he assured them that, "before they have done with the agitation, they might even find themselves in prison. It is not improbable that they may be insulted and even injured bodily. To suffer such insult and injury would be their pride" (Joshi 1988: 223–224). Gandhi, acting like a parent, was trying to make leftovers look like a feast.

The bejeweled Indian woman: from bondage to freedom

An important area in which Gandhi felt that women could help the nationalist cause was by raising funds for his various political campaigns and for social uplift work. His appeal was mostly to affluent women. They could help in two ways: first, they could donate their jewelry, one asset over which they had sole control. This act would provide funds for the cause, help women live a simpler life more in keeping with life in Gandhi's new order, and teach them the "joys" of giving or sacrifice. Thus it would have material and spiritual consequences. Second, the women could help collect funds, since Gandhi thought that men were less likely to refuse appeals by women than appeals by men.

But to convince the women to part with their jewelry, Gandhi had to change deeply entrenched habits that went back several centuries. Again he sought the help of the epic heroines. "Think of Sita," he told the women at Sonepur in 1927.

> Do you imagine she went about with Rama in his 14 years' forest wanderings with heavy ornaments like you? Do you think they add to your beauty? Sita cared for the beauty of her heart and covered her body with pure khaddar (homespun). . . . Free yourselves of these shackles and relieve the poverty of people who have no clothes, much less ornaments to wear.
>
> (Joshi 1988: 147)

He pointed out in an article in *Navajivan* in 1929 that jewelry was a form of bondage; heavy arm and ankle ornaments slowed women's movements and ear and nose rings made it easy for her husband or even her child "by firmly taking hold of a nose or ear ornament," to render her helpless (Joshi 1988: 212). Furthermore, Gandhi wrote, spending money on gold and silver jewelry made little economic sense either for the individual or for the nation, for money spent on jewelry meant loss of that much capital for investment. He covered all bases: he provided women with personal, altruistic, and nationalistic reasons for donating their jewelry to the cause. Many women heeded his demands and gave him their jewelry and the bags of cash they had collected.

Recruiting women to "purify" tradition

Gandhi's emphasis on social reform to make India "fit for self-rule" made women, whom he considered the custodians of Indian culture and conscience, a crucial target of his appeals. Moreover, a number of the social ills to which Gandhi turned his attention fell really in the "private" or "domestic" arena. Issues like child marriage, remarriage of child widows, dowry, purdah, treatment of Bhangis (sweepers whom Gandhi called Harijans), and prohibitions against inter-caste dining, affected individuals on a personal level. Most encounters with Bhangis occurred in the home when they came to clean the latrines; it was women who arranged marriages and taught their daughters to observe purdah; and because women were the family cooks, inter-caste dining would be difficult without their cooperation. For his reforms to succeed, therefore, Gandhi needed to win women over to his cause.

To do so, he started a dual campaign to illustrate that what women considered to be sacred injunctions spelt out in the *smritis* were actually "verses inserted by persons accepted as *smritikars* (authors of smritis) in the period of our degeneration . . . I look upon myself as an orthodox Hindu and my attack proceeds from the desire to rid Hinduism of its defects and restore it to its pristine glory" (CWMG, vol. 14: 204). Gandhi took pains to explain at the various meetings of women he attended, that "true" Hinduism maintained that all human beings, be they women, *sudras*, widows or Brahmins, were equally worthy. All souls were the same. However, equality did not mean similarity. Gandhi believed in the doctrine of equal but different.[5] He was careful to point out that, unlike Christians who wanted to destroy Hinduism, he wanted to rid it of untruths to make it stronger. "It is easy to demonstrate the grandeur of the *smritis* minus these verses" (CWMG, vol. 14: 204). Thus he hoped to solicit the women's support for his battles against what he regarded as ills of Hindu society by reconstructing a dharma that he claimed was based on early, "authentic" sections of the *smritis*. It was important for the creation of the Indian community/nation that his reconstructed dharma question those Hindu practices that by legitimizing inequality *divided* rather than united the Indian people. At the same time, it was crucial that he not denounce the traditional gender and caste systems, for such denunciations would have split the Hindus.

Gandhi's reconstruction of the Hindu dharma involved cleansing existing Hindu practices of injunctions that sanctioned untouchability, child marriages, restrictions against remarriage of child widows, and women's and *sudras'* illiteracy. Gandhi believed that the key to the acceptance of his reconstructed dharma lay in women's hands for it was women who, by teaching their children "correct" values and conduct, perpetuated these practices. As he explained at a women's meeting in Kathlal,

> It is not in the hands of the Brahmins, or of men, to preserve dharma. It is entirely in the hands of the women to do so. The foundation on which society rests is the home and dharma is to be cultivated in the home. The fragrance in the home will spread all over society. . . . Women are the presiding deities of the home. If they do not follow dharma, the people would be totally destroyed.
>
> (CWMG, vol. 20: 63)

Temple entry was a way of publicizing discrimination against the untouchables and part of his overall goal of eradicating untouchability completely. He believed that to do so, women's support was essential. In 1934 at a women's meeting in Ahmedabad, Gandhi claimed,

> Men tell me: "We do wish to give up untouchability. But do you wish to create domestic quarrels? We are willing to have Harijans in our houses. But what can we do if those who are in the house for all twenty-four hours would not allow them?" So, if women realize that untouchability is a sin and has to be wiped out, men would not be

able to hold fast to it. It is beyond the powers of men. This is the experience of most men.

(Joshi 1988: 289)

Not only did women have to be convinced themselves, but they had to be recruited to convince others also. Again, it was their "natural" traits and traditional role that, according to Gandhi, made them suitable for the "battle" to gain access to temples for the untouchables. They had "good powers of persuasion"; they could "convince the bonafide temple-goers that true religion will open the hearts of the people and the gates of the temple to every human being and will brand no one as an outcaste" (Joshi 1988: 286).

Balancing tradition and national needs

So important was women's involvement in the national movement for Gandhi that in response to the question, if a woman may "in the teeth of opposition by her husband undertake national service? Or must she only go as far as the husband will permit her?" Gandhi states unequivocally that she should listen to her conscience rather than her husband. Of course, his much-revered Sita obeyed Rama even when she knew he was wrong to abandon her after she had proven her chastity. But in Gandhi's schema the husband ranked lower than the nation. Since the national cause was a "higher" cause, it was all right for women to step outside their homes on appropriate occasions to work for it. When their help was not needed, they were to return to their homes to teach their children how to be good citizens. They were to engage in politics when male leaders called them to shoulder that duty; they were not to take on lives as politicians and public administrators. Indeed, one year before independence, when the end of the British Raj was imminent, Gandhi was uncertain about women engaging in national politics by standing for elections to the legislatures and so on. (Joshi 1988: 340, 342). It is instructive to recall that when the South Africa government passed the Marriage Act (1913) which recognized only marriages performed according to Christian rites or those registered with the government, it was Kasturba, Gandhi's wife, who led women to court arrest by demonstrating against the Act. Gandhi, by his own admission, was apprehensive at first about women taking such action. His reasons were that he was concerned for Kasturba's health and that he lacked confidence in the women's ability to complete successfully what they were undertaking: "If at the last moment they flinched, their prominence might seriously damage the cause they sought to advance" (Joshi 1988: 371). It was finally decided to let the "ladies" proceed with their plan but under no circumstance were they to divulge their names until they were *safely* in jail. Thus their men could be saved from embarrassment if the women failed.

The women's success revealed their mettle. Besides, after imprisonment, the women returned to their homes and "the usual routine of an Indian woman's life. ... They are the same patient, dutiful women that India has produced for centuries" (Joshi 1988: 370). Thus these women demonstrated that inclusion of women in the "struggle" could be both effective and non-threatening to the traditional family. Kasturba's initiative in South Africa paved the way for Gandhi's appeals to women in India. But, as Kishwar argues, women in India "remained auxiliary and supportive. They did not come out for direct action as women had in South Africa" (Kishwar 1985a: 1698). However, Gandhi's appeals to them, his references to their "special" traits, and the importance of their contributions to the nationalist cause could not help but empower them by improving women's perception of themselves.

By and large, the empowerment of women was limited to the domestic arena. Gandhi made it clear that he did not

> envisage the wife, as a rule, following an avocation independently of her husband. The care of the children and the upkeep of the household are quite enough to fully engage all her energy. In a well-ordered society the additional burden of maintaining the family ought not to fall on her. The man should look to the maintenance of the family, the woman to household management; the two thus supplementing and complementing each other's labours.
>
> (Joshi 1988: 292)

While Gandhi claimed that assigning men and women different roles did not imply inequality – he insisted that "wives have all the rights which husbands enjoy" (Joshi 1988: 293) – his tone when speaking to and about women was often patronizing and even authoritarian. It almost seems that while Gandhi revered "the Indian *woman*" epitomized by Sita, Draupadi, and Damyanti, his views of women such as those he met at meetings were less than favorable. For example, on several occasions he complained that staying cooped up in the women's quarter because of purdah meant that women did not know how to behave when they assembled to hear him. "I have the privilege of addressing hundreds of meetings of women, attended by thousands. The din and the noise created at these meetings make it impossible to speak with any effect to the women who attend them. ... And when silence is restored it becomes difficult to interest them in many every day topics" (Joshi 1988: 149).

Gandhi scolded the women at the meetings for being "lazy," "provincial," "extravagant," "hypocritical," and fond of "gossip" and "jewelry." He was never satisfied with the amounts of money they raised, accusing them of being too fond of their luxuries and jewelry to part with them. He often played on their guilt to gain their support. He believed they did not have organizational skills and so needed to be "guided" by men. At one point, when asked if women were "to be given the wheel as a revolutionary weapon as he had said it was in the hands of a Jawaharlal [Nehru]?" he answered, "No. How could it be such in the hands of an ignorant woman? But if every woman in India span, then a silent revolution would certainly be created of which a Jawaharlal *could make full use*" (Joshi 1988: 339, emphasis added). The reason for his patronizing tone can be found in Gandhi's claim, "I believe, *I know your sex and your needs better than you do yourselves*" (Joshi 1988: 339, emphasis added). Gandhi believed that he knew what was good for women as is evident in his responses to letters that women wrote to him and his articles and speeches referring to women. But what seems to me to be particularly revealing was his statement at the Kasturba Memorial Committee Meeting on January 11, 1946, that the Trust's goal of making women self-reliant and self-sufficient "did not mean that men would go down, but if womenfolk improved and raised themselves up, men would automatically be raised *higher*" (Joshi 1988: 335, emphasis added).

Women in independent India

In this chapter I have tried to illustrate why women were crucial to Gandhi's political goals and how they were used for the national cause of winning independence. But what was Gandhi's *swaraj* supposed to do for women? As independence drew near he outlined programs that women were to participate in. He was not really interested in women standing for election to legislatures. Instead he wanted them to "attend to the improvement of the condition of the village womenfolk. They must attend to the health and sanitation of the villages and to the education and culture of the womenfolk" (Joshi 1988: 336). All these tasks were in keeping with what Gandhi considered "natural" to women. Like the advice contained in the Gita, the one Hindu work that he was profoundly affected by, he believed that we should "be happy in the state to which we are born and do the duty for which nature has destined us" (CWMG, vol. 71, 209).

In addition to focusing on "sanitation and hygiene," women were to get rid of evil customs (among which he listed "useless expenditure on jewelry"), and he underscored the need to teach women "the care and upbringing of children, discipline in their own lives in every department including eating" (Joshi 1988: 339). However, the woman's first obligation was to her own family. Responding to the question on whether the wife or dependent of a government servant could devote time to national work, Gandhi made it clear that she should do so only if there was no danger of "her property being confiscated or the education of her children suffering. If any woman thought that by doing constructive national work her children stood to lose privileges they might otherwise get from the Government, she should not undertake the work" (Joshi 1988: 336). In fact, he pointed out that "they [women] would serve the country even by doing household duties" (Joshi 1988: 334).

Gandhi believed in equal pay for men and women, though because he defined women's tasks as different from those of men, it was not clear how equal pay was to be implemented. Appropriateness of different tasks for men and women was further recognized and affirmed in Gandhi's blueprint for girls' and women's education:

> The duty of a woman is to look after what in English is called the hearth and home. Man has never performed this task . . . Hence it is my confirmed opinion that women should get a distinct kind of education. The two [men and women] have separate spheres of activity and their training, therefore, should also be different. This does not imply that the work of one is inferior while that of the other is superior; the spheres of the two are complementary.
>
> (CWMG, vol. 61: 125)

However, Gandhi firmly believed in legal equality for all Indians regardless of gender or caste.

Though women were to receive equal legal rights and reign supreme in the domestic sphere, Gandhi denied them power over their bodies except for their right to take their own lives to protect their honor. The reason for this can be traced to Gandhi's views of women's sexuality and the place that view occupied in his overall politics and ideology. He did not perceive women as having any sexual needs. Indeed a case could be made that he wanted to preserve gender but to eliminate sex, except for procreation. His attitude toward female sexuality was especially evident in his speeches and writings about contraceptives, abortion, *brahmacharya* (chastity), and rape. To Gandhi, "woman" was not "prey to sexual desire to the same extent as man. It is easier for her than for man to exercise self-restraint." Therefore, instead of teaching her about contraceptives and abortion, he believed that one needed to teach her "the art of saying no even to her husband, to teach her that it is no part of her duty to become a mere tool or a doll in her husband's hands" (Joshi 1988: 297). It was only when women could be chaste like Sita that India could have *Ramarajya* (the ideal state) (Joshi 1988: 181).

To Gandhi the "sexual act" was the "obscene act" (Joshi 1988: 269). It was also an act that, because it entailed loss of semen, sapped man's creative energies, making him weak and ineffective. Such men had lost India to the British. To regain its independence and keep India free, chaste women were needed to restrain men's sexual drive. For Gandhi believed that women were stronger than men were and therefore could help the latter observe *brahmacharya*, self-control. If one followed Gandhi's logic, one would conclude that it was *because* women had not been able to restrain men that India was colonized. It was women's fault after all!

Gandhi placed great store in chastity – he believed that chastity was a woman's strongest weapon; if a woman was truly chaste she could not be raped. He wrote in *Navjivan* in 1922:

There certainly are brutish men in the world who commit such crimes [rapes], but that man does not exist nor will he ever be born who can force himself upon a woman who values her chastity. . . . The woman who calls upon Rama when in danger will surely be protected by Him. Which evil man will dare to approach a woman who is prepared to die? Her eyes will shine with such light that any vicious man will be unnerved by it. . . . When someone wishes to dishonour a woman . . . [she has] a right to commit suicide. *It is indeed her duty to do so.*

(Joshi 1988: 99, emphasis added)

In 1927 he had relaxed his position somewhat. In a letter to a woman correspondent he wrote:

a woman's virtue is violated through both the man and the woman acting voluntarily, and if the woman is self-controlled and pure in mind, violation of her virtue is impossible. This is true in two senses. One is that the Shastras proclaim, and it must be believed, that the body of one whose mind is pure is protected by the mind itself. . . . Ravana could not outrage Sita's modesty . . . [because] he knew that if he tried to assault her body it would be burnt to ashes. . . . And the second meaning is that, if a woman's mind is pure her virtue is not violated and she is not stained by sin, even though she may have been raped.

(Joshi 1988: 157)

A number of women continued to challenge Gandhi on his views about rape. To them it sounded as if he was "blaming the victim." In 1932, he wrote, "personally I believe that a woman, if she has the courage, would be ready to die to save her honour" (Joshi 1988: 271). What is surprising is that his comments on rape did not include anything about the rapist. Perhaps to him, since men were naturally endowed with strong sex drives and women were not, it was the latter's responsibility to restrain the men by their purity, as Sita had done with Ravana. He was against abortion even when pregnancy was a result of rape.[6]

Gandhi's emphasis on self-control and chastity had a practical outcome. In his asrama, and among his political workers – *satyagrahis* – he demanded these virtues; indeed the *satyagrahis* were trained to lead chaste lives – married couples were to treat each other as brother and sister, akin to the relationship he had established with his wife at the age of 31. Self-control, the obverse of chastity, was to be cultivated through a regimen of discipline and diet. At one point Gandhi insisted that men treat women as if they were mothers or sisters. His downplaying of sex made women feel safer working with male *satyagrahis* (CWMG, vol. 50: 210–211), thus facilitating their involvement in the nationalist movement. His support of conventional gender roles made women's work in the public arena less threatening and more acceptable to men. However, in practice, Gandhi's principle of "equal but separate" improved women's position about as much as African Americans' position was improved by similar "separate but equal" rulings by the US Supreme Court. In other words, "equal but separate" is not equal.

Conclusion

Despite Gandhi's glorification of women as mothers, wives, and domestic "queens," women's involvement in the Indian nationalist struggle did extend their horizons beyond the home and made them conscious of their place in Indian society.[7] But when the politics of *satyagraha* with its emphasis on chastity, self-control, renunciation, non-violence and, above all, suffering, brought thousands of women into the political arena, it did so for specific purposes – propagation of *swadeshi* (homespun), boycott of foreign cloth, picketing of shops selling liquor and foreign cloth, raising funds, and working for what Gandhi called the "constructive program" in the villages. Typically, after a specific campaign receded, the women returned to their regular lives. At no point did Gandhi challenge their traditional roles. Such issue-based participation has continued to characterize Indian women's involvement in politics. Since independence, following Gandhi's example, women have used extra-constitutional means to publicize specific issues that affect their lives: in the 1970s women protested against rising food prices and scarcity of cooking oil and kerosene. They encircled (gherao) government offices and demanded relief (Kishwar and Vanita 1984; Omvedt 1980). The protesting women, however,

> placed the issues of food and unemployment within the framework of woman's traditional role as wife and mother . . . [the] protests . . . expressed women's frustration and anger with the material conditions that threatened their ability to fulfill their gender-ascribed role; women were not protesting against the traditional differentiation of roles. Like Gandhi's non-violent, non-cooperation, and khadi (homespun) movement, this brand of activism posed little threat to the male–female hierarchy, though it politicized women across the board.
>
> (Bald 1986: 209)

During the last few years, urban Indian women have come out of the comfort of their homes to demonstrate against eve-teasing, rape, and dowry-murders. These protests, unlike those during the nationalist movement, were organized and directed by autonomous groups that appeared around the country in response to specific situations. Similarly, women in villages have come together to register objections to development projects that ignore women's needs for fodder, clean water, and fuel. The most publicized were the Chipko movement to protect the forests from being felled (Bald 1985), and the recent unsuccessful attempts by men and women to stop the construction of the World Bank financed Narmada dam. Gandhi had let the proverbial genie out of the bottle (or home?) and it/she was difficult to put back in any permanent way. But while Gandhi may have politicized thousands of Indian women it is only recently that Indian women, from different regions, classes, and castes, have taken the initiative themselves to fight for their rights, though by and large they tend to see their rights within the framework of the gender roles defined by Gandhi.

Notes

1 This point, which Gandhi reiterates a number of times in different contexts, has been stressed in most of the more recent studies of Gandhi's views on women (see Bald 1986; Katrak 1992; Patel 1987; Kishwar 1985a).

2 An example of Gandhi's references to the primacy of the woman's conscience occurs in the context of a question whether a wife should undertake national service even if her husband objected. At that time Gandhi claimed that national service was a higher good than the family.

3 In particular I am indebted to Pushpa Joshi (1988) for her wonderfully comprehensive anthology of Gandhi's writings and statements on women and A. T. Hingorani's collection of Gandhi's works entitled *To the Perplexed* (1966).

4 By a curious route, here Gandhi was arriving at somewhat similar conclusions as Engels did in *The Origin of the Family, Private Property and the State* (1972). Like Engels, Gandhi was connecting women's loss of power, albeit of a moral kind, with their loss of economic power.

5 Gandhi believed that the *varnashramadharma* (caste-system) had much to commend it. He viewed it as an organic division of society where each member performed tasks to which he or she was naturally suited and all tasks were equally valuable and necessary. In such a system no task was superior to the another, rather, people who performed different tasks lived in harmony with each other – mutually dependent on each other – the hallmark of a community.

6 When in 1947 Gandhi learnt that thousands of women had been raped and/or abducted by Muslims and Hindus, he wanted families and the society alike to take the "fallen" women back and help to rear their children.

7 The framers of the Indian constitution, who legalized equal rights between the sexes and established equal pay for equal work, recognized women's contributions to the nationalist struggle. Despite the law, however, even government-owned enterprises pay women less than men, and customs of the Hindu, Muslim, and Sikh communities continue to work against legal equality between the sexes. See Bald (1985: 42–50).

6 Communalism, nationalism, and gender

Bhartiya Janata Party (BJP) and the Hindu right in India

Geeta Chowdhry

One of the distinguishing features of politics in the 1990s has been the rise of the Bhartiya Janata Party (BJP), representing the Hindu right, as a political force in northwestern and central India. The shaping of political relations in India by the BJP in alliance with the Vishwa Hindu Parishad (VHP) and the Rashtriya Swayam Sevak Sangh (RSS), collectively called the Sangh Parivaar,[1] has been based on a nationalist call. The nationalism of the Hindu right is based on the (re)construction of the social landscape in at least two complementary ways: first, the reconstruction of religious identities in which a monolithic, victimized, Hindu identity is juxtaposed against a monolithic, villainous, Muslim identity; and second, accompanying historical revisions, because religious reconstruction has required a rewriting of history in essentially communal ways. Although there are differences between the BJP's moderate and liberal factions' acceptance of the VHP and RSS stand on communalism, communalism is essential to their collective stand on nationalism.[2] This chapter claims that although communalism remains at the forefront of the right-wing Hindu political and social agenda, gender is inextricably woven into the (re)constructions of religion and history on which this movement's claims of nationalism and communalism have rested.[3]

The various approaches to communalism in India can be classified into three broad categories, those that implicitly argue that communalism is something "culturally specific like the caste system or the god Krishna," those that see communalism as a pathology of modernity (Fox 1996), and those which while agreeing with the second, focus primarily on the gendered nature of communal discourse.

Scholars in the first category suggest specific ways in which communalism has manifested itself in India, thereby keeping the analysis very specific to India. For example, Fox (1996) claims that communalism is represented as "the excrescence of Indian tradition, an atavism or primitivism." Others characterize communalism as a pathology of Indian nationalism (Chandra 1984; Chatterjee 1986).

The second approach, which Fox associates himself with, analyzes communalism as a pathology of modernity (Nandy 1990). Here, communalism manifests itself as an institutional force under colonization (Pandey 1990). For Fox, communalism is the "inherent weakness or constitutional weakness ... bound to come out sooner or later when modernity has disenchanted the world" (Fox 1996: 237).

The third approach, which identifies the gendered nature of communal discourse, grows out of the second approach but emphasizes the gendered aspects of colonial discourse. However, it focuses primarily on the myriad ways in which gender is used in communalist discourse in India (Sarkar and Butalia 1995). It is this third approach that this chapter utilizes and develops.

Nationalism and communalism

The origins of communalism can be traced back to the colonial enterprise in India. Although Indians have historically utilized religious identification as the basis for social, political, and economic mobilization, the "activity of organizing antagonistic Muslim and Hindu collective identities" was first observed around the cow slaughter movement in the 1890s. During this movement, Hindu groups attacked Muslims in Northern India (Ludden 1996b: 13). Indeed, the institutionalization of communalism was promoted egregiously by British imperialist power in India. The equation of India with Hindus under the colonial regime, the reporting of anti-colonial riots as communal riots, colonial documentation and writing of separate legal codes for Muslim and Hindu populations, and the colonial creation of separate electorates for Hindu and Muslim populations are all evidence that communalism was a guiding principle of the colonial enterprise in India (Pandey 1990).

After thirty-five years of quiet on the communal front following Indian independence, communalism erupted as a major political force in India in the 1980s. In the 1970s and 1980s the Congress Party, the dominant party in India since 1885, lost its stranglehold over Indian politics as the discrepancies between public promise and party performance became apparent to the Indian public (Kohli 1990). Communalism in India has arisen as "the struggle to reconstruct India politically" intensified in the 1980s and 1990s (Ludden 1996b: 18).

> The struggle is centrally concerned with the legitimacy of the state, the distribution of state resources, power in society and justice. ... *Hindutva* has emerged as a solid competitor for popular loyalties and the RSS and the BJP have increased their power, in significant measure because they have successfully used non-parliamentary means, including violence to win elections.
>
> (Ludden 1996b, 19) (see note 10)

Discourse on the relationship between nationalism and communalism in India has gained currency, as communalism has become a major political force. In the eleventh Lok Sabha (House of the People) elections held in May 1996, the BJP platform was dominated by nationalist discourse.[4] Discussing topics that ranged from identity and culture to economy and gender, the BJP election manifesto appealed to the nationalism of Indians. In the introduction, which spelled out the "vision, faith and commitment" of the BJP, the manifesto declared that "the present millennium began with the subjugation of our ancient land; let a reinvigorated, proud, prosperous and strong India herald the next millennium" (BJP 1996: 6). It ended with an appeal to all "patriotic Indians" to assist the BJP in the task of nationalist reconstruction (BJP 1996: 80). Giving the concept of nationalism concrete form, the BJP specifically addressed issues of *surajya* or good governance, *swadeshi* or economic nationalism, *suraksha* or defense of the territorial integrity of India, *shuchita* or anti-corruption agenda, and *samrasata* or empowerment as embodying nationalism in their campaign (BJP 1996: 6).[5]

> Our Manifesto reflects the application of these four concepts in good governance and their role in molding the nation we dreamt of on the dawn of independence – a prosperous and strong India, a country where every citizen regards this land of ours, this Bharatbhoomi, that stretches from the Indus to the seas, as his sacred motherland.
>
> (BJP 1996: 6–7)

Hindutva, what the BJP has called cultural nationalism (BJP 1996: 6) and what anti-communalists see as a clarion call for establishing a Hindu nation, integrates these four concepts under the umbrella of nationalism (Kapur and Cossman 1995: 84). They see *Hindutva* as woven into the lives of the citizens of India: "*Main Hindutva ko iss dharti se judi whoi manavta manta hoon*" (I see *Hindutva* inextricably woven into the humanism of this land) (Advani 1996).

Claiming that "one people, one culture" is the basis of the BJP's cultural nationalism, the BJP calls *Hindutva* a "unifying force" that will create a national identity and ensure national cohesion. In the tradition of early modernization thinkers, *Hindutva* defined in this way becomes a common denominator, a seemingly harmless concept essential for the development of a nation. The BJP orchestrates the discourse on *Hindutva* to make it appear essential for the unity and the survival of the nation.[6] The success of the BJP in establishing the discourse on *Hindutva* as devoid of religious meaning and therefore innocuous cannot be minimized. This is evident from the controversial judgments of the Supreme Court of India in two high profile cases.[7] In the 1996 Supreme Court case 130, Dr. Ramesh Yashwant Prabhoo v. Prabhakar K. Kunte as well as in 1992 Supreme Court Case 169, Manohar Joshi v. Nitin Bhaurao Patil, the Supreme Court has held that *Hindutva* cannot be seen as coterminous with religious fundamentalism but rather that it stands for a uniform culture:

The word "Hindutva" is used and understood as a synonym of "Indianization", i.e. development of a uniform culture by obliterating the differences between all the cultures coexisting in the country. The words "Hinduism" or "Hindutva" are not necessarily to be understood and construed narrowly, confined only to the strict Hindu religious practices unrelated to the culture and ethos of the people of India, depicting the way of life of the Indian people.

(SCC 1996: 1, 134)

The word "Hindutva" by itself does not invariably mean Hindu religion and it is the context and the manner of its use which is material for deciding the meaning of the word "Hindutva" in a particular text.

(SCC 1992: 171)

Although the Supreme Court sought to distinguish between *Hindutva* and Hinduism, the court itself used the terms interchangeably, thus forcing us to deduce that Hinduism, *Hindutva*, and Indian national identity were also synonyms (Nauriya 1996). It is obvious from its judgments that the court failed to recognize that such an equation implies the obliteration of non-Hindus from the category of Indians. This is an extraordinary oversight given the intellectual and communal antecedents of the term *Hindutva*.

Hindutva first rose to prominence through the writings of Veer Savarkar. *Hindutva: Who is a Hindu?* was written by Savarkar in 1923. Identified as one of the architects of the RSS, Savarkar defined the boundaries of *Hindutva* and circumscribed its usage for modern India by equating it with communalism. In this document, Savarkar listed three principles as essential for *Hindutva*: *pitrabhoomi* (fatherland), *jati* (blood line),[8] and *sanskriti* (culture). The first principle claimed that to be a Hindu one should be born within the land of "*Bharatvarsha*" which stretches "from the Himalayas to the cape" or from "Indus to the seas." There is nothing unique in Savarkar's use of birth within defined territorial (*jus soli*) as entitlement to citizenship. What is unique is his use of the term "fatherland" to define India when most nationalist writers refer to India as *Bharatmata* or "motherland." The second concept, *jati*, claims that to be a Hindu one should establish lineage from "natural," as opposed to converted, Hindu parents. Although this concept attempts to exclude on the basis of religion it is also the basis on which the RSS makes a distinction between Muslim converts and original Muslims or *Babur ki aulaad* (the children of Babur), the emperor who established the Mughal dynasty in India. Since most Muslims in India were converted, Indian Muslims can claim links to Hindutva on the basis of *jus soli* and lineage. It is the final concept, shared culture that combines *sanskriti* (culture) with *punyabhoomi* (sacred lands), that becomes the most critical criterion in establishing the basis of exclusionary communalism. It clearly implies that only those whose sacred lands (sacred to their religion) lie within the fatherland really have the moral basis for

constituting a nation (Deshpande 1995). This criterion of citizenship privileges religious/cultural citizenship rather than territorial citizenship. Under
it Muslims, Christians, Jews, and others whose holy lands lie outside the
spatial boundaries of *punyabhoomi* are excluded both from *Hindutva* and
from citizenship of the fatherland, i.e. India.

Similar sentiments echo in the writings of the RSS and, more subtly,
in the writings and campaigns of the BJP. The insiders, those who are
able to equate their land of birth with the sacred lands of their religion,
are "appropriate citizens," whereas the outsiders, those whose "fatherland"
is not the same as their sacred lands, are suspect in terms of their civic
status and their patriotism. Patriots and traitors are defined by their religious affiliations. One of the architects of the RSS, Dr. K. B. Hedgewar,
writing during the time of non-cooperation with the British and the struggle
for Indian independence, referred to Muslims as "*yavan (demon) snakes.*" He
was convinced that "Indian Muslims had proved themselves Muslims first
and Indians only secondarily" because they had withdrawn their support
for the Indian independence movement after Turkey ended the *Khilafat*
movement (Pandey 1993).[9] Currently, the RSS trains cadres to prepare
for the formation of a Hindu *Rashtra* (nation). Communalism is at the core
of RSS nationalism today.

The current link between the Hindu right's communalism and nationalism is perhaps most clearly articulated in a speech given by Sadhavi
Rithambra, a VHP woman member, at Hyderabad, in April 1991:

> As far as the construction of the Ram temple is concerned some people
> say Hindus should not fight over a structure of bricks and stones. They
> should not quarrel over a small piece of land. I want to ask those people,
> "if someone burns your national flag will you say 'oh, it doesn't matter.
> It is only two meters of cloth, which is not a great national loss.'" The
> question is not of two meters of cloth but of an insult to the nation. Ram's
> birthplace is not a quarrel about a small piece of land. It is a question of
> national integrity . . . He (the Hindu) is fighting for the preservation of a
> civilization, for his Indianness, for national consciousness, for the recog-
> nition of his true nature. We shall build the temple.
>
> (quoted in Kakkar 1996: 157)[10]

The communalism of the BJP also is couched in nationalistic terms although
here it is more sophisticated and subtle. Sushma Swaraj, the spokesperson
of the BJP, was one of the candidates who addressed the issue of communalism directly during her 1996 campaign. Before an audience composed
mostly of Muslim women, Swaraj declared that the BJP really did not
discriminate against Muslims. However, she said that it irked the BJP that
Muslims did not support India but instead rooted for Pakistan during the
two Indo-Pakistan wars and during the various cricket matches held
between the two countries.[11]

The BJP's espousal of the communal cause is particularly visible in its 1996 Election Manifesto. The manifesto dedicates a section to "Illegal Immigration: Demographic Invasion – A Threat to Our Security," in which the BJP declares that illegal immigration, in particular Bangladeshi immigration, is a threat to the security of the Indian nation because it threatens the demographic balance of the country. Deportation of illegal Bangladeshi immigrants is emphasized as a solution to this threat (BJP 1996: 39–40). What appears as a nationalistic, although mean-spirited, proposal takes on communal hues when compared to the BJP's discussion of Chakma refugees from Bangladesh. Whereas the BJP advocates repatriating Bangladeshis, many of whom are Muslims seeking economic refuge, they propose to set up refugee camps for Chakma refugees who are Buddhists. They advocate full citizenship for Chakma refugees who do not want to return to Bangladesh and seek the repatriation of those who do only after obtaining guarantees from the Bangladeshi government for their security. Communal allegories highlight the distinctions made between the two groups of refugees. Whereas Bangladeshi Muslims are portrayed as a security threat to India, Chakmas are portrayed as a displaced community (BJP 1996: 36, 66–67). Religion is the basis of this distinction.

The section on minorities in the 1996 BJP Election Manifesto states that BJP policies would be guided by "justice for all, appeasement for none." Underlying this statement is the message that the policy of "pseudo-secularism" introduced by Jawaharlal Nehru, India's first prime minister, and followed by successive Congress and non-Congress Party governments, has really meant the "politics of appeasement" of Muslim and other minorities (Davis 1996: 42).[12] Lal Krishan Advani, President of the BJP and a clever political strategist, has been the backbone of this assault on Nehruvian concepts of secular democracy.

> Nehru's thinking made Indian nationalism an amorphous thing. . . . Democracy and liberalism as preached by Nehru were denuded of their Indianness. So Hindu bashing became synonymous with secularism. I believe that India is what it is, because of its ancient heritage. Call it Hindu or call it Bhartiya (Indian). If nationalism is stripped of its Hinduness, it will lose dynamism.
>
> (quoted in Malik and Singh 1994: 41)

The BJP asserts that, in contrast to the "politics of appeasement" practiced by previous governments, BJP nationalism based on "one nation, one people, one culture," will lead India into the 21st century. The conflation of Hinduism with India is the goal of the Hindu nationalist project that portrays Muslims as "invaders" and "foreign transplants." However, this is a fallacious argument because Islam "is as old in India as in Turkey. Indian Islam is older than American Christianity and European Protestantism. Indian Islam is no more derivative than Chinese or Japanese Buddhism" (Ludden 1996b: 5).

The Hindu Right's construction of Muslims as a monolithic population with loyalties to Pakistan is based on "an inclination to construct a Muslim identity around Islam" (Hasan 1995). However Muslims, like members of other communities, interact with the socio-economic environment as secular actors contingent on the positions they occupy in society. For example, Muslim farm laborers may have much more in common with Hindu farm laborers than with Muslim landlords. However, the discourse of communalism sacrifices the class identity of Muslims on the altar of religious identity.[13] Communalist discourse constructs a monolithic Muslim population with Islamic identity as its only defining characteristic.

Historically this has not been the case. Examining the evidence gathered during the first all-India census in 1881, Mushirul Hasan declares that Muslims did not form a monolithic geographic, linguistic, political, economic, or social entity. Like Hindus, Muslims were also composed of multiple and distinct communities within India. Colonial political arrangements advocating separate electorates for the Muslims, the Congress Party's response to these projects, and the ensuing alliance between liberal Muslims and the Ulema (clergy) to ensure their own participation and leadership, fostered the construction of a monolithic Muslim identity. Islam was used as the common ground for this identity (M. Hasan 1995).

Focusing exclusively on institutions like the Muslim League and on individuals like Mohammad Ali Jinnah, who was the architect of Pakistan, the Hindu right identifies every Muslim with the two-nation theory. This is historically inaccurate. Many Muslims who were members of the Indian National Congress opposed the two-nation theory. The Jamia-Milia Islamia (National Muslim University) housed many Muslim intellectuals who were greater supporters of Gandhi's non-cooperation than of Jinnah's two-nation theory. They were a living testimony to the multiculturalism that they espoused, housing within the university radicals and reformists from many religious and economic backgrounds (M. Hasan 1995). Thus, the "slate of traitors" is socially constructed through an inaccurate rewriting of history to create a monolithic Islam and a monolithic Hinduism in India.

Rewriting history and religion? Nationalism/communalism, identity politics and gender

The privileging of Hindus and the villainization of Muslims in the discourse and politics of the Hindu right rests on the assumption that Hindu and Muslim identities are monolithic and homogeneous. Gender is integral to the creation of these assumptions and the female body has often been the contested site of the communal agenda.

Prominent in the Sangh Parivar's narrative on Muslim identity are three interrelated themes: first, the Muslim male "threat" to and violation of the "honor" of Hindu women; second, the demographic threat; and third, the "state" of Muslim women, as a consequence of the immutable oppression of Muslim women by Muslim men condoned by an emasculated Indian state practicing the politics of "minority appeasement." The use of the female body to establish cultural identity, honor, and nationalism is not unique to the Hindu right. It follows a patriarchal pattern shared by regimes over the world.[14] The current emphasis on these themes by the Hindu right involves gender as the focal point of communalist histories.

Threat to and violation of Hindu women

The specter of "the rape of Hindu women by lustful Muslim men" has served to construct three interconnected communities: victimized Hindu women devoid of agency; emasculated Hindu men "incapable of defending their women and incapable of raping Muslim women"; and the community of Muslim men characterized by "sensuality, lust and religious aggression." V. D. Savarkar's (1971) influential work *Six Glorious Epochs of Indian History* rewrote Indian history and the history of Islam in ways that highlighted these reconstructed identities:

> [a] suicidal morbidity had completely possessed the Hindu for a long time. This morbidity paralysed their own offensive and counter-offensive might. . . . Having only learnt by rote the maxim to give food to the hungry and water to the thirsty is a virtue, the Hindus went on giving milk to the vile poisonous cobras and vipers. Even while the Muslim demons were demolishing Hindu temples and breaking to pieces their holiest of idols like Somnath, they never wreaked their vengeance upon those wicked Muslims, even when they had the golden opportunities to do so, nor did they ever take out a single brick from the walls of Mosques. The Muslim women never feared retribution or punishment at the hands of any Hindu for their heinous crime. They (Hindus) had a perverted idea of women's chivalry [sic].
> (Savarkar 1971: 167–169, quoted in Purshottam Agarwal 1995)[15]

Savarkar interprets Islam and the religious duty of Muslims without reference to the Quran, Hadith, or the Sharia. He suggests that Islam teaches a religious aggression that manifests itself in the abduction, rape, and conversion of Hindu women to Islam (Savarkar 1971). Through the political rhetoric of nationalism, he condemns the whole Muslim community to the status of "the phallic other" (Mukhia 1996).

> With this same shameless religious fanaticism, the aggressive Muslims of those times considered it their highly religious duty to carry away forcibly the women of the enemy side, as if they were commonplace property, to ravish them, to pollute them, and to distribute them to all and sundry, from the Sultan to the common soldier and to absorb

them completely in their fold. This was considered a noble act, which
increased their number.

(Savarkar 1971: 174–175, quoted in Purshottam Agarwal 1995)[16]

The same depiction of victimized Hindu women and criminal Muslim
men continues in the *Organizer*, the magazine of the RSS. Writing about
the horrors of the partition of India in 1947, the *Organizer* declares that
Muslim men engaged in a customary and "age-old practice of Muslims,"
that is, the abduction and rape of women. In contrast, rape by Hindu
men is dismissed as an aberration, an act of weakness by a few individuals who may have "sheltered" abandoned Muslim women during partition
but then "handed them over" to the appropriate authorities as soon as
the Indian government started the "recovery" process for victims (Butalia
1995; Menon and Bhasin 1993).

   Before, during and after the Babri Masjid (Babri Mosque) and Ram
Janmabhoomi (the birthplace of Ram) conflicts, a similar creation of
Muslim identity by communalist forces was visible. In 1969, during
Hindu–Muslim riots in Ahmedabad, Hindus were ordered to "wipe those
out who have dishonored your mothers and sisters" (Mukhia 1996). In an
interview, B. L. Sharma of the VHP Indraprastha unit in new Delhi "had
woven an entire anti-Muslim tirade around the figure of the repeatedly
raped or threatened Hindu woman" (reported in Sarkar 1995). Speeches
by Sadhavi Rithambara and Uma Bharati, both outspoken women *sanyasins*
of the *Hindutva* movements, exhort Hindu men to fight their emasculation
and take revenge for the wrongs meted out to Hindus by Muslims.[17]
Rithambara declares that Muslims inflict cruel punishments on Hindu
women, whereas the "impotence" of Hindu men does not permit them
to kill Muslim men.

> In Kashmir the Hindu was a minority and was hounded out of the
> valley. Slogans of "Long Live Pakistan" were carved with red-hot iron
> rods on the thighs of our Hindu daughters.
>   We [Hindus] have religious tolerance in our very bones. Together
> with our three hundred and thirty million Gods, we have worshipped
> the dead lying in their graves. Along with Ram and Krishna we have
> saluted Mohammed and Jesus ... We have never said, "O World!
> Believe in our Upanishads, Believe in our Gita. Otherwise you are an
> infidel and by cutting the head of an infidel one gains paradise."
>   (quoted in Kakkar 1996: 160)

Krishna Sharma, of the VHP's women's wing, commands that "if they
[Muslims] rape 10–15 of our women we must also rape a few [of theirs]
to show them that we are no less" (interviews conducted by Anita and
Vasudha, 1995). Implicit in this statement is the message that Muslims
rape Hindu women as a matter of course while Hindu men do not rape

Hindu or Muslim women. Explicitly, Sharma is clearly inciting Hindu men to rape Muslim women as a form of revenge.

The discourse of the Hindu right ignores actual events to present a gendered version of history in which the Hindu is emasculated by Hindu teachings of tolerance and non-violence. Implicit in these discourses is the assumption that Hindu men do not wrong women, whether Muslim or Hindu. In contrast, Islam and Muslims are portrayed in villainous terms as teaching and practicing violence, especially violence against women. Intolerance and forced religious conversions are seen as fundamental to Islam. Rape and forced conversion of Hindu women are portrayed as central to the Islamic enterprise in India.

The identity of Muslims created by the Hindu right is made to depend on a caricature that parallels Western caricatures and phobias about Islam. Historically, the Islamic enterprise in India was not primarily a religious enterprise, but rather a geopolitical exercise of conquest. If religious conversion and the victimization of women occurred during the process, then the Muslim invaders and settlers were no different from any other rulers at war, whatever their religious persuasion.

Similarly the portrayal of Hinduism and Hindu men as inherently non-violent not only is erroneous, but also rests on a fictitious homogeneous Hindu past. The imagined community of Hindus, or what Romilla Thapar (1992a) has called "syndicate Hinduism," is a recent invention (post-second millennium) which attempts to dismiss the diversity and divisions within Hinduism for political purposes. According to Thapar, Brahmanical Hinduism, which the Hindu right portrays as "syndicate Hinduism," did not in fact preach *ahimsa* (non-violence), despite references to it during the era of Upanishads. The doctrine of *ahimsa* was associated with Sraminism (a sect within Hinduism) but was more foundational to Buddhism and Jainism than to Hinduism. The claim that religious persecution is a hallmark of Islam and is absent from Hinduism is not upheld in historical sources. The writings of the Chinese pilgrim, Hsuan Tsang, who visited India in the seventh century CE, testify to the persecution of the Sramans by the Saivite Brahmins. The destruction of Buddhist monasteries and Stupas, and the killing of Buddhist monks, is attested to in the writings of the twelfth century historian Kalhana. Similar persecution of the Jain establishment by Hindu Saivaite sects is documented by Thapar (1992a) for Tamil Nadu. Desai (1957) has documented Jain persecution by the Lingayat Brahmins in Karnataka and persecution of untouchables by the Brahmanical sects is documented in Government of India (GOI 1980). Finally, the unequal treatment meted out to women by the Brahmanical sect is described in Manusmriti.[18]

The rape of Muslim women by Hindu men during the partition of India and over the course of the Babri Masjid-Ram *janmabhoomi* episode is well documented (Butalia 1995; Kakkar 1996; Menon and Bhasin 1993). The complicity of Hindu women in gang rapes of Muslim women and the tearing open of pregnant wombs has also been well documented. Thus the image of Hindu pacifism and Muslim aggression is clearly based on a fictitious rendering of history for the sake of a communal cause.

Muslims as a demographic threat

This discourse suggests that Muslims pose a demographic threat to India because of their high fertility rates and is based on the claim that Islam does not allow Muslims to use birth control. The social practice of triple talaaq (divorce by repudiation) and polygamy,[19] both linked by the Hindu right to Islam, also are said to promote the explosion of the Muslim population in India. This theme is apparent in numerous documents and speeches produced by the Hindu right.

> The Hindu was dishonored in Kashmir because he was in a minority. But there is a conspiracy to make him a minority in the whole country. The state tells us Hindus to have only two or three children. After a while they will say do not even have one. But what about those who have six wives, have thirty or thirty-five children and breed like mosquitoes and flies.
>
> (Rithambara quoted in Kakar 1996: 162)

Shambhu Prasad, a member of the VHP from Gujerat, claimed that the Muslim population in India is increasing because of the Muslims' "backward outlook on life" and their religious-cultural practices. He asked Hindu women to abandon birth control so that the Hindu population could keep up with the Muslims (Bidwai *et al.* 1996).

Muslim identity is thus defined, in part, by a mythical population discourse that obfuscates as much as it reveals. It is true that fertility rates for Muslims are greater than fertility rates for Hindus. However, these are aggregate numbers and by themselves do not tell us much. For example, a larger percentage of the Muslim population is poor. Research on population finds higher fertility rates among the poor. So, it is possible that if we disaggregate fertility data by class and religion, we would find that the fertility of Muslims and Hindus of the same social class are comparable. Even if fertility rates for Muslims are higher than for Hindus, Muslims constitute only 12 percent of the total population whereas the Hindus constitute 80 percent. Thus the bogey of a Muslim "takeover" is revealed as another communalist myth.

The state of Muslim women

Debates surrounding the formulation and implementation of a Uniform Civil Code (UCC) are used to articulate "the state of Muslim women" and to reconstitute the identity of the "Hindu community" contra "the

Muslim community." Article 44 of the Indian Constitution states that "the State shall endeavor to secure for all its citizens a Uniform Civil Code throughout the territory of India." However, the UCC is not listed in the Constitution as a "fundamental right" which can be enforced in a court of law, but rather as a "directive principle of state policy," which means it is only recommended. The difficulty of mandating a UCC is based on the conflict of any proposed code with the different personal status laws (referred to as personal laws in India) of the majority as well as minority communities in India. Because Articles 25 and 26 of the Constitution of India guarantee freedom of religion, and Article 29 guarantees minorities the right to conserve their culture, it was decided that a UCC would violate the sanctity of such guarantees.

Despite these concerns, a Hindu Code was introduced as a bill in parliament during the 1943–1944 sessions. It was not discussed by the constituent assembly until 1951, when Jawaharlal Nehru was forced to withdraw it because of opposition within the Congress Party. The bill was finally passed by the parliament as five separate Acts in 1956 (Baird 1981; Som 1994).

> The Hindu Code bill made significant departures from traditional laws in that it allowed intercaste marriage, reinforced monogamy and made divorce possible. Nevertheless, the constitution distinctly anticipated a single civil code for all citizens of India, and the Hindu Code was only a halfway house to this end; the issue of marriage, divorce, and inheritance still is a part of a system of personal laws, applicable solely on the basis of religious identity. In spite of limitations and anomalies, the Hindu Code Bill nevertheless conferred a semblance of equal rights on Hindu women in the sphere of property, marriage and so on.
>
> (Hasan 1993: 6)

Muslim women and women from other religious minorities were left under the umbrella of religious laws since the difficulty of ensuring cultural and religious autonomy to already threatened minority groups led the state to adopt a "secular non-interference" policy with regard to personal laws of minority communities. In doing so, the state was in fact siding with the revivalist organization of Muslim clergy in India, the Jamait-al-Ulema-i-Hind. This organization has opposed the need for reform of personal law in order to maintain the sanctity of the Sharia and the identity of the millet (religious community) (Z. Hasan 1993). It is not surprising that personal and family law as defined by the clergy and upheld by a part of the Muslim population in India has become a battlefield for identity politics.[20] The limitations of secularism, which while protecting religious and cultural diversity, also protects gender inequalities, are obvious. It is paradoxical that secularism, which guarantees equal treatment of different religions by the constitution, is predicated on the unequal treatment of women of different religions. In essence, this non-interference in Muslim personal law has created a two-tier judicial system for Hindu and Muslim women. Hindu women belong to the upper tier since they are given some protection from Hindu personal laws by the laws of the Indian state; the lower tier is for Muslim women who are fully subject to the personal laws of the Muslim community.[21]

In recent years, the UCC debate has erupted again with respect to two Supreme Court cases, namely the Shah Bano case and the Sarla Mudgal case.[22] Shah Bano, a 73-year-old Muslim woman, had sued her husband, plaintiff Mohammad Ahmad Khan, for maintenance under the Criminal Procedure Code. The code guarantees the maintenance of wives, children, and parents who are destitute and unable to maintain themselves. The Madhya Pradesh High Court decided in favor of Shah Bano, ruling that Mohammad Ahmad Khan pay her a modest maintenance. In his appeal to the Supreme Court, the plaintiff alleged that he had repaid Shah Bano's dowry and had also maintained her during the *idda* period (three months following the divorce), as he was required by the Muslim personal law. Thus he was no longer responsible for her maintenance. In April 1985, the Supreme Court upheld the judgment of the High Court and awarded Shah Bano Begum the sum of Rs. 179.20 ($14.00 approximately).[23] Interpretations of the Muslim personal law and scholarly interpretations of the Quran were used by the Supreme Court to justify its decisions regarding maintenance for divorced women and the issue of *mahr* or dowry (AIR [*All India Reporter*] 1985: 14–24).[24] In addition, Chief Justice Y. V. Chandrachud observed in his deliberations that

> It is also a matter of regret that Article 44 of our Constitution has remained a dead letter ... A common civil code will help the cause of national integration by removing disparate loyalties to laws that have conflicting ideologies. No community is likely to bell the cat by making gratuitous concessions on the issue. It is the State that is charged with the duty of securing a uniform civil code for the citizens of the country and unquestionably it has the legislative competence to do so ... The political courage to use that competence is quite another [issue] ... Inevitably the role of the reformer has to be assumed by the courts.
>
> (AIR 1985)

This judgment as well as the Supreme Court's negation of Muslim personal law sparked off countrywide protests from "fundamentalist" Muslim groups like the All India Muslim Personal Law Board, Jamait-a-Ulema-i-Hind, the Jamait-e-Islami, and the Muslim League (Z. Hasan, 1989). "Progressives" within the Muslim community – a large percentage of Muslim women, academicians, writers, journalists, film personalities, experts in Sharia laws – supported the judgment and signed a memorandum indicating that providing support to a destitute and divorced

Muslim women in no way interfered with Muslim personal law or Islamic law. The government of Rajeev Gandhi initially hailed the decision. However, losses in the 1985 by-elections and the government's decision to open the premises of Babri Masjid to Hindu worshippers (see note 10) forced the Rajeev government not only to reverse its position but also to introduce a Muslim Women's Bill in parliament. This bill, in essence, denied Muslim women the right to avail themselves of the Criminal Procedure Code in maintenance proceedings.[25] The government explained its introduction and support of the Muslim Women's Bill by saying that Muslims were not ready for change, clearly an effort to cover up its capitulation to Hindu and Muslim fundamentalist forces.

A decade later, on May 10, 1995, the Supreme Court of India revived the debate on the UCC in its judgment in Sarla Mudgal and Ors. v. Union of India and Ors (JT 1995 (4) SC 331). Sarla Mudgal, the President of Kalyani, an organization working for the welfare of needy families and women in distress, together with three other petitioners, raised issues regarding the legality of second marriages conducted after Hindu men had converted to Islam without divorcing the wives whom they had previously married under Hindu law. The Supreme Court ruled that second marriages which occurred after the husbands' conversion to Islam were null and void since the first marriages contracted under the Hindu Marriage Act had not been dissolved. The judgment of Justice Kuldip Singh stated that

> a marriage celebrated under a personal law cannot be dissolved by the application of another personal law to which one of the spouses converts and the other refuses to do so ... It is obvious from the various provisions of the Act that the modern Hindu Law strictly enforces monogamy ... A second marriage by an apostate under the shelter of conversion to Islam would nevertheless be a marriage in violation of the provisions of the Act ... it is no doubt correct that the marriage solemnised by a Hindu husband after embracing Islam may not be a strictly void marriage under the Act because he is no longer a Hindu, but the fact remains that the said marriage would be in violation of the Act which strictly professes monogamy.
>
> (JT 1995 (4) SC 334–335)

The opinions of Justice Kuldip Singh and to a lesser extent of Justice R.M. Sahai were based on a dualistic juxtaposition of Hindu "modern" law and Hindu community with Muslim personal law and the Muslim community in which Hindu law and Hindu community were upheld as models. The judgment also suggested that the Hindu, Sikh, Buddhist, and Jain communities had relinquished their commitment to their own personal laws for the sake of national integration and unity. Thus the issue of patriotism was raised once again in reference to the Muslim community.

The Hindus along with Sikhs, Buddhists and Jains have forsaken the cause of national unity and integration, some other communities would not, though the Constitution enjoins the establishment of a "common Civil Code" for the whole of India . . . Those who preferred to remain in India after the partition, fully knew that the Indian leaders did not believe in two-nation or three-nation theory and that in the Indian Republic there was to be only one nation – Indian Nation – and no community could claim to remain a separate entity on the basis of religion.

(JT 1995 (4) SC 331)

The religious leaders of the Muslim community were clearly incensed at the interference of the courts in Muslim personal law issues. In a move to preserve patriarchal privilege, the All India Muslim Personal Law Board successfully displaced the discussion of a UCC from issues of gender justice to issues of minority identity. The courts assisted in this displacement of Muslim women from public discourse by conflating threats to national integration and national unity with the persistence of polygamy. Judicial references to Jinnah's two-nation theory, echoing the inflammatory and communal rhetoric of the Hindu right, also assisted in deflecting attention from Muslim women to the deeply contested politics of citizenship and Muslim minority rights in a majority Hindu state.

In addition, the judgment also placed the blame for Hindu bigamy squarely on the shoulders of the Muslim community and Muslim personal law allowing up to four marriages.

Till the time we achieve the goal – uniform civil code for all the citizens of India – there is an open inducement to a Hindu husband who wants to enter into second marriage while the first marriage is subsisting, to become a Muslim. Since monogamy is the law for Hindus and the Muslim law permits as many as four wives in India, errant husband embraces islam to circumvent the provisions of the Hindu Law and to escape from penal consequences.

(JT 1995 (4) SC 334)

The position of the Hindu right on the UCC is similar to the position of many liberal and feminist groups in India that seek the imposition of a UCC to ensure gender justice.[26] However, the Hindu right's concern for "the state of Muslim women" is but thinly veiled communalism. The Hindu right focuses on polygamy in Islam, Hindu men's access to polygamy through conversion to Islam, and divorce by repudiation as the source of Muslim women's inequality and insecurity. Again, the representation of Muslims as a monolithic community engaging in repudiation and polygamy is not borne out by evidence. A survey of Muslim women in Delhi demonstrated that among the 200 respondents, all but one was a partner in a first marriage. For 94 percent (187) of the respondents, it was also their husband's first marriage. Only 4 percent (8 cases) represented second marriages after a divorce, while 2 percent of respondents were partners in a second marriage after the death of a first wife. In only one case was the respondent a fourth wife (Bano 1995).

Representing Muslims as a monolithic and "backward" community opposed to change does not have an empirical base. During the Shah Bano case, Muslim women demonstrated all across India to declare their support for Muslim women's right to maintenance. The Committee for the Protection of the Rights of Muslim Women was formed with members from Trivandarum, Delhi, and Calcutta (Z. Hasan 1989). Prominent Muslim men and women from all spheres of life signed a memorandum declaring their support for a Muslim woman's right to secure maintenance from her ex-husband. This demonstrates the existence of multiple Muslim communities with varied positions on women's rights. Placing the blame for India's fragmented personal law regime on the Muslim community reinforces the conflation of gender justice with cultural and religious identity while obfuscating the issues at hand.

In its eagerness to blame Hindu polygamy on Islam, the Hindu right does not discuss other ways in which Hindu polygamy is manifested. Most Hindu males committing bigamy do not resort to conversion. They use loopholes inherent in the Hindu Marriage Act to marry more than once without getting a divorce (Kishwar 1995; Sangari 1995). Because many Hindu marriages are not registered in court, the petitioner needs to provide the testimony of the priest who conducted the marriage to prove that it occurred. Generally, obtaining the testimony of priests is extremely difficult for poor women, primarily because they cannot provide monetary compensation for such services. In addition, priests do not want to get involved in legal cases if they fear their trade might suffer as a result of their involvement. Thus it is easy to dismiss common law marriages as non-existent, thereby legalizing another wife (Agnes 1995). If the Hindu right were seriously interested in justice for women, it would take issue with the Hindu Succession Act, which does not allow women to be joint owners of ancestral property.[27] In addition, it could also focus attention on *sati* and other forms of domestic violence.[28]

The discourse of the Hindu right co-opts the language of feminism, using the exclusion of the Muslim community from the UCC to highlight the state of Muslim women and, at the same time, to spearhead an attack on a "backward Muslim community." Feminists have made efforts to distance themselves from the Hindu right by focusing on an optional civil code (Chaachi *et al.* 1995; Kishwar 1995) that would provide individuals with the choice between following the personal law of the community and a "genuinely non-discriminatory Civil Code" of India. Although an optional civil code could provide some of the protection promised by the UCC, it remains mired in the particularistic, oppressive, and confining constructions of gender mandated by religious authorities. Even though women by themselves or with men, have historically "bargained with patriarchy" to create space for redefining gender roles, a gender-justice program based on a non-recognition of structural relations of power in the community is likely to remain only a window dressing (Sangari 1995, 1996). It is more likely that women will be pushed to accept a personal law of the community over the UCC. It is also likely that religious and cultural communities will only rarely seek to alter ingrained patriarchal practices. Although the Hindu Code Bill, as discussed earlier, passed despite opposition from conservatives within the Hindu community, the issue of Muslim minority status and the Hindu right's espousal of reform in the Muslim community muddies the waters on the UCC. On the one hand, to pose the "women question" within the constructs of religious or customary plurality is self-defeating given patriarchal practices. On the other hand, the "women question" cannot be resolved within the legal constructs of the UCC without leaving it open to capture by communalists. Thus the interplay of gender, religion, and nationalism by the Hindu right locks the "women question" in a struggle over which dimensions shall define identity.

The Hindu right, which has so ardently supported the claims of Muslim women, has also contested the claims of broadly based Indian feminism and has dismissed the movement in general. However, the Hindu right utilizes the language of feminism in the service of communalism to create "Muslim men" and "Muslim cultures" as an inferior "Other." In a practice similar to the colonizers' "civilizing mission" in which colonization was justified as "the white man's burden" of saving whole cultures from uncivil practices, the Hindu right has created a discourse of "uncivil and unpatriotic practices" to justify the undermining and the eradication of Muslim culture in India.[29] Although women have been the objects of this discourse, its situation in the politics of religious identity obliterates women in the struggle for gender rights.

Conclusion

In this chapter I argue that the conflation of nationalism and communalism by the Hindu right is based on the creation of a monolithic victimized Hindu identity and a monolithic villainized Muslim identity. These identities rest on historical and religious reconstructions in which gender is the centerpiece. Whether the focal point is the victimization of Hindu women by Muslim men or the oppressed state of Muslim women, Muslim men are constructed as the "uncivilized Other." The Muslim community is constructed as "uncivil," "unpatriotic," and not to be trusted because its allegiance lies outside of India. These efforts towards social construction of Muslim and Hindu identity are based on a communal discourse aimed at the political mobilization of upper caste Hindus.

Recently, efforts were made by the BJP towards including lower caste Hindus in the Hindutva enterprise. A case in point is the BJP-BSP (Bahujan Samaj Party) coalition forming the government in Uttar Pradesh in 1997. The Bahujan Samaj Party's membership is largely comprised of Dalits (the oppressed), also known as "untouchables." This has introduced some fissures between the VHP and the BJP/RSS "family" because the VHP is more wedded to the idea of upper caste supremacy than the BJP, whose agenda is more political than cultural.

The gender implications of the Hindu right's communal enterprise have paradoxically relegated gender justice to a tertiary position within its own institutional politics and among fundamentalist segments of the Muslim community. By emphasizing the "backwardness" of the Muslim community *vis-à-vis* Muslim women, and by juxtaposing this "backwardness" against the "progressive" nature of the Hindu community and its acceptance of a reformed Hindu family law, the Hindu right evades responsibility for improving the situation of Hindu women. The purportedly exalted status of Hindu women also rests on the creation of a mythical past in which women and *nari shakti* (woman power) were the wellsprings of family and community. It is now alleged that Western influence and commercialism have objectified Hindu women, making it necessary to restore Indian women to their rightful, culturally granted positions. By refusing to recognize the structural locations of gender injustice in Indian society, the Hindu right is able to advocate policies that imply no structural changes to ensure gender justice. The Hindu right's emphasis on a UCC has also made some Indians, including feminists and "progressive" Muslims, wary of imposing a code that interferes in a community's right to cultural self-determination. Ironically, gender justice and women's rights have become victims of this discourse on minority rights.

Notes

1   These are Hindu nationalist organizations. The Rashtriya Swayamsevak Sangh (RSS or the National Volunteer Corps) was founded in 1925 by Hegdewar to help Hindu men "resist the temptations of a secular society" (Kolodner 1995: 235). It has become associated with V. D. Savarkar and his espousal of "*Hindutva*." Golwalkar founded the Vishwa Hindu Parishad (VHP or the World Hindu Association) in 1964 seeking to "Hinduize" Indian politics. In 1951, the Bhartiya Jana Sangh (BJS or the Indian People's Organization) was founded as a Hindu nationalist political party. Although it was the first Hindu political party whose leadership had links with the RSS, it was not able to emerge as a significant political force. The BJS joined the Janata coalition to oppose Indira Gandhi in the 1977 elections. This coalition was united in its opposition to the "emergency" imposed by Indira Gandhi in 1975, but suffered from ideological divisions, personal ambitions, and conflict over the "dual allegiance" of BJS members to the RSS and the Janata party. The BJS withdrew support from the Janata government, leading to its collapse and new elections which returned Indira Gandhi and the Congress (I) to power. Soon after the Bhartiya Janata Party (BJP) was formed. Several prominent members of

the BJP are also members of the VHP and RSS. Atal Bihari Vajpayee has been a lifelong member of the RSS. Vijayraje Scindia, an ex-Maharani of the Gwalior gharana, is a member of the VHP.

2   Although the term "communalism" derives from the word "community," the two have evolved into distinctive terms. "Community" evokes positive images of identity derived from belonging to a group that is ascriptive or acquired. Community identities can be multiple – for example, sex, religion, color, class, language, sexual preferences and the like. "Communal" derives its identity-based politics from religious communities, suggesting the social construction of these identities for political mobilization (Bidwai *et al.* 1996: 7). Communalism conveys images of religious bigotry based on notions of supremacy, segregation, and polarized constructions of religious identity as well as the political mobilization of groups based on such distinctions.

3   In the 1996 parliamentary elections, the national platform of the BJP was much less open in its hostility towards Muslims in India when compared with its militant position during the Babri Masjid (mosque)–Ayodhya Mandir (temple) dispute (see note 10). Indeed after the BJP was asked to form a government the President's speech did not mention the Mandir–Masjid issue at all. The Prime Minister himself came out unequivocally in favor of the concept that all citizens are equal before the law. As fair as this appears on the surface, however, equality in fact became a smokescreen for undoing protective laws.

4   The Lok Sabha or the House of the People is the Lower House of the Indian parliament. The upper house is called the Rajya Sabha or the Council of States. The people directly elect the Lower House and the leader of the majority party in the Lok Sabha becomes the Prime Minister.

5   Mr. Lal Krishna Advani, a stalwart of the BJP, later led the 1992 *rath yatra* to Ayodhya and was instrumental in the destruction of Babri Masjid. He led a *surajya rath* across the country espousing that the BJP was the only party that could provide good governance to the Indian people.

6   The equation of "one nation, one culture" with unity is orchestrated so carefully that I found even some of the strong critics of BJP supporting its idea of a unified Indian culture.

7   In Supreme Court Case (SCC) 130, Ramesh Yeshwant Prabhoo v. Prabhakar Kashinath Kunte, with Bal Thackeray v. Prabhakar Kashinath Kunte, the Supreme Court upheld the judgment of the Bombay High Court that the appellants Prabhoo and Thackeray had engaged in corrupt electoral practices because they had appealed for votes on the basis of religion and thereby had flagrantly violated the secular principles of the constitution of India (Supreme Court Cases 1996, 1:130–168).

8   Although the most commonly and widely used translation of *jati* is "caste," Savarkar has used it to mean bloodline.

9   The *Khilafat* movement was significant in the struggle for Indian independence. The Indian National Congress supported the Turkish-led *Khilafat* movement, which was centered on the right to choose the Caliph or the Khalifa. RSS historians have alleged that Muslims supported the Indian national struggle only because the Indian National Congress supported the khilafat movement and that Muslim support ended with the demise of the *Khilafat* movement. It is certainly misleading to declare that Indian Muslims withdrew their support of the Indian independence movement when the struggle for the Caliph ended. Indian Muslims were continuously involved in the struggle for Indian independence while the RSS never took an active role in the movement (Chandra 1984).

10   Rithambara refers to the Ram Janmabhoomi (birthplace) and Babri Masjid (mosque) conflict in India.

On December 6, 1992, after several years of political posturing and communal incitement by the Hindu right, about 300,000 people gathered in the small town of Ayodhya, Uttar Pradesh, birthplace of the Hindu God Rama. For several years, Ayodhya was the site of communal controversy fueled by Hindu fundamentalist claims that the Babri Masjid (mosque) built in 1528 by Mir Baqi for the Mughal king Babar, was constructed on the site of a temple commemorating the birthplace of Ram. In the events that followed, Hindu *kar sevaks* (workers for the cause) destroyed the Babri Masjid while police did nothing to stop the destruction. In the violence that followed 1,700 people were killed and 5,000 injured (Ludden 1996a).

11 Heard at the rally by the author. Clearly, such stereotyping of Muslims in their unwavering support of Pakistan is based on notions of religious citizenship rather than civic citizenship.

12 Although Jawaharlal Nehru and other members of the constituent assembly were unable to include the concept of secularism in the preamble of the Indian constitution, Nehru is still credited with introducing the concept of the secular state into India. He has also been critiqued for introducing a Western concept into India. Indira Gandhi introduced the word "secular" into the constitution of India along with socialist in 1970s. Some claim that, unlike the Western usage of "secular" to imply separation of church and state, the Indian usage stands for *sarv dharam sambhav*, which means that all religions are equal in the eyes of the state. This implies that the state can intervene in religious affairs to guarantee the equality of religions in India.

13 The precedence that religious identity takes over other identities in South Asia is one of the legacies of colonialism. It is also manifested in "orientalist" writings about India. For a discussion of the creation of an Islamic identity see Mushiral Hasan (1995).

14 When the Christian right in the United States wants to highlight the issue of declining morality it uses the "abortion" issue as its example. When the Islamic fundamentalist Shiaini regime of Ayatollah Khomeini in Iran wanted to demonstrate its opposition to the west, it forced the segregation and veiling of women.

15 According to the Hindu right, Muslims committed many heinous crimes. The pillaging of Hindu temples during the invasions of the early thirteenth century, the rape of Hindu women during the early invasions as well as during the partitioning of India, and forced conversions to Islam are cited as examples. Muslim women also participated in crimes against Hindu women.

16 Muslims also have their own stereotypes about Hindus:

> If a Hindu woman or child walks through a Muslim street, the Muslim will let them go; thinking the fight is between men and should not involve women, children and the aged. A Hindu does not think like that. It is enough for him to see the other person is a Muslim before he strikes without regard for age or gender.
>
> (quoted in Kakkar 1996: 126)

17 The term *sanyasin* (female)/*sanyasi* (male) means one who has renounced the world. The vow of celibacy is important for acquiring *sanyasin* status. Uma Bharati, sometimes referred to as the "sexy sanyasin," is a BJP Member of Parliament. Sadhavi Rithambara, also a member of the BJP, chose the name "Sadhavi," "celibate," as an adult. Ironically, her second name, Rithambara, refers to a celestial beauty who serves the gods by seducing ascetics who are perceived as a threat to the established pantheon. The speeches of Rithambara and Bharati were distributed on cassettes during the Babri Masjid and Ram

Janmabhoomi conflict. The Government of India has banned them for their hateful messages.

18 Manusmriti is a Brahmanical text dated between the second century BC and second century AD. It codifies the teachings of the sage Manu and is fairly comprehensive in its discussion of the human condition. These teachings are patriarchal and have exercised tremendous influence on Hindu law (Roy 1995).

19 Triple talaaq refers to one method of divorce under Islam. According to Muslim personal law, a Muslim man can divorce by declaring three times that he divorces his wife. Muslim men are also permitted to have up to four concurrent marriages.

20 It has been suggested that in exchange for non-interference in Muslim family law, Nehru was able to secure the inclusion of a ban on cow slaughter (Gopal 1988; Mahmood 1977).

21 Other minority women – for example, Christians – also come under the jurisdiction of the personal laws of their community.

22 Other Supreme Court cases also raise these issues. See, for example, Jordan v. S. S. Chopra.

23 Because Shah Bano sued under the Criminal Procedure Code and not under civil law, the obligation of the state and judicial bodies to uphold Articles 25 and 26 was minimized. This judgment was in part based on two earlier decisions of the Court which upholding the applicability of section 125 of the Criminal Procedure Code, namely Bai Tahira v. Ali Hussain Fidalli Chotia (1979) and Fazlunbi v. V. Khader Vali (1980).

24 The judgment quotes extensively from different translations to show that the Quran places Muslim husbands under an obligation to look after their divorced wives. In addition, the Chief Justice disagrees that *mahr* is a settlement after divorce. Using scholarship on Muslim personal law, he shows that *mahr* is a dowry settlement agreed to by the husband at the time of marriage and that the customary practice of part at marriage and the rest at divorce does not change the nature and purpose of *mahr* (AIR 1985, Supreme Court 945).

25 Rajeev Gandhi's government had lost the 1985 by-elections and was fearful that continuing to support the Supreme Court verdict would alienate Muslim voters from the Congress Party.

26 Feminist groups have distanced themselves from the mandatory Uniform Civil Code because of the communal overtones it had acquired from the backing of the Hindu right. Several groups suggested an optional civil code as the answer that would provide an individual the choice between personal law or the Uniform Civil Code. Clearly, the issue of "choice" is problematic from several theoretical and empirical positions. For example, in patriarchal systems, can choice by coerced?

27 See Bina Agarwal (1995) for a detailed discussion of women's land rights in South Asia.

28 Vijaya Raje Scindia, a member of the BJP and the VHP, made extremely controversial statements about sati during the Deorala sati case. Distinguishing between voluntary and coerced she implicitly condoned voluntary self-immolation by widows.

29 This paragraph paraphrases Leila Ahmed's (1992) discussion of colonialism in Egypt. Lord Cromer, the British representative in Egypt, used the oppression of women in Islamic societies as the centerpiece of his defense of the Western colonial enterprise. Interestingly, this "savior" of Egyptian women was a founding member and one time President of the Men's League for Opposing Women's Suffrage in Britain (Ahmed 1992: 144–168).

7 Ulster's Red Hand

Gender, identity, and sectarian conflict in Northern Ireland

Mary K. Meyer

The Red Hand's my emblem
the Sash is my song
to the Republic of Ireland
We'll never belong
We have only six counties
But we're proud and true
and will always be loyal
to that Red Hand so true

And the Red White and Blue boys
That part of our cause
It gave us our freedom
religion and laws
We'll fight to defend it
with heart and with hand
and we'll never be driven
from this Ulster land[1]

The politics of Northern Ireland are unambiguously gendered, yet gender has remained a largely ignored variable in explaining the ongoing conflict between the province's "two communities." Some recent scholarship in Northern Ireland has highlighted women's historical exclusion from the formal political structures of the state and women's marginalized yet significant informal political participation in grassroots/community organizations.[2] This research demonstrates that Northern Ireland's political system is very conservative, patriarchal, and essentially closed to women, despite a limited but vibrant women's movement. Some feminists have gone as far as to characterize Northern Ireland as an "armed patriarchy."[3] However, our interest here is not so much the role of women in/outside of the formal and informal political structures in Northern Ireland or in the course of the Troubles. Rather, we shall examine the gender constructions found in sectarian identities and symbols. While no single variable can possibly explain the complex layers of conflict in Northern Ireland, such an examination can show how central gender politics is to the perpetuation of the "Troubles." Such a gender analysis not only illustrates the circumscribed spaces for women in the conflict but also reveals the deeper nature of the political projects of the "two communities" in Northern Ireland.

Both the Protestant/unionist/loyalist identity and the Catholic/nationalist/republican identity are constructed and highly gendered, albeit in different ways. The Protestant/unionist/loyalist identity draws heavily on masculine/warrior symbols with virtually no room for feminine symbols, thus reflecting the staunchly patriarchal values of unionism, its preoccupation with allegiance to the British state, and its exclusion of women from political leadership. The Catholic/nationalist/republican identity draws on masculine symbols but also makes room for powerful feminine symbols, thus reflecting (creating?) more space for women to participate in the nationalist struggle. By considering the gender constructions used in the sectarian symbol systems and identities, it may be possible to locate and explain the political spaces available – or not available – to women. More importantly, such an analysis reveals the deeper nature of the conflict as a political one centering on state versus nation rather than about equally competing ethnic identities or nationalisms *per se*. Finally, it suggests that there are deeper obstacles to resolving the "Troubles" in Northern Ireland than those traditionally recognized.

Defining concepts

Gender and the nation-state

Gender is slowly being recognized as a variable or unit of analysis (like class or race/ethnicity) that should be included to understand complex social phenomena. Recent feminist scholarship demonstrates that gender is a historical social construction that is malleable and varies from place to place. Gender constructions rooted in history, culture, class, and political power structures both reveal and assign values to women's and men's social roles, and they define expectations and rules governing "proper" womanhood and manhood. In Western societies, gender constructions, while complex, usually are defined in terms of polar opposites, wherein "masculine" values such as strength, firmness, loyalty, bravery, autonomy, and rationality are opposed to "feminine" values such as weakness, softness, fickleness, superstition, dependency, and emotionality (especially love). Under patriarchy, "masculine" values are privileged in the public/political sphere and thus play an important part in the political marginalization and subordination of women, whose supposed "feminine" characteristics are more "suited" to the private sphere of the home. Such gender constructions reveal and reinforce the "citizen-warrior" values associated with men in producing and controlling the state (*patria*) and the "mother" values associated with women in reproducing the home, family, and nation.

Pettman (1996: 11–23) and other feminist theorists have shown how states are engaged in the construction of this public/private divide and regulate gender relations, with serious implications for the politics of citizenship for women. There are also important implications for the gendering of nation, nationalism, and the state.

Recent literature on gender and nationalism appears to be divided with regard to the gender constructions, symbolism, and meanings associated with "nation" and "nationalism." According to Parker *et al.* (1992b: 4), George L. Mosse was apparently one of the first scholars to look at the links between nationalism and sexuality, while Benedict Anderson (1991) was one of the first to employ the term "gender" in his study of nationalism, even though he had "relatively little to say about gender or sexuality." Parker *et al.* (1992) have asserted that

> nationalism favors a distinctly homosocial form of male bonding. Mosse argues that "nationalism has a special affinity for male society and together with the concept of respectability legitimized the dominance of men over women." For Anderson this recognition is deeply implicit: "The nation is always conceived as a deep, horizontal comradeship. Ultimately, it is this *fraternity* . . . that makes it possible . . . for so many millions of people, not so much to kill, as willingly to die for such limited imaginings." Typically represented as a passionate brotherhood, the nation finds itself compelled to distinguish its "proper" homosociality from more explicitly sexualized male–male relations, a compulsion that requires the identification, isolation, and containment of male homosexuality.
>
> (Parker *et al.* 1992b: 6; emphasis in original)

While these observations about the gendering – or at least sexualizing – of nationalism are insightful, they may not be very useful for understanding the ways in which nation is gendered. As presented by Parker *et al.* Mosse's argument seems to have more to do with how the (patriarchal) state harnessed nationalism to serve its purposes in carving out the nation-state (along with women's subordination). Anderson (1991) elucidates this point in his discussion of the state's historical role in constructing an "official nationalism" in order to define and legitimize its claim to sovereign authority over a population within its borders. However, Anderson's argument is only accidentally concerned with gender. His single mention of the term "gender" and his use of such terms as "comradeship" and "fraternity" do not constitute a gender analysis of nation or nationalism, which the rest of his book omits, even if his postmodern approach to the phenomenon does open space for others to do so. Anderson's more important contribution is his insistence that nationalism is not a political ideology like liberalism or fascism but should be treated like such anthropological concepts as "kinship" or "religion." He defines "nation" as an "imagined political community – and imagined as both inherently limited and sovereign" (Anderson 1991: 5–6). Anderson is also important because of his rich examination of the complementary roles of print capitalism and the state in constructing such imaginings by standardizing national languages, developing national literatures and presses, creating public educational systems, mapping territories, collecting census data, and so on, both in Europe and in colonial territories.

Contrary to Parker *et al.*'s assertion, traditional representations of the "nation" have been typically associated with female gender constructions and women's bodies, as illustrated in such nineteenth-century symbols of nation-as-woman as Britannia, Columbia, Germania, Hibernia, and others. Recent feminist scholarship also finds feminine gender values associated with the nation, even if it was the patriarchal state that constructed such values. Drawing from the framework of Nira Yuval-Davis and Floya Anthias (1989) in *Woman–Nation–State*, V. Spike Peterson (1994) identifies "five gender-differentiated dimensions along which women have typically been situated in relation to nationalist processes." Women have been viewed as: (1) biological reproducers of group members; (2) social reproducers of group members and cultural forms; (3) signifiers of group differences; (4) participants in political identity struggles; and (5) members of society generally (Peterson 1994:78; see also Pettman 1996).

As biological reproducers under patriarchy, women "mother" the nation, "an extended family writ large" (Moghadam, quoted in Peterson 1994: 81). Women's bodies become privatized and sexualized as reproducers of the nation; women's membership in the group is thus contingent upon their generative/genealogical blood sacrifice as biological bearers of children. As social reproducers of group members and cultural norms, women's state-sanctioned roles as mothers and teachers are meant to transmit family and group histories as well as cultural practices, myths, stories, and values that socialize children into the imagined identities of the group. As signifiers of the group and of group difference, a woman's body represents the personification of nation-as-female, "ever in danger of violation – by 'foreign' males" (Peterson 1994: 80) and in need of protection by male citizen-warriors. As participants in political identity struggles, women have always played a role in nationalist struggles; however, this role is often marginalized, forgotten, or ignored altogether. As members of society, women's (feminist) goals may conflict with nationalist objectives, with women often being pressured to "wait" (e.g. for equality with men) until nationalist goals are achieved (Peterson 1994).

On closer consideration, in the first three dimensions, women or their bodies represent the sexualized/biological blood-ties that demarcate the nation, a word that comes from the Latin *natio* < *natus*, born, and *nascar*, to be born. In the last two dimensions, women are subordinated to the nationalist cause, which is led by men seeking political independence, autonomy, and self-determination – the essential principles of state sovereignty.

If nation is thus gendered and represents the imagined horizontal kinship/blood relations that delimit group homogeneity and denote the mothering values associated with feminine characteristics (love, bonding, caring, sacrifice within and between generations), the "state" is also gendered. The state represents the hierarchical (vertical) authority relations based on force (government, laws, courts, police, military) over a separate well-defined territory and population. Since the emergence of the modern state system with the Peace of Westphalia (1648), the state has claimed absolute sovereignty over its land and the population living inside its territorial boundaries. The centralizing state of the early modern period (seventeenth century) sought to break the power of the Church as well as the private feudal loyalties of lord and vassal. In the place of these feudal authority relations, the state erected a new hierarchy of obedience and allegiance for those living inside the territorial boundaries it claimed. The English civil wars of the seventeenth century inspired Thomas Hobbes to theorize about the Leviathan – the totalizing, centralizing sovereign state that would define political authority and public space, defend territorial boundaries, guarantee internal public order, and create a civic religion to fix the loyalties and obedience of citizens to the state. The public political space – the body politic – constituting the sovereign state was conceived as a male body; it is both generated and defended through war by male soldiers. In the eighteenth and nineteenth centuries, "citizen" became the public, legal, and ideological male embodiment of political actors in the state (*patria*) while "nation" remained the privatized, sexualized, and domesticated female embodiment of the "people's" imagined kinship, along with the rest of the flora and fauna of the national territory.

In the patriarchal state (in this sense a redundancy), the nation and territory are to be demarcated, tamed, controlled, protected, and defended through hierarchical authority relations that value domination, force, and the warrior values associated with masculine characteristics (strength, valor, bravery, loyalty, discipline, autonomy, rationality, and so on). Full citizenship is reserved primarily for males, whose blood sacrifice as citizen-soldiers – as warriors – for the state to protect the nation(al borders) from penetration or violation by foreign males is privileged and rewarded. Boundary maintenance through interstate war becomes the *ultima ratio* of the state, and patriotism (not nationalism *per se*), which glorifies the military victories of the state and the blood sacrifice of its citizen-soldiers, becomes the highest manifestation of citizen loyalty to the state.

Under Western patriarchy, then, the "nation" represents the horizontal kinship and naturalized blood relations that idealize group homogeneity and are essentialized by the female symbols and feminine values associated with mothering. The "state" represents the vertical and hierarchical power relations based on force that idealize sovereignty and are defended by the male symbols and masculine values associated with soldiering. The "nation-state" brings both horizontal and vertical – both feminine and masculine

– axes together to create an inherently limited and autonomous political community ensured by force.

Sectarianism in Northern Ireland

The gendering of state and nation along these lines is a useful starting point for studying the way in which the conflict in Northern Ireland is gendered. The conflict is usually characterized as one based on sectarianism, which in its narrow sense refers to divisions and bigotry based on religious faith. But the divisions between the "two communities" in Northern Ireland are very old and very complex, involving religious, economic, cultural, and political cleavages. Nevertheless, the identities of the "two communities" in Northern Ireland are defined firstly in religious terms, Protestant versus Catholic, and secondarily in political terms, unionist/loyalist versus nationalist/republican.

Sectarianism has been "an often misunderstood" and "to a great extent under-theorised term" (Shirlow and McGovern 1997: 178). Sectarianism is increasingly being defined by Northern Ireland scholars as a form of ethnic conflict, where "religion has become the "boundary marker" for ethnic divisions" (Sales 1997: 61, quoting Shirlow and McGovern 1997). As Mark McGovern and Peter Shirlow (1997) put it,

> If we examine sectarianism as a specific form of ethnic difference this allows theoretical perspectives developed in relation to the study of ethnic relations, divisions, and conflict to be employed in the analysis of sectarian social relations. Such a conception of sectarianism ensures that, whilst religious affiliation is established as a primary discourse of ethnic separation, religion is not recognised as the "subject" of conflicting interest but as a symbol of conflict, representing a means to identify, express, historically root, "legitimate" and "give meaning" to resource competition.
>
> (McGovern and Shirlow 1997: 178)

As Rosemary Sales (1997: 61) notes, "the categories 'Protestant' and 'Catholic' have a particular social meaning in Northern Ireland. Increasingly, the labels are being replaced by 'from the Protestant community' or 'the Catholic community,' emphasising their ethnic, rather than religious significance."

It is significant that scholars and political leaders in Northern Ireland have come to frame sectarianism in this way and discuss the conflict between the "two communities" in terms of ethnicity; however, there are several problems with this framing of the conflict. First, it coincides with the political and academic tendency since the end of the Cold War of framing nearly all contemporary civil conflicts in terms of ethnicity. But this obscures the "imagined" nature of community identity as delineated by Anderson and risks essentializing group difference in Northern Ireland. This is because "ethnicity" itself is a problematic term to define.

The term "ethnic" comes from the Greek words *ethnicos*, meaning national, gentile, or heathen, and *ethnos*, meaning either race or nation. Thus, at one level, while it can be seen as a more or less equivalent term for "nation," emphasizing the imagined kinship ties of a group and delineating insiders and outsiders, at another level ethnicity is a term that seems dangerously to essentialize cultural difference in terms of biology. Its use by early Western anthropologists in studying non-western colonial societies ("cultures") and by contemporary "ethnic brokers" both on the far right and among minority group leaders reifies, naturalizes, biologizes, and often racializes cultural difference. As Pettman (1996: 73) notes, "it is difficult to separate out 'race,' ethnicity, and nationalism in many instances."

Moreover, identity processes based on ethnicity lead to the danger of "ethnic absolutism," "if identities are essentialized or if culture is used to claim virtue or naturalized goods" (Pettman 1996: 76). As identity politics homogenize and naturalize ethnicities, this process also becomes gendered: women again become markers of community difference and their bodies become territories to be controlled, violated by, or defended against attacks by males of the other group. Thus, the recent political and intellectual construction of the "Protestant community" and the "Catholic community" in terms of ethnicity only serves to deepen, and risks essentializing, the divisions between people further. Such constructions perpetuate separation, segregation, and the process of "Othering," even while they are thought to be "politically correct" and "respectful" of conflicting but equally legitimate "traditions" (this is known as "parity of esteem" in Northern Ireland). At the extremes, such constructions lead to or promote an absolutism that justifies violence against the essentialized Other. But the conflict in Northern Ireland is not so easily ethnicized.

Protestants have historically been in the majority in Northern Ireland, whose border was deliberately drawn according to census data by the British government at the time of partition (1921) to include Protestant communities in the province and ensure a loyal, Protestant majority in political power. Thus the British state carefully linked religious affiliation and political loyalty in creating Northern Ireland.[4] However, the "Protestant community" includes a wide range of religious, class, and political memberships and interests, from the mainstream Protestant denominations (Church of Ireland; Methodists; Presbyterians) to smaller independent churches (embracing Free Presbyterians, Pentecostalists and evangelicals); from upper class elites and urban professionals to urban working class and poor rural farmers; from left- to right-wing political parties; and of course both men and women. Under other circumstances, the deep class cleavages within such a community could be expected to have a significant destabilizing political impact. However, the common bond holding this very diverse community together is the desire to maintain

Northern Ireland's political and economic union with Great Britain. This bond and allegiance to union with Britain drives the politics of the Protestant community, overriding all other divisions.

The hegemonic political tendency within the community is unionism, which includes several political parties with the word "unionist" centrally placed in their names. For example, the Ulster Unionist Party (UUP) is the largest, mainstream unionist party ("official" unionism). The Democratic Unionist Party (DUP) (Ian Paisley's party) and the United Kingdom Unionist Party (UKUP) are both far right. The Progressive Unionist Party (PUP) (and the now defunct Vanguard Unionist Party (VUP)) embraces a more left-wing, working class ideology. At its extreme, unionism embraces "loyalism," which refers to the more hard-line supporters "willing to countenance draconian state action or the use of paramilitary violence" to maintain Northern Ireland's constitutional bond to the British state. Loyalist paramilitary forces include the Ulster Volunteer Force (UVF), the Ulster Defence Association (UDA), and the Loyalist Volunteer Force, among others. Loyalist ideology is blatantly sectarian in nature and "is inevitably predicated upon the negative categorisation of Catholics" (McGovern and Shirlow 1997: 177–178). To the extent that there is a Protestant "community" that shares a common identity, it has been shaped in contradistinction to the Catholic "community," whose aspirations are feared to be a political reunification of Northern Ireland with the rest of Ireland. Such a prospect would then make Protestants a minority and significantly weaken their political power.

The "Catholic community" has historically been a minority in Northern Ireland; however, recent demographic data suggest it is now about 40 percent of the total population in the province. Like the Protestant community, the Catholic community includes a wide diversity of class, rural/urban, and political interests. While the Catholic community is more homogeneous in religious affiliation, many are not practicing Catholics; a distinction has recently been made between "religious Catholics" and "cultural Catholics" to reflect this reality. The term "cultural Catholic" refers to the fact that, in general, the Catholic community embraces a well-defined Irish ethno-cultural or national identity. This community is also referred to as the "nationalist" community. Most nationalists in Northern Ireland seek some form of autonomy or at least power sharing for Irish Catholics in Northern Ireland, while some seek full political reunification with the Republic of Ireland.

The mainstream nationalist political party is the Social Democratic Labour Party (SDLP), which embraces a non-violent political strategy within the current constitutional structures to achieve equal rights, justice, and power sharing for Catholics in Northern Ireland. Further to the left, Sinn Féin rejects the legitimacy of British rule and British military occupation in Northern Ireland and seeks full reunification of Ireland under one republican, socialist government. This republican wing within the

Catholic/nationalist community is linked politically with the Provisional Irish Republican Army (IRA), a descendant of the original IRA that fought for Irish independence in the early twentieth century. Other republican paramilitary groups exist (e.g. Continuity IRA and more recently the Real IRA), but the "Provos" have been the predominant republican "military force." The Provisional IRA sees itself fighting a just war for the republican cause, and while some of the violence it has used has killed or maimed many Protestant civilians, it has tended to target primarily British military and security forces or symbols of the British state.

If sectarianism in Northern Ireland is a form of ethnic difference, and if ethnic groups, like nations, are "imagined communities" that "involve the social construction of an origin, and the idea of a common fate, as a basis for community" (Sales 1997: 61), then the Protestant and Catholic communities can be expected to have different stories, symbol systems, meanings, and identities that form the basis for carving out the "Us" from the "Them." Moreover, as social constructions rooted in history and patri-archal social relations, we can expect that these different community markers will be gendered. By analyzing the gender constructions privi-leged by the two communities in telling their "stories," we can gain a deeper insight into the spaces for women in each community's identity and struggle. Moreover we can gain deeper insight into the nature of the conflict itself in order to tell whether it is an "ethnic" conflict, a political conflict, or some other kind of conflict.

Gender and sectarian symbols in Northern Ireland

Northern Ireland is home to a particularly rich terrain of politically symbolic texts and rituals that mark community boundaries and identities. From the myths and stories about each community's origins to the famous street murals painted on the sides of buildings in Belfast and Derry to political marches and street protests, activists from both sides of the conflict produce a plethora of signs that mark territory and announce identity. Once one is sensitized to gender as a social construct and begins to look for representations of women and men in these symbol systems, the almost total absence of women or female imagery in unionist/loyalist markers is striking. Conversely, the frequent presence of women and female imagery in nationalist/republican political markers is equally striking.

The Protestant community: identity as a celebration of the state

There is a fundamental crisis of identity in the "Protestant community." It asserts a "British" identity based on a claim of citizenship in the United Kingdom of Great Britain and Northern Ireland (the full and formal name of the state to which the province belongs), but it lacks a clear national or ethnic kinship with "English," "Welsh," or "Scottish" people or a clearly defined ethno-national kinship identity of its own.

Some loyalists have sought to address this gap by investing in the symbolism of the Red Hand of Ulster or by inventing a new myth of origin for the province. The Red Hand occupies a central place in the flag of Ulster, which hangs prominently in loyalist neighborhoods and working class housing estates. The Red Hand is the oldest symbol of unionist and loyalist organizations. It represents the story of the struggle between two ancient chieftains for the possession of Ulster.[5] The land was to be given to the chief who first touched it. As they approached the land by sea, one of them cut off his own hand and threw it on the beach. The ancient O'Niell clan adopted this symbol to represent its claim to rule Ulster (Bryson and McCartney 1994: 41). The Red Hand has since become the symbol of Ulster and of unionist/loyalist claims to possession of the province. The paramilitary Ulster Volunteer Force (UVF) crest includes the Red Hand surrounded by the words, "UVF – for God and Ulster." Significantly the bloodied hand, standing upright with its palm facing forward as if taking an oath, is less a symbol of ethnicity than it is a symbol of allegiance to state power. The only "blood tie" here is the self-mutilation of a male war chief intent on gaining possession of a certain territory. Women are conspicuously absent from this story.

A less popular but revealing effort by some unionists and loyalists to construct an ethnic identity and a founding myth for their community is found in the controversial writings of Ian Adamson and the recent rewriting of the story of Cúchulainn, an ancient Celtic male hero who has traditionally been part of the Irish nationalist/republican story.[6] Adamson asserts that the original inhabitants of Ulster were not the Gaels but the Cruthins, who were related to the Picts in Scotland. The Cruthins were later invaded by the Gaels, forcing the former into easternmost parts of Ulster and some back to Scotland. The seventeenth century Ulster Plantation "brought many Presbyterian Scots who may be justly considered as returning to the home of their ancestors" (Ian Adamson, quoted in McAuley 1994: 92). Adamson thus constructs an "Ulster Scots" identity based on a story of "homecoming." Loyalists in the paramilitary Ulster Defence Association have taken this story a bit further in claiming Cúchulainn (the Hound of Ulster) as an ancient Cruthin warrior. When Queen Mebh (Maeve) of Connacht invaded Ulster from the west of Ireland, Cúchulainn singlehandedly resisted her armies (Buckley and Kenney 1995: 48–51; McAuley 1994: 92; Rolston 1995: iii). In the loyalist version of the ancient epic, the lone male hero, now representing the ancestors of the "Ulster Scots," defends the land from the invading female, representing the Gaelic-Irish, and her armies.

The stories of the Cruthin and Cúchulainn began to appear regularly in the loyalist paramilitary UDA's magazine Ulster in the late 1970s; however, this attempt to create a founding myth for the Protestant community has had limited popular appeal. James McAuley (1994: 92–96) notes that this may be explained partly by the traditional use of Cúchulainn in republican iconography (hence its alienness to loyalists) and partly by the lack of a sense of history and historical identity in the loyalist community. However, its lack of popular appeal may also be explained by the fact that these stories have no room for women except as the embodiment of the enemy nation. If our discussion of the gendered nature of "nation" under patriarchy is correct, there can be no true sense of a community identity based in a founding myth without the presence of women as generative or constitutive members of the group.

For most unionists and loyalists, the more relevant founding stories of the Protestant community are focused around the Williamite–Jacobite wars of 1688–1692, particularly the Siege of Derry (1688) and the Battle of the Boyne (1690).[7] Derry, known as the "Maiden City," was the site of the earliest (1608) Protestant "Plantation" (implantation, colony) created by the British state in Ulster. A fortified wall was built around the city to separate and protect the Protestant settlers from the "native" Catholic population. When the Catholic armies of James II besieged the city in 1688, Colonel Robert Lundy, "the treacherous governor" of Derry,

> wavered with indecision, uncertain whether to support King James or King William, but his mind was made up for him when a group of apprentice boys shut the gates. For many months, the loyal Protestants held out, enduring fierce deprivations. They were short of food and had only the crudest weapons, but somehow the Maiden City remained intact. . . . In the end, help for the city was at hand. The *Mountjoy*, a Williamite ship, burst the boom that had been set across the River Foyle. Then, following the arrival of William's army, the city was relieved, freeing the Protestants from the forces of oppression and Catholicism.
>
> (Buckley and Kenney 1995: 46–47)

Buckley and Kenney (1995: 52–53) have noted the sexual imagery in this story of the Seige of Derry, where the threatened rape of the Maiden City is resisted until "a more benign quasi-sexual intruder," William III, arrives in his ship, curiously named the *Mountjoy*. But Buckley and Kenney do not go far enough in their explication of the sexual metaphor. William III is more than a "benign quasi-sexual intruder." In this version of the story he is the rightful lord of the Maiden City and takes what is already his. More importantly, Buckley and Kenney overlook the significance of the apprentice boys in the story. The loyal male youths (who are also virginal) close up the city to defend its honor, subjecting it to "fierce deprivations," until King William and his forces could arrive. Women remain invisible; there are no heroic women actors in the drama except for the stony female figure of the walled city itself. The apprentice boys are the real heroes of this story, and their actions have been commemorated in some form since the late seventeenth century. Every December the loyalist organization calling itself the "Apprentice Boys of Derry" commemorates the closing of the city gates and burns an effigy of the "traitor" Lundy; in August they commemorate the relief of the city by marching atop its thick stone walls (Jarman and Bryan 1996: 11).[8]

The Apprentice Boys' semi-annual commemoration of the Seige of Derry is complemented by the numerous Orange lodges' commemorations of the decisive Williamite victory over Catholic forces at the Battle of the Boyne in 1690 on July 12 as well as other significant military events throughout the year (e.g. the Battle of the Somme and Armistice Day). These commemorations take the form of public marches and parades led by drum and fife bands. The most controversial of these marches and parades are those that pass through Catholic/nationalist areas or neighborhoods, such as the Garvaghy Road in Portadown or the Lower Ormeau Road in Belfast, along routes that the Orangemen assert are "traditional." The Orange marches not only are controversial political and sectarian events, but also are highly gendered.

The Orange lodges are male only institutions ("brotherhoods") with Masonic overtones,[9] organized hierarchically with several layers of authority (Jarman and Bryan 1996: 6–9). The Orangemen tend to be middle-aged, middle class men, although younger men have been joining Orange lodges in recent years as the marches have become more conflictual. Their marching regalia (dark suits, orange sashes, bowler hats, white gloves; lodge banners; Union flags) has been fixed since the end of the nineteenth century. Enthusiasts are seen as "curators of a highly elaborate tradition that includes rituals and other genres of symbolism" (Buckley and Kenney 1995: 173). Their rituals, emblems, and banners use symbols based on biblical texts, particularly from the Old Testament, the most common of which are stories about heroic men.[10] Yet Jarman and Bryan (1996) note that joining the Orange Institution

> is a political decision as well as a religious one, and for most Orangemen parading in public is the focus of their membership. Indeed, many Orangemen would not regularly attend church or their Orange lodge meetings. Parades are therefore quite clearly political expressions and are understood in that way by the majority of participants. The Orange Institution is political.
>
> (Jarman and Bryan 1996: 7)

It is also a site of sectarianism. The Orange Institution has close if complex connections both to the Church of Ireland and the main unionist parties, the UUP and the DUP, whose politicians are often at the forefront of defending the "rights" of Orangemen to "practice their religion" by marching on the "Queen's highways."[11]

A few important marches begin in April, but the main marching season of the Orange Order is from June through September, with July 12 being the most important marching day and the Drumcree March on the Sunday before the 12th the most controversial.[12] They may include a religious service at a local Protestant church, but the marches always follow a route through a significant piece of territory. The marchers often end up with a large picnic or outdoor celebration back in "Protestant" or neutral territory where family members may join in. Women and children typically play the role of supportive spectators at points along the parade route.

Leading the parade is a marching band, typically with loud Lambeg drums accompanied by snare drums, fifes, flutes or other instruments. Today, most marching bands are distinct from the Orange lodges and are hired specifically for the march. Since the 1960s, they have been independent, self-organizing bodies attracting younger, working class males specializing in "blood and thunder" or "kick the Pope" marches. These marching bands "offer an alternative, less official, social network" than the Orange Orders, "and their involvement in parades is in many senses more 'active,' and therefore more attractive, to younger and more alienated groups" (Jarman and Bryan 1996: 13). These bands often are linked to loyalist paramilitary organizations, commonly displaying UVF flags or other insignia in their color party (Bryson and McCartney 1994: 114–116) and adopting names like "Young Conquerors." Significantly, while the marching bands are predominantly male, "the colour party is normally female. As well as making political statements with the flags, it is therefore a way to involve girlfriends and potential girlfriends," much like female majorettes in American high school or college marching bands (Bryson and McCartney 1994: 115). These young women therefore provide decoration and affirmation to the parading men and boys.

The marching bands have also taken the responsibility for street decoration in preparation for local marches, painting street curbs red, white, and blue, and hanging red, white, and blue bunting and other loyalist flags in Protestant neighborhoods, thus marking out loyalist territory (Bryson and McCartney 1994: 130). These street decorations are complemented by impressive murals painted on the sides of buildings in loyalist working class areas in Belfast. There is a long tradition of painting (and periodically repainting) murals of King William III on the sides of buildings across the province in preparation for the July 12 celebrations. Belinda Loftus (1990) and Bill Rolston (1992, 1995) have shown how frequently the image of King William III has appeared in unionist and loyalist art and how little variation exists in representations of him. He is paradigmatically portrayed as riding a galloping white horse into battle or across the River Boyne, sword drawn and wearing a white-plumed hat. Although their number has declined in recent years, murals of "King Willie" continue to appear.

In the 1980s and 1990s, however, other themes have appeared in loyalist murals, which "belong" to loyalist paramilitary organizations such as the

Ulster Volunteer Force, the Ulster Defence Association, and the Loyalist Volunteer Force (LVF). Common to all these murals are the insignia of the loyalist paramilitaries and other statist symbols, such as the Red Hand of Ulster, the Crown (representing the British state), the Ulster flag, Union Jack, and other flags, crests, shields, and guns.[13] The most frequent and menacing figures in these murals are the armed and faceless male bodies representing the loyalist paramilitaries themselves. Always wearing bala-clavas to hide their faces, typically dressed in black, their rifles aimed and cocked in phallic readiness, these warriors signal their defense of Ulster. Yet "Ulster" is always represented by the Red Hand, flags, or shields, never as land or people. Some of these murals include the silhouetted figures of soldiers from earlier times (e.g. World War I/Battle of the Somme, the "B-Specials," and so on), or war memorial-like tombstones, commemorating a "fallen soldier." One remarkable UDA mural in East Belfast shows the slumped, half-naked figure of Cúchulainn, "Ancient Defender of Ulster from Irish Attacks over 2,000 yrs ago [*sic*]", generating an offspring – a UDA male soldier in combat fatigues and carrying a gun – as one of "Ulster's Present-Day Defenders." This atavistic depiction of male self-genesis may be unusual, but the absence of women or feminine symbols of any sort in the picture is not. Throughout the loyalist murals, there is a total absence of women and female imagery. Instead, their symbolism is cold, lifeless, faceless, and dehumanized. Rolston finds the prominence of inanimate objects and the "stark absence" of human beings – aside from the hooded gunmen – in recent loyalist mural art significant. "It was as if loyalist mural painters no longer knew where loyalist people fitted. ... [T]he flags, shields, etc. seemed sure, indisputable, immovable. Yet the very robustness of this representation again disguises an under-lying identity problem" (Rolston 1995: ii–iii).

The loyalist murals, the unionist founding myths, and the Orange marches celebrate an identity that is statist and martial. Their symbolism is starkly male and militaristic. They have no space for female symbols except as a stony walled city under siege or the embodiment of the enemy nation, and no place for women except as marginalized onlookers or deco-rations in parades that become ceremonies of identity with the state. Their common bond is loyalty to the union with Britain and a territoriality that commemorates the military victories of the British state. The only apparent kinship ties are the masonic bonds of brotherhood within and between Orange lodges or the comradeship of the loyalist bands and paramilitary organizations. There are of course unionist and loyalist women who iden-tify with and support Orangism, through their fathers', husbands', or sons' participation. And as the Orange marches have become more controver-sial in recent years, women have become more visible in coming out to support them. However, without a more central place for women in its membership, organizational structures, and symbol system, Orangism cannot be the basis for an "ethnic" or "national" identity. And without

Plate 1 UDA loyalist paramilitary mural, East Belfast: Cúchulainn giving birth to UDA paramilitary

Plate 2 UFF loyalist paramilitary mural, North Belfast: "Simply the Best." The curb has been painted red, white, and blue.

Plate 3 UVF loyalist paramilitary mural, North Belfast: "Compromise or Conflict."

Plate 4 Nationalist/Republican mural, West Belfast: Mother Ireland and *An Gorta Mór* (The Great Hunger/Famine)

Plate 5 Republican mural, Derry City: The New "Mother Ireland?"
Commemoration of Bernadette Devlin McAliskey and street protesters
at the Battle of the Bogside, 1969

Plate 6 Republican/Sinn Féin mural, West Belfast: The ten dead hungerstrikers and an armed provo. "They may Kill the Revolutionary but
NEVER the Revolution"

any visible female imagery, the symbol systems of unionism and loyalism cannot provide the kinship bonds that create any sense of community. At best, these symbol systems are a highly patriarchal form of patriotism; at worst, their atavism approaches a form of fascism.

The Catholic community: identity as a celebration of the nation

Unlike the Protestant community, there is no crisis of identity in the "Catholic community" in Northern Ireland. The political symbol systems of the Catholic community are "Irish"; however, as a minority group in Northern Ireland, it has not always been safe for Catholics to admit to having an Irish national identity or citizenship.[14] Nevertheless, "cultural Catholics" have studied the Irish language, are familiar with its literature, sometimes listen to traditional Irish music, participate in Irish national sports (Gaelic football, hurling, camogie), and know their Irish history. There are complex historical economic, social, and political reasons for this, however. The separate Catholic school system and institutions like the Gaelic Athletic Association (which is organized island-wide) are important factors in perpetuating this identity, as is the discrimination that Catholics have experienced historically in Northern Ireland. Although there are patriarchal and occasionally militaristic aspects to the political symbolism used by nationalists and republicans, it also incorporates many important female representations, as signs both of the vulnerability and endurance of the community.

Unlike unionists and loyalists, who have only recently sought to construct a founding myth, nationalists have a ready-made, long constructed, and highly stylized nationalist story in the North. It is (partly) shared by people living south of the border and has been reinterpreted and reconstructed as the historical, material, and political context in the North changes. This narrative includes a prominent place for strong women – fighting women, from the ancient Celtic Queen Mebh (who fought Cúchulainn) to Gracey O'Malley (who resisted Elizabethan intrigues) to the Countess Constance Markievicz (who fought heroically in the 1916 Easter Uprising with the IRA). Moreover, the image of a woman has represented both Ireland and the Irish nation from the beginnings of the independence movement in the late eighteenth century, if not earlier. Sometimes depicted as a young maiden surrounded by lush vegetation, sometimes as an older woman suffering famine, sometimes as an ancient Celtic heroine, Eire, Hibernia, or "Mother Ireland" is a powerful cultural and political symbol (see Loftus 1990).

Buckley and Kenney (1995: 45–53) have noted that a central theme of Irish nationalist history in the North is that of recurrent invasions of Ireland by outsiders (Danes, Anglo-Normans, English/British). The personification of Ireland as a woman (e.g. Róisín Dubh or Caitlín Ní hUallacháin) thus evokes the rape metaphor, particularly in telling the story of the British state's invasion, conquest, and oppression of the native Irish people. From this perspective, the Ulster Plantation in Derry was an illegitimate implantation/penetration/violation of Eire/Mother Ireland by outsiders. The vulnerability and weakness of the Irish could not be defended by King James II's Catholic armies, leading to further depredations against the natives who lost land, freedom, and even their language.

An old Jacobite love song, Siubhail a Rún (Come My Love), evokes this gendered version of history but carries it a step further. A tearful maiden sings, half in English, half in Irish, that "when King James was forced to flee/The Wild Geese spread their wings to sea/And bore my *buachaill* [dear boy; boyfriend] far from me/*Is go dhé thú, a mhuirnín slán* [A blessing go with you my beloved]." She wishes "the king would return to reign/And bring by true love back again/I wish and wish, but wish in vain/*Is go dhé thú, a mhuirnín slán.*" She then vows to dye her "petticoat red/And round the world I'll beg my bread/Till I find my love, alive or dead/*Is go dhé thú, a mhuirnín slán*" (in Healy 1977: 12–13). In this song, the woman had sold everything she owned to buy a sword for her lover, but with the Jacobite armies defeated, he is lost; the conquest of defenseless Ireland now forces her to begging and even prostitution until she can find the one she really loves. She is now homeless and wanders the world in search of her protector.

Belinda Loftus (1990) has illustrated how artistic representations of Mother Ireland have changed over time, from vulnerable to fecund, from suffering to transcendent. One notable lithograph from 1916 titled "The Birth of the Irish Republic" depicts seven male soldiers in a bunker, some wounded, some firing guns. Rising out of this group into a ray of light from the sky (heaven?) is a resplendent young woman. In one hand she holds the Irish tricolor, which blows from her gown, framing her head in a kind of halo; she also wears a sandal with a Celtic design (see Loftus 1990: 65). This nationalist lithograph is significant. Not only does it include a woman's body centrally placed in the picture, but also it depicts male soldiers giving rise/birth to her and defending her through their blood sacrifice. Here the gender symbolism of state and nation come together to produce the Irish Republic. This birthing is markedly different from the loyalist mural depicting Cúchulainn as the sole progenitor of a UDA paramilitary gunman.

Another female figure sometimes used in the Irish national story is the Madonna. Some observers have criticized the "sentimental" and "patriarchal" image of Mother Ireland and the "meek, submissive figure of the Virgin Mary" in such nationalist iconography (Morgan and Fraser 1994: 82). However, the Virgin Mary is not necessarily a meek and submissive figure. She can also be seen as a powerful intercessor and an almost goddess-like protector who is strong enough to suffer with her people to alleviate their pain. There was a noteworthy mural in Belfast depicting the Virgin Mary watching over Bobby Sands, one of the dying H-Block hungerstrikers, who is himself depicted in a Christological way (Rolston 1992: 30). Sentimental? Yes. Patriarchal? Sure. Weak and submissive? No. These depictions of women icons are remarkable compared to the highly masculinized loyalist symbols. There is no comparable female icon in the Protestant/unionist/loyalist symbol system.

These female icons in Irish national symbolism are shared on both sides of the border. In Northern Ireland, however, republican symbolism today rarely uses overtly religious themes. It is mainly secular and very political. There is a recent mural in Derry depicting a larger than life Bernadette Devlin McAliskey holding a megaphone as two male youths surrounded by rising smoke throw stones while another young woman prepares for street battle. This mural memorializes Devlin's role during the Battle of the Bogside (1969) in encouraging residents to defend "Free Derry" against attacks by state security forces and thus immortalizes her as the new, Northern, Mother Ireland.

Several other republican murals portray historical republican women, such as the Countess Markiewicz, less famous local women standing up to British security forces, or those killed (along with men and children) on Bloody Sunday (January 1972) by British troops. One Sinn Féin mural in Belfast presents three republican women activists, one of whom holds a rifle, under the caption, "We must grow tough but without ever losing our tenderness," suggesting several layers of gender meanings (see Rolston 1992: 34). While these murals may still be playing with Mother Ireland themes, their portraiture of actual women stresses women's active participation in the republican movement. Still other murals in Belfast and Derry have highlighted revolutionary women from other parts of the world (Nicaragua, South Africa), stressing solidarity with similar "people's struggles" elsewhere.

Unlike the loyalist murals, republican mural art is populated with the figures and faces of men and women, boys and girls, famous leaders and ordinary people. It often includes a great deal of written text to "educate" the community about its history, the political struggle, and its heroes, including women. Republican mural art also makes extensive use of Celtic designs, draws on Celtic folklore, and often includes the Irish language in its written text (Loftus 1990; Rolston 1992, 1995).

There are a number of older republican murals that are more militaristic in nature, with stark, black silhouettes of armed "provos" that are reminiscent of some loyalist paramilitary murals. But these are few in number compared to the rest of the republican murals, which present more realistic, humanized, and "softened" images of republican males. One mural along the Falls Road immortalizes the ten male hungerstrikers, with smiling portraits of each one, their names, the dates they died, and their ages at death. Alongside this homage is another mural showing a provo holding the Irish flag, which waves behind him; he wears camouflage and holds a rifle in his other arm. Despite this militaristic theme, the young man is presented full-faced with bare forearms – a much more humanized depiction than that of loyalist paramilitaries wearing balaclavas and showing no skin. This image is framed with the caption, "They may kill the Revolutionary but NEVER the Revolution."

Most of the steely, cold, faceless, military figures in republican mural art represent British troops and the Royal Ulster Constabulary (RUC) – the security forces of the state. One mural in Derry shows the mostly hidden faces of an RUC officer and a British army soldier beating a naked human figure that is remarkably androgynous in its depiction. The victim has long flowing hair and is shown full-face, outlined by a beard, but the rest of the body is drawn in such a way as to be not entirely clear whether it is meant to be a male or female figure. However, in more recent murals appearing since the first IRA ceasefire (1994–1996), even the RUC and British army soldiers are presented in more humanized, even comical ways, with messages like "*Slán Abhaile*" (good-bye) or "Time to Go" painted in the picture.

It is significant that several recent murals in nationalist/republican areas in west, central, and north West Belfast depict lively, even festive scenes with cartoon characters or representations of men, women, and children walking, dancing, or playing along roads lined with trees or buildings and plenty of blue sky above. These cheerful scenes are almost devoid of overtly political messages but seem to emphasize the centrality of the neighborhood's identity. One such mural along the Falls Road celebrates the "Forest of Belfast," with a young couple, four children (three girls and a boy), and a dog strolling down a stone path through the forest complete with bumble bees, flowers, and a small stream. Attached to the mural is a sign with the Irish word *Saoirse* (freedom). Another mural along the side of the building that houses the Lower Ormeau Road Residents Association near central Belfast depicts a lively community scene, with a score of people working, biking, walking, and playing along the road lined with the red brick buildings of the neighborhood. A large male bricklayer in blue overalls stands ready with the cement while two voluptuous and scantily dressed female figures push a stroller or wave to onlookers while children play in the background.

Nearby, another very recent mural reprises an older and more overtly political theme by depicting a menacing file of Orangemen marching down the road. The leader has the form of a skeleton wearing Orange marchers' regalia and carrying a sign reading "One Way" while half a dozen black silhouettes (one of whom holds the hand of a child) wearing hats and orange sashes march behind. The ghoulish parade is about to trample the figure of a woman in a green jacket and long red hair as she kneels in the middle of the road, her protest sign saying "Peace Justice" knocked or dropped from her hands as she pleads for the marchers to stop. In this mural, the Orange parade passes a building that has its own mural painted with the words, "What part of NO don't you understand?" The imagery of sexual assault against the nationalist community by faceless Orange marchers in this mural leaves little to the imagination. This mural also acknowledges the role of women activists of the Lower Ormeau Road as well as their counterparts of the Garvaghy Road in Portadown, who have organized street demonstrations and women's peace camps to protest Orange marches through their neighborhoods.

These examples illustrate the rather developed nationalist identity of the republican movement in Northern Ireland. The images are gendered, but include strong women and men as well as land, trees, and roads as constitutive of the nationalist community. They are lively and dramatic. They demonize the British state, security forces, and the Orange Order and glorify the armed struggle, where women also have an important place not only as observers or supporters but as active participants and heroines. These idealized images are of course forms of propaganda in the service of a political project led primarily by men seeking a reconstitution of the state. But it is significant that these public art forms give so much space to representations of women. Like loyalist murals, this republican art marks out nationalist/republican "territory," along with green, white, and orange curb painting and Irish national flags, but it is a territory that is "peopled" rather than one that is held by and for the lifeless symbols of the state.

Conclusion

People who study the conflict in Northern Ireland often have a difficult time classifying its nature. It is said to be a "sectarian" conflict that pits "two communities" against each other defined broadly along religious affiliations, but it is not primarily about religion. Rather, it is a constitutional conflict over the legitimacy of the state structures governing the people living in the region. There are two "imagined" communities, but defining them in terms of ethnicity is problematic. There is a well-developed ethnonationalist "Irish" identity within the Catholic community that is used by republicans to legitimize, rally, and further their political project, but not all Catholics favor political reintegration with the rest of Ireland or believe it is realistic to do so. On the other hand, there is a crisis of identity within the Protestant community, which lacks a clear sense of "ethnicity." Despite efforts by some loyalists to construct an ethnic identity for the Protestant community, such an identity has remained elusive. To the extent that there is an identity within the Protestant community, it is defined as the negative of the "Other" community. It is "not Irish"; it identifies with the British state; at its extremes it is "anti-Catholic" and sectarian – "any Catholic will do" as a target of loyalist violence. "Sectarianism" in Northern Ireland remains an undertheorized term.

A gender analysis of the political symbolism of the "two communities" can reveal better how they construct their group identities. Such an analysis reveals that from loyalist public murals and street decorations to the con-struction of an "Ulster-Scots" founding myth to the marches of the Orange Order, the "imagined" Protestant community's symbols are highly masculinized. The Protestant community identifies primarily with the masculinist symbolism of the state, celebrates the state's military victories over the Irish nation, and lacks the female imagery that is central to the construction of a national identity. It also reveals that the Catholic commu-nity has a positive national identity that incorporates strong female imagery as essential to the construction of the group. The gendering of the symbol systems of both communities is patriarchal in the sense that it is deeply embedded in Western associations of the state with masculinized warrior values and of the nation with feminized kinship values. They reveal that the conflict is about state versus nation, not ethnicity *per se*. These gendered symbol systems also reveal that there is very little space for women to participate in the unionist/loyalist political project, while there is much more space for women to participate in the nationalist/republican political project. Although politics and society in Northern Ireland remain highly patriarchal, forcing women in both communities into traditional social roles and marginalized political participation, unless the unionist/loyalist community can incorporate women into its institutional structures and symbol systems, its lifeless patriotism is doomed to fail.

Notes

1 Lyrics to a Loyalist song, quoted in McAuley (1994: 98).
2 See e.g. Democratic Dialogue (1996), Evason (1991), McWilliams (1995), Miller *et al.* (1996), Morgan and Fraser (1994), Rooney and Woods (1995), Sales (1997), Wilford (1996), Wilford *et al.* (1993), Women and Citizen Research Group (1995).
3 According to Monica McWilliams (1995: 34, fn 7), Cathy Harkin coined the term "armed patriarchy" when working with Women's Aid in Derry between 1977 and 1981.
4 The Tower Museum in Derry City displays a fascinating pair of government maps from the time of Partition showing census data marking out the Protestant population from the Catholic population in Ulster and the demarcation of the border creating "Northern Ireland" with its Protestant majority.
5 Ulster is one of the four ancient provinces in Ireland. In the 1921 partition of the island, six of its nine counties became "Northern Ireland" while the other three counties became part of the "free state" or Irish republic.
6 Cúchulainn is the hero of the Gaelic-language epic *Tain Bo Cuailnge* (Buckley and Kenney 1995: 49).
7 Derry was renamed Londonderry by the British crown at the time of the Plantation. Both names are still used today, usually – but not always – indi-cating the political identity/allegiance of its user. The politics of this name are quite complex.
8 The first Apprentice Boys club was created in 1714, but the present organi-zation originated in 1814. Many of its members also belong to the Orange Institution. The Apprentice Boys of Derry are not formally linked to any particular political party. It is the smallest but most important loyalist order

in London/Derry, with an estimated 12,000 members (Jarman and Bryan 1996: 11).

9 The first Orange Order appeared in the 1790s; Orange lodges grew in number and organization in the nineteenth century. Today there are some 1400 Orange lodges with around 40,000 members. According to Bryson and McCartney (1994: 113), there is a Women's Orange Order, but they provide no details about the organization and I have not yet found any other reference to it. It remains invisible during the Orange marches.

10 For example Noah, Abraham and Isaac, Jacob, Joseph, Moses, Joshua, Gideon, David, Elijah, Jehu, and Daniel (see Buckley and Kenney 1995: 187–190).

11 The Orange Order and related institutions (the Royal Purple Arch and the Royal Black Institution) "can claim to represent and in some ways typify Ulster Protestantism. Their aims . . . are to uphold Protestantism as a religion and to uphold the interests of Northern Ireland's protestants" (Buckley and Kenney 1995: 173).

12 The Drumcree March is held in Portadown and draws thousands of men from Orange lodges all around the province. It begins with a march to the (Anglican) Church of Ireland at Drumcree, just outside of town, for a religious service. It returns back through Portadown via a different route, taking it down the Garvaghy Road, which has become a predominantly Catholic-nationalist neighborhood. Increasingly violent clashes have occurred during the Drumcree marches since 1996 as nationalist residents assert their "right to be free from sectarian harassment" and Orangemen insist on their "right to practice their religion" and march down the "Queen's highways" and along their "traditional routes."

13 I wish to thank Mr. John Hoey, who graciously took me around loyalist and republican neighborhoods in Belfast to show me many of these murals for this research.

14 A Catholic elections officer told me in May 1997 that while registering voters in the North, he discovered that Catholics are reticent to give their nationality as "Irish" (the other choice on the form is "British") unless they are subtly reassured that it is legal – and safe – to do so.

8   From subjects to citizens

Women and the nation in Kuwait

Mary Ann Tétreault and Haya al-Mughni

Kuwait is a rapidly modernizing country where women enjoy many of the same social and civil rights guaranteed to men.[1] However, Kuwaiti women are deprived of many of the political rights enjoyed by Kuwaiti men. Although they are entitled to participate as voters and as candidates in the administration of local cooperative stores, women cannot run for the national legislature or vote for its members. In the summer of 1999, during an unanticipated suspension of the parliament, the Kuwaiti ruler issued a decree conferring full political rights on Kuwaiti women. As we discuss later in this chapter, the decree itself was voted down by the parliament; subsequently, a virtually identical parliamentary initiative also was defeated, though by a narrower vote. At the time of writing, Kuwaiti women are still without full political rights. Even so, the events of the past year have mobilized many Kuwaitis, men as well as women, into an intensified effort to achieve them.

The struggle to achieve women's political rights has been a perennial issue in Kuwaiti politics since the adoption of the 1962 constitution and the subsequent passage of laws governing elections under its aegis. Like the US constitution, Kuwait's constitution does not discriminate between women and men with respect to their citizenship rights but a number of laws adopted under that constitution, such as those regulating elections, do discriminate against women. Yet the parliament has resisted repeated appeals for enfranchisement by women eager to enjoy the full panoply of rights conferred on men by the constitution. That, coupled with the surprising 1999 initiative by a regime otherwise indifferent, and sometimes even hostile to, citizen demands for democratization, highlights the prominence of gender as an axis of conflict in Kuwaiti society.

Gender politics in Kuwait acts as a proxy for other kinds of group antagonisms. For example, gender discrimination occurred in the same context

An earlier version of this chapter was published in 1995 in *British Journal of Middle Eastern Studies*, 22: 1 and 2, under the title "Gender, Citizenship, and Nationalism in Kuwait."

in which increasing numbers of tribal men were granted formal citizenship and enfranchised by the regime as a means to bolster its power in what has been an independent and often contentious parliamentary body. This history of political preference for tribal men over all women contributes to the ongoing antagonism between those men who perceive themselves as upholders of tradition and the women whom they see as dangerously modern. Economic uncertainty adds to this antagonism. The Kuwaiti economy began to falter following the crash of an informal local stock market in September 1982, and weakened further in response to a decline in world oil prices culminating in a price collapse in 1986. Although oil prices have both risen and fallen since then, some of Kuwait's class antagonisms continue to be managed by masking them under the guise of gender conflicts (al-Mughni 1993).

At the same time, Kuwait, like other Middle Eastern countries, experienced an upsurge in support for Islamist political movements following the 1978–1979 revolution in Iran. In domestic conflicts between Kuwaiti Islamists and Kuwaiti secularists, gender not only is a metaphor for other social and political conflicts but often becomes the primary battleground on which Islamists challenge the legitimacy of secularist political groups. Gender was a primary axis of conflict between secularists and Islamists in the 1992 parliament (Tétreault 1997, 2000), and the strongest opposition to the amir's proposal to give women political rights came from Sunni Islamists in and outside of parliament. The amir's action calls into question the state of what had been assumed to be a tacit alliance between the ruling family and Sunni Islamists, especially those associated with the Muslim Brotherhood or Ikhwan.

During the late 1970s, the Kuwaiti regime sought to harness Islamist enthusiasm to its own campaign to weaken democratic opposition in Kuwait. Changes in Kuwait's electoral law led to the growing prominence of Islamists in the Kuwaiti parliament beginning in 1981 (Gavrielides 1987). This, along with the experience of the 1990–1991 Iraqi invasion and occupation during which women were highly visible actors in the resistance inside and outside Kuwait while the tribal *badu* acquired reputations as cowards and slackers, increased antagonism between these two groups (Longva 1996; Tétreault 2000). Following the invasion, Islamism became even more powerful inside and outside of Kuwait. In the 1992 and 1996 parliaments,[2] Islamists challenged the regime and the secular opposition directly on gender issues. They won some important victories, the most significant of which was to pass a law mandating gender segregation in Kuwait's post-secondary schools (Tétreault 1997, 2000; Tétreault and al-Mughni 2000). The uneasy alliance between the Kuwaiti regime and elements of the Islamist opposition was based on the identity of Kuwait as a traditional tribal state. Now that the regime has chosen to position itself as a champion of women's political rights, these alleged longstanding political alliances are suddenly undermined.

Citizens, subject, and nationals

The concept of citizenship in the modern world is complicated by the conflicting claims of individuals, groups, and complex organizations. Among these, the nation-state, an entity that defines its material existence as a specific territory (Ruggie 1986) is the most important. "State" and "citizen" were not always mutually exclusive concepts. Aristotle (1986) saw the state as a plurality of citizens who come together for self-sufficiency in a political association aiming at the highest good. Since the eighteenth century, however, the state increasingly has come to be seen as separate from civil society (Keane 1988; Wood 1994). Political theorists who imagine state–society relations to be the result of a contract between citizens and rulers, visualize as discontinuous what to the ancients and even to some of their contemporaries in the early modern era was a seamless web of relationships embedding the citizen in the state (Pateman 1988b; Wood 1994). To these "contract theorists," the interests of the state and those of the citizen diverge, making them competitors for resources, authority, and power. Consequently, state interests in the survival of government, regime, and the integrity of control over territory and populations are seen to be in conflict with citizens' interests in the survival of individuals, families, and the moral and material bases for life. In this view, the citizen actually is conceptualized as a resource of the state which uses citizens and the material bases of their lives to defend and aggrandize itself. The modern notion of separation between state and civil society reflects this perception that there is a fundamental conflict of interests between the two.

Both of these models of state–citizen relations are enormously simplified. Neither "state" nor "citizen" is a unitary concept. States can be disaggregated into institutions, governments, and regimes and each of those also can be broken down further, for example, into parties, agencies, and other formal and informal divisions where a divergence in interests results in a breakdown of unitary identification and behavior. Similarly, citizens are not simply rivals – or possessions – of the state. Sometimes as individuals though more frequently as groups or corporations, citizens join in alliances with, capture, or are co-opted by some parts of the state to further their mutual interests (e.g. Gilpin 1981; Lindblom 1977; Lowi 1969). The distinction between state and civil society is, therefore, flexible in practice and should be in any theory developed to explain relations between them.

Another distinction important in an analysis of state–society relations is the one that separates citizen from subject. The notion of citizenship goes back to ancient conceptions of the state as a corporate expression of the interests and desires of a community of persons any male member of which at any time could, at least theoretically, govern (Aristotle 1986; James 1986; Wood 1994). Consequently, a citizen is a free person, an autonomous participant in political life. In contrast, a subject is not free but rather is "subjected" to the will of another. The subject is a member of a political order that Benedict Anderson (1991) calls "the dynastic realm," not a government, but a whole world.

> [I]n fundamental ways "serious" monarchy lies transverse to all modern conceptions of political life. Kingship organizes everything around a high centre. Its legitimacy derives from divinity, not from populations, who, after all, are subjects, not citizens. . . . [I]n the older imagining, where states were defined by centres, borders were porous and indistinct, and sovereignties faded imperceptibly into one another.
>
> (Anderson 1991: 19)

In the dynastic realm, time is nonlinear rather than a chain of cause and effect. Thus, events like Abraham's sacrifice of Isaac or the crucifixion of Christ are either mirror images or similar points in cosmic cycles (Anderson 1991). Dynastic cycles governed by concepts such as the Mandate of Heaven, or life cycles during which parents produce children to take their places in a cosmically regulated pattern of recapitulation without change – without "progress" – are the divinely ordained pathways of a virtuous life (Marr 1981). In this sense, the monarch also is a subject, of the divine will that organizes the world. But the political center imposes a double subjection on all those who are not the monarch. Not only the divine will but also the will of the monarch who represents the divine will on earth constitute legitimate limits on the autonomy of the subject.

"Tradition" is the term we use to refer to the remnants of the dynastic realm in the modern world. When we speak of "tradition" and "traditional life," we speak implicitly of timelessness and subjection. We envision persons whose positions in life are determined by qualities independent of their individuality. Indeed, we do not see individuality – what Hannah Arendt (1965) called "plurality" – as characteristics of such people. Although we might not attribute their "traditional" qualities to divine will, we employ terms such as "nature" or "culture" that amount to much the same thing. Hidden beneath the gloss of "tradition" are the assumptions of the dynastic realm: the interconnected concepts of legitimate subjection and an inherent absence of progress or "development."

The ancient concept of citzenship has been revived in the modern period with the same flaw that characterized the notion in classical Athens: it is a gendered concept (Mosse 1985; Pateman 1988b; Peterson 1994; Yuval-Davis and Anthias 1989). Aristotle (1986) differentiated between male and female citizens with respect to their relative autonomy, believing that the nature of female citizens as emotional beings incapable of reason obviated autonomy and required them to be ruled by men (also Ortner 1974). The meaning of citizenship for women under these circumstances had little to do with civil or political rights; it was concerned primarily with ensuring the citizenship of legitimate male offspring (Patterson 1991).

The concept of "nationality" as an identity conferred by birth, marriage, and/or naturalization is similarly independent of notions of citizenship rights (Anderson 1991; Guy 1992). During the twentieth century, nationality began to be closely regulated by states as wars, refugee movements, and other political changes such as decolonization, led nation-states to restrict and regulate population movements across their boundaries. Consequently, state bureaucracies were charged with classifying individuals as "citizens" of specific nation-states, a classification conferring entitlements and obligations but not necessarily equally to every person carrying a passport from the same state.[3]

"Nationalism" refers to a psychological identification similar to kinship that binds people to one another regardless of boundaries drawn by nation-states or which government issues one's passport. Liah Greenfeld (1992) associates the development of nationalism with modernity and the spread of a democratic ideology that includes a notion of citizenship as distinct from "subjecthood." She says that nationalism originated as a revolution in consciousness that took place in sixteenth century England, and attributes its widespread attractiveness to its egalitarian values. Both Greenfeld and Anderson emphasize the importance of literacy and the development of an egalitarian popular culture transmitted and reinforced by reading and writing as critical to the spread of nationalism to other countries. Greenfeld calls nationalism the hallmark of modernity because it is a created symbolic order based on a conception of sovereignty as inhering in a people rather than in a ruler. She sees nationalism as fundamentally independent of kinship and interest (Greenfeld 1992: 10, 18). Whether one agrees with Greenfeld's state-centered conceptualization of nationalism, or one regards nationalism as a primordial identity as Anthony Smith (1991a) and Walker Connor (1994) argue that it is, the legitimacy of the modern nation-state rests on the belief that its regime and government rule with the consent of the governed (Weber 1995).

Citizenship, nationality, and gender

Nothing in Greenfeld's or Anderson's analyses would lead us to expect that the rise of nationalism coincided with an expansion of citizenship rights for women. As Pateman (1988b) and others (e.g. Hunt 1992; Okin 1989) point out, the myths of origin positing the existence of a "social contract" between nations and their rulers in modern societies are based on an ideology of monogendered equality: brotherhood. Thus, the social contract between citizen and state in modern liberal theory from Locke to Rawls rejects only half of the dynastic concept of patriarchalism: paternal patriarchy, the "rule of the fathers." Liberal theory replaces that half of patriarchialism with fraternity, but it is silent on the subject of masculine or conjugal patriarchy, the submission of women to their husbands (Pateman 1988b). Until the twentieth century and virtually everywhere in the world, wives were the subjects of their husbands just as children were the subjects of their fathers, and neither were autonomous citizens (e.g. Boswell 1988; Mason 1994; Mill 1929; Okin 1989; Tétreault 1994). Consequently, when we equate nationalism to kinship, we overlay the egalitarian model of fraternity with the hierarchical model of patriarchy. The resulting confusion helps to obscure the oppressive communalism of many nationalist movements.

The normative and positive absence of women from theories about citizenship was and still is echoed in practice and in laws that discriminate between women and men with respect to nationality as well as civil rights and responsibilities. Until the twentieth century, most states did not grant civil status and rights to women (Guy 1992; Mayer 1995). According to Donna Guy (1992), what prompted the extension of citizenship to women was their emigration across the borders of European states to new homes outside Europe. Despite European women's departure from their natal states, they continued to be seen as coming from and, in some sense, representing these states.[4] This is because nationality as an identity inheres in individuals per se, regardless of where they are, rather than in populations occupying a specific territory (Anderson 1991). As a result, "the condition of . . . [a nation's] women living abroad, whether as respectable wives or as socially marginal prostitutes, affected the rights and inherent restrictions of citizenship beyond national frontiers" (Guy 1992: 202). The subjection of "their" women to the laws of another state pushed European states to grant citizenship to women, as they did to men, but not as part of a democratization project. Rather, female citizenship legitimized these states' intervention in the affairs of other sovereign states as a means to protect those women – and their own honor. This process also reinforced the connection between women and vulnerability, both the woman's and the state's through hers. The connection between sexuality and nationality is strong for other reasons as well. Nationality not only is a bureaucratically conferred identity, but also confers entitlement to distributions by the state of valuable resources, and raises concerns about the transfer of citizenship from parents to children.

Nationality is an outcome of the global domination of the nation-state,[5] a bounded unit in a finite universe of other, similar, units (Anderson 1991). Although nationalism and subjection are compatible with porous boundaries and sovereignties that fade imperceptibly into one another, citizenship and nationality are differently imagined. Citizenship, unlike subjection, is horizontal, bounded, and exclusive, based on the conception of individuality as an inter-unit equality analogous to sovereignty (Ruggie 1986). Nationality, unlike "the nation," is a quality of the person, secure within the boundaries of body and mind no matter where he – or she – is located ethnically or geographically.

Citizenship and nationality in Kuwait

Citizenship is a contested concept where state-formation is incomplete, a condition regarded as widespread among the countries of the Middle East (e.g. Bromley 1994). In Kuwait, for example, the social contract myth is patriarchal in both senses of the term, producing a conflict between images of Kuwait as a nation-state and as a dynastic realm (al-Mughni 1993; al-Naqeeb 1990; Sharabi 1988). The Kuwaiti nation is envisioned as a family, a multilevel hierarchy with the ruler at its head, rather than as a band of brothers of equal status. Within the national family, the ruling family enjoys a constitutionally protected status and many informal privileges that are greater than those of other Kuwaiti nationals whose rights as citizens are thereby limited (Crystal 1990; Tétreault 1991, 1995b).

In Kuwait, the family, like the state, is patriarchal. The family, rather than the person, is constitutionally defined as the basic unit of society. The subjection of Kuwaiti women within the family, though limited by law and constitution, is analogous to the subjection of all Kuwaiti citizens to their rulers, which also is limited by law and constitution. Women's subjection is connected to their role in sexual reproduction, one that is construed as problematic in a universe where the concept of penetration is analogous to images of threat. The control of women's bodies – who can penetrate them and determine the status of their issue – is a problem that transcends "morality" or even "social control." Rather, it is a matter of national security.

The national security dimension of gendered nationality is highly threatening in Kuwait. Although outsiders think of Kuwait as rich, Kuwaitis perceive their nation as small and vulnerable, with today's wealth an accident contingent on forces external to state and society and therefore fundamentally insecure (Tétreault 1995a). Kuwait's deeply embedded culture of insecurity coevolved with the patriarchal tribalism characteristic of its social order.[6] State policies aimed at restricting the number and kind of persons eligible to receive citizen entitlements resonate with tribalist interpretations of the proper positions of women and outsiders in the life of the community.

All states restrict the entitlements and rights of outsiders, but many are increasingly troubled by the effects on the national political economy of limiting the rights of female citizens. This also is true for Kuwait. The education of women and consequent changes in their social expectations, together with the need for trained and competent nationals to fill strategically important positions, are negated by the state's efforts to define nationality and citizenship in a premodern way. This tension embeds Kuwait in a contradiction whose logical conclusions for the survival and prosperity of the state are problematic regardless of how the tension is resolved.

Nationals and expatriates

Kuwaitis became a minority in their own country following the discovery of their oil resources. Labor imported for a broad range of economic development projects soon outnumbered Kuwaiti nationals. By 1965, as the result of the in-migration of expatriate workers and their families, Kuwaitis made up only 36.1 percent of the population (Kuwait Ministry of Planning 1992: 27).[7] Kuwait's last pre-invasion census, taken in 1985, showed that the proportion of nationals had fallen to 27.7 percent. Large proportions of these non-Kuwaitis were long-time residents. In 1985, 57 percent of non-Kuwaiti Arab residents aged 30 years and over had lived in Kuwait for ten years or more, and about 41 percent of all non-Kuwaiti Arab residents actually had been born in Kuwait (Shah and al-Qudsi 1990). An important domestic economic factor helping to explain the rapid growth of the foreign labor force is a large wage differential favoring Kuwaitis. Foreign workers are much cheaper to employ and, as a result, make up the vast majority of private sector employees (Crystal 1992; Ismael 1982; Longva 1997; Tétreault 1995a, 2000). State agencies are urged to increase the relative proportion of nationals among their employees by adopting ambitious "Kuwaitization" programs (Tétreault 1995a), but even though government officials talk about Kuwaitization in the private sector, they have been slow to provide rational incentives to encourage it.

The Nationality Law of 1959, amended several times since then, allows foreigners to obtain Kuwaiti nationality through naturalization. Arabs and non-Arabs (primarily Persians) living in Kuwait prior to 1945 and remaining residents until the Nationality Law was promulgated were able to obtain Kuwaiti nationality. Those who came to Kuwait after 1945 had to complete at least twenty years of residency and qualify under other criteria such as being fluent in Arabic, being capable of earning a living, and being a Muslim before applying for Kuwaiti nationality. Until it was amended in 1980, the Nationality Law limited the number of such naturalized persons to fifty per year. Even after that, the rate of naturalization did not rise to any significant extent (Crystal 1992: 86).

Naturalized Kuwaitis and their children, along with second-category citizens (these are male citizens who came to Kuwait or registered their nationality after 1920) and their male offspring, were not entitled to vote or to run for elective office. In 1994 the nationality law was amended again to permit the sons of naturalized citizens who were born after their fathers had been granted citizenship to vote and to run for office. During the 1996 elections for the National Assembly, approximately 20,000 such persons voted for the first time (Tétreault 2000).

Restrictions on naturalization coupled to a relatively liberal policy toward refugees prior to the mid-1980s, contributed to the emergence of a stateless class of persons, the *bidun* (in Arabic, "without" – that is, without nationality). *Bidun* are recognized as permanent residents but hold no nationality documents other than a laissez-passer permitting them to leave and reenter the country. The *bidun* are Kuwaiti subjects but not Kuwaiti citizens. Before 1986, *bidun* enjoyed many of the same economic rights as Kuwaitis; subsequently, restrictions were imposed curtailing their rights to attend state schools and hold jobs in the state sector. This policy was adopted to force *bidun* to disclose their nationality and produce corroborating documents, but many insisted that their families had been nomads having neither nationality nor documents. The exact number of *bidun* is not known. According to Rashed al-Aneizi (1994), prior to the Iraqi invasion, there were about 225,000 *bidun* in Kuwait. After liberation, the number dropped to about 117,000 because many either left the country or declared a nationality. In 1996, in response to criticism of the status and living conditions of *bidun* in Kuwait following liberation, the government established a committee under the Ministry of Interior to develop criteria for naturalizing some *bidun* and regularizing the status of those permitted to remain as resident aliens without citizenship. However, as we write in the summer of 1999, the status of Kuwaiti *bidun* remains unresolved.

Foreigners cannot vote, run for the National Assembly (parliament), or hold offices in labor unions, public welfare associations such as cooperatives, or state-chartered voluntary associations. State concern about the growing domestic influence of Arab nationalists had prompted the government, in the late 1960s, to remove non-Kuwaitis from positions of authority in voluntary associations (al-Mughni 1993). As Jill Crystal rightly argues,

> [Arab workers'] political sense of entitlement, as members of the large Arab nation, make them in practice more of a threat to the state. This larger shared loyalty to one Arab nation (not state) has its roots not only in a shared cultural history but also in a shared opposition to colonial rule and in the history of the shared political movement for Arab independence that was defeated by Britain and France. It found political expression not only in recurrent movements for political integration but also in the lip service paid to Arab nationalism by leaders of virtually every Arab state ... Kuwait and Saudi Arabia came increasingly to link entitlement to state sovereignty, whereas ... the poorer states increasingly stressed this larger Arab identity as a justification for sharing ... [state] revenues.
>
> (Crystal 1992: 83, 85)

Industrial and commercial laws adopted in the 1950s and 1960s have limited the extent of non-Kuwaiti ownership of productive capital. Foreigners were required to have Kuwaiti partners who were allocated a minimum of 51 percent of any investment. There continue to be restrictions on residency based on salary levels. According to the 1987 Immigration Law, a foreign man employed in the public sector had to earn at least KD 450 per month and one employed in the private sector a minimum of KD 650 per month to be permitted to bring his family into the country.[8] Some whose wages fall below the levels demanded bring their wives on separate visas issued to *khadimat*, domestic servants, which requires that they be sponsored by a Kuwaiti *khafeel* or by another legal resident whose salary meets a higher standard (Shah and al-Qudsi 1990; interviews by Tétreault 1990, 1992).

The government initiated a modern system of education in the 1950s in part to increase Kuwait's ability to satisfy labor force requirements domestically and thereby reduce dependence on foreign workers. The 1962 constitution guarantees every Kuwaiti national, male and female, the right to an education and the right to work. Free education was made available from primary school through university training, including the opportunity for qualified students to study abroad. Prior to the 1990 Iraqi invasion, a citizen unable to obtain work in the private sector could always find a secure job in the state sector, though this has become more difficult since liberation because of budgetary pressures. A social security system, supported by employers and the state, provides retirement pensions paying a minimum of 65 percent and a maximum of 95 percent of a Kuwaiti employee's highest monthly salary. Although the quality and quantity of entitlements available to Kuwaiti women are inferior to what is available to Kuwaiti men (Tétreault and al-Mughni 1995, 2000), all Kuwaitis enjoy benefits substantially greater than what are available to *bidun* and foreigners residing in Kuwait.

The wage differential between foreign and national employees, plus the effective guarantee of a secure state-sector job to Kuwaitis, had perverse effects on the quality of the labor force. Rather than reducing the proportion of foreign workers, these policies led to a "de-skilling" of the Kuwaiti labor force. The result was to concentrate Kuwaitis in service positions in the state sector while the bulk of productive work continued to be performed by expatriates. At the same time, it also increased the state's ability to prevent and control the formation of opposition groups based on class:

> The fact that the same organization, the state, is at once employer, law enforcer, and social services provider ... also means it is much easier for this organization to monitor, prevent, and control class-based behavior, that is, to keep workers in line, than it would be were these roles more scattered.
>
> (Crystal 1992: 74)

A similar encouragement of dependency on the state grew out of the national welfare policy. Kuwait's extensive welfare system assists middle- and low-income families, elderly people, disabled people, divorced women, widows, prisoners' families, and unmarried girls. Programs include public housing, rent subsidies, subsidies for water and electricity (which, like local telephone service were, until recently, provided free of charge to citizens), and a monthly allowance based on the number of children in a family.[9] These social assistance programs were designed to promote family stability and attack the causes of poverty by encouraging education, training, and employment. But according to Hassan Hammoud (1987) they also have a perverse effect on work incentives because they award needy families more in welfare benefits than they can earn from employment. In this way they increase dependency.

The state's welfare policies, in intention and effect, created a privileged class of Kuwaitis whose rights to education, employment, and other benefits are protected and guaranteed by the government. Jacqueline Ismael (1982) and Anh Nga Longva (1997) argue that the non-Kuwaiti population has been used as an instrument to legitimize the regime and consolidate its power. By ensuring the well-being of the Kuwaiti minority as against a disfranchised, economically disadvantaged, foreign majority, Kuwait's monarchy justifies its continuation in power. Crystal (1990, 1992) argues that the generous allocation of social services to Kuwaitis also reinforces patriotism, state-centered nationalism, and feelings of loyalty to the state. Kuwait's welfare policies thus help to maintain the boundaries between Kuwaitis and non-Kuwaitis. More importantly, they create a sense of superiority among the privileged citizens, which is an important element of Kuwaiti national identity. However, they have been less successful in generating consistent loyalty to the regime.

National identity and Islam

Kuwait's welfare policies also have been less than uniformly successful in producing national unity among social groups. There are significant divisions among Kuwaitis (Gavrielides 1987), between Shi'a and Sunna, between the rich and the not-so-rich, between *badu* (tribal populations) and *hadhar* (city dwellers), and between *bidun* and citizens.[10] The state's struggle to establish a sense of national unity and reinforce national loyalty is expressed by its vigorous propagation since the 1970s of the concept of *al-'usra al-waheda*, the "one – that is, united – family" as the dominant national symbol. The concept of *al-'usra al-waheda* resonates with images of traditional Kuwaiti families whose members lived closely together under the wing of the family's patriarch. Kuwaiti children are taught to call the amir "baba Jaber," that is, "father Jaber," the head of Kuwait's one united family and the nation's highest authority to whom everyone owes obedience and loyalty. Halim Barakat (1993) notes a profound similarity between the image of the father in the family and the image of God in Islam. Hisham Sharabi (1988) claims that the recursive patterns of patriarchalism in religion, state, society, and family support the continuation of autocratic and of authoritarian regimes in the Arab world, a conclusion supported by Eric Wolf (1982) for other cultures.

The Islamization of Kuwaiti society became a policy of the government beginning in the late 1970s, during a period when the regime faced criticism for closing down the parliament and suspending a series of constitutionally mandated civil liberties. The government felt pressed to associate itself more closely with Islam for several reasons. Among them was the growing strength of Islamist movements in Kuwait, and their affiliation with the political opposition in reaction to the suspension of the constitution and parliament. Another was that popular adherence to Islamic values and principles suited the interests of the regime. Unlike Arab nationalists who place a high value on democracy and individual rights, Islamists call for *intima'* (cultural belonging), discipline, the preservation of traditional family forms, and obedience to political authority, values that reinforce the position of the regime. In contrast, the secular opposition challenges the regime by making persistent demands for democratization (Tétreault 1995b, 2000).

The popularity of Islamist movements was enhanced by growing criticism of the social liberalism of the 1960s, widely regarded as responsible for generating a host of social problems. As Kuwait modernized, the divorce rate and juvenile deliquency rose. Alcohol consumption, though illegal, became widespread. Perhaps the most worrisome problem to many Kuwaitis is that traditional family relations, based on the principle of ta'a (obedience to the patriarchal head), seemed to be breaking down. Many regard such social problems as the result of the attractiveness of Western values and the growing (though still limited) participation of women in the labor force (al-Rahmani 1996). Domestic critics, both religious and secular, see both as root causes of women's alleged neglect of their family responsibilities, the erosion of family ties, and the weakening of national unity.

Since the 1960s, Muslim reformers, particularly those in the Social Reform Association, had campaigned vigorously for strict adherence to Islamic mores and the institution of the Shari'a as the source of legislation. They called for the prosecution of zina (generally translated as "adultery" but, in more conservative interpretations, a term that also can refer to touching, talking to, or being alone with unrelated men – see Ahmed 1992:44, 120). They demanded as well the separation of the sexes and the veiling of women in public spaces; the prohibition of alcohol importation, manufacture, and consumption; and laws governing the collection of *zakat*, the religious tax whose payment is one of the five pillars of Islam.

Muslim revivalists preach the virtues of a hierarchical ethical order. In this order, Muslim women, veiled and obedient, are everywhere subordinate to men and confined to roles dictated by their biological constitution. Their most natural and essential role is that of mother. The family is their natural domain, where they are maintained and protected by their husbands. Islamists do not oppose the participation of women in the paid labor force entirely, however. They agree that there may be a need for Kuwaiti

women to work, but only in positions where they neither compete nor associate with men, such as in sex-segregated institutions like girls' schools where
they serve – and compete against – women only (al-Mughni 1993).

Kuwaiti women and the state

The state supports religious norms defining the main duty of men as
supporting their wives and children and the main duty of women as looking
after their families, but the practical translation of these norms into law
has been, at best, inconsistent. For example, in 1986, the National Assembly
approved legislation allowing civil servants up to two years of maternity
leave at half pay. This reflected the desire of a majority of the parliament
to raise the participation of Kuwaiti women in the labor force as a way
to reduce dependence on foreign workers.[11] The very next year a new
personal status law, drawn in accordance with the Maliki interpretation
of Islam, made it the legal responsibility of husbands to support their wives
and children.

Changes in popular attitudes make it easier for Kuwaiti women to work
for pay and still conform substantially to religious and social norms. Native
women's labor participation rate increased from 2 percent in 1965 to more
than 25 percent in 1993, with a large proportion of female workers
employed as teachers in government schools (Shah 1994). Other labor
policies intended to enhance national security, such as the post-liberation
expulsion of demonstrably loyal Palestinian workers, eased temporarily
competition in the national labor force, and expanded job opportunities
for Kuwaiti women outside education (Tétreault, interviews 1992, 1994).
In its report for the second quarter of 1996, the National Bank of Kuwait
(NBK) noted a more rapid labor force growth rate for women than men
during the previous eighteen months (NBK 1997:11–12).

But even though Kuwaiti women are asked by their government to
perform a dual role as mothers and as paid workers, they still are effectively without formal political rights. The electoral law passed in Kuwait's
first post-independence parliament restricted the right to vote and run for
office to Kuwaiti men over 21 years of age. This law continued in force
despite decades of women's campaigning for full political rights (Tétreault
1993a) and was challenged credibly for the first time only in 1999, and
not by a proposal originating in the parliament but by an amiri decree
requiring parliamentary approval to go into effect. Also, Kuwaiti women
continue to face wage discrimination. Nasra Shah and Sulayman al-Qudsi
(1990) report that even when women have higher educational qualifications
than men, their wages still fall below the male average. Kuwaiti working
women also are denied the same social benefits that Kuwaiti men are entitled to. For example, they do not receive child allowances if their husbands
also work in the state sector. An apparent contradiction to the bias in
benefits favoring male over female workers is a new law passed by the

1992 parliament permitting working mothers to retire with full benefits after fifteen years regardless of their age. However, the effect of this law is that at the same time Kuwaiti women are entering the labor force at a faster rate than Kuwaiti men, the parliament adds to family and other social pressures to get them out as quickly as possible. The goal of limiting women's employment rights also is visible in calls for restricting access by women to engineering majors and in the passage of a 1996 law requiring gender segregation at all Kuwaiti post-secondary schools.

Defining women as dependent on men acquits the state from any responsibility to support them. It is only when women lack male support and are unable to earn an income that the government steps in to help. Working women and those with husbands or fathers deemed able to support them are denied government assistance, thus limiting their ability to leave abusive family situations or to provide for their children in cases of desertion. In 1992 alone, 308 applications submitted by women declaring their need for state support were denied on the grounds that the women either were employed or should have been able to obtain assistance from a male relative (al-Mughni, interviews 1993).

Female welfare beneficiaries receive monthly income support as well as rent subsidies. In 1993, 5,344 divorced women and widows (out of a total population, male and female, of more than 600,000 persons)[12] received such benefits (al-Mughni, interviews 1993). Even so, Kuwaiti women are not entitled to own government-supplied or subsidized houses, a privilege restricted to male heads of households (*rab al-'usra*). When a husband dies, the house goes automatically to the wife and the children if there are children. If there are no children or after the children are grown and leave home, the house is repossessed by the state unless the widow can show that relatives of the deceased head of household are living with her in the house.[13]

Residential segregation is practiced throughout Kuwait. Areas specifically reserved for female welfare beneficiaries effectively ghettoize these women in blocks of flats in remote areas. Their geographic isolation mirrors their social rejection and has generated a host of problems for divorced mothers and widows. Their anomalous situation in a society where adult women live with parents, spouses, or adult children has stigmatized them as "unworthy mothers" and women of low morals (Tétreault and al-Mughni 1995).

Other marginalized Kuwaiti women are those who have married non-Kuwaitis. In Kuwait, as in other Arab and Islamic states, citizenship is passed from father to child. Kuwaiti women married to foreigners are mothers of non-Kuwaiti children who, like themselves, are denied the political, economic, and social protections to which Kuwaiti men are entitled. Adult children and non-Kuwaiti spouses of Kuwaiti women are treated like any other expatriates and have no right to remain in Kuwait unless they receive residency permits from the state on the same basis as other foreigners seeking Kuwaiti residence (Tétreault, interviews 1994). The children of Kuwaiti women and non-Kuwaiti men are denied admission to government schools and the university. In 1982, Kuwaiti women married to non-Kuwaiti men lost their right to apply for government housing. Their right to housing loans was rescinded in 1993. Despite individual and collective attempts by Kuwaiti women to secure some rights for their non-Kuwaiti spouses and children, the government remains impervious to their requests. As a result, increasing numbers of Kuwaiti women in this situation are emigrating with their families to Canada and Great Britain in search of a better life.

Women and civil society in Kuwait

In Kuwait, "civil society" is a term that until 1999 included only male nationals as fully entitled participants. Male foreigners and male *bidun* continue to experience restrictions on their political and economic activities similar to those placed on foreigners in other countries. The assumption supporting this differential treatment in Kuwait is that such persons actually "belong" somewhere else, that they are members of other civil societies, other nations, and not of Kuwait's civil society and nation. Kuwaitis believe that claims by foreigners to citizen entitlements should be made to the government in their country of nationality rather than to the government of a country they are merely visiting. This view comports with psychological models of nationalism as well as with legal models of citizenship under international law, although the plight of the *bidun* constitutes an important exception internationally and in the minds of some Kuwaitis as well.

Such an assumption cannot be used to excuse or explain restrictions on rights for Kuwaiti women. The assumptions underlying their unequal treatment belong to the dynastic realm and do not correspond to modern understandings of citizenship and civil society. Under the formulations still guiding the treatment of Kuwaiti women under Kuwaiti law, women are part of nature rather than civilized society. A Kuwaiti woman has no nationality that belongs to her absolutely. She is Kuwaiti by virtue of having a Kuwaiti father but can lose her status as a Kuwaiti if she marries a foreigner even though she still may be entitled to live in Kuwait. Many Kuwaitis see this as natural, saying that if a woman wants to remain a Kuwaiti she should not marry a foreigner. The fact that her divorce or widowhood restores a woman's Kuwaiti nationality does not dilute the social or legal impact of this model of the Kuwaiti woman. She continues to be seen as little more than a vessel for the transmission of nationality between men across generations rather than as a civil person in her own right.

The lack of civil status for Kuwaiti women also was expressed in laws denying them political rights. Even so, elite women have been visible in a number of public arenas for more than a generation and women's views on a variety of issues are published in the press. The president of Kuwait University is a woman, a vice president of the Kuwait Petroleum Corporation is a woman, and other elite women also hold powerful positions in government agencies. Yet, as one of us has noted in a previous work (al-Mughni 1993), the privileges of elite women have been slow to trickle down to other Kuwaiti women. Elite women in Kuwait have used their positions to maintain the social status quo and preserve their own class privileges. Despite differences among women, the reality for all Kuwaiti women is that their status and survival continue to depend entirely on their relationship to men. In this context, the law and those who participate in making laws hold the key to a systematic improvement in the rights of Kuwaiti women.

The 1996 success by Kuwaiti parliamentary Islamists in passing the gender segregation law led to an upsurge of interest in Kuwait's women's movement, enough to stem the growth in the number of Islamists returned to the parliament in the October 1996 election, but not enough to reverse it (Tétreault 1997). Women continued to demand their political rights throughout the lifetime of the 1996 parliament, but their efforts were thwarted by Islamist domination of key legislative committees. Meanwhile, the 1996 parliament even more than its contentious predecessor, blocked government attempts to reduce parliamentary authority over fiscal policy. Despite government assertions that the state's fiscal difficulties were due to structural deficits growing out of overly generous entitlement programs, opposition leaders pointed to bad management and what they termed "the theft of public funds" as equal contributors to budget deficits. Repeated clashes between parliamentarians and cabinet ministers – some of whom were members of the ruling family – induced the amir to dismiss the parliament on May 3, 1999 and call for new elections.

On May 16, nearly two weeks after the parliament was suspended, the amir issued the decree conferring full political rights on women. Amiri decrees promulgated during a parliamentary recess must be approved when the body reconvenes. However, this procedure is constitutional only if the decrees themselves are "urgent" (Article 71). Such a claim was difficult to make for the women's rights decree: women would not have been able to vote until the next regularly scheduled election in 2003 even if the decree had been approved. With regard to a number of other equally far-ranging decrees, the claim of urgency also was clouded, in part by the fact that substantial parliamentary opposition to the government's positions on them already was both strong and publicly known. Among these was a measure that effectively would have reversed the nationalization of foreign oil holdings by permitting foreign direct investment in oil production in Kuwait. As a result of the context in which women's political rights were proposed, the parliamentary response reflected not only the usual legislative ambivalence toward (if not outright disagreement with) the notion of female political autonomy, but also a reaction against the association of women's rights with what were criticized as unconstitutional attempts by the amir to force through a large number of radical changes in economic and social policy.

Even so, from May 16, when the women's rights decree was announced, to November 30, when a virtually identical measure went down to defeat a week after the decree itself was rejected by the parliament, women's rights dominated public discussion of domestic political issues. This discourse included all sorts of positioning as members lined up for and against the women's rights decree in expected ways – Islamists and tribalists against, and many liberals for. However, a few lined up in unexpected ways, chief among them the former speaker, liberal Ahmad al-Sa'doun, who had become the *bête noire* of the regime. These opponents promised to oppose the women's rights decree along with others they regarded as non-urgent and therefore as illegitimate encroachments on the parliament's legislative authority. These constitutional hard-liners were among the few Kuwaitis attempting to broaden the focus of discussion to include other aspects of the policy agenda implied by the full complement of legislation proposed by the amir during the parliamentary interregnum.

However, it also is true that, despite all of the attention to Islamist and tribalist opposition to women's political rights, a number of Kuwaiti liberals also had records opposing female enfranchisement. Their views were grounded on the belief that, on the whole, women are more conservative than men and thus that allowing women to vote would work against the interests of liberal candidates (interviews by Tétreault 1990, 1992). It would not be surprising if this expectation regarding female conservatism also was shared by the amir. A similar motivation prompted the naturalization and enfranchisement of large numbers of tribal residents prior to the 1981 election marking the end of a parliamentary recess imposed in 1976. The resulting "desertization" of Kuwaiti domestic politics (Ghabra 1997) set the stage for two decades of clashes over gender and other "lifestyle" issues in the parliament and in Kuwaiti society.

Whether the eventual enfranchisement of Kuwaiti women will be similarly effective in embedding strongly traditional forces in domestic political life remains to be seen, however. Among tribal Kuwaitis, the effects of modernization can increasingly be seen to include the "embourgeoisement" of boys and girls in the rising generation. As these young persons reach their political majority, they reveal an expanding degree of individualism and independence unimaginable at the time their fathers were awarded citizenship. Modernity also has affected the political orientations of young persons in the ruling family, some of whom have recently taken public positions in opposition to their governing elders. Kuwaiti women experience the same modernizing forces as other groups in their society. Unlike their male counterparts, however, exclusion from political life has prompted many Kuwaiti women to see their coming achievement of first-category political rights as the key to their achievement of individual autonomy. Expectations that the feminization of Kuwaiti politics can halt the erosion of support for traditional rule may be dashed even more quickly than the expectations that desertization could accomplish this goal.[14]

Conclusion

The gap between the level of human and civil rights guarantees for Kuwaiti women, as opposed to Kuwaiti men, often is explained as the result of "tradition," a catch-all term that conceals the reality of subjection behind a veil of nostalgia. Especially potent in a region where imperialism left so much political, social, and economic chaos in its wake, appeals to tradition find strong support in populations devastated by global economic restructuring and disaffected from marginally legitimate, inept, and self-aggrandizing political regimes. One reason for the appeal of – and to – tradition in the Middle East is that religion, which does enjoy widespread popular legitimacy, is credited as being the foundation of traditional values. Tradition and religion thus appear to be synonymous, even though religious leaders are quick to adopt modern ways to compete for authority against both autocratic regimes and aspiring secular reformers (Mernissi 1992).

On the whole, however, in the Middle East as elsewhere, religious institutions have lost power to states in educational, judicial, and economic arenas, although they continue to play a prominent role regulating personal status and "private" behavior. These are areas over which most states are willing to share or even concede authority as part of a "social contract" describing a balance of power between religion and the state in situations where each has sizable constituencies but neither can mobilize enough support to rule alone (e.g. Gause 1994; Jorgensen 1994; Tétreault 1995b). Such a strategy brings double benefits to the state. It simultaneously pacifies religious opponents and pushes secular opponents into a corner marked off as socially radical and therefore even less legitimate than the regime. The strategy also benefits religious leaders. It gives them authority over highly salient aspects of daily life while it undermines secularists' claims to represent the community.

The subjection of women also bridges divisions among men by uniting them to protect what Maxine Molyneux (1985) calls strategic gender interests, that is, the interests they all share as men who benefit, individually and collectively, from female subordination. Some evidence for this can been seen in the mobilization of Kuwaiti secularists in opposition to the extension of voting rights to women prior to the 1992 parliamentary elections (Tétreault 1993a: 283). Among the secularists' rationales for their opposition was that because Islamists have more wives than secularists, the enfranchisement of women could tip elections against secularist candidates. A similar assumption is likely to have influenced the sudden and unexpected decision by the amir to override the legislature by decreeing political rights for women during a parliamentary recess. Fundamental principles such as whether political rights are integral to the human rights that every Kuwaiti should be entitled to ought to have motivated both sides in their debates on this issue. However, abstract principles were invoked to support another rationale, that is, that the amir should not have made this change by issuing an unconstitutional decree but instead should have permitted the parliament to do it in a legal way.

Other interests bring into question the extent of any practical effects of female enfranchisement. Since the mid-1980s, Kuwait's generous welfare policy has strained the capacity of the economy to provide all the bene-fits and services to which male citizens are entitled. Even before the Iraqi invasion, young men had to wait years for a house, forcing many to post-pone marriage. Budgetary shortfalls increased as the result of the invasion, occupation, and liberation of Kuwait. For example, Kuwait's direct payments to members of the coalition amounted to $23 billion, and many of its blue-chip overseas portfolio holdings had to be liquidated to finance the expenses of the occupation, liberation, and post-war reconstruction. Payments to citizens, some in the form of new entitlements, also reduced the government's capacity to keep up with mandated social benefits without running deficits (Tétreault 1992, 1995a). As a result, post-liberation parlia-ments have fought with the government over the terms under which the imposition of taxes, user fees, and even the expropriation of zakat paid by Kuwaiti corporations can be imposed to augment the state's oil and investment income.[15]

The extension of full citizenship status to women would open the possi-bility that people who now are denied a range of welfare benefits could become eligible for them overnight. A parliament suddenly vulnerable to pressure from women voters and female electoral opponents also could extend civil rights protections that would enable women to challenge men in court over such issues as equal employment rights and wage discrimina-tion. While current preoccupations with budget deficits might cloak the results of such changes under concerns about how expensive they would be, the deeper threat that female citizenship poses to men, and not only in Kuwait, is sexual rather than economic. If women had full civil rights, the necessity for them to acquiesce to male domination would be attenuated. Women could demand equal rights in marriage, challenging a host of reli-giously sanctioned practices from polygyny to repudiation that lie at the root of female subordination in the Kuwaiti family. Full rights for Kuwaiti women would enable them to avoid marriage altogether, secure in their own government-subsidized homes, supported by income from their guar-anteed jobs, and looking forward to independence even in old age sustained by their generous pensions. The thought alone is revolutionary.

The inextricable logic of extending full rights to women in virtually every society comes up against the reality of social, political, and economic orders constructed on the basis of female subordination (Rubin 1975). Susan Okin (1989) shows how such orders are defended, even by liberals, as necessary to induce the kind of self-sacrifice required to bear and rear children and to transmit culture from one generation to the next. A similar self-sacrifice is required to field armies, armies that throughout history have been disproportionately composed of men (Elshtain 1987; Pateman 1988b).

Arguments against women's rights in Kuwait also rely on appeals to tradition to keep women in their "natural" place. Similar appeals to tradition are used to discredit those who press for democratization. The conflation of tradition with Islam deploys the power of religion and the interests of the mosque on the side of a monarchy interested in keeping Kuwaiti society embedded in the dynastic realm rather than allowing it to evolve toward an egalitarian modernism that would threaten its authority. Arguments for continuing the gender differentiation of citizenship rights that appeal to self-sacrifice and tradition are unlikely to remain persuasive as women's voices assume greater prominence in domestic political discourse. Self-sacrifice by definition cannot be institutionalized. When this is attempted, what results is compulsion, the smothering rather than the expression of a person's essential nature. Tradition, in Kuwait as in other Muslim societies, is both ambiguous and contested, including traditions that describe the status of women (e.g. Ahmed 1992; al-Mughni 2000; Spellberg 1994). This is why the legal rights of women vary among Muslim countries just as they do among countries whose societies are shaped by other religious traditions (Mayer 1995). In the end, it is neither self-sacrifice nor tradition that explains the subordinate position of women in Kuwait. It is the self-centeredness of those who used to monopolize social, economic, and political power. As this monopoly cracks under the pressure of women seeking to realize their political aspirations, Kuwaiti civil society will reform and the meaning of citizenship will be enriched.

Notes

1 Social rights in this context include jobs, salary parity with men in identical positions, and social services such as education and health care. Civil rights commonly refer to free speech and press, the right of assembly, and privacy rights. Political rights allow the citizen to participate in governance, and include such rights as voting, service on juries, and eligibility for political office. See Marshall (1950).
2 Parliaments in Kuwait are referred to by the year of their election.
3 Differential treatment of nationals is not based on gender alone. For example, the state of Israel distinguishes among nationals according to whether they are Jewish or "Arab" as well as whether they are male or female (Tekiner 1994).
4 This kind of representation is discussed in Habermas (1991: 5–9) and refers to an emblematic role – standing for something. In this context, we can think of the demeanor and behavior of an American or a Kuwaiti abroad as being seen by foreign nationals as somehow representing or standing in for how American or Kuwaitis are and behave generally.
5 The concept "nation-state" is contested in the literature on nationalism and ethnicity. One view, associated with those such as Anderson (1991) and

Greenfeld (1992), is that nationalism inheres in the state as a political entity. Others, most prominently Walker Connor and Anthony Smith, believe that nationalism is an ideology that is not simply analogous to kinship but is based on a belief that actual kinship exists. Connor (1994: 90–100) points out that few nation-states actually feature the coincidence of a territory with a population sharing the same ethnonational heritage (1994: 90–100). Thus, he distinguishes between "nationalism" and "ethnonationalism."

6 Eric Wolf (1982) argues that kin-organized societies have more rigid in-group/out-group boundaries under conditions of scarcity than when resources are abundant.

7 Percentages are calculated from the data supplied in Kuwait Ministry of Planning (1992: Table 11).

8 On February 4, 1995, the cabinet endorsed new family visa regulations that raised salary requirements for expatriates wishing to bring their families to Kuwait. At the same time, the government increased annual charges for bringing in various family members. The new policy was defended as a way to stimulate the domestic economy and reduce the number of men living on their own in Kuwait, but its impact is difficult to project given the simultaneous rise in salary requirements and the imposition of higher charges per non-Kuwaiti resident.

9 The state also provides every male Kuwaiti a low-interest loan for home construction and financial incentives to marry and bear children. Married Kuwaiti men working in the state sector receive a KD 50 per month allowance per child (about $170.00 US).

10 The integration of *bidun* into the Kuwaiti population through their high rates of participation in military and police forces puts them in a different category from foreigners with nationality living in Kuwait.

11 This provision never became law because the National Assembly was dissolved shortly afterward.

12 The total number of Kuwaitis in 1992 was 626,150 as reported in Kuwait Ministry of Planning (1995: 56), Central Statistical Office *Annual Statistical Abstract*.

13 Even while a husband is living, access to housing is heavily regulated by the state. For example, childless couples must live in state-owned apartments rather than houses, access to which goes preferentially to families with children. This policy reinforces social norms according to which unmarried children, particularly unmarried daughters, live with their parents. See Tétreault and al-Mughni (1995).

14 These trends are explored in greater detail in Tétreault (2000).

15 The *zakat* is the Islamic charitable tax that is collected from individuals and companies. Companies are supposed to pay at the rate of 2.5 percent of assets.

9 (Gender) struggles for the nation

Power, agency, and representation in Zimbabwe

Sita Ranchod-Nilsson

This chapter grows out of a period of rethinking my earlier work on African women's participation in the liberation struggle in Zimbabwe. In the late 1980s I set out to locate African women's participation in Zimbabwe's rural-based struggle for national liberation within a broader context of rural political economy. My research focused on the connections between women's roles in peasant agriculture, gender relations within households, and the many ways in which rural African women participated in the liberation struggle. This work drew upon a substantial body of literature on women's involvement in nationalist struggles that had been published during the previous decade. This literature highlighted women's active participation in nationalist movements throughout the former colonial world, and illuminated the "hidden" forms of women's participation and women's agendas that emerged from their involvement in nationalist struggles (see Eisen 1984; Geiger 1987, 1990; Jayawardena 1986; C. Johnson 1986; O'Barr 1976; Stacey 1983; Van Allen 1974, 1976). However, recent feminist scholarship, influenced by postmodern concerns with language, representation, and subjectivity, has shifted scholarly attention away from women's political agendas and collective organizing in the context of nationalist movements, to the multiple and even contradictory ways in which identities are implicated in the very idea or construction of "the nation." This work has powerfully demonstrated that nations have shifting meanings and boundaries. These are premised on particular notions of family, sexuality, and citizenship that are, in turn, based upon particular ideas about masculinity and femininity (see Eisenstein 1996; Gaitskell and Unterhalter 1989; McClintock 1993; Peterson 1994; Yuval-Davis and Anthias 1989). The emphasis has shifted from conceptualizing women as an interest group or constituency that participates in a social movement in exchange for greater access to state decision-making authority and resources, to broader exploration of the ways in which conceptual categories like "the state" and "citizen" are based upon particular gender identities.

The recent scholarship on women and nationalism, or gender and nationalism, also is influenced by the almost unavoidable engagement with postmodernism that characterizes much of contemporary feminist scholarship. While it is not within the scope of this chapter to put forth a description of postmodernism that would in any way do justice to the intellectual history and debates associated with it, two debates within feminist scholarship related to postmodernism are relevant to the problem addressed in this chapter. First, postmodern theorists criticize essentialist categories and universal theorizing. They argue that all knowledge is limited, based on the subjective experience of the individual self as situated within particular discursive and material contexts (see Butler 1990; Marchand and Parpart 1995; Nicholson 1990). Those concerned with feminist politics and social change criticize the emphasis on subjectivity and difference. If the category "women" does not exist, or if it loses coherence through an emphasis on difference, the very basis for political action is undermined (Alcoff 1988; Bordo 1990; DiStefano 1990). A second, related concern involves the emphasis on representation and discursive practices in constituting or constructing the subject/self. In the absence of universal truths, knowledge is local and constrained by language or discourse – "a historically, socially and institutionally specific structure of terms categories and beliefs – . . . where meanings are contested and power relations determined" (Scott 1988). The emphasis on representation and discursive practices raises questions about the role of individual and collective agency. If power is articulated primarily through discourse, what role, if any, does political activism play in altering social relations (Alcoff 1988; Fraser and Nicholson 1990)?

It is this problem, how to reconcile issues of subjectivity, representation and agency, that I want to address in this chapter using women's involvement in the national liberation struggle in Zimbabwe as a case study. Perhaps the central question becomes what is the meaning of gender dimensions of representation for the cultural construction of nations and the ways in which we understand women's activism, struggle, and involvement in nationalist movements? Is women's active participation misguided because it is undertaken in support of a political goal – the realization of state power by the nation – that is based upon their subordination? Is it even possible to identify a "women's agenda," or do multiple and even inconsistent agendas coexist? How can we reconcile women's active participation in nationalist struggles, participation that indicates the existence of such "women's agendas," feminist and not, with the broader issues of representation that, more often than not, clearly depict images of women in spaces associated with the household, with caretaking and nurturing, and with an overall position that is subordinate to men? The answers to these questions have clear implications for the ways in which we situate women's involvement in nationalist movements as well as for our understandings of citizenship and the gender dimensions of state power.

During most of the 1970s Zimbabwe, then Southern Rhodesia, was embroiled in an armed liberation struggle that eventually came to envelop most of the rural areas of the country. Despite the self-proclaimed socialist ideology of the Zimbabwe African Nationalist Union (ZANU), one of the main liberation movements that went on to control the government after independence, subsequent scholarship has most frequently identified the struggle as primarily nationalist with, at best, only limited transformative goals (Astrow 1983; Davies 1988; Mandaza 1986; Stoneman 1988; Sylvester 1990, 1991). This type of liberatory or anti-colonial nationalism was widespread throughout the colonized territories following World War II. Recognizing this, we need to consider the ways in which the goals of African liberation, or at least political independence from white settler rule, created particular dynamics within African nationalist movements. The construction of nations and national identities in this context might create very different dynamics from those shaped in more contemporary nationalist movements based primarily on ethnic, religious, and/or racial identities – examples include contemporary ethnonationalism in the former Yugoslavia or the racist, anti-immigrant sentiments expressed by Jean-Marie Le Pen and the National Front party in France.[1] While all nationalisms are based upon the demarcation of categories of "us" and "them," the ways in which gender identities get played out can be quite different. For example, in a number of armed anti-colonial struggles, nationalist gender ideology included "warrior women" who took up arms in defense of home and children (Eisen 1984; Gaitskell and Unterhalter 1989; Stacey 1983; Urdang 1979, 1989). However, in other nationalist movements there is no place for warrior women. There "the good nation-alist woman" is one who bears children for the nation, rears them to be loyal citizens, and suffers a mother's anguish when they are struck down in the nation's defense (McClintock 1993; Wells 1991).

This chapter begins by offering brief descriptions of what I have iden-tified as two general bodies of feminist literature dealing with nationalism and by describing in more detail my concerns about women's agency in nationalist movements. Then, I move to the case of Zimbabwe and describe how women's agency and their agendas constituted an integral part of the rural struggle. This material is based primarily on my own collection of oral data and analysis of the experiences of women in Wedza district.[2] Albeit limited, this glimpse into particular forms of women's participation and women's own imaginings about the nation suggests that women did have clear visions of how they wanted their lives to change as a result of their involvement in the nationalist movement. The final section suggests possible ways of reconciling the two bodies of literature and working toward a feminist perspective on nationalism that does not discount or overlook women's agency or women's own imaginings of the nation.

Feminist literature on nationalism

Feminist scholarship on nationalism has gone through at least two distinct phases. The first phase, during the 1970s and early 1980s, focused on women's active participation in national liberation struggles throughout the formerly colonized world. Case studies of these movements highlight women's meaningful, though often hidden, forms of participation; the connections between modernization, feminism, and nationalism; and the location of politics within the household. The second phase, influenced by postmodernism, post-colonial studies, and cultural studies, emerged in the late 1980s and focuses on the construction of the nation and the ways in which specific gender identities are embedded in the particular meanings of "the nation." These embedded gender meanings inform not only nationalist movements, but also continuing struggles over just who constitutes "insiders" and "outsiders" and where the fluid identity boundaries of "the nation" get drawn.

What I am referring to as the first phase of feminist scholarship on women's involvement in nationalist struggles involved primarily case studies of women's participation in anti-colonial movements. In parts of Africa, Asia, and the Middle East, modernization framed the assertion of national identities in ways that allowed for a limited coexistence of feminist and nationalist goals. Women's circumstances as a result of colonial capitalist expansion, together with the assertion of democratic rights in nationalist movements, set the stage for (limited) feminist struggles for political equality and policy reforms such as equality for women in the legal process, removal of discriminatory practices in employment and education, and the right to vote. In these early movements, women's struggles for autonomy and political rights were caught in the balance between local bourgeoisies and traditional political and religious authorities. Where the former dominated, nationalist movements promised limited legal reforms in the areas of political participation, education, property rights, and gender-based discriminatory practices. Where the latter dominated, limited reforms were also promised, but, more importantly, women were used as highly emotive symbols for the nationalism movements as guardians of national culture, tradition, and the family (Jayawardena 1986).

Other early works on women's involvement in anti-colonial struggles highlighted women's use of "traditional" forms of political protest (O'Barr 1976; Van Allen 1974; Wipper 1975–1976). In these cases, such as the Igbo "women's war" in Nigeria, women's symbolic power associated with so-called "traditional" practices was made all the more powerful when juxtaposed with "modernized" forms of political authority. Later work on women and nationalism established the significance of women's organizations in the development of nationalist movements (C. Johnson 1986; Walker 1982). For example, Susan Geiger's work on women activists in the Tanganyika African National Union (TANU) drew attention to the centrality of women's dance groups to nationalist organizing in Dar es Salaam. The dance groups "embodied nationalist principles" and provided strong support for TANU as well as networks through which the nationalist movement could mobilize (Geiger 1987). In this case the role of women's dance groups as significant organizations for mobilization challenged conventional conceptions of political space.

In several countries that experienced armed nationalist struggles, such as Mozambique, China and Vietnam, peasant women were able to push revolutionary movements to address their concerns within the context of broader transformative goals (see Eisen 1984; K. Johnson 1983; Stacey 1983; Tétreault 1994; Urdang 1979, 1989). In these cases the goals motivating women's involvement included access to community-based economic and political resources, and also transformations within the household through changes in state policies affecting marriage, property, and child custody.

This rich case study literature fundamentally altered understandings of both the forms and the location of participation in nationalist movements. No longer could explorations of nationalist politics be limited to describing membership in or activities in connection with nationalist organizations. These investigations of women's participation in nationalist movements revealed that domestic politics also shaped their dynamics and often in fundamental ways (Ranchod-Nilsson 1994: 77–82). As a consequence, the goals of nationalist movements, particularly for women, are not solely associated with the political structures and policies of the state but also with changes on the domestic front. This literature also demonstrated that nationalist movements involved both conflict between "colonizer" and "colonized" and conflict between men and women within nationalist movements. As Cynthia Enloe (1993) points out, "By taking women's experiences seriously, feminists have disclosed that women and men within nascent communities often struggle with each other over *whose* experiences . . . will define the community in its new national manifestation" (Enloe 1993: 232–233, emphasis in original).

While this early work on women and nationalism challenged the location, form, and focus of nationalist politics, it remained situated in broader narratives of class struggle, national independence, modernization, and state consolidation. In case after case women appeared to be losers because they were politically marginalized during periods of state consolidation following successful nationalist movements. Whether consigned to under-funded ministries or ghettoized in separate party organizations, "women's interests" never remained central to nationalist movements after those movements gained control of state power (Jacobs 1989; Kruks *et al.* 1989; Van Allen 1974; see also Geisler 1995). Women who were active in nationalist organizations on "equal" terms with men became less-than-full citizens after the attainment of state power. Ironically, most were chased back into the home by new constructions of "the good nationalist woman."

The second wave of feminist scholarship on nationalism does not focus on the activities undertaken by women in nationalist movements. Rather, it explores the ways in which gender shapes the construction of national identities. In the introduction to their substantial reader on nationalism, Eley and Suny (1996) write the following about feminist contributions to the study of nationalism:

Even more revolutionary in its effects on historical thinking [than recent scholarship on class interests], feminist theory has taken on the most naturalized of all categories, gender, and destabilized our understanding of the "natural" roles and capacities of women and men. The multiplicity, fluidity, contextual and contested qualities of identities that studies of gender have highlighted have undermined any notion of a single all-embracing primary identity to which all others must be subordinated at all times and costs.

(Eley and Suny 1996: 10)

Whereas much of the literature on nationalism emphasizes the conditions under which and/or the ways in which collective identities of nations are formed in opposition to outside groups, feminist scholarship has concentrated on the constructions and reconstructions of gender differences and hierarchies within what are generally construed to be "homogeneous" groups.

This literature has brought to light numerous ways in which women are implicated in the social constitution of "the nation." As biological and social reproducers women's bodies are claimed by the nation and in consequence often become battlegrounds in nationalist conflicts (Eisenstein 1994; McClintock 1993; Yuval-Davis and Anthias 1989). Because women biologically reproduce members of national collectivies, under what conditions, when, how many, and whose children women will bear become issues of national importance (to men) and civic duty or outright oppression (to women) (Peterson 1994; Tétreault 1997a). As mothers, women are the producers and transmitters of national culture (Gaitskell and Unterhalter 1989; Sharoni 1995). Through restrictions on sexual and marital relations, women reproduce the boundaries of national groups (Yuval-Davis and Anthias 1989). As the symbolic bearers of the nation, women also "define the limits of national difference and power *between* men" (McClintock 1993: 2, emphasis in original). So not only do women serve as powerful symbols of the nation, but also their bodies are used to demarcate national boundaries through pronatalist policies that make women's biological capacities into patriotic duties, or through campaigns of sexual violence and terror meant to denigrate those outside "the nation" (Stiglmayer 1994; Tétreault 1997a).

Because the very idea of the nation is premised on gender inequality, specifically the subordination of women, those writing about the gendered nature of nations are almost entirely pessimistic about the possibilities of women asserting their own agendas, feminist or not, in the context of nationalist movements. But reconciling women's activism in support of nationalism continues to pose a dilemma. Zillah Eisenstein (1996) acknowledges this uneasy alliance in the context of anti-colonial movements but sees the coexistence of anti-colonial feminist interests with nationalist movements as no more than "an intermediary step." She writes, "I continue to believe that no nationalism can fully include a multiracial/woman-specified democracy" (Eisenstein 1996: 15). Enloe (1993) also acknowledges this dilemma noting that while nationalism serves to perpetuate the privileging of masculinity,

> too many women have broken out of the confines of domesticity and have carved out a space in the public arena for me not to weigh carefully the anti-patriarchal consequences of that activism, even if they fall short of full emancipation and are achieved in spite of, not in harmonious alliance with, patriarchal nationalist men.
>
> (Enloe 1993: 230).

African women's involvement in nationalism in Zimbabwe

The case of Zimbabwe's struggle for national liberation provides a historically and culturally specific context in which to explore the dilemma posed in the previous section of this chapter. African women were very involved in the struggle for national liberation in a number of ways. During the early nationalist period, wives of African political leaders participated in auxiliary organizations that basically carried over domestic roles associated with food preparation and social gatherings to political movements. Later, during the armed struggle, young African women fled across the borders to the training camps of the military movements, the Zimbabwe African National Liberation Army (ZANLA) and the Zimbabwe People's Liberation Army (ZIPRA), to undergo military training and become armed combatants.[3] ZANLA trained male and female fighters together and also sent mixed groups of combatants back into the country.

The rural mobilization model was based on a Maoist strategy for winning the hearts and minds of the peasantry through infiltrating rural villages. Because many rural areas, including Wedza district, had high rates of male out-migration, it was especially important for the combatants to gain the support of rural women. Women supported local bands of guerrillas by providing domestic services such as cooking and laundry. They also hid combatants, carried supplies and weapons, and provided information about local "sell-outs" or informants and the location and number of Rhodesian troops. Elsewhere, I have argued that women combatants and rural women supporters participated in the national liberation struggle for a variety of reasons that reflect the ways in which gender and generational differences were configured by colonial and customary practices (Ranchod-Nilsson 1992b, 1994). But, in the course of making these connections, women combatants and rural women supporters also revealed their own agendas for changes they wanted to see in the new nation. In the course of discussing the liberation war and their participation in it, many women clearly articulated their hopes for different – improved – living circumstances following independence. If one takes seriously women's agency in all the many ways they participated as activists in the nationalist movement, it makes sense to ask if that agency was consistent with a construction of "the nation" that, as recent feminist scholarship has powerfully argued, is premised on women's subordination within the family and within the nation.

As mentioned earlier in this chapter, the liberation struggle in Zimbabwe was primarily a nationalist struggle. Notwithstanding the claims of some movement activists that they supported "African socialism" or "scientific socialism," this was first and foremost a struggle for African control of the state (Astrow 1983; Mandaza 1986). Led by educated urban elites, this particular form of nationalism also relied on the support and input of the rural population. Terence Ranger (1985) has identified this form of nationalism as "peasant nationalism," the consciousness developed as the result of the struggle to retain "the peasant option" in the face of colonial policies of land alienation and forced cultivation methods.[4] It was expressed within the idiom of "traditional" religion, which was also the most important factor shaping the dynamics of rural mobilization (Ranger 1985; see also Lan 1985). Thus, this struggle involved the (re)creation and assertion of an African cultural identity within the struggle for political control of the state.

But this nationalist, or peasant nationalist, struggle should not be conceptualized in a linear or teleological fashion. Scholarship on Zimbabwe's guerrilla war has demonstrated that, in many ways, the struggle for national liberation was neither unified nor always clear about political goals. The liberation war was waged by political movements that, despite the creation of the Patriotic Front in 1978, had different ideological goals, different strategies for rural mobilization during the guerrilla war, and different regional bases of support among the population (Astrow 1983; Bhebe and Ranger 1995; Lan 1985; Martin and Johnson 1985; Moore 1991; Ranger 1985). Other scholars have demonstrated how the conflict between Africans and the white minority regime of Ian Smith and the Rhodesian Front was only one axis along which much broader social conflicts, or one revolution among others, got played out during the national liberation struggle. For example, Kriger (1988, 1992) argues that rural mobilization during the liberation war was shaped more by local tensions based on gender, generation, and lineage than on the ideological message of the liberation movements. She argues that rural dwellers were motivated less by the political goals of the guerrillas than by a combination of fear of the guerrillas and opportunities created by the breakdown of rural political authority to settle scores on the local level. Sylvester (1990) rejects an "ideal-typical model of revolution," that is in any way "teleological, holistic or binary." Instead, she understands the liberation struggle as a series of revolutions in the Gramscian sense. Multiple revolutions unfolded simultaneously and included struggles within the peasantry based upon gender, generation and lineage tensions (Sylvester 1990). These works suggest that even within this particular form of anti-colonial nationalism there were multiple spaces for women's activism inside and outside the organized nationalist movements. They also call into question the political strength of the nationalist movements and, hence, the extent to which any particular understanding of "the nation" dominated the liberation struggle.

African women participated in the liberation struggle in many different ways; factors such as age, education, marital status, household configuration, and whether and how they participated in rural agriculture shaped their choices among various forms of activism. Women assumed positions as armed combatants, members of the general staff, refugees in camps, rural supporters in villages – even in the government's protected villages known as "keeps" – and *chimbwidos*, the teen-aged girls who often traveled with the combatants in rural areas, despite the misgivings of their parents.[5] In this section I focus on female combatants and rural women supporters living in villages because women filling these roles were predominant among those I interviewed in Zimbabwe.

Large numbers of African women joined the liberation movements, underwent military training together with men, and fought side-by-side with them during the war. According to some estimates, by the middle of the war (about 1977), between one-quarter and one-third of the thirty thousand Zimbabwe National Liberation Army combatants were women, and thousands of other women lived and worked in the camps in non-military capacities.[6] A number of women even held positions of authority within the hierarchies of the military command structure and the general staff. The involvement of large numbers of primarily young African women combatants was not so much the result of active recruitment or commitments to gender equality on the part of the liberation movements. To the contrary, ZANU/ZANLA may have come to its rather limited commitments to "women's liberation" – which were most clearly articulated in 1978 and 1979, just eighteen months before the ceasefire – more as a result of practical considerations related to the number of young women crossing the border to join the liberation army than as a guiding principle for social transformation (Ranchod-Nilsson 1992b).

In the early period of the armed struggle, African women were not trained as combatants. They participated primarily by carrying supplies across the border to Zambia because the Rhodesian authorities were unlikely to suspect that women would be activists. But by 1973, young women were in training to become combatants in ZANLA. Training women had a strategic purpose: to mobilize the rural population and to shame rural men into joining the struggle. Between 1973 and 1976, the numbers of young women and men who left secondary schools to cross the borders and join the military movements grew dramatically. Many of the young women left rural boarding schools with groups of their friends; others followed brothers and boyfriends; still others were kidnapped by groups of combatants operating inside the country. I also found some evidence to suggest that at least some of the young women who joined the military movement did so to escape "traditional" marriage practices and the lack of educational and employment opportunities for women in rural areas.

One consequence of the dramatic growth in the numbers of both male and female recruits was that traditional gender hierarchies were officially disregarded in terms of military command structures and also in the division of labor within the camps. Women commanders were to be obeyed in the same way male commanders were obeyed, and both men and women participated in camp duties such as cooking, fetching drinking water, and gathering firewood. A male ex-combatant suggested that the military training created a kind of equality between men and women:

> We trained together in Tanzania . . . after the training we were all just alike. No one ever said, "ah this woman is doing that" because you see they were also given posts like . . . she's a commander and I'm not a commander. She could give orders . . . and [this] was rare in our culture. So, from there I think we built up togetherness or some equality during that time.
>
> (interview in Harare, November 20, 1988)

A female ex-combatant named Tainie Mudondo describes her experience in similar terms:

> There is something I want to say about life in the camps: there was no difference between men and women. If there was any job to be done, like fetching water or wood, both men and women were detailed to do it, although fetching wood and water is traditionally women's work.
>
> (quoted in Weiss 1986: 90)

These new gender relations did not develop without some difficulties, particularly during the early stages of the war when some male commanders used their positions of power to gain sexual access to women combatants and other women in the military camps. Although female fighters did acquire a kind of equality with men in the military camps, when they were fighting inside the country these women did not always assert their equality with either their male counterparts or with rural authorities. Nevertheless, toward the end of the war, ZANU was publicly advocating "women's liberation" as part of a broader goal of building socialism. At the first ZANU Women's Seminar in May 1979, Robert Mugabe, ZANU's leader and Zimbabwe's current president, praised women for their participation in the armed struggle, saying that the war had become "as much a process towards the liberation of the nation as towards the emancipation of women" (Mugabe 1979: 22).

For women combatants, their experiences in the military camps and ZANU's rhetoric about women's liberation led many to expect that, after independence, the new nation they had been fighting for would recognize in policy and practice the equality of men and women. Many young women who became combatants had left their homes to join the military struggle because they knew that they were being denied educational and economic opportunities by the confluence of interests between the colonial state and African patriarchal authorities. These women expected that after proving themselves in the military struggle, they would no longer be denied access to these opportunities. Moreover, those young women who had fled their homes to avoid marriage and "traditional" marriage practices expected changes in the social practices associated with *lobola*, or brideprice.[7] They resisted this form of marriage that, for too many women, meant being under the complete control of a man and his family, and many articulated a desire for marriage without *lobola* (Ranchod-Nilsson 1992b, 180–184).

African women who lived in Wedza district during the national liberation struggle were also active participants in the movement, but their agendas reflected somewhat different interests than those expressed by the young women combatants. Women who remained in the rural areas during the war were older than those who became combatants, if only by a few years, and most of them were agricultural producers. Like the women combatants, their concerns also were shaped by colonialism and African patriarchal practices but in very different ways.

Wedza district is located approximately 170 kilometers southeast of Zimbabwe's capital, Harare (known as Salisbury before independence in 1980). Its location on a high plateau meant that agricultural conditions, both for growing crops and for grazing cattle, were relatively good. Wedza district's close proximity to the capital also meant that, in the communal areas, rates of male out-migration were relatively high.[8] Consequently most of the people living there during the war were women, and they were the ones mobilized by the liberation forces. From 1976 until the ceasefire in 1979, Wedza district was simultaneously occupied by ZANLA and by Rhodesian soldiers. Neither side could claim to control the territory; instead local residents described the Rhodesian soldiers as being in control during the day while the combatants were in control during the night. This created an extremely tense situation for local villagers who were literally caught between these two opposed armed forces.

A few women in the district had been active in African nationalist politics before the movements were driven underground by the Rhodesian Front in 1962, and they were able to articulate nationalist positions on education, employment, and political rights. Many more rural women, however, got their information about the war from wildly disparate sources and, therefore, did not – could not – simply reiterate the goals of the nationalist movements. Some rural women knew about nationalist movements from Rhodesian propaganda that painted frightening pictures of terrorists and *gandangas*, strange people with tails (see Frederikse 1982); others got information from

the families of young relatives who had left school to join the military struggle; still other women relied on information from their own children who
came home from boarding schools during holidays with stories about meeting the combatants at their schools. Nevertheless, their own experiences
combined with their interaction with the combatants, did result in clearly
articulated visions by rural women of changes they wanted in connection
with their support for the nationalist struggle. While some of these changes
were consistent with the agenda of the liberation movements articulated
by the combatants, others were based on the experiences and desires of the
rural women themselves.

At all-night village mobilization sessions known as *pungwe*, groups of
guerrillas explained why they had come to liberate African people from
the white settlers and from colonial rule. For the most part, despite their
initial fears, women responded positively to the combatants' agenda of
grievances over lost land, lack of education and employment opportunities, and racial discrimination. The village residents formed support
committees to collect money, food, and other supplies for local combatant
groups, and to carry food and supplies to the camps and do combatants'
laundry. Women figured prominently in these village efforts. In one village,
women even claimed that their support committee was far superior to one
in a neighboring village, where the committee was led by men, because
the women had more organizational experience and better communication
skills as a result of their participation in African women's homecraft clubs
(Ranchod-Nilsson 1992a). Women also came up with clever ways of smug-
gling food and other supplies to the guerrillas – hiding guns in the middle
of a bundle of firewood or wrapping them in blankets to look like babies
(see also Staunton 1990; Weiss 1986).

The combatant's mobilizing efforts were framed in terms taken from
cultural nationalism and carried out through the idioms of traditional religion and family life. These idioms revealed assumptions about proper
gender identities for men and women. Combatants referred to themselves
as the children of the parents at the *pungwe* as well as calling themselves "the children of Zimbabwe." Rural women, then, were celebrated
as "mothers of the revolution," both during the liberation struggle and,
later, after independence. The combatants celebrated women's strong
maternal ties to them, their figurative children, and to the land. The liberation movements revered rural women who took on a maternal role *vis-à-vis*
combatant groups. After the war, they were similarly revered by the state
as well. But not all women fit the role of the revolutionary mother. Women
accused of witchcraft or prostitution were, in many cases, treated as "sell-
outs" and publicly punished by guerrilla groups.

But African women did not just passively respond to the demands of
guerrillas. On the contrary, their own accounts of their involvement suggest
that they had clear agendas for political change that they wanted to insert
into the broader programs outlined by various combatant groups. As the

guerrillas established their authority in rural areas they were confronted with local problems they had not anticipated – women went to them with domestic problems involving, among other things, lack of financial support from their husbands, domestic abuse, jealousy over their husbands' girl-friends, and unwanted divorces. In their advice and intervention, the guerrillas were most often sympathetic to women, attempting to resolve disputes in a number of ways that varied from village to village and over time. In some cases, they spoke privately with the husband or with the husband and wife together, in other cases, disputes were discussed publicly at *pungwes*. Sometimes, guerrillas reasoned with men, threatened them, and even beat them. Women occasionally expressed fear that the guerrillas would kill their husbands, although I never located any evidence of a husband who had been killed in this context.

An examination of rural women's accounts of their experiences in the national liberation struggle reveals their own ideas about "the nation" and a clear vision of the ways in which they hoped their lives after the war would be substantially different from what they had become under late colonialism. Rural women in Wedza had little interest either in equality between men and women or in "scientific socialism." They sought to regain control over their economic livelihoods and domestic authority. According to anthropologist David Lan (1985), the grievances of rural dwellers were expressed in two main desires: "to regain the lost lands and *to regain the control which the people had lost over their lives*" (Lan 1985: 123, emphasis added). The issues of domestic conflict that women raised with the guerrillas suggest that they were conscious that within their households they had lost significant status previously associated with marriage, age, and women's community roles as religious leaders and artisans. If rural women were imagining "the nation" as they put themselves at risk to support combatant groups during the liberation war, their own accounts suggest that the nation they imagined was based on reconfigured ideas of masculinity and femininity. These ideas were not composed in terms of western feminism or notions of gender equality. Rather they concentrated on allowing women to regain authority in their households that they felt was rightfully theirs, such as control over their own mobility and sexu-ality, and access to resources that would allow them to fulfill what they themselves identified as their "traditional" responsibilities.

Women combatants and rural women supporters thus did not share the same agenda during the liberation war. Also, the climate of pervasive fear that dominated all rural interactions during the war meant that there were few opportunities for rural dwellers, male or female, to express their shock at and disapproval of women combatants. Rural guerrilla groups were, however, aware that women combatants posed a challenge to rural patri-archal relations. In many cases, women combatants did not deal directly with rural villagers. But the post-war experience of female ex-combatants suggests that their military involvement, their fighting, training, and travelling with the male combatants, as well as the overall challenge to patriarchal authority posed by the youthfulness and sexuality of the guerrillas, was incompatible with accepted gender identities and roles (Geisler 1995; Jacobs 1989; Ranchod-Nilsson 1997). Women ex-combatants returning to rural villages were more likely to be greeted with suspicion and disapproval from family members, particularly men, than with the cheers and accolades befitting heroes (Weiss 1986).

From these accounts it is clear that women combatants and rural women supporters in Wedza district did not share the same vision or imagining of the new nation they were fighting for or of their places within it. Young women combatants were keenly aware of issues of gender equality, and this awareness was reinforced by some of their experiences as activists in the liberation movements. The youthful make-up of the armed movements also reinforced a challenge to parental, more specifically patriarchal, authority which for at least some women combatants was associated with the eradication of oppressive marriage practices (see Kriger 1992; Ranchod-Nilsson 1992b; Ranger 1985). Women combatants also wanted better access to education and economic opportunities as well as mobility that had been denied by a combination of colonial and African patriarchal interests. To some extent, these desires were reflected in ZANU's public lauding of women combatants and its public commitments to women's equality toward the end of the liberation war. But it is important to point out that these commitments, although public, were not part of, and in many cases were even contradicted by people's experiences in rural areas during the war.

Rural women's agendas for change were in many ways quite different. Rural women with primary responsibility for agriculture wanted increased access to land and decision-making authority in connection with their agricultural labor both within the household and *vis-à-vis* local government authorities. They wanted fair prices for their agricultural products, and access to education for all of their children, particularly their daughters, and also for themselves.[9] In addition, women wanted access to waged employment, increased social mobility, and an end to what they viewed as a sexual double standard – women are constrained by suspicion about their sexual behavior framed as intimations that they might be prostitutes, while men have few social sanctions associated with their sexual activities. The public airing of domestic disputes by rural women suggests that, for many of them, the new nation meant altered gender relations within households in connection with multiple issues: division of labor, economic authority, sexuality, and mobility.

To the extent that women participated in the national liberation struggle in varied capacities, they expressed multiple, and even contradictory visions of and hopes for their lives in the new nation. These multiple perspectives could coexist without coming directly into conflict during the liberation war because the liberation movements remained factionalized throughout the long struggle. And even though ZANLA guerrillas, and, later, the government of Robert Mugabe and ZANU(PF), celebrated "mothers of the revolution" (and, to a much lesser extent, the "warrior women" combatants), these images and representations are only two-dimensional cut-outs as compared to the complex understandings women had of "the nation," far too narrowly imagined to account for women's active involvement in the national liberation struggle.

Agency and representation

In the case of women's involvement in Zimbabwe's national liberation struggle, women's political agency cannot be understood exclusively as a reflection of a gendered construction of "the nation." While the iconography of the nation was in large part based on images of women either as "mothers of the revolution," or as "warrior women," these images were, in many ways, contradictory and neither vision was ubiquitous during the war. Within ZANU/ZANLA, the movement that dominated guerrilla activity in Wedza district, "warrior women" presented a blatant challenge to rural patriarchal authority and, consequently, did not figure prominently in rural mobilization efforts. Throughout the country women took advantage of multiple spaces in the nationalist struggle – within competing movements, military camps and rural villages – to insert their own agendas and desires into the many nascent discourses about "the nation." While some of their concerns clearly involved access to state power and resources, other concerns were centered on the local gender dynamics of communities and households. Even though rural women may have considered themselves "mothers of the revolution," their concerns, revealed within the context of the rural struggle, went far beyond the narrow, domestic realm implied by the image of "mother."

The struggle to dominate how these myriad candidates for inclusion were combined to define "the nation" did not take place until after independence in 1980 when ZANU transformed itself from a liberation movement into a governing party. This party has maintained political power since independence by creating and recreating categories of insiders and outsiders largely in terms of references to the country's liberation struggle. Occupants of each category have shifted dramatically during this period. This is particularly true with respect to African women, whose experiences have not lived up to their expectations or "imaginings" during the nationalist struggle.

Initial government policies and practices held some promise – for example, the new government created a Ministry of Community Development and Women's Affairs, initially staffed by many enthusiastic, professional women. It passed laws giving women the status of adults, property rights in marriage and maintenance payments from men who fathered their children; and it embarked on massive programs to make education and primary health care universally accessible. However, over time, these efforts grew anemic, suffering from lack of funding, lack of enforcement, and a general lack of interest on the part of policymakers. At the same time, more troubling trends emerged involving repeated government round-ups of women alleged to be prostitutes, recurring public attacks blaming women for a host of social problems ranging from domestic violence to "baby-dumping," and, recently, an emerging public discourse about Zimbabwe's "cultural crisis" that seems to boil down to women not knowing their appropriate place – which is within the household, under the control of a man (Ranchod-Nilsson 1997; also see Geisler 1995). Rural women have also been short-changed in the government's very limited attempts at land resettlement (Jacobs 1989).

These trends suggest that women are not full citizens of the nation regardless of their political agency and active participation in the nationalist struggle. The divergence between expectations and outcomes is a function of the divergence in how participants experienced and understood the movement. A detailed understanding of the ways in which the gender story unfolded in the context of the struggle for national liberation in Zimbabwe demonstrates how and why a single, coherent cultural framework of "the nation" began to emerge only after independence. Prior to that, multiple frameworks coexisted each holding out different gender possibilities for the new nation. During the war, women took advantage of the political spaces open to them to assert their own desires for change within households, within local communities, and at the level of the state. Any assessment of change resulting from women's participation in the nationalist movement would, therefore, have to address changes, not only in state policies and institutions, but also changes in gender relations within households.

The two bodies of literature referred to in the first section of this chapter provide useful insights into women's participation in nationalist movements that need not be conceptualized in mutually exclusive ways. In this case, the construction of "the nation" may have been based on gender hierarchy/male supremacy, but during the liberation war, the evidence suggests that no single vision of "the nation" dominated the multiple factions that made up the "liberation movement," and the multiple sites of political conflict. Women's active participation helped shape competing visions of "the nation" that only partially centered on state power. Given a different constellation of victorious forces, an entirely different Zimbabwean nation might equally well have emerged.

Notes

1   Some of the differences I am suggesting are quite subtle. For example, although the nationalist movement in Southern Rhodesia was primarily anti-colonial, it also involved internal conflicts based upon ethnic, lineage, and regional identities crucial in shaping the dynamics of both the rural struggle and of later

configurations of who was "inside" and "outside" the nation (see Kriger 1988, 1992; Sylvester 1990; Werbner 1991).

2 Because my information comes from one district, generalizations about women's participation in other areas of the country, unless otherwise noted, are speculative and require further research.

3 A high degree of international involvement, class division among Africans and, to a certain extent, the politicization of ethnic differences led to deep factions within and changing alliances among several liberation movements. However, toward the end of the war, there were two main military movements, ZANU and ZAPU and their military wings, ZANLA and ZIPRA. Only ZANU/ ZANLA were operative in Wedza district, and my discussion reflects this. However, I do not wish to imply that ZANU/ZANLA were the only ones who fought the war. That clearly was not the case.

4 Ranger uses the term "peasant option" to refer to the choice of African agricultural producers to participate in commodity production on their own terms as entrepreneurs in the market (Ranger 1985: 25). This can be contrasted with the colonial imperative to draw Africans into capitalist economic relations as rural and urban laborers instead of as agricultural producers.

5 During the war, guerrilla groups organized rural youth separately into *chimbwidos*, young women supporters, and *mujibas*, young male supporters. These young people acted as liaisons between the rural civilian populations and the groups of guerrillas. Because of their close ties to the guerrilla groups, these young men and women often exceeded their authority. In addition rural parents were particularly upset about chimbwidos traveling with guerrillas and staying at their bases because they did not want their daughters to have sexual relations with the guerrillas.

6 These figures are taken from Gay Seidman (1984) and Olivia Muchena (1984) respectively. These figures may be overstated by the inclusion of women who were living in the camps as refugees or in capacities other than as military personnel (personal communication, Norma Kriger, 1989).

7 For analyses of the ways in which the colonial codification of African customary law altered African marriage practices in ways that were particularly detrimental to women see Elizabeth Schmidt (1990) and Martin Chanock (1982).

8 The colonial state alienated vast stretches of African land and subsequently designated land in racial terms. Europeans were allocated large tracts for commercial farms whereas Africans were allocated much smaller plots held communally and meant to meet only bare subsistence needs. These latter areas are generally located in parts of the country that are more densely populated and have poorer agricultural conditions than other parts of the country. During the colonial period such areas were known as "native reserves," and later became known as "communal areas." District authorities did not keep track of male labor migration during the colonial period. Studies conducted in Wedza district after independence in 1980 yield varying figures such as 41 percent of households have a male "head of household" working away from home (Callear 1982), that half of the men in a survey identify themselves as migrant laborers (Truscott 1985) and, in my own sample, that 63 percent of women surveyed reported that their husbands migrated to towns for employment (Ranchod-Nilsson 1992b).

9 See Elizabeth Schmidt (1992) for a discussion of how Africans, and particularly African women, were systematically disadvantaged in colonial agricultural policies.

10 Citizen-soldiers or republican mothers

US citizenship and military obligation in an era of "choice"

Cheryl Logan Sparks

The recent barrage of sexual harassment and assault charges within the United States military comes despite a concerted and apparently sincere effort by the Department of Defense to improve the treatment of women in their ranks. The campaign to recruit and retain more women has increased the percentage of female enlistees to 20 percent, and retention and promotion rates are rising steadily. Over 80 percent of job categories in the US military are now open to women as a result of changes in combat restrictions. Sensitivity training and sexual harassment courses have been incorporated into the regular training schedule throughout the military, and all branches, except the Marine Corps, currently employ a "gender-integrated" basic training program.[1]

Although these efforts are laudable, many critics argue that the only way to reform gender relations within the military is for women and men to be truly equal. As retired Army Major Lillian Pfluke has noted, "women are still totally excluded from any position that engages in direct ground combat. So you have the "haves" and the "have-nots." Any time you have two classes of people, you're going to have some kind of tension. You have some people thinking they're superior to the others."[2] Unfortunately, the steps that the military has taken toward integrating women may have heightened that tension, leaving many male soldiers feeling not only that they are superior, but also that their rights are being trampled in the military's scramble to attract and promote more women. Since the 1970s, the US military has adjusted physical fitness standards to accommodate women or allowed women to meet a "gender norm" instead of the male-defined minimums. This policy sparked considerable resentment among military men, reinforcing their view that women soldiers cannot compete physically. A more serious source of friction, however, may be their perception – whether right or wrong – that women share equally in the benefits offered by the military, but do not face an equal level of risk, since they are excluded by law from the ground-combat positions that are usually considered the most dangerous.[3] Still, despite a widespread belief that women are being favored under the current system, most military men in the United States continue to oppose allowing women in ground-combat positions. Military women (most of whom have no personal desire to engage in active combat) generally concur, although they are more likely to argue that women who desire and who are qualified for front-line positions should have the *option* to serve (Harrell and Miller 1997; Moskos 1990).

Since there is, however, virtually no chance that the United States would adopt a policy granting male soldiers a similar option to avoid combat arms assignments, allowing women to choose whether or not to participate would do little to alter the perception that they receive special treatment (see Burk 1995; Moskos 1993). As sociologist Charles Moskos (1990) noted in his study of women in the US Army:

> The core question – the one avoided in public debate, but the one that the women soldiers I spoke with in Panama were all too aware of – is this: Should every woman soldier be made to confront exactly the same combat liabilities as every man? All male soldiers can, if need arises, be assigned to the combat arms, whatever their normal postings. True equality would mean that women soldiers would incur the same liability. To allow women but not men the option of entering or not entering the combat arms would – rightly or wrongly – cause immense resentment among male soldiers; in a single stroke it would diminish the status and respect that female soldiers have achieved.
>
> (Moskos 1990)

A study by Laura Miller (1997) suggests that there is indeed a growing resentment among men in the Army, many of whom believe that women are the "favored gender" in the military at this time. Although Miller notes that structural analyses of the military indicate that this is far from true, some male soldiers feel that they are being treated unfairly and therefore adopt tactics that are typical of oppressed groups. One such behavior is harassment of the group that is seen as being more powerful; thus, Miller suggests that male soldiers' perceptions that they are the victims of gender bias may lead them to sexually harass the female soldiers who, in their view, are taking unfair advantage of the system.

A similar feeling of resentment is apparent in many of the young men who are required to register with the US Selective Service after their eighteenth birthday. They contend that *civilian* women – who are automatically exempted on the basis of sex – are also receiving preferential treatment when it comes to military obligation. One young draft registrant, Auren Hoffman (no date), summed up this sentiment in a recent editorial:

> As a patriot and an American, I understand the necessity of registering for the draft. Also, my financial aid depended on my registration – so I was doubly interested in signing up to be eligible for the draft. After reading the Selective Service papers, I found out that only men

had to register. I have to admit, I was dumbfounded. Today, over four years later, I still do not understand the logic of not requiring women to register. . . . Our armed forces are making strides to include women in combat and other key positions. Why then should women escape the draft? . . . I doubt that such a policy would stand up in court. It is blatant bias and [the] inference that only men add value to the armed forces is discriminatory, wrong, and has no place in our society.

Hoffman may be correct in stating that the policy could no longer withstand a legal challenge. Although the US Supreme Court ruled that the males-only registration policy was constitutional in *Rostker v. Goldberg* (1981), that decision rested heavily on the argument that the draft is intended to fill combat positions, which women could not legally hold at that time. When President Clinton requested a re-examination of the situation in 1994, in light of the recent changes opening some combat positions to women, the Department of Defense (1997) claimed that the policy remains "justifiable," given women's continued exemption from front-line positions. This does not guarantee that the courts would agree, however, and the policy remains a bit tenuous even under current combat rules. If the combat exclusion is entirely discarded at some point in the future, young women would almost certainly be required to register for the draft.

Underlying the resentment of both draft registrants and male soldiers is the perception that women have a greater degree of "choice" in determining their level of responsibility for the national defense. American men see their options as being restrained by the government. They *must* register because they are male and they *must* accept combat duty because they are male.[4] American women, on the other hand, can choose whether to enter the military during time of war and have greater latitude in deciding how much danger they will face. Some also argue that women can "choose" to become pregnant when hostilities are imminent, thus evading combat or even deployment. Thus, those who criticize the fairness of the current system maintain that women get all of the benefits of US citizenship and all of the benefits of military service without incurring the full range of liabilities and responsibilities.

The obvious counterpoint to this argument is that women get short-changed in so many other areas of civic and social life that any preferential treatment in the area of military obligation does not even begin to balance the scale. While this is true, military service has, throughout American history, played a central role in the determination of citizenship. The strong historical connection between the obligation to risk one's life for the state and citizenship in that state thus raises the question of whether women can be fully accepted as citizens (or as soldiers) if they continue to be excused from this requirement solely because of their sex.

Obligation, citizenship, and gender

The issue of obligation to authority lies at the very core of political theory, so it is not particularly surprising that many volumes have been written addressing the duties that citizens owe to the state. Few of these, however, deal with the very different ways that we conceptualize this obligation for men and women. Again, this is not surprising, since the "citizens" discussed by early political theorists were clearly male heads-of-households. Indeed, the virtues that are required in the ideal citizen are often depicted as the antithesis of feminine attributes – as when Hobbes says that men who run from battle are of "womanly courage" and Machiavelli states that a prince will be despised if he gains a reputation of being effeminate. Much of the work by feminist political theorists over the past several decades has been devoted to sorting out exactly what happens to these canonical texts when women (not as family members, but as autonomous citizens) are added to the mix. In many cases, the theory becomes an unrecognizable mess, because it depended at its core on strict adherence to a system of separate spheres of activity for men and women.[5]

One would expect the situation to be different in contemporary political theory. But the modern works that deal explicitly with issues of citizenship and obligation, including Michael Walzer's (1970) *Obligations: Essays on Disobedience, War, and Citizenship,* pay scant attention to the fact that one half of the citizens they are discussing are women, who are excused en masse from the most onerous duty required by the state.[6] As Linda Kerber (1995) notes, our concept of civic obligation has generally included four specific duties: "the obligation of allegiance (and its corollary, the obligation to refrain from treason), the obligation to pay taxes, the obligation to serve on juries, and the obligation to risk one's life in military service" (1995: 27). Women have always been held accountable to some degree for the first two duties, but the last two obligations to the state – both of which remove the woman from the home at least temporarily – were traditionally waived in deference to the presumably higher claim of the husband. Under early American law, wives were treated much the same as property, and it was held that the husband's right to the labor and services of his "property" would be infringed if his wife was required to perform civic duties outside the home. Jury service, the less burdensome of the two public obligations, was extended to women only after suffrage was won, and then on a piecemeal basis. A few US states began allowing women to serve on juries during the early 1920s, but this was generally framed as a right, not an obligation. As late as the 1970s, some states continued to grant women an automatic exemption if they claimed their services were needed at home, making it very difficult for women accused of a crime to truly be heard by a "jury of their peers." Only after the US Supreme Court's decision in *Taylor v. Louisiana* (1975) were states required to change their laws so that women were automatically included in the pool of potential jurors and faced an equal obligation to serve when called.

In a similar fashion, the *right* to participate in most areas of military service has gradually been extended to women over the course of the twentieth century, but the *obligation* to serve – even in non-combat roles – has remained conspicuously absent. It would appear that, in this one instance, the body politic has been willing to waive its usual insistence that rights must be paired with duties to the state. Many justifications are given for this exception to the rule, ranging from women's presumed inferiority in combat situations to the necessity of someone remaining at home to assume the jobs that men vacate when they go off to war – although there would, of course, be fewer vacancies to fill if half of those required to fight were female. Behind most of these arguments, however, lies the deeper realization that even if women prove themselves capable of fulfilling any male role during war-time, the reverse is not true – men cannot give birth to the next generation of soldiers.

Life-givers and life-takers

The idea that women are the biologically designated "life-givers" – and men, therefore, the "life-takers" – is deeply seated in our culture.[7] David Horowitz, a frequent writer for the *National Review*, typifies this view, arguing that any claim of a right to participate in combat is inherently flawed because

> there are definite limits to equal rights and equal opportunity when biology is involved. Do American males have the right to bear children? Do they have an equal opportunity with women to do so? Do they have an equal aptitude for combat? Ninety per cent of those arrested for violent crimes are male. Obviously males have a distinct advantage over females in mobilizing an existing instinct for aggression.
>
> (David Horowitz 1992: 46)

This "life-giver" and "life-taker" analogy is also one of the most common refrains in contemporary arguments against women assuming a more active role in military combat. As one high-ranking US military officer expressed it:

> Combat is finding . . . closing with . . . and killing or capturing the enemy. It's KILLING. . . . And women CAN'T DO IT! Nor should they even be thought of as doing it. The requirements for strength and endurance render them UNABLE to do it. And I may be old-fashioned, but I think the very nature of women disqualifies them from doing it. Women give life. Sustain life. Nurture life. They don't TAKE it.[8]

Other proponents of this view go even further, arguing that this division is a product of evolution that goes beyond reproduction, as "men and women developed separate and distinct physical, emotional, and biological characteristics because of the different demands of their roles – women as child-bearers, homemakers, nurturers; men as warriors and hunters" (Sasser 1992: 40).

It is clear to most dispassionate observers that these depictions are true merely of *some* women and *some* men under specific conditions, but this dichotomous view of male and female roles is widely accepted in the US military – and not by male soldiers alone. Interviews with military women (and especially enlisted women) show that they have rather traditional views of gender roles in general, but particularly when it comes to the issue of combat:

> That's the nature of human beings. A man is going to be dominant over a woman.

> I don't believe that women have it in them to just take up a gun and shoot somebody they don't even know. Some men don't either. But men are trained that they may have to fight. We weren't, and I don't think that will change.

> Women have always, always been the nurturer. You nurture, you take care of, that's been ingrained in you from the time you were a little bitty thing. To deliberately go out and be the hunter is a role that I think women would have trouble with.[9]

The American public also appears reluctant to put women in the role of the "hunter." Although opinion polls indicate that around 55 percent of the public favors allowing women to go into combat if they *choose* to, they are very uncomfortable with the idea of imposing this burden on those women who prefer to be "nurturers." Any suggestion that women could be conscripted for military service instantly evokes comments about motherhood, the continuation of the species, and basic differences in the natures of men and women. During the Persian Gulf War, viewers were bombarded with media images of military mothers leaving tearful children as they were deployed. Commentators rarely mentioned that women were only 6.8 percent of the entire US contingent, or that a far greater number of military *fathers* were being taken from their families, as they have been throughout history when the nation required their service.[10]

The sole consolation for many observers was that the women heading off to war had, after all, volunteered for a career in the military and should have anticipated the potential costs to their children and families. Since there was no need to reinstate the draft during the Gulf War – and since women continue to be safely exempt from registration – we were able to avoid the issue of what could happen in the not-too-distant future when the women being deployed are not volunteers, but conscripts. We will not always have this luxury, however, so it may be useful to consider why the issues of motherhood and civic obligation continue to be so closely inter-twined in US political culture.

Maternal obligation

In her discussion of the gendered nature of citizenship in the US and else-where, Cynthia Enloe (1992) states that Americans tend to equate "first-class citizenship" with self-sacrifice and the state-ordained use of violence, both of which "have been imagined in American culture to be masculine domains" (Enloe 1992: 15). Enloe emphasizes that the "selfless sacrifice" must be violent in nature in order to qualify one for citizenship of the highest order, and this is probably true. A century ago, however, women's rights activists were willing to make a few compromises, settling for what we would today consider "slightly-less-than-first-class" citizenship by emphasizing the sacrifices that women could and did make on behalf of the state. The arguments that suffragists used to justify granting women the vote played on the powerful ideological notion of separate spheres, which continues to strongly influence our conceptions of citizenship and obligation.

Few of those who currently insist that women should be exempted from combat would maintain that they should therefore be denied all rights of political participation. During the struggle for suffrage, however, the fact that women did not bear the same burden of civic duties and risks made it quite easy for opponents to justify different treatment in the political realm – women did not share equally in political responsibilities, thus they had no automatic claim to equal political rights. Anti-suffragists made a specific connection between the obligation to protect the state and the right to choose its leaders, arguing that women must be willing to assume the responsibility of military service if they desired the right to vote. In 1866, when the US Congress was debating the issue of whether to include women in proposed amendments that would enfranchise black males, Senator Morrill of Maine declared that the "ballot is the inseparable concomitant of the bayonet. Those who practice the one must be prepared to exercise the other. To introduce woman at the polls is to enroll her in the militia; to transfer her from the class of non-combatants to the class of combatants" (as cited in Stanton *et al.* 1882: 564). His view was echoed by many of his colleagues, including Senator Williams of Oregon, who emphasized the relationship between obligation to the state and the right to participate in its government:

> Women do not bear their proportion and share, they cannot bear their proportion and share of the public burdens. Men represent them in the Army and in the Navy; men represent them at the polls and

in the affairs of the Government; and though it be true that individual
women do own property that is taxed, yet nine-tenths of the property
and the business from which the revenues of the Government are
derived are in the hands and belong to and are controlled by the men.
Sir, when the women of this country come to be sailors and soldiers;
when they come to navigate the ocean and to follow the plow; . . .
when they love the dissoluteness of the camp and the smoke and the
thunder and the blood of battle better than they love the enjoyments
of home and family, then it will be time to talk about making the
women voters; but until that time, the question is not fairly before the
country.

(as cited in Stanton *et al.* 1882: 109–110)

Suffragists noted ironically that many of the Congressmen who clung stead-
fastly to the "ballots and bullets" thesis had not hesitated to purchase
substitutes to fulfill their own military obligation during the recent Civil
War, and also pointed out that this basis for excluding women from the
polls would logically exclude men who were physically incapable of military
service or who, like most members of Congress, were too old to fight. The
opponents of women's right to vote prevailed, however, and the connection
between the political right of suffrage and the political obligation to fight
became one of the mainstays of the anti-suffragist repertoire during the
next five decades of the battle for the ballot.

It is important to note that most suffrage advocates did not question
the idea that nature assigned a distinct set of duties to men and women,
nor did they disagree with the view that women's physical and emotional
differences precluded them from many activities, including military combat.
What they did question was the notion that this difference precluded
them from political participation, especially since women rendered an
equally risky and equally vital service – their own form of blood-sacrifice
for the nation:

Every soldier that is born brings some woman down to the very gates
of death. Thirty-five thousand women every year in Massachusetts
encounter pains and risks to life, which if brought together would
surpass the pangs and sufferings of any battle-field in the war of the
great rebellion – and all this to keep the ranks of the civilians
and the soldiers full. And shall these mothers now be taunted with
the idea that they are disqualified to vote till they go out and shoot
somebody?[11]

Some suffragists even argued that mothers had a *greater* claim to the ballot
than those who rendered military service. In her speech before the 1887
Convention of the National Woman Suffrage Association, Lillie Devereaux
Blake asked:

Which every year does most for the State, the soldier or the mother who risks her life not to destroy other life, but to create it? Of the two, it would be better to disfranchise the soldiers and enfranchise the mothers. For much as the nation owes to the soldiers, she owes far more to the mothers who in endless martyrdom make the nation a possibility.

(Stanton *et al.* 1882: 115)

These comments concerning the risks of childbirth were not simply a rhetorical counterpoint to anti-suffrage arguments. During the suffragists' era, pregnancy was actually quite similar to the draft – a life-threatening risk that few could avoid. While the chance of dying in any given war may have been greater than that of dying during any given pregnancy and delivery, women were usually "drafted" repeatedly during their lives. By 1900, the number of live births per woman had fallen to around five, and the risk of maternal death per pregnancy was estimated at approximately one death for every 154 live births, making the chance that a mother would die in childbirth during her lifetime somewhere around one in thirty (see Leavitt 1986: 129–154). The danger was thus quite real, and by the early 1900s, giving birth to the next generation of soldiers was widely accepted by the public and by national leaders as the feminine equivalent of battle. As President Theodore Roosevelt put it, the woman who gave birth to and nurtured a child was rendering the state "a great and indispensable service which involves pain and discomfort, self-abnegation, and the incurring of risk of life" (as cited in Kerber 1995: 33). The eventual consensus was that the dangers faced by female citizens in their service to the republic were different from – but essentially equal to – those faced by men, and a certain balance was achieved.

One reason that suffragists and legislators were eventually able to strike a bargain on this issue was that suffragists had gradually been shifting their primary focus from a claim of rights to a claim of duties. Early suffragists had encountered considerable resistance from the women who claimed to have "all the rights they needed," so they turned to what many saw as a more compelling argument – that women, as the "purer" sex, had a duty to seek suffrage so that their votes could help clean up the nation. The emphasis on duty was especially important when equating the sacrifice of mothers with the sacrifice of conscripted soldiers. At the turn of the century, childbirth was not a matter of planned and conscious choice – nor did most people believe that it should be. In his discussion of motherhood as a civic service, Teddy Roosevelt explicitly compared "the woman who flinches from childbirth" to "the soldier who drops his rifle and runs in battle" (as cited in Kerber 1995: 33). An individual woman who refused to bear children, like the individual soldier who defected in battle, was not an immediate threat to the nation, but if these attitudes were adopted on a wide scale, the nation would be left weak and unprotected.

Civic obligation and motherhood in the era of "choice"

By the late 1970s, however, several major social changes had rendered the comparison of childbirth to combat virtually meaningless. During both world wars and the Korean War, women volunteers were increasingly engaged as participants in war, and although they were in fairly traditional service roles, they were in frequent danger. The dividing line between combatants and non-combatants was blurred beyond recognition after the war in Vietnam, as US soldiers were encouraged to treat women, children, and elderly people as justifiable targets of war. The chemical weapons used, and the looming possibility of nuclear war, made it clear that women and children were no longer an automatically protected class.

An important – but rarely acknowledged – factor underlying the changing perceptions of women's military obligation was that childbirth was no longer the severe threat to women's lives and health that it had been in the early decades of the century. Maternal mortality rates had dropped dramatically – from an estimated one maternal death for every 154 live births in the early 1900s to one maternal death for every 4,800 live births in 1974.[12] Hospitalization was now the norm and anesthesia was common – although still a painful ordeal for many, it was difficult to argue that childbirth brought every woman to the "very gates of death." Furthermore, with the advent of easily accessible birth-control and legal abortion, the decision to bear children was increasingly posited as a *choice*, not an *obligation*. It was certainly not seen as an obligation to the state – especially after the US Supreme Court's decision in *Roe v. Wade* (1973) made it clear that a woman's right to control her reproductive life took precedence over any interference by the government, at least in the early stages of pregnancy. American women might choose to bear the sons who would be the next generation of soldiers, but it was rarely suggested that they were shirking their duty to the nation if they decided to have only a few children, or none at all.

The draft was ended around the same time as the decision in *Roe v. Wade*, so there was a brief space of time where both women and men were officially excused from their traditional "military" obligations. In 1979, however, Congress ignored President Carter's request that women, as well as men born after 1960, be required to register for the draft. The exclusion was challenged in court by several men who claimed that the Act's gender-based discrimination violated the due process clause of the Fifth Amendment. Women's groups, including the National Organization for Women (NOW), filed *amicus curiae* briefs arguing that women should be included, but the attempt was futile. Opponents of the Equal Rights Amendment (ERA) seized on this issue, and their claims that the ERA would not only mandate female registration for the draft, but also require women to fight in combat positions, helped to defeat the ratification effort in several key states.

Throughout the struggle to ratify the ERA, women's "equal right to fight" remained on the agenda. There was, however, little attention to the issue of whether women had an obligation to fight. Although NOW and other US women's organizations protested women's exclusion from the draft, the feminist community has been pretty ambivalent about the relationship between women and military service over the years – some taking the position that women should avoid collaborating with the paternalistic war machine of the state and others arguing that women should be allowed to participate on an equal basis – if they desire. The lack of consensus on the proper "feminist" approach has resulted in a general silence on this issue from many feminist organizations, leading some military men to suspect ulterior motives:

> Is it asking too much to demand that women at least register for potential combat? Here is the feminists' opportunity to right a wrong in grand and dramatic fashion. But where are they? They're not doing much to counter critics' complaints. They are more interested in preferential treatment than equal treatment.
>
> (Hutcheson 1995)

One reason that many feminists have not stepped forward to "right this wrong" is that, like most people on the liberal side of the political spectrum, they believe that draft registration is a relic of the Cold War that should be ended. Furthermore, it can also be argued that there are other, more urgent, issues facing the feminist community, especially since men are being required only to register for a potential draft – an act that the US Selective Service Administration is quick to remind us is as simple as filling out a postcard. The feminist groups that address military issues have, for the most part, concentrated on the admittedly major tasks of ensuring that women in the military are protected from discrimination and securing the right of women to volunteer for equal military participation. This strict focus on rights does, however, ignore the trickier question of whether women have an equal *obligation* to serve their country in times of war.

Conclusion

The progress of women in the United States toward equal citizenship has been difficult, and it has required compromises along the way. In order to convince society that women were entitled to participate in government, suffragists focused on the one service to the state that men could not perform – giving birth – as a way of circumventing the claim that those who did not serve in combat had no right to cast a ballot. Evoking the image of the "Republican Mother" was a successful strategy, but it reinforced several notions that have returned to haunt contemporary efforts to expand women's rights. First, positing childbirth as the feminine equivalent of battle stressed the differences, rather than the similarities, between men and women as citizens, and guaranteed that American conceptions of citizenship would continue to be heavily gendered. Second, as the inherent risk of childbirth has steadily declined, this justification for women's equality as citizens has virtually disappeared – all that remains is the underlying ideological notion that one cannot be both a "life-giver" and a "life-taker." Finally, the idea of childbirth as a civic *obligation* is no longer relevant. Although we continue to stress that male citizens are obligated to bear arms to protect the state, few women would easily accept the idea that their citizenship is based upon a duty to make babies for the state.[13]

As there has been, and almost certainly will be, no suggestion that women forfeit their right of suffrage given the changed circumstances surrounding childbirth, it could be argued that this is simply a historical curiosity with little relevance to the present. Unfortunately, the fact that American women's duties to the state are different from those of men continues to shape the debate over whether women can demand equal rights, both inside the military and out. Military men, like the feminist community, have shown a considerable degree of ambivalence when it comes to women in combat. On the one hand, most would prefer that combat continue as a male domain, with men retaining an exclusive lock on the benefits, prestige, and opportunities for advancement that go hand in hand with the risks. For many, this would also protect an institution that has traditionally served as an integral part of the very definition of masculinity. However, as the US military has stepped up its efforts to ensure equal opportunities regardless of gender, women are increasingly seen as competitors, and the idea that women should be allowed to share the benefits of military service, but not required to share equally in the risks, evokes a certain amount of anger.[14]

Men cannot choose to assume the inherently female role of "life-giver," so they resent any changes that allow women to choose (and thereby alter) the traditionally male role of "life-taker." Even more frustrating is the fact that women can choose to accept neither role – or both roles. It is probably not a coincidence that much of the hostility toward women in the US military revolves around the issue of pregnancy and childbirth – ranging from the assumption that women get pregnant to avoid unwanted assignments to the fact that the military grants new mothers additional leave, an option not available to new fathers. To many of the most conservative soldiers, motherhood and military simply do not mix, and the idea of a maternity uniform is an insult to everything the "uniform" is supposed to represent.

Military women acknowledge that there is little hope of changing these "old-timers" – their ideas on the proper place of men and women, and on the role of the military, are so entrenched that the only point of encouragement is that they will eventually retire. The younger generation of military men are more progressive in their ideas about women's role in the military, but they are also more likely to insist that women have an obligation to carry an equal share of the burdens and risks of service (Harrell and Miller 1997). Resentment over women's perceived advantages in the military is certainly not the only reason for the high rates of discrimination and persecution that women face, but it is a contributing factor. It gives the "old-timers" an easy scapegoat for explaining their actions, and may be eroding the more egalitarian views of the younger generation of military men.

What is more troublesome, however, is that our current policies may also be alienating a far larger number of young *civilian* men who are generally supportive of equal rights. In conversations with draft-age male undergraduates in the United States, those who claim support for the male-only registration almost invariably believe that military women should remain in support positions because they are incapable – either physically or emotionally or both – of handling the conditions of combat. From their perspective, defending the country is, simply put, a man's job. Conversely, the young men who are most inclined to resent the fact that they – but not their sisters – are required to register for the draft are usually those with the most enlightened views on the abilities of women. They champion the right of women to participate in combat, noting that brains can be just as important as brawn in modern warfare, and they insist that they would be perfectly willing to follow a woman into battle. Given their belief that women are their equals, they find it difficult to justify a policy that obligates men, but exempts women. The most common reaction from female students is general discomfort with the entire topic – the vast majority of women do not want to register, but most admit the inherent unfairness of demanding equal rights without accepting equal responsibilities.[15]

Clearly, a decision needs to be made on draft registration. The ideal solution would be to get rid of this remnant of the Cold War era and thus eliminate the problem entirely. Unfortunately, this does not seem likely. When US Representative Peter DeFazio of Oregon proposed legislation in 1995 that would abolish the Selective Service Board, he met strong resistance not only from some of his colleagues in the House of Representatives, but also from President Clinton, who touted draft registration as "low-cost insurance" against an uncertain future. More important to congressional defenders of the program, however, was its symbolic benefits. It was proclaimed a "rite of passage," a "patriotic duty," and an opportunity for young people "to show they want to serve their country." Repeatedly, the representatives referred to the over 98 percent compliance rate among "our young people" – never explicitly dealing with the fact that one-half of them are exempted from registration and that many of the young men register only because they forfeit significant benefits if they refuse.[16]

If the US Government insists on keeping the registration requirement – as seems likely – there is no viable reason to maintain it for men only, since over 80 percent of the positions are now open to women and the Selective Service Board has admitted that women in certain professions, such as medicine, would probably be called into service if a draft was ever authorized. The male-only registration serves no purpose other than to remind both young men and women that the requirements of citizenship vary according to gender and that the government does not (despite its claims to the contrary) truly see women as equal. Exempting women from any of the obligations of citizenship suggests that they are citizens of a different – and, inevitably, inferior – sort.

Notes

1 Although reports from the military indicated that gender-integrated training was actually beneficial to both male and female recruits, a 1996 report from a civilian committee appointed by Congress reached an opposite conclusion. The committee, chaired by former US Senator Nancy Kassebaum-Baker, has recommended that the program currently followed by the Army, Air Force, and Navy, which keeps male and female trainees together at all times, be altered so that sleeping quarters and certain aspects of physical training are handled separately. The committee cites high incidences of sexual contact between the troops, and notes that the rules some units have adopted, where male and female recruits train together but are not allowed to interact verbally or physically, do not serve the purpose of furthering unit cohesion or providing a hospitable training environment for either male or female recruits. There is no indication as yet whether any of the services will follow the recommendations of the committee. Report to the Chairman, Subcommittee on Military Personnel, Committee on National Security, House of Representatives. "Basic Training – Services Are Using a Variety of Approaches to Gender-Integrated Training." June 1996; Dana Priest. (1997) "Civilian Committee on Military Favors Separate Female Training: Need to Bolster Cohesion, Discipline Cited." *Washington Post*, December 16: A01; see also William Raspberry. (1997) "Military Reform Skeptic." *Washington Post*, December 26: A29; Mark Thompson. (1998) "Boys and Girls Apart." *Time.* January 5.
2 Maj. Lillian Pfluke, as cited in Larry Margasak. (1996) "Women in Combat Suggested as Solution." *The Daily Iowan.* November 25: 8A.
3 Although military women are required to serve in a theater of war if so ordered, they continue to be exempted by law from ground combat and are generally given a greater degree of choice in determining how close they come to actual battle. Judith Wagner Decew (1995) also notes that many military men feel that they must carry "more than their share of some undesirable duties because women trained to do them are precluded from that service."
4 Except, of course, for the more fortunate in society who have the financial resources or political influence necessary to avoid their military service obligations. During the war in Vietnam, many young men (including quite a few of our current national leaders) either evaded the draft by remaining in college or managed to secure non-combat positions as a result of family connections. Similar policies, including the purchase of "substitutes," were common in previous wars. Under the current Selective Service policy, there is no attempt to seek out and prosecute those who do not register for the draft, although a

fine of up to $250,000 and/or a prison sentence of up to five years could be imposed if convicted. The only penalty that is actively being enforced is that you are ineligible to receive federal (and most state-level) financial aid for education or most types of federal and state employment if you fail to register – again, a penalty that disproportionately impacts those from lower and working class backgrounds (Department of Defense 1997).

5 Rousseau, Kant, and Machiavelli immediately come to mind as writers whose theories of the state become very shaky if you admit women to full citizenship and participation. Among the many works that examine the impact of women on these theories are Susan Moller Okin (1979), Jean Bethke Elshtain (1981) and Carole Pateman (1989).

6 Judith Shklar (1991) does address the fact that our conceptions of citizenship are gendered, but never really deals with why women are differently obligated when it comes to military service or the implications that this may have on society's perception of their citizenship.

7 Elshtain (1987) gives an excellent overview of the way that women and men have been stereotyped as "life-givers" and "life-takers" in western political thought, and provides some thought-provoking counterexamples.

8 Testimony before the House of Representatives by General Robert H. Barrow, former Marine Commandant, 1991.

9 The quotes from military women are taken from a collection of interviews conducted between 1985 and 1991 by Dorothy and Carl Schneider as part of the Women in the Military Oral History Project at Schlesinger Library, in Boston. I explore this issue more fully in "Maternal Forces: Gendered Perceptions of War and Violence in Military Women," presented at the 1995 Conference of the Southern Political Science Association.

10 For more on the media's handling of the Gulf War, see D'Ann Campbell (1992) and Cynthia Enloe (1992).

11 "Recommendation of the Joint Special Committee on Woman's Suffrage, Commonwealth of Massachusetts, 1869," as cited in Edith M. Phelps (1912).

12 Maternal mortality figures for 1974 are taken from the 1988 US House of Representatives Hearings on the Surrogacy Arrangements Act of 1987, p. 175.

13 The cultural categories of "life-givers" and "life-takers" may also help to explain the stereotype that women in the military are lesbians. Military women are choosing to fulfill the *male* type of obligation to the state, therefore they must not be planning to fulfill the standard *female* obligation of motherhood.

14 Mary Ann Tétreault (1988) notes that women in Vietnam were perceived as competitors when given the chance to serve on equal terms with male soldiers. The prestige and potential advancement offered by combat assignments are cheapened if women are also made eligible, and the number of these assignments available is decreased (Tétreault 1988: 61). A similar problem results if prestige and advancement are no longer predicated on having served in combat – a change that many women in the military have encouraged. A recent study of cohesion among male and female troops suggests that discrimination and harassment may actually worsen as more women enter traditionally male job specialties due to the male soldiers' perception that their position is being threatened. See Leora N. Rosen *et al.* (1996).

15 These observations are drawn from discussions and informal surveys in my American Government and most of my political theory classes since 1994.

16 These quotes are taken from the House Debate on Draft Registration. US House of Representatives. July 27, 1995. Text of the debate is available online at the Central Committee for Conscientious Objectors homepage. (www.libertynet.org/ccco/)

11 Women warriors

The paradox and politics of Israeli women in uniform

Edna Levy

Military service has been conceptually and historically linked to full membership in the democratic collective. To defend the homeland is the ultimate obligation of the citizen. In Israel, where security and defense are ongoing concerns and most Jewish men and women must by law serve in the military,[1] this connection between army service and citizenship is a strong social and cultural value. To be a "real Israeli" is to have served in the Israel Defense Forces (IDF) (Horowitz and Lissak 1989; Kimmerling 1984; Peri 1983; Schiff 1992).[2]

Yet even though the laws of universal conscription apply to Jewish women as well as to Jewish men, women do not reap the benefits of this alliance between soldiering and citizenship. Despite the rhetoric of equality (which often cites women's service in the military as "proof" of sex equality in Israel), Israeli women are not full and equal participants in public life. The labor market is highly segregated according to sex, with women concentrated in middle-status occupations and underrepresented in both high- and low-status occupations (Izraeli 1991: 169). Israeli women earn about 76 percent of men's salaries (Semyanov and Kraus 1993:107; Yishai 1997)). In recent decades this earnings gap has widened: in 1978 women's hourly wage was 78 percent of men's; by 1988 women earned only 72 percent of men's wages (Izraeli 1991). Women are underrepresented in politics as well, consistently occupying only seven to eleven seats in the one hundred and twenty-member Knesset (Etzioni-Halevi and Illy 1993). In the fourteenth Knesset, elected in June 1996, women occupy only nine Knesset seats, and Limor Livnat is the sole female member of the cabinet. Despite women's slow but steady advances in parliamentary representation across the globe, as well as the theoretical advantage that a system of proportional representation (such as Israel's) may offer women candidates (Etzioni-Halevi and Illy 1993), women in Israel are gaining little ground in terms of political representation.

How is it that women's military service does not translate into concrete political, economic, or social benefits for Israeli women? The first answer is that the type of service that women perform in the military only reinforces traditional female roles of nurturer and supporter. Not only are women in the IDF prohibited from combat, but also the tasks that they do perform are deeply gendered: women are the social workers, the instructors, the teachers, and the secretaries. The few women who perform "manly" jobs receive a large degree of media attention; however, most women in the IDF are service providers for men in uniform.[3]

But this gendered division of labor within the IDF is not the whole story. Army service is also gendered in more informal, though no less powerful, ways. Specifically, the public image of the IDF soldier – as it appears in the mainstream Israeli media – is built upon a gendered system of meaning. It is the meaning of soldiering at this public, cultural level – and the way in which gender underwrites this imagery – which I explore in this chapter. This public imagery of the soldier is part of the system that sustains both the primacy of the military within Israeli society and the partial exclusion of Jewish Israeli women from national life. The arguments here rest on content analysis of newspaper pictures and articles relating to military service that appeared in two of the three major Israeli dailies in 1995,[4] and on television reports broadcast during that same year. Relevant articles and newspaper photographs from years other than 1995, and publications other than these two daily papers supplemented this primary data collection.

The discussion begins with an exploration of the images of the soldier body, arguing that male bodies are most often displayed as active while female bodies are more often immobile and contained. Both the images of the soldier body and depictions of male and female sexuality portray the male as the norm and the female as an "accessory." The political consequence of this subject/object gender distinction is to limit the potential for women's participation in public life.

These portrayals restrict both women's and men's sense of their proper place in the national community. They tend to encourage men to be public actors and initiators and invite women to be ornaments of public life and facilitators of men's actions. Compared to legal restrictions or institutionalized practices, the profusion of different images of male and female soldiers performs a less obvious role in restricting men's and women's public life. The power of such images lies in their taken-for-granted and unquestioned "naturalness."

Feminist scholarship has convincingly pointed out that not only formal restrictions on citizenship but also forms of imagining the ideal citizen and the relationship between citizen and nation are heavily underwritten by gender. Theorists such as Carole Pateman (1989), Susan Okin (1979), and Anne Phillips (1991) have explored the masculinity inherent in democratic notions of the individual; Nira Yuval-Davis (1997) and Anne McClintock (1995) have examined the feminization of the symbol of the nation and the masculinity of the citizen who serves "her." My analysis seeks to build upon these lines of thought by exploring one aspect of everyday discourses about citizenship in the Israeli case. Thus this is a study of the micro-processes of the workings of ideology, as Dick Hebdige (1979) defines the term:

> Ideology by definition thrives *beneath* consciousness. It is here, at the level of "normal common sense," that ideological frames of reference are most firmly sedimented and most effective, because it is here that their ideological nature is most effectively concealed.
>
> (Hebdige 1979: 11, emphasis in original)

Ideology is essentially unarticulated; it is that unquestioned set of assumptions that permeates society as a whole and invisibly guides our understandings of the world around us. It is the apparent naturalness of ideological forms that renders them so powerful. As Hebdige (1979: 13) comments, ideological forms "are shrouded in a 'common sense' which simultaneously validates and mystifies them." In this vein, Yanagisako and Delaney (1995) argue that the intersection and overlap of apparently distinct discourses – in this case, the discourse of gender and the discourse of military duty to the nation – result in the decreased visibility of power relations. Power is naturalized through such superimposition. Thus the power of the state over the citizenry as well as the power imbalance between Jewish Israeli men and women is hidden through the alignment of soldiering with traits that are taken for granted as male.

Women are not physically prevented from participation in national life as full and equal citizens by these common cultural images. Yet female citizenship is definitely restricted by them. The flood of gendered imagery – of women smiling and serving, of men running and firing – reflects and reinforces public assumptions of what it means to be a full participant in Israeli life. These images are part of a hegemonic discourse that defines the boundaries of the collective. And while this discussion focuses on the effect of images of soldiering on Jewish Israeli women, similar dynamics of informal cultural exclusion apply as forcefully to others, such as ultra-orthodox Jews, Israeli Palestinians, and new immigrants, all of whom may enjoy formal citizenship status but are similarly discursively excluded from full membership in the national community.

Gender, as I use the term here, is the meaning that a culture assigns to biological sex differences. But it is more – gender is a system of meaning that shapes the way we think about, interpret, see, and understand the world around us. In this symbolic system, human qualities are divided into sets of opposites that are presented as mutually exclusive – strong/weak, rational/emotional, abstract/concrete, public/private. In each pair, the first term is associated with the male, the second with the female. Furthermore, socially and culturally, there is a clear ranking here – of strong over weak, of rational over emotional, of the masculine over the feminine (Cohn 1993; Connell 1995). This symbolic system of meaning underwrites the imagery of soldiers and soldiering that pervades the Israeli media.

Bodies in motion and bodies as form

The images of the ideal soldier that flood the mainstream Israeli media almost daily are of moving bodies – bodies running, firing, sweating. There are specific external clues that point to this active body – dirt on the face or uniform, a stern facial expression, a weary or alternately alert stance. Yet the imagery is not about appearance, but action. Soldier bodies are bodies on the move. Control and discipline of the self make bodies move more efficiently.

Male soldier bodies are almost always depicted according to this action framework. But if he runs, she smiles. Female soldier bodies wink, pose, and look good. Body stance, facial expression, and props to lean on or hold do not imply movement or exertions, but signal a passive body that is all appearance. Control and discipline do not build up women soldiers' strength and stamina, but keep women's bodies slim, neat, and looking pretty.

Bodies-in-motion is a dominant motif in images of male soldiers appearing in major daily newspapers. Rarely do we see non-combat male soldiers at work, or combat soldiers at rest (unless they have upon them some evidence of exertion, such as dirt, or are in high positions of command). At the same time it is common in the press to hear soldiers complain about the lack of action. Active movement is set up as the norm of soldiering, its ultimate performance. Consequently, inaction is portrayed together with a certain level of frustration. As one soldier serving at an outpost in Lebanon says to the television cameras, "Everyone's disappointed that there's no action" (*Weekly Diary* [TV] May 17, 1996).

Consider these words from another soldier in Lebanon, and note the emphasis on physical aggression and the link with sexuality:

> You feel like if you don't have it [an active encounter with the enemy] it won't happen, it's as if you passed it, it went, missed, you didn't fulfill your potential. To walk – everyone can walk. To carry loads – everyone can carry loads. But these twenty seconds of engagement, of coming into contact, of attack, for this we wait all the time. This is our – this is our wettest dream.
> (Ohed Katz, Golani soldier, *Weekly Diary* [TV] March 3, 1995)

The desired soldier body in this case is active and moving and also decidedly male. This soldier's use of the phrase "our wettest dream" clearly marks the battlefield as an arena only for men.

When it comes to images of women in uniform, the emphasis is on outward appearance. In newspaper pictures, women soldiers are standing still, smiling, neatly dressed, sometimes even in sexually suggestive poses. They are often participating in formal ceremonies. In most such pictorial representations, appearance takes precedence over exertion. "Portraits" – posed pictures – of women soldiers appear often in the press. These women are neatly dressed, well coifed, usually wearing make-up and almost always smiling. Often they have just graduated from an IDF course. They frequently appear in pairs. Women marching or standing at attention in military ceremonies also are common images. These women usually wear skirted uniforms, and also are immaculately dressed and clean.

Undoubtedly, when male soldiers graduate from IDF courses they too press their uniforms and wash their faces. But pictures of such neatly presented men rarely appear in the press. Instead, men's pictures often show them on their last hike towards graduation, often unposed. Pictures of male soldiers in ceremony are certainly less common than the ones of female soldiers.

This emphasis on physical appearance runs through the written accounts of female soldiers as well. One typical article refers to the "beauties" on a base, "of all colors and heights, mostly thin and shapely," and describes one woman soldier thus: "Maron, [like] Botticelli's Venus that emerged from the water, red-amber hair, light eyes, beautiful, quiet" ("Strength in Action," *Ma'ariv* 1996).

This article, and others like it, refers often to dieting: "They nibble mostly toasts and count for each other how much they ate the day before." To the extent that dieting is a theme describing women soldiers, it reinforces the femininity of these young women. Dieting is what Susan Bordo has called a "discipline of perfecting the body as an object" (Bordo 1993: 179). To diet is to suppress bodily desires and necessities in order to alter the body's external appearance. It is to exercise control and discipline. And while the control and discipline of military training is aimed at superior physical ability (of the individual or of the coordinated group), the control and discipline of dieting is aimed at the form of the body as object.

The gendered distinction between exertion and external form is also apparent in the ways that dirt and weapons figure in popular imagery of the IDF soldier. Dirt and dishevelment signal an active (male) body, while cleanliness and neatness signal a passive (female) body. Weaponry in use is an extension of a vigorous (male) body, while weapons as ornaments on bodies (or, alternately bodies as ornaments on weapons) indicate a stationary (female) body.

For example, in one typical picture published in *Yediot Achronot*, the male soldiers are rumpled, wrinkled, slouching. Their uniforms are disheveled – we see unsnapped snaps, open pockets. Boots are muddy and so too are pant knees and legs. Dirt and dishevelment are markers of the active body, the body at work, doing what soldiers do. In contrast, women are more often shown neat and clean. This neatly ordered – presentable – body is an inactive body.

In a particularly blatant reversal of the dirty man/clean woman dichotomy, a picture of a muddy female soldier appeared in the newspaper *Yediot Achronot* (May 13, 1995). "The Chocolate Soldier" (as the caption reads) is smiling into the camera and clutching a machine gun close to her body. Close-fitting clothing and mud accentuate the outline of her body. She has mud on her face and body, but not from hard physical labor. This mud came from the Dead Sea Spa. Compare this picture to a picture of the crack "Egoz" fighting force (*Ma'ariv* December 5, 1996). In this photograph, a muddy male soldier crouches and aims a rifle, staring in the direction of the supposed target. His body form is not visible to the viewer – this is a close-up of his hands, face, and weapon. In these two cases, mud on the female soldier is an external sign of the regimen of beauty; mud on the male soldier is an external sign of the exertion necessary to fight. These pictures also show a marked contrast in body stance – the woman is standing and posing, while the man is aiming and firing (in accompanying photographs men are shown running and jumping as well).

Comparing the two pictures of muddy soldiers highlights another theme: the relationship between soldier and weapon. The woman soldier holds her gun close to her body, as if she was hugging it. She is not using it as a weapon. The male soldier, in contrast, is aiming and firing his gun. Her gun is a prop; his is an extension of his body's strength and activity.

In general, when men hold guns, they are either in use – being cocked or fired – or draped across the body as if they were simply a piece of clothing, an extension of the army uniform. For men, guns are tools. In contrast, weapons are often ornaments for women. Women soldiers hold guns erect, display them, and hug them. Just as the weapons are ornaments on their bodies, the women too are ornaments on the weapons. They drape themselves over or salute missiles, smile in front of planes. The sexual inferences are not too hidden. Compare for a moment two pictures that appeared in the same newspaper on the same day (*Ma'ariv* November 22, 1996). On the front page a photo shows male soldiers at work defending an outpost in Hebron. Their weapons are at the ready. On the back page a beauty queen smirks as she salutes (a parody of army discipline?) and decorates the machinery.

This distinction between action and appearance is clearly conveyed to teens. Before they are old enough to be drafted, young Jewish men understand that becoming a soldier involves physical exertion. The emphasis on the physical that runs through media accounts is paralleled in social practice: even before entry into the IDF, young Israeli men train and exercise in anticipation of their pending call-up to the army (Gal 1986: 59). The army explicitly encourages this emphasis on physical training for men through its outreach materials. In the IDF and Ministry of Education pre-army training seminar presented to Jerusalem area high school students in 1994, the young men – but not the young women – were instructed on how to exercise effectively to avoid injury. Similarly, in commercially available guidebooks for the new recruit, the same pattern recurs. However, the guidebook aimed at young women (Almog 1993), written by a former head of the Women's Corps, has a whole chapter entitled "Looking Good!"[5] which includes advice on how to select shampoos and perfumes, and admonitions such as "for the next two years, take care to preserve your outward appearance, for you are a [female] soldier, who represents the Israel Defense Forces in the nation" (Almog 1993: 171). There is almost no mention of physical training in the guidebook for women. In contrast, a guidebook aimed at young men (Ravia and Rosen 1987) has a whole chapter titled "Preparing for the Draft" which talks only about physical training – and not, for example, about psychological or emotional readiness. The chapter includes a detailed fitness schedule, complete with charts and diagrams.

The mainstream media as well as materials tailored to a teenage audience tend to portray men's bodies in uniform as active and women's bodies in uniform as static. Yet other common types of images also complicate this framework. Women's bodies sometimes appear in the press as active initiators (although these may be undercut by the style of the presentation), and women's sexuality is often described as actively in service to men. These represent alternate forms of intersection between gender and the soldier body. The different styles of presentation and imagery tend to reinforce a subservient and limited notion of women's citizenship.

Simulated soldiers

While most images of women in uniform are appearance-oriented, some show images of women performing non-traditional tasks or portrayed in non-traditional ways. They show women in full battle gear, grimacing under the weight of a stretcher as they tramp through the mud. Women are photographed running, firing rifles, operating heavy machinery, disheveled, dirty. What do these images tell us about the gendering of soldiering? Are these pictures "proof" that real soldiering is, in fact, open to both sexes? No.

The media fascination with women who perform pseudo-male jobs in the IDF is perhaps an indication of the extent to which such images do not fit social and cultural expectations. These images are newsworthy because they break gender stereotypes and they are interesting because of their shock value. A full-page article, "The Blond Undercover Agent" (*Yediot Achronot* October 22, 1995), is devoted to an undercover woman operating in the territories, whose job and activities are no different than those of her male coworkers. When the first women cadets underwent a Border Police training course, the print and television media followed closely and reported on their progress from their first day until their graduation ceremony.

The extent to which such women are anomalies or parodies of "real" soldiers is highlighted repeatedly by the way in which their appearance is framed by the media. When appearing on television shows or interviewed in the press, the questions asked (or captions under pictures) are often delegitimizing. Interviewers ask these young women about the physical difficulties of their jobs, or refer to the "messiness" of the task: "Isn't it very physical work?" and "You really get down in the grease?" are typical queries (*Soldier's Day Programming* [TV] July 9, 1995). By asking such questions of women, the press reinforces the analogy between dirt, physical exertion, and masculinity. Between the two mutually exclusive understandings of male and female soldiering, there is little room to maneuver. Given the "double bind" of gender (Bordo 1993) unconventional women can be only tokens, or worse, parodies. Such women are brought onto television shows or highlighted in feature articles in the press precisely because they are unconventional. The media treatment reveals that the dichotomous constructions of gender – and these women's violation of those gender categories – is the news here.

Other pictures of women doing "serious" army training or work appear sometimes as a direct consequence of manipulation of the media by the IDF. Consider that several pictures appearing during the same time period (late January–February 1995) depict women on the move, sweating and disheveled; women breaking the male-action versus female-appearance imagery. But this is no sign of a breakdown of the categories of gender. Rather, these pictures were released by the IDF Spokesman's office and appeared in the mainstream media within two weeks after IDF Colonel Gershon HaCohen said to Jerusalem teens that "men were always fighters and women were always whores" (*Yediot Achronot* January 26, 1995). The scandal occupied the front pages of the daily papers for days. It riveted the Israeli public, evoking demonstrations, sharp reactions from politicians, and demands that the Colonel be released from the IDF (he was not – once the scandal no longer received front-page coverage, Colonel HaCohen was promoted). The public discussion centered on whether women were in fact necessary and useful to the IDF. It is no wonder that the IDF Spokesman's office, which had a history of sponsoring photo-opportunities of women soldiers scantily clad in pseudo-porn poses, suddenly offered a few photos of women doing serious army work.

Interestingly, the IDF did not release pictures of women soldiers on the job as radio operators, teachers, or social workers – jobs much more common for women to hold. In the wake of this public debate over the necessity of women in the IDF sparked by a comment from an IDF officer dismissing women as whores, the message of the IDF is loud and clear: yes, women *are* doing the "real work" in the army, and that "real work" is combat (read: male).

The argument thus far has been that "manliness" is built into the imagery of the soldier. The emphasis on the women soldiers' appearance portrays women as objects – as form, not content, as symbols, not actors. This is part of a more general dynamic in which women – their skills, charm, and sexuality – are the accessories to the "real soldiers": the men. Women are *accessories* in the IDF, in both meanings of the word – women are support staff as well as ornaments of male soldiers. Most of the jobs that women perform in the Israeli army (teacher, clerk, social worker) involve nurturing or supporting male soldiers. And women – specifically women's physical appearance – also serve as status symbols of male soldiers' prestige. Women inductees learn through formal lectures and informal social practices that one of their primary roles in the IDF is to "soften" the brutal face of the military machine.

This theme of women as naturally able to temper the harshness of the military is a common and oft-repeated one. One writer remembers that at the end of her basic training course, the Chen (Women's Corps) Chief Officer told the soldiers that "the job of the girl is to bring spark and style" to the IDF. The very name of the Women's Corps reveals the intention that women's femininity be harnessed for military needs. "Women's Corps" was chosen in part because its Hebrew acronym, "Chen," means "charm" (Yuval-Davis 1985: 660). A government publication explaining the military purpose of women's service in the IDF states that female soldiers are to "help in the areas of crystallizing the morale of the units and taking care of the soldiers of the units" (*The Government Report of the Committee on the Position of Women* 1978, cited in Yuval-Davis 1985: 661).

According to mainstream media accounts, women's beauty is also a marker of the male hierarchy within the IDF. The media describe as common practice within the army the assignment of the prettiest clerks to the most prestigious units. High-ranking officers have models serving as their secretaries ("Tel Aviv Time," November 1995); departments within the air force are also reported to have had a system of assigning the best-looking female clerks to the most prestigious units within the corps ("My IDF," *Ma'ariv* January 20, 1995). Amira Dotan, a former Chief Officer of the Women's Corps, commented that even while many female clerks are no longer needed in the IDF, commanders surround themselves with pretty clerks ("The Lie of Chen," *Yediot Achronot* January 24, 1995). The woman's outward appearance is a status symbol of the men in the unit; she is a trapping of power and prestige.

The connection between appearance and sexuality is that the "nurturing function" of women is often understood as sexual. Whether or not the IDF "officially *encourages* implicit sexual relations" as claimed by Nira Yuval-Davis (1985: 663, emphasis in original), the theme of women in uniform as sexual providers is a common one in the press. One label applied to women in the IDF, and often quoted in the press, is "fresh mattresses." One woman who served as a clerk for the prestigious Givati brigade is quoted:

> It's like an unwritten rule that they only take good looking girls to be company clerks. They want you to be nice to the soldiers and spoil them, and I don't mean just by giving them cake.
>
> (*Jerusalem Post* February 3, 1995)

Accounts of women soldiers sleeping with high-ranking officers attract media curiosity ("To be a Brigadier-General's Lover is Status," *Ha'aretz* March 20, 1985). Even though a study of sexual activity of men and women during years of service found that men were more sexually active and more promiscuous than women, the headline still read: "What do women soldiers do at night?" (*Yediot Achronot* July 12, 1995). In this understanding of women's soldiering, women's sexuality is not much different than women's sensitivity or prettiness; all are resources that make men's difficult job of soldiering a little more pleasant.

Within a context describing women as sexual providers and sexual objects, it is not surprising that sexy pictures of pretty female soldiers have appeared often in the press. The women in these pictures – women who are serving in the IDF – are scantily clad, sometimes holding a rifle erect, and they stand in sexually suggestive poses. The tolerance of such imagery – by the IDF and the public at large – can occur only within a context where women in uniform are sexual objects.

After years of frequent sexy shots in the press, the IDF began reprimanding women soldiers who appear in such photographs.[6] The imagery that now appears is less blatant but, nonetheless, still sexual. Interestingly, the reasons given by the IDF for the new policy include concern for maintaining respect for military *weaponry*. Colonel Amos Gilad of the IDF Spokesman's Department, comments to the press:

> A women soldier who is standing, portrayed as a sexual object, in a wet shirt or covered in mud that accentuates her curves, and holding a rifle – this is definitely a form of pornography. It places the weapon that the (male) soldiers sweat over as a mockery and scorn. It also harms the honor of women.
>
> ("The Lie of Chen," *Yediot Achronot* January 24, 1995)

The images are considered "a form of pornography" because of the dishonor they accord the IDF itself, and most particularly, the weaponry over which IDF soldiers "sweat." In Gilad's words, the rifle – an object, a symbol of the physical exertion of the male soldier – should be accorded at least as much honor as the human being objectified in the picture.

Perhaps Gilad intends to affirm that he has no higher respect for the weapon than the woman. But consider this contradiction: while individual women soldiers today are reprimanded for appearing in sexualized pictures in the press, male soldiers who hang pin-up posters of (non-IDF) women in offices and outposts are not similarly disciplined. Apparently, the major offense of the pictures of wet women in uniform and the "chocolate soldier" is the dishonor to the IDF – and not the objectification of women.

Although women soldiers as sexual objects is a common theme in media portrayals of the IDF, not just any form of sexuality is so compatible with the military ethos. Male homosexuality is, for example, much less tolerated than female sexiness. In contrast to the years of IDF tolerance of sexy pictures of women in uniform, the army was quick to expel from his combat unit the first man to display his homosexuality openly in the press by appearing in a sexy pose during Gay Pride Week in 1993. Why are sexualized images of women soldiers tolerated, while one sexy image of a homosexual male soldier caused such swift and severe punishment? The different reactions of the IDF to the two phenomena reveal the degree to which compulsory heterosexuality underwrites the system of meaning that defines good soldiering, the meaning of the military, and gender relations. Simply put, in order for a woman soldier to soften the IDF with her charm and smiles, there must be some (imagined) sexual tension between her and the men around her. It is within this context of the symbolic order of gender – and especially its heterosexual component – that the frequent appearance of near-pornographic images of sexy women soldiers in the mainstream media makes sense.

The links between images of women as passive and/or sexual objects and their actual and assumed role within the IDF as nurturers of male soldiers implies a whole host of assumptions about women's and men's place in the nation. The idea of soldiers running to the battlefront to defend their nation is interconnected with notions of masculine strength and sexual aggression and feminine weakness and service to men. The images of sexy female soldiers reflect and reinforce on a daily basis the gendered nature of national belonging. Any digressions from this frame-work – such as depictions of male soldier homosexuality or women fighting on the battlefield – threaten the symbolic order of gender and nation.

Women's sexuality, fertility, and femininity are part of the story of soldiering in another sense: they are also the actual or symbolic goods over which war is waged. Women's bodies – as fertile reproducers of the nation and the sexual possessions of men – are imagined as resources to be protected from the enemy (see Eisenstein 1996; Huston 1982). "Our women" are part of the national assets to be protected. Within this dynamic, women are not the defenders, but the defended. They are not active agents, but property to be shielded from harm. The gendered iconography of the nation relies upon the sense of something to be protected – and most often, in Cynthia Enloe's (1994) word that "something" is "womenand-children."

This place of women's bodies in the story of war is highlighted in discussions or references to war and rape. Feminist analyses of rape – both wartime rape and rape in general – have argued that rape is not about sex but power (Brownmiller 1975; MacKinnon 1987: 85). Rape during wartime is often a symptom of rage and hatred towards enemy *men*. "Women's bodies constitute the battlefield where men communicate their rage to other men" (Rejali 1996: 366). The way in which the potential rape of women IDF soldiers is addressed in public discussions underlines this feminist analysis. Israeli women are not allowed to serve in combat in part because they may fall captive to the enemy. As captives they would be subject to rape by enemy soldiers. (a conquering of the Israeli male's territory) and impregnation with non-Israeli children (a perversion of the glorification of the woman as reproducer of the nation).

In February 1995, during a discussion of a proposed bill allowing women to volunteer for combat units,[7] then Prime Minister (and former war-hero) Yitzhak Rabin opposed women's combat service, asking "If they are captured, who will take responsibility?" (*Yediot Achronot* February 6, 1995). The comment was not silently accepted by the Israeli public – men and women wrote critical newspaper editorials arguing that such an outlook perpetuated a double standard unfair to women and men alike – but it did echo a common theme regarding the reasons why women do not serve in combat. The fear and threat is of the sexual assault of "our" women if they fall captive.

Three discursive constructions – of the enemy, of soldiering, and of women as reproducers of the nation – underlie this general social concern with women prisoners of war (POWs). Arab captors, so the Israeli social understanding goes, are expected to rape their prisoners. Consider, for example, woman Member of Knesset (MK) and Minister of Labor Ora Namir's explanation: "We shouldn't forget that Ben Gurion's generation instructed that women will not serve in combat units, after the incidents of rape, murder, and abuse of women's corpses in the [1948] War of Independence" (*Ha'aretz* February 2, 1995). Similarly, the rape of an American woman soldier captured during the Gulf War has been touted as "proof" that Arabs will rape Israeli women soldiers if they fall captive (for example, see "After the Supreme Court Case," *Yediot Achronot* June 30, 1995). This portrayal of the Arab enemy is implicitly contrasted to the supposedly more humane treatment by Israelis of Arab soldiers captured during war (A. Bloom 1991: 137).

The rape of a woman soldier is frightening for the Israeli public, in part because this is precisely the sort of action that making war is meant to prevent. Even outside of Israel, making war is about defending the home – and women and children are symbols of the home (Enloe 1994; Stiehm 1982). The enemy can also rape male soldiers, but, as terrible as this possibility is, it does not evoke the same outcry by the Israeli public. Why? One answer is, as discussed above, that the rape of a woman symbolizes the winning of the battle in some sense, the incursion of the enemy into "our" territory – the bodies of our women. As sociologist Daphna Izraeli is quoted in the press, the rape of women POWs is understood somehow as a usurpation of (Jewish) Israeli property:

> The sex of the women is taken as something that belongs to her Jewish man and not a strange man. An enemy's abuse of a woman soldier shocks us more than sexual abuse of a male soldier.
>
> ("Be nice/pretty and serve coffee," *Davar* February 10, 1995)

At least one man lamented the double standard encapsulated by Rabin's public question: "Who will be responsible for women POWs?", arguing that if he were to fall captive, he too deserves that someone be responsible ("[Female] Fighters," *Ma'ariv* February 10, 1995).

This double standard of concern for potential sexual assault of men and women at the hands of the enemy does not reflect a general social valuing of women's sexuality or the right of women to protection from violence. If this was the case, then the sexual assault and violence against women that occurs daily within Israel's borders would not be tolerated (see Sharoni 1994). In the wake of Rabin's comments about "responsibility for women POWs," one feminist commentator pointed out that the public concern with women POWs cannot be understood to be about the safety and sexual autonomy of Israeli women:

> Israel puts up very well, every day, with all kinds of assaults against women. It manages to live quite well with the reality of women being murdered by their spouses, at a rate that exceeds the killing of Israelis by the enemy.
>
> (Esther Herzog, "Women POWs? Unthinkable,"
> *Jerusalem Post* February 1995)

Apparently, Herzog comments, the right to assault and sexually abuse Israeli women is a privilege of the male citizenry. If Herzog is right, then the resistance to women's combat service has another explanation: the fear that arming and training women to defend the homeland could be turned against the male citizenry's "right" to women's bodies and used instead for self-defense. One of the first women to be trained in the Border Police course feels empowered by her physical fitness:

> If I were attacked by a rapist in a dark alley, I would now know how to deal with him. Instinctively I would choke him, one blow and he'd get the message. He'd find out he's not dealing with a loser.
>
> ("Wonder Women," *The Jerusalem Post Magazine* June 7, 1996)

Women fighters threaten not only the "manliness" of fighting, but also the social power imbalance within Israeli society. By challenging the gendered iconography that underwrites the nation itself, women fighters may challenge the very identity of the nation.

Another reason why the potential for rape of female and male soldiers is treated differently is linked to the reproductive abilities of women. A raped woman can become pregnant with the enemy's child, a perversion of a central social value in Israel: bearing Jewish children. Orit, a woman soldier who trains infantrymen for combat, recognizes this danger in her comments about the ban on women in combat:

It's nonsense – the business of POW. If they want us to be in combat, then order us to put in an IUD [intrauterine (contraceptive) device] for five years, and maybe I'll think about it seriously.

("A Woman of Valor," *Yediot Achronot* 1994)

Orit offers to restrict her own biological functions in order to take up the mantle of combat soldiering. Her comments build upon the common understanding of the danger of falling captive – and the danger of pregnancy with an enemy child – and twist this discourse by expressing her willingness to (temporarily) sterilize herself for the right to fight. Such a willingness to sacrifice reflects the centrality of soldiering in the Israeli consciousness. It also represents an alternate discourse regarding fertility and the obligation of women to the nation.

Israeli women do not, like their male counterparts, achieve entry into the national collective through their role as soldiers. Rather, their Israeliness is defined through the act of birth and mothering.[8] Women as well as men in uniform repeat this distinction between the proper role of women and their service to the nation as reproducers – not fighters – within the IDF. As the head of the IDF Women's Corps put it, "There is a special role for the Jewish woman as a mother and the center of the family. I fight for equal opportunities for male and female soldiers, but we must recognize that there are certain differences" (Dotan 1993: 140). Orit's comments about the IUD do not represent a critical alternative to this discourse, but rather an attempt to achieve Israeliness – belonging in the collective – as a man. She can do so only by erasing her womanhood, by temporarily immobilizing her reproductive functions.

To sum up the arguments thus far, the contrast between men's active bodies and women's ornamental bodies is complicated by other dynamics of representation. Specifically, women soldiers may be presented as active but these images tend to be undermined through the style and form of representation. Such images of active women soldiers serve as parodies of true soldiering and thus highlight the equivalence between masculinity and soldiering. In addition, women's bodies serve men in uniform in multiple ways. Female sexuality is not only the antithesis of soldiering but also the particular prize for men at the front. In this way (along with their labor at the homefront and in the delivery room), women's bodies serve the men who serve the nation. Women's sexuality and fertility are the very goods to be protected by the soldier, a component of the national treasure that battles are meant to defend. These complex and interconnected relationships between gender, bodies, sexuality, and soldiering reflect and replicate particularly restricted forms of citizenship for Jewish Israeli men and women.

Men's and women's bodies and the body politic

What does the flood of gendered imagery – of running male soldiers and smiling female soldiers – mean for real men and women in Israel? What does the soldier body (as it is portrayed in the mainstream media) imply for the imagining of the body politic? What forms of participation or membership in the national community are facilitated or encouraged, and what forms are precluded or limited?

The portrayal of the soldier body – and the rigid differentiation between male and female body imagery – is more than simply a matter of media style. The individual body that appears in the media at the very least signals how the individual member of society is imagined – as actor or observer, participant or spectator, as vigorous or docile. The predominance of images of sweating, moving, running male soldiers opens up the possibility for real men to act in the social and political world. The dearth of active images of female soldiers diminishes the potential of real women to act. Instead, the objectification of women soldiers – the emphasis on their outward appearance and immobility – legitimizes women's position as passive ornaments of public life.

Of course these images do not physically prevent women's political activity or participation. Neither do they force men into public life. What they do is less overt – but no less powerful. Gendered images help regulate the norms of behavior for men and women; they legitimize some forms of participation and de-legitimize others; they define certain activities as natural for one sex and not the other. They limit what can be imagined.

For example, when President Ezer Weizman dismissed Member of Knesset Shulamit Aloni, he did not refer to her intellect, abilities, or political position. Instead he drew attention to her physical appearance, calling her a "bulging, dried up old lady" (*Yediot Achronot* February 3, 1995). The images of soldiers explored here are part of the system of meaning that makes it possible to dismiss a woman's – but rarely a man's – political views by reference to appearance.

The way in which the imagery of soldier bodies is gendered mimics the way in which gender underwrites the democratic project. Classic democratic thought has been built upon assumptions and categories of gender, understanding men as actors in the public sphere and women as objects, possessions of the male actors. Thinkers such as Carole Pateman (1988a) and Anne Phillips (1991) have argued that while the notion of the universal individual has been presented as a gender-neutral idea, the individual so envisioned has historically and theoretically always been male. As Phillips points out, however we choose to define the abstract individual of democratic thought – as rational, independent, or autonomous – these traits "all turn out to have a sexual history. For contemporary feminists, the individual is highly suspect. Behind his supposedly gender-free guise, he remains unmistakably a man" (Phillips 1991: 33).

The exclusion of women from the category of "individual" rests upon a distinction between subject and object, between visible public agency and invisible private passivity. Women are not the autonomous property-owning individuals who freely enter into social contracts with each other. Instead, women are included in democratic theory as part of the owned property itself. And while the formal rights of women to vote and participate in the democratic collective may have been granted not long ago, the underlying distinction between actor and object still operates, making women's full inclusion in the democratic project "ambiguous and uncertain" at best (Phillips 1991: 34).

The images of soldiers in the Israeli media parallel this theoretical and historical distinction between male and female. The male soldier is the active initiator, the one who does the job of soldiering, much as the (male) citizen is the participant in the public arena. The female soldier is more often an object, discussed and portrayed as a static form. She is an object in soldiers' clothing, much as the female citizen is a non-individual object in the public arena who is not fully allowed to participate.

The imagery of the soldier body is, then, a model for acceptable behavior by real men and women. It also replicates the gendered distinction between action and inaction that underwrites democratic thought. Viewed from a different angle, and leading to other insights into the gender of national belonging, the soldier body is the body politic writ small.

The way in which the individual body is portrayed can be seen as a reflection of the imagining of the social collective. Mary Douglas (1973), among the first to undertake a sociological study of the body, argued for this interplay between macro and micro levels of analysis:

> The social body constrains the way the physical body is perceived. The physical experience of the body, always modified by the social categories through which it is known, sustains a particular view of society. There is a continual exchange of meanings between the two kinds of bodily experience so that each reinforces the categories of the other.
>
> (Douglas 1973: 93)

Rumpled clothing or made-up faces have political meaning insofar as they signal attributes of the collective body. And to the extent that images of male and female soldier bodies are rigidly drawn and mutually exclusive, men and women occupy different places in the collective body.

In Israeli political culture, as in many democratic nations, the relation of political to military institutions is coded in the language of the body as a distinction between mind and muscle. Policy is debated and decided in the political arena and is carried out by the army. Political actors use their heads and decide policy; military men use their bodies and execute that policy. When this distinction is challenged, as when a prominent group of Israeli rabbis declared that religious soldiers had an obligation to disobey military commands to evacuate Jews from certain areas, the military and political reaction is swift and unequivocal: "Every soldier can have his own political opinion, but when he is drafted to the army, he acts according to only one authority – his commander who gets his direction from army command" (Main Officer of Education and Gadna, Tat-Aluf Shalom Ben Moshe, quoted in *Yediot Achronot* July 9, 1995).

This distinction between mind and muscle is a key factor in the conceptual separation of military and political power. This analytical distinction is an aspect of public discussions as well as academic analyses (see for example Kimmerling 1984; Lissak 1984). It underlies the notion of the army in a democratic society as a politically neutral executor of the national will. Following Douglas's (1973) insight that the relationship between body parts signals social hierarchy, the imagery of the active male soldier signals the differentiation between governmental and military power. As an active exerting body, the male soldier signifies the enactor of the political will. He is emblematic of the military as the "muscle" of the body politic.

This discussion provides a clue into the link between military service and national belonging. The individual male soldier gains entry into the community, the nation, by first displaying his willingness to act physically, literally to flex his muscles, on behalf of the nation. And women, whose military service is depicted as inactive or symbolic, are excluded from this track of entry. What then is the connection between the imagery of the individual female body and the way in which the collective social body is conceived? Rather than signaling participation in public life, images of the inert female body plug into and reinforce the conception of woman as *symbol* of the nation, while the female body as sexual provider for men reinforces the notion of women as *supporter* of the male citizen.

Women gain entry into the Israeli collective as "support staff" to the main (male) participants – most obviously as mothers, but also as wives and sisters. Jean Bethke Elshtain (1987) argues that two prototypical symbols guide our imagining of war and our own identities, the Just Warrior and the Beautiful Soul. These two idealized symbols are heavily and thoroughly gendered, argues Elshtain: "Women in western culture have served as collective, culturally designated 'beautiful souls'"(Elshtain 1987: 4), an image laden with notions of purity, innocence, and passivity. Worrying, supportive, mourning mothers and wives of soldiers, militantly patriotic women, even women peace activists or pacifists, all are often understood within the imagery of the Beautiful Soul trope. Elshtain's formulation does not reflect the role of women's sexuality in national life. Yet here too women serve as support staff for actively engaged male participants. Women's sexuality, like their nurturing skills, are depicted as in service to male soldiers and as goods to be protected by men in battle. Sexuality, like beauty and reproductive abilities, is the antithesis to soldiering and also the very prize that soldiering is meant to protect.

Israeli women are imagined as facilitators, enablers, reproducers of the nation, but not players. Often the nation is imagined as female and the relationship of citizen to nation is modeled after some ideal heterosexual love. In Israeli literature and everyday media imagery, women are often conceived of as the pure, untainted "home" to be protected or defended in war. The way in which female soldier bodies are portrayed does not challenge but rather reinforces this dichotomy between male defender and female nation. The predominant imagery of women soldiers as passive and well groomed – as objects, not actors – fits into this connection between idealized femininity and the nation. Women are not seen as participants, but as signifiers, much as the flag or the seal or some other object. The order and cleanliness of the female body is not incidental – it signifies the purity of the nation (and the national mission) and also the purity and innocence of the women "back home." In so doing, it discursively limits the real potential for women to participate as full and equal citizens of the Israeli nation.

Notes

1 Jewish and Druze men serve for a minimum period of three years; Jewish women serve for a minimum of twenty-one months. Increasingly, the IDF is exempting more youth from service by raising the minimum educational or psychological criteria that already are more stringent for women than for men. This discrepancy, combined with the option of exemption on religious grounds, readily available to women but not to men unless they are students in ultra-orthodox institutions, means that only 50–70 percent of Jewish Israeli women serve, while 80 percent of Jewish Israeli men serve (Izraeli 1997; Oron 1995).

2 This analysis refers only to the impact of gender on Jewish Israeli women's place in the collective. See Sharoni (1994, 1995) for discussions of the impact of militarism on Israeli and Palestinian women; Smooha (1984) and Smooha and Kraus (1985) for discussions of its impact on Jewish Israelis of non-European descent; Kretzmer (1987), Lewin-Epstein and Semyanov (1993) and Wolkinson (1991) for discussions of Arab-Israeli citizens that touch on the effects of militarism.

3 This sexual division of labor within the modern IDF has strong historical roots. See Jorgensen (1994) and Anne Bloom (1991) for more complete discussions.

4 These two newspapers are *Ha'aretz* and *Yediot Achronot*, chosen because of their different formats and target audiences. *Yediot Achronot* is published in tabloid format and leans towards more colorful stories; *Ha'aretz* has a more traditional layout, focuses on editorials and foreign news, and avoids sensationalism (Tal 1995). The Israel Advertising Association has called *Ha'aretz* a "quality" paper and *Yediot Achronot* a "popular" paper.

5 This is a rough translation. The chapter title, "Yofi Lakh!" can be translated more literally as "Good for You," but contains the insinuation of physical appearance, since "yofi" literally means "beauty."

6 For example, the "chocolate soldier" was reprimanded for appearing in the press. In coordination with the Women's Corps, the Spokesman's Office has also ceased inviting press photographers to IDF "fun days" – which take place at hotel pools and beaches and have often been sources of the "sexy" pictures.

7 In May 1994 several Members of Knesset, representatives from right and left

parties alike, proposed an amendment to the law of compulsory service which would allow women to volunteer for any job within the army and to be considered "according to her abilities, and not according to her sex." That same month, another MK (from one of the ultra-orthodox parties) proposed an amendment to the same law that would cancel women's service in the IDF entirely.

8 For more on this link between motherhood and national belonging see Berkovitz (1992) and Yuval-Davis and Anthias (1989). The dynamic is not uniquely Israeli; see, for example, McClintock (1995) for a discussion of the South African case, and Afshar (1989) on the Iranian case.

References

Adorno, Theodor W., Else Frenchel-Brenswick, D. J. Levinson and R. N. Sanford. (1950) *The Authoritarian Personality*. New York: Harper.

Advani, Lal Krishan. (1996) *10 o'clock Evening News*. Door Darshan, India. April 24.

Afshar, Haleh. (1989) "Women and Reproduction in Iran," in Nira Yuval-Davis and Floya Anthias (eds.) *Woman–Nation–State*. London: Macmillan.

Agarwal, Bina. (1995) *A Land of One's Own: Women and Land Rights in South Asia*. New Delhi: Oxford University Press.

Agarwal, Purshottam. (1995) "Surat, Savarkar and Draupadi: Legitimizing Rape as a Political Weapon," in T. Sarkar and U. Butalia (eds.) *Women and the Hindu Right: A Collection of Essays*. New Delhi: Kali for Women.

Agger, Inger. (1994) *The Blue Room*. London: Zed Books.

Agnes, Flavia. (1995) "Hindu Men, Monogamy and Uniform Civil Code." *Economic and Political Weekly*. 30: 50: 3238–3244.

Ahmad, Aijad. (1995) "Culture, Nationalism, and the Role of Intellectuals: An Interview with Aijaz Ahmad." *Monthly Review*. 47: 3: 48.

Ahmed, Leila. (1992) *Women and Gender in Islam: Historical Roots of a Modern Debate*. New Haven, CT: Yale University Press.

AIR (*All India Reporter*). (1985) Supreme Court 945=1985 Cri. L.J. 875-M.L.R. (1985) 202. Mohd. Ahmed Khan, Apellant, v. Shah Bano and Others, Respondent. The Supreme Court of India, Criminal Appellate Jurisdiction.

Alcoff, Linda. (1988) "Cultural Feminism versus Poststructuralism: The Identity Crisis in Feminist Theory." *Signs*. 13: 3: 405–436.

—— and Elizabeth Potter (eds.) (1993) *Feminist Epistemologies*. New York: Routledge.

Alexander, M. Jacqui. (1994) "Not Just (Any)*Body* Can Be a Citizen: The Politics of Law, Sexuality, and Postcoloniality in Trinidad and Tobago and the Bahamas." *Feminist Review*. 48: 5–23.

—— (1997) "Erotic Autonomy as Politics of Decolonization," in M. Jacqui Alexander and Chandra Talpade Mohanty (eds.) *Feminist Genealogies, Colonial Legacies, Democratic Futures*. New York: Routledge.

—— and Chandra Talpade Mohanty (eds.). (1997) *Feminist Genealogies, Colonial Legacies, Democratic Futures*. New York: Routledge.

Allen, Beverly. (1992) "Terrorism Tales: Gender and the Fictions of Italian National Identity." *Italica*. 69: 2 (Summer): 161–176.

—— (1996) *Rape Warfare: The Hidden Genocide in Bosnia-Herzegovina and Croatia*. Minneapolis: University of Minnesota Press.

Allport, Gordon. (1954) *The Psychology of Prejudice*. Reading, MA: Addison-Wesley.

Almog, Hedva. (1993) *Becoming a Soldier in Israel's Women's Corps*. Jerusalem: Keter.

Anderson, Benedict. (1991) *Imagined Communities*, 2nd edn. London: Verso.

al-Aneizi, Rashed. (1994) *The Bidun in Kuwait. (Al-Bidun fi al-Kuwayt.)* Kuwait: Qurtas.

Anita, S. Manisha and Kavita Vasudha. (1995) "Interviews with Women," in T. Sarkar and U. Butalia (eds.) *Women and the Hindu Right: A Collection of Essays*. New Delhi: Kali for Women.

Anthias, Floya and Nira Yuval-Davis. (1992) *Racialized Boundaries*. London: Routledge.

Antic, Milica. (1992) "Yugoslavia: The Transitional Spirit of the Age," in Chris Corrin (ed.) *Superwomen and the Double Burden*. Toronto: Second Story Press.

Arendt, Hannah. (1951) *The Origins of Totalitarianism*. New York: Meridian.

—— *On Revolution*. New York: Compass.

—— (1977) *Eichmann in Jerusalem: A Report on the Banality of Evil*. New York: Penguin.

Aristotle. (1986) *Politics*. Trans. Hippocrates G. Apostle and Lloyd P. Gerson. Grinell, IA: Peripatetic Press.

Armstrong, John. (1982) *Nations before Nationalism*. Chapel Hill, NC: University of North Carolina Press.

Astrow, Andre. (1983) *Zimbabwe: A Revolution Lost its Way?* London: Zed Books.

Bacchetta, Paulo. (1993) "All Our Goddesses Are Armed." *Bulletin of Concerned Asian Scholars*. 25: 4: 38–51.

Baird, Robert. (1981) "Uniform Civil Code and the Secularization of Law," in R. Baird (ed.) *Religion in Modern India*. Delhi: Manohar.

Bald, S. R. (1985) "Feminization of the Women's Movement in India." *Willamette Journal*. 2: 31–54.

—— (1986) "From Satyartha Prakash to Manushi: An Overview of the 'Women's Movement' in India," in D. Basu and R. Sisson (eds.) *Social and Economic Development in India: A*. New Delhi/Beverly Hills/London: Sage.

Banerjee, Sumanata. (1993) "'Sangh Parivar' and Democratic Rights." *Economic and Political Weekly*. 28: 34: 1715–1718.

Bano, Sabeeha. (1995) "Muslim Women's Voices. Expanding Gender Justice under Muslim Law." *Economic and Political Weekly*, 30: 47: 2981–2982.

Barakat, Halim. (1993) *The Arab World: Society, Culture and State*. Berkeley, CA: University of California Press.

Barber, Benjamin. (1984) *Strong Democracy*. Berkeley, CA: University of California Press.

Basu, Amrita. (1993) "Feminism Inverted: The Real Woman and Gendered Imagery of Hindu Nationalism." *Bulletin of Concerned Asian Scholars*. 25: 4: 25–36.

—— (1995) "Feminism Inverted: The Gendered Imagery and Real Women of Hindu Nationalism," in T. Sarkar and U. Butalia (eds.) *Women and the Hindu Right: A Collection of Essays*. New Delhi: Kali for Women.

Basu, Tapan, Pradip Datta, Sumit Sarkar, Tanika Sarkar and Sambuddha Sen. (1993) *Khaki Shorts and Saffron Flags: A Critique of the Hindu Right*. New Delhi: Orient Longman.

Beauvoir, Simone de. (1952/1974) *The Second Sex*. Trans. H. M. Parshley. New York: Vintage.

Bem, Sandra Lipsitz (1993) *The Lenses of Gender*. New Haven, CT: Yale University Press.

Bennington, Geoffrey. (1990) "Postal Politics and the Institution of the Nation," in Homi Bhabha (ed.) *Nation and Narration*. New York: Routledge.

Bennis, Phyllis. (1993) "Command and Control: Politics and Power in the Post-Cold War United Nations," in Phyllis Bennis and Michel Moushabeck (eds.) *Altered States: A Reader in the New World Order*. New York: Olive Branch Press.

Bennoune, Karima (1994) "Algerian Women Confront Fundamentalism." *Monthly Review*. 46: 4: 26–49.

Berkovitch, Nitza. (1992) "Women and the State: Constituting the Female Subject in the Legal Discourse in Israel." Paper presented to the American Sociological Association Conference. Pittsburgh, PA.

Bhabha, Homi. (1990) *Nation and Narration*. London: Routledge.

—— (1994) *The Location of Culture*. New York: Routledge.

Bhartiya Janata Party. (1994) *Kashmir in Peril*. (no place).

—— (1996) *Election Manifesto*. (no place).

—— (no date) Speeches of Shri Atal Bihari Vajpayee, Swamy Chinmayanand and Shri Lal Krishan Advani, Ayodhya Issue, publication no. 122.

Bhattachardee, Anannya. (1992) "The Habit of Ex-Nomination: Nation, Woman, and the Indian Immigrant Bourgeouisie." *Public Culture*. 5: 1: 20, 30, 31.

Bhebe, Ngwabi and Terence Ranger (eds.). (1995) *Soldiers in Zimbabwe's Liberation War*. London: James Currey.

Bidwai, Praful, Harbans Mukhia and Achin Vanaik (eds.) (1996) *Religion, Religiosity and Communalism*. New Delhi: Manohar.

Blee, Kathleen. (1991) *Women of the Klan*. Berkeley, CA: University of California Press.

Block, Robert. (1993) "Killers." *New York Review of Books*. 40: November 8: 9.

—— (1994) "The Tragedy of Rwanda." *New York Review of Books*. October 20: 3–8.

Bloom, Anne. (1991) "Women in the Defense Forces," in B. Swirski and M. Safir (eds.) *Calling the Equality Bluff: Women in Israel*. New York: Pergamon.

Bloom, Mia M. (1998) "War and the Politics of Rape." Unpublished paper.

Bloom, William. (1990) *Personal Identity, National Identity and International Relations*. Cambridge: Cambridge University Press.

Bologh, Roslyn Wallach. (1987) "Marx, Weber, and Masculine Theorizing," in Norberto Wiley (ed.) *The Marx–Weber Debate*. Beverly Hills, CA: Sage.

Bordo, Susan. (1990) "Feminism, Postmodernism, and Gender-Scepticism," in L. Nicholson (ed.) *Feminism/Postmodernism*. New York: Routledge.

—— (1993) *Unbearable Weight: Feminism, Western Culture, and the Body*. Berkeley, CA: University of California Press.

Borneman, John. (1994) "Towards a Theory of Ethnic Cleansing: Territorial Sovereignty, Heterosexuality and Europe." *Working Papers on Transitions from State Socialism*. New York: Mario Einaudi Center for International Studies, Cornell University.

Boswell, John. (1988) *The Kindness of Strangers: The Abandonment of Children in Western Europe from Late Antiquity to the Renaissance*. New York: Vintage.

Braidotti, Rosi. (1997) "Comments on Felski's 'The Doxa of Difference': Working through Sexual Difference." *Signs*. 23: 1: 23–40.

Brass, Paul. (1985) *Ethnic Groups and the State*. New York: Barnes & Noble.

—— (1991) *Ethnicity and Nationalism: Theory and Comparison*. Newbury Park, CA: Sage.

Brennan, Timothy. (1990) "The National Longing for Form," in Homi Bhabha (ed.) *Nation and Narration*. London: Routledge.

Breuilly, John. (1982) *Nationalism and the State*. Manchester: Manchester University Press.

Bromley, Simon. (1994) *Rethinking Middle East Politics*. Austin, TX: University of Texas Press.

Brown, Karen McCarthy. (1994) "Fundamentalism and the Control of Women," in John Stratton Hawley (ed.) *Fundamentalism and Gender*. New York: Oxford University Press.

Brown, Wendy. (1988) *Manhood and Politics*. Totowa, NJ: Rowman & Littlefield.

Brownmiller, Susan. (1975) *Against Our Will: Men, Women and Rape*. New York: Fawcett Columbine.

Bryson, Lucy and Clem McCartney. (1994) *Clashing Symbols? A Report on the Use of Flags, Anthems and Other National Symbols in Northern Ireland*. Belfast: Institute of Irish Studies for the Community Relations Council, Queen's University.

Buckley, Anthony and Mary Catherine Kenney. (1995) *Negotiating Identity: Rhetoric, Metaphor, and Social Drama in Northern Ireland*. Washington, DC and London: Smithsonian Institute.

Burk, James. (1995) "Citizenship Status and Military Service: The Quest for Inclusion by Minorities and Conscientious Objectors." *Armed Forces and Society: An Interdisciplinary Journal*. Summer: 503–530.

Butalia, Urvashi. (1995) "Muslims and Hindus, Men and Women: Communal Stereotypes and the Partition of India," in T. Sarkar and U. Butalia (eds.) *Women and the Hindu Right: A Collection of Essays*. New Delhi: Kali for Women.

Butler, Judith (1990) *Gender Trouble*. New York: Routledge.

—— (1993a) "Endangered/Endangering: Schematic Racism and White Paranoia," in Robert Gooding-Williams, (ed.) *Reading Rodney King, Reading Urban Uprising*. New York: Routledge.

—— (1993b) *Bodies that Matter*. New York: Routledge.

—— (1999) "Against Proper Objects", *differences* 6(2 and 3): 1–26.

Caldicott, Helen. (1986) *Missile Envy: The Arms Race and Nuclear War*. New York: Bantam.

Calhoun, Craig. (1997) *Nationalism*. Minneapolis: University of Minnesota Press.

Callear, Diane. (1982) "The Social and Cultural Factors Involved in Production by Small Farmers in Wedza Communal Area, Zimbabwe." Report no. 17. Division for the Study of Development. Paris: Unesco.

Campbell, D'Ann. (1992) "Combating the Gender Gulf." *Minerva Quarterly Report*. Fall/Winter: 13–41.

Castle-Kanerova, Mita. (1992) "Czech and Slovak Federative Republic: The Culture of Strong Women in the Making," in Chris Corrin (ed.) *Superwomen and the Double Burden*. Toronto: Second Story Press.

Chaach, Amrita, Farida Khan, Gautam Navlekha, *et al.* (1996) "Reversing the Option: Civil Codes and Personal Laws." *Economic and Political Weekly*. 31: 20: 1180–1183.

Chakravarti, Uma. (1990) "Whatever Happened to the Vedic Dasi?" in Kumkum Sangari and Sudesh Vaid (eds.) *Recasting Women*. New Brunswick, NJ: Rutgers University Press.

Chandra, Bipan. (1984) *Communalism in Modern India*. Delhi: Vani Educational Books, Vikas.

Chanock, Martin. (1982) "Making Customary Law: Men, Women and Courts in Northern Rhodesia," in Margaret Jean Hay and Marcia Wright (eds.) *African Women and the Law: Historical Perspectives*. Boston, MA: African Studies Centre, Boston University.

Charney, Craig. (1994) "Democracy Won." *New York Times*. April 27: A17.

Chatterjee, Partha. (1986) *Nationalist Thought and the Colonial World: A Derivative Discourse?* Delhi: Manohar.

—— (1989) "Colonialism, Nationalism, and Colonialized Women: The Contest in India." *American Ethnologist*. 16: 4: 622–33.

—— (1993a) *The Nation and the Fragments: Colonial and Post Colonial History*. Princeton, NJ: Princeton University Press.

—— (1993b) *Nationalist Thought and the Colonial World*. Minneapolis: University of Minnesota Press.

Chodorow, Nancy. (1978) *The Reproduction of Mothering*. Berkeley, CA: University of California Press.

—— (1995) "Gender as a Personal and Cultural Construction." *Signs*. 20: 3: 516–544.

Chow, Rey. (1991) *Women and Chinese Modernity*. Minneapolis: University of Minnesota Press.

Cigar, Norman. (1995) *Genocide in Bosnia*. College Station, TX: Texas A & M University Press.

Cohen, Ronald and Elman, R. Service (eds.) (1978) *Origins of the State*. Philadelphia, PA: Institute for the Study of Human Issues.

Cohen, Stuart. (1995) "The IDF: From a 'People's Army' to a 'Professional Military' – Causes and Implications." *Armed Forces and Society*. 21: 2 (Winter).

Cohn, Carol. (1989) "Sex and Death in the Rational World of Defense Intellectuals," in Diana E. H. Russell (ed.) *Exposing Nuclear Phallacies*. New York: Pergamon.

—— (1993) "Wars, Wimps and Women: Talking Gender and Thinking War," in Miriam Cooke and Angela Woollacott (eds.) *Gendering War Talk*. Princeton, NJ: Princeton University Press.

—— (1998) "Gays in the Military: Texts and Subtexts," in Marysia Zalewski and Jane Parpart (eds.) *The "Man" Question in International Relations*. Boulder, CO: Westview Press.

Coles, Robert. (1986) *The Political Life of Children*. Boston, MA: Atlantic Monthly Press.

Collins, Patricia Hill. (1992a) *Black Feminist Thought: Knowledge, Consciousness and the Politics of Empowerment*. Boston, MA: Unwin Hyman.

—— (1992b) "Learning to Think for Ourselves: Malcolm X's Black Nationalism Reconsidered," in Joe Wood (ed.) *Malcolm X, In Our Own Image*. New York: St. Martin's Press.

Connell, R. W. (1995) *Masculinities*. Cambridge: Polity Press.

Connelly, Joan Breton. (1994) "Parthenon and Parthenoi: A Mythological Interpretation of the Parthenon Frieze." Unpublished paper.

Connolly, William E. (1974) *The Terms of Political Discourse*. Lexington, MA: Heath.

Connor, Walker. (1978) "A nation is a nation, is a state, is an ethnic group, is a . . ." *Ethnic and Racial Studies*. 1: 4: 378–400.

—— (1994) *Ethnonationalism: The Quest for Understanding*. Princeton, NJ: Princeton University Press.

Coole, Diana H. (1993) *Women in Political Theory* 2nd edn. Boulder, CO: Lynne Rienner Press.

Copelon, Rhonda. (1994) "Surfacing Gender: Reconceptualizing Crimes against Women in Time of War," in Alexandra Stiglmayer (ed.) *Mass Rape.* Lincoln: University of Nebraska Press.

Corrigan, Philip and Derek Sayer. (1985) *The Great Arch: English State Formation as Cultural Revolution.* Oxford: Basil Blackwell.

Crystal, Jill. (1990) *Coalitions in Oil Monarchies: Rulers and Merchants in Kuwait and Qatar.* New York: Cambridge University Press.

—— (1992) *Kuwait: The Transformation of an Oil State.* Boulder, CO: Westview.

Davies, Rob. (1988) "The Transition to Socialism in Zimbabwe: Some Areas for Debate," in Colin Stoneman, (ed.) *Zimbabwe's Prospects.* London: Macmillan.

Davis, Angela. (1992) "Black Nationalism: The Sixties and the Nineties," in Gina Dent (ed.) *Black Popular Culture.* Seattle, WA: Bay Press.

Davis, Richard H. (1996) "The Iconography of Rama's Chariot," in David Ludden (ed.) *Contesting the Nation: Religion, Community and the Politics of Democracy in India.* Philadelphia: University of Pennsylvania Press.

Decew, Judith Wagner. (1995) "The Combat Exclusion and the Role of Women in the Military." *Hypatia.* Winter.

de Lauretis, Teresa. (1987) "The Female Body and Heterosexual Presumption." *Semiotica.* 67: 3–4: 259–279.

de Lepervanche, Marie. (1989) "Breeders for Australia: A National Identity for Women?" *Australian Journal of Social Issues.* 24: 3: 163–182.

Democratic Dialogue. (1996) *Power, Politics, Positionings: Women in Northern Ireland.* Report no. 4. Belfast: Democratic Dialogue.

Dent, Gina. (1992) "Black Pleasure, Black Joy: An Introduction," in Gina Dent (ed.) *Black Popular Culture.* Seattle, WA: Bay Press.

Department of Defense. (US). (1997) "The Selective Service System: Why Women Aren't Required to Register." April 14. (http://www.sss.gov/women.html).

Desai, P. B. (1957) *Jainism in South India.* Sholapur, India.

Deshpande, Satish. (1995) "Communalizing the Nation-Space: Notes on Spatial Strategies of Hindutva." *Economic and Political Weekly.* 30: 50: 3220–3227.

Deutsch, Karl. (1966) *Nationalism and Social Communication,,* 2nd edn. New York: MIT Press.

Devji, Faisal Fatehali. (1992) "Hindu/Muslim/Indian." *Public Culture.* 5: 1(Fall): 3, 7.

Dinnerstein, Dorothy. (1976) *The Mermaid and the Minotaur: Sexual Arrangements and Human Malaise.* New York: Harper Collins.

DiStefano, C. (1990) "Dilemmas of Difference: Feminism, Modernity, and the Postmodern," in Linda Nicholson (ed.) *Feminism/Postmodernism.* London: Routledge.

Dizdarevic, Zlatko. (1994) *Portraits of Sarajevo.* New York: Fromm International.

Doob, Leonard. (1964) *Patriotism and Nationalism: Their Psychological Foundations.* New Haven, CT: Yale University Press.

Dotan, Amira. (1993) "Amira Dotan: Israel's First Female General," in B. Swirski and M. Safir (eds.) *Calling the Equality Bluff.* New York: Pergamon.

Douglas, Mary. (1973) *Natural Symbols.* New York: Vintage.

Doyle, Michael W. (1986) *Empires.* Ithaca, NY: Cornell University Press.

DuBois, W. E. B. (1969) *The Souls of Black Folks.* New York: Signet.

Ehrenreich, Barbara. (1997) *Blood Rites: Origins and History of the Passions of War*. New York: Metropolitan.

Einhorn, Barbara. (1993) *Cinderella Goes to Market: Citizenship, Gender and the Women's Movement in East Central Europe*. New York: Verso.

Eisen, Arlene. (1984) *Women and Revolution in Vietnam*. London: Zed Books.

Eisenstein, Zillah. (1994). *The Color of Gender*. Berkeley, CA: University of California Press.

—— (1996) *Hatreds: Racialized and Sexualized Conflicts in the Twenty-First Century*. New York: Routledge.

Eley, Geoff and Ronald Grigor Suny. (1996) "Introduction: From the Moment of Social History to the Work of Cultural Representation," in Geoff Eley and Ronald Grigor Suny (eds.) *Becoming National*. New York: Oxford University Press.

Elias, Diana. (1994) "Kuwaiti Papers Expose Punishment Imbalance." *The Australian*. 7.

Elshtain, Jean Bethke. (1981) *Public Man, Private Woman: Women in Social and Political Thought*. Princeton, NJ: Princeton University Press.

—— (1987). *Women and War*. New York: Basic Books.

—— (1992) "Sovereignty, Identity, Sacrifice," in V. Spike Peterson (ed.) *Gendered States: Feminist (Re)Visions of International Relations*. Boulder, CO: Lynne Rienner Press.

Engels, F. (1972) *Origin of the Family, Private Property and the State*. New York: Pathfinder Press.

Engineer, Asghar Ali. (ed.) (1987) *The Shahbano Controversy*. Hyderabad, India: Orient Longman.

Enloe, Cynthia. (1983) *Does Khaki Become You? The Militarisation of Women's Lives*. Boston, MA: South End.

—— (1987) "Feminist Thinking about War, Militarism, and Peace," in Beth B. Hess and Myra Marx Ferree (eds.) *Analyzing Gender*. Newbury Park, CA: Sage.

—— (1990) *Bananas, Beaches and Bases: Making Feminist Sense of International Politics*. Berkeley, CA: University of California Press.

—— (1992) "The Politics of Constructing the American Woman Soldier as a Professional 'First Class Citizen': Some Lessons from the Gulf War." *Minerva Quarterly Report*. Spring: 14–31.

—— (1993) *The Morning After: Sexual Politics at the End of the Cold War*. Berkeley, CA: University of California Press.

—— (1994) "The Gendered Gulf," in Lauren Rabinovitz and Susan Jeffords (eds.) *Seeing Through the Media: The Persian Gulf War*. New Brunswick, NJ: Rutgers University Press.

Enzensberger, Hans Magnus. (1994) *Civil Wars, From L.A. to Bosnia*. New York: New Press.

Erikson, E. H. (1969). *Gandhi's Truth*. New York: Norton & Norton.

Esman, Milton. (1977) *Ethnic Conflict in the Western World*. Ithaca, NY: Cornell University Press.

Etzioni-Halevi, Eva and Ann Illy. (1993) "Women in Legislatures: Israel in Comparative Perspective," in Yael Azmon and Daphna N. Izraeli. (eds.) *Women in Israel*. New Brunswick, NJ: Transaction.

Evason, Eileen. (1991) *Against the Grain: The Contemporary Women's Movement in Northern Ireland*. Dublin: Attic Press.

Fallows, James. (1989) *More Like Us*. Boston, MA: Houghton Mifflin.

—— (1993) "Looking at the Sun." *Atlantic Monthly*. 272: 5: 78.

Fanon, Frantz. (1963). *The Wretched of the Earth*. New York: Grove.

Fausto-Sterling, Anne. (1992) *Myths of Gender: Biological Theories about Women and Men*. 2nd edn. New York: Basic Books.

Ferguson, Yale H. and Richard W. Mansbach. (1996) *Polities: Authority, Identities and Change*. Columbia, SC: University of South Carolina Press.

Fitzgerald, Frances. (1972) *Fire in the Lake: The Vietnamese and the Americans in Vietnam*. Boston, MA: Little, Brown.

Fox, Richard G. (1996) "Communalism and Modernity," in D. Ludden (ed.) *Contesting the Nation: Religion, Community and the Politics of Democracy in India*. Philadelphia: University of Pennsylvania Press.

Fraser, Nancy and Linda Gordon. (1994) "A Genealogy of Dependency: Tracing a Keyword of the US Welfare State." *Signs*. 19: 2: 304–336.

Fraser, Nancy and Linda J. Nicholson. (1990) "Social Criticism without Philosophy: An Encounter between Feminism and Postmodernism," in Linda J. Nicholson (ed.) *Feminism/Postmodernism*. London: Routledge.

Fraser, Steven (ed.). (1995) *The Bell Curve Wars*. New York: Basic Books.

Frederikse, Julie. (1982) *None But Ourselves: Masses vs. Media in the Making of Zimbabwe*. New York: Penguin.

Funk, Nanette and Magda Mueller. (1993) *Gender Politics and Post-Communism*. New York: Routledge.

Gaidzanwa, Rudo. (1993) "Citizenship, Nationality, Gender and Class in Southern Africa." *Alternatives*. 8: 1: 39–60.

Gaitskell, Deborah and Elaine Unterhalter. (1989) "Mothers of the Nation: A Comparative Analysis of Nation, Race and Motherhood in Afrikaner Nationalism and the African National Congress," in Nira Yuval-Davis and Floya Anthias (eds.) *Woman–Nation–State*. London: Macmillan.

Gal, Reuven. (1986) *A Portrait of the Israeli Soldier*. New York: Greenwood Press.

Gal, Susan. (1994) "Gender in the Post-Socialist Transition: The Abortion Debate in Hungary." *East European Politics and Societies*. 8(Spring): 271.

Gandhi, M. K. (1965–1969). *Collected Works of Mahatma Gandhi*. Vols. 1–90. New Delhi: Government of India.

Gause, III, F. Gregory. (1994) *Oil Monarchies: Domestic and Security Challenges in the Arab Gulf States*. New York: Council on Foreign Relations.

Gavrielides, Nicolas. (1987) "Tribal Democracy: The Anatomy of Parliamentary Elections in Kuwait," in Linda Layne (ed.) *Elections in the Middle East: Implications of Recent Trends*. Boulder, CO: Westview.

Gay, Peter. (1995) *The Bourgeois Experience: Victoria to Freud*. Vol. III. *The Cultivation of Hatred*. New York: Fontana.

Geertz, Clifford. (1963) *Old Societies and New States*. New York: Free Press.

Geiger, Susan. (1987) "Women in Nationalist Struggle: TANU Activists in Dar es Salaam." *International Journal of Historical Studies*. 20: 1–26.

—— (1990). "Women and African Nationalism." *Journal of Women's History*. 2: 1: 227–244.

Geisler, Gisela. (1995) "Troubled Sisterhood: Women and Politics in Southern Africa." *Journal of African Affairs*. 94: 545–578.

Gellner, Ernest. (1983) *Nations and Nationalism*. Ithaca, NY: Cornell University Press.

Genew, Sneja and Anna Yeatman (eds.). (1993) *Feminism and the Politics of Difference*. Boulder, CO: Westview.

Gevisser, Mark. (1994) "Who is a South African?" *New York Times*. April 26: A23.

Ghabra, Shafeeq. (1997) "Kuwait and the Dynamics of Socio-economic Change." *Middle East Journal*. 51: 3: 358–372.

Gilpin, Robert. (1981) *War and Change in World Politics*. New York: Cambridge University Press.

Gilroy, Paul. (1987) *There Ain't No Black in the Union Jack: The Cultural Politics of Race and Nation*. London: Hutchinson.

—— (1992) "It's a Family Affair," in Gina Dent (ed.) *Black Popular Culture*. Seattle, WA: Bay Press

Giroux, Henry. (1993) *Living Dangerously: Multiculturalism and the Politics of Difference*. New York: P. Lang.

Gleason, Gregory. (1991) "Nationalism in our Time." *Current World Leaders*. 34: 2: 213–234.

Glenny, Misha. (1993) "Bosnia: The Tragic Prospect." *New York Review of Books*. 40: November 4: 38–49.

Goldberg, David Theo. (1993) *Racist Culture*. Oxford: Blackwell.

Goldhagen, Daniel Joshua. (1996) *Hitler's Willing Executioners: Ordinary Germans and the Holocaust*. New York: Alfred A. Knopf.

Goldstone, Jack A. (1986) "The English Revolution: A Structural-Demographic Approach," in Jack A. Goldstone (ed.) *Revolutions: Theoretical, Comparative, and Historical Studies*. New York: Harcourt, Brace, Jovanovich.

Gopal, Sarvapelli. (1988) "Nehru and the Minorities." *Economic and Political Weekly*. 23: 45, 46 and 47: 2463–2466.

Gordon, Linda. (1990) *Women, the State and Welfare*. Madison, WI: University of Wisconsin Press.

Government of India. (1980) *Reservations for Backward Classes: Mandal Commission Report of the Backward Classes Commission*. New Delhi: Akalank.

Greenfeld, Liah. (1992) *Nationalism: Five Roads to Modernity*. Cambridge, MA: Harvard University Press.

Greven, Philip. (1992) *Spare the Child: The Religious Roots of Punishment and the Psychological Impact of Physical Abuse*. New York: Vintage.

Grewal, Inderpal and Caren Kaplan (eds.). (1994) *Scattered Hegemonies: Postmodernity and Transnational Feminist Practices*. Minneapolis: University of Minnesota Press.

Gurr, Ted. (1994) *Ethnic Conflict in World Politics*. Boulder, CO: Westview.

Guy, Donna. (1991) *Sex and Danger in Buenos Aires: Prostitution, Family, and Nation in Argentina*. Lincoln: University of Nebraska Press.

—— (1992) "'White Slavery': Citizenship and Nationality in Argentina," in Andrew Parker *et al.* (eds.) *Nationalisms and Sexualities*. New York: Routledge.

Habermas, Jürgen. (1991) *The Structural Transformation of the Public Sphere: An Inquiry into a Category of Bourgeois Society*. Trans. Thomas Berger and Frederick Lawrence. Cambridge, MA: MIT Press.

Haeri, Shahla. (1993) "Obedience versus Autonomy: Women and Fundamentalism in Iran and Pakistan," in Martin E. Marty and R. Scott Appleby (eds.) *The Fundamentalism Project*. Vol. 2. *Fundamentalisms and Society: Reclaiming the Sciences, the Family, and Education*. Chicago: University of Chicago Press.

Halperin, David M. (1990) *One Hundred Years of Homosexuality*. New York: Routledge.

Hammoud, Hassan R. (1987) "Kuwait," in John Dixon (ed.) *Social Welfare in the Middle East*. London: Croom Helm.

Haraway, Donna. (1988) "Situated Knowledges: The Science Question in Feminism and the Privilege of Partial Perspective." *Feminist Studies*. 14: 575–599.

Hardacre, Helen. (1993) "The Impact of Fundamentalisms on Women, the Family and Interpersonal Relations," in Martin E. Marty and R. Scott Appleby (eds.) *The Fundamentalism Project.* Vol. 2. *Fundamentalisms and Society: Reclaiming the Sciences, the Family, and Education.* Chicago: University of Chicago Press.

Harrell, Margaret C. and Laura L. Miller. (1997) *New Opportunities for Military Women: Effects upon Readiness, Cohesion, and Morale.* Washington, DC: The Rand Corporation.

Hart, Lynda. (1994) *Fatal Women: Lesbian Sexuality and the Mark of Aggression.* Princeton, NJ: Princeton University Press.

Hasan, Mushirul. (1995) "Muslim Intellectuals, Institutions and the Post-Colonial Predicament." *Economic and Political Weekly.* 30: 47: 2995–3000.

Hasan, Zoya. (1989) "Minority Identity, Muslim Women Bill Campaign and the Political Process." *Economic and Political Weekly.* 24: 1: 44–50.

—— (1993) "Communalism, State Policy and the Question of Women's Rights in Contemporary India," *Bulletin of Concerned Asian Scholars.* 25: 4: 5–15.

Hassim, Shireen. (1993) "Family, Motherhood and Zulu Nationalism: The Politics of the Inkatha Women's Movement." *Feminist Review.* 43 (Spring).

Hawley, John Stratton (ed.) (1994) *Fundamentalism and Gender.* New York: Oxford University Press.

Healy, James N. (ed.) (1977) "Shule Aroon/Siubhail a Rún." *Love Songs of the Irish.* Dublin: Mercier Press. 12–13.

Hebdige, Dick. (1979) *Subculture: The Meaning of Style.* London: Routledge.

Hechter, Michael. (1975) *Internal Colonialism: The Celtic Fringe in British National Development, 1536–1966.* London: Routledge & Kegan Paul.

Hedges, Chris. (1995) "War Turns Sarajevo away from Europe." *New York Times.* July 28: A4.

Hekman, Susan J. (1990) *Gender and Knowledge: Elements of a Postmodern Feminism.* Cambridge: Polity Press.

Heng, Geraldine and Janadas Devan. (1992) "State Fatherhood: The Politics of Nationalism, Sexuality, and Race in Singapore," in Andrew Parker *et al.* (eds.) *Nationalisms and Sexualities.* New York: Routledge.

Herbst, Jeffrey. (1989) *State Politics in Zimbabwe.* Berkeley, CA: University of California Press.

Hingorani, A. T. (ed.). (1966). *To the Perplexed* (Collection of M. K. Gandhi's Writings and Speeches). Bombay: Bharatiya Vidya Bhavan.

Hirsch, Marianne. (1994) "Pictures of a Displaced Girlhood," in Angelika Bammer (ed.) *Displacements.* Bloomington: Indiana University Press.

Hobbes, Thomas. (1981) *Leviathan.* New York: Penguin.

Hobsbawm, Eric J. (1990, 1992) *Nations and Nationalism since 1780: Programme, Myth, Reality.* New York: Cambridge University Press.

Hockenos, Paul. (1993) *Free to Hate: The Rise of the Right in Post-Communist Eastern Europe.* New York: Routledge.

Hoffman, Auren. (no date) "Women and the Draft." *Contraband Magazine.* (http://members.aol.com/CntrabndMag/draft.html).

Horowitz, Dan and Moshe Lissak. (1989) *Trouble in Utopia.* Albany, NY: State University of New York Press.

Horowitz, David. (1992) "The Feminist Assault on the Military," *National Review,* Oct. 5, p. 46.

Horowitz, Donald. (1985) *Ethnic Groups in Conflict.* Chapel Hill, NC: Duke University Press.

Hunt, Lynn. (1984) *Politics, Culture, and Class in the French Revolution*. Berkeley, CA: University of California Press.

—— (1992) *The Family Romance of the French Revolution*. Berkeley, CA: University of California Press.

Huntington, Samuel. (1993a) "The Clash of Civilizations?" *Foreign Affairs*. 72: 3: 22–49.

—— (1993b) "If Not Civilizations, What?" *Foreign Affairs*. 72: 5: 186–194.

Huston, Nancy. (1982) "Tales of War and Tears of Women." *Women's Studies International Forum*. 5(3/4): 271–282.

Hutcheson, Maj. Keith A., USAF (1995) "Drafting True Equality: Why Not Make Women Register for the Selective Service System?" *Armed Forces Journal International*. December. (http://afji.com/Mags/1995/Dec95Draft.html)

Hutchinson, John. (1987) *The Dynamics of Cultural Nationalism: The Gaelic Revival and the Creation of the Irish Nation State*. London: Allen & Unwin.

—— and Anthony Smith (eds.) (1994) *Nationalism*. London: Hutchinson.

Ignatieff, Michael. (1994) *Blood and Belonging: Journeys into the New Nationalism*. New York: Farrar, Straus & Giroux.

Isaacs, Harold. (1976) *Idols of the Tribe: Group Identity and Political Change*. New York: Harper & Row.

Ismael, Jacqueline. (1982) *Kuwait: Social Change in Historical Perspective*. Syracuse, NY: Syracuse University Press.

Iyer, R. (ed.). (1986). *The Moral and Political Writings of Mahatma Gandhi*. Vols. I and II. Oxford: Clarendon Press.

—— (ed.). (1987). *The Moral and Political Writings of Mahatma Gandhi*. Vol. III. Oxford: Clarendon Press.

Izraeli, Dafna. (1991) "Women and Work: From Collective to Career," in Barbara Swirski and Marilyn P. Safir (eds.) *Calling the Equality Bluff: Women in Israel*. New York: Pergamon.

—— (1997) "Gendering Military Service in the Israeli Defense Forces." *Israel Social Science Research*. 12: 1.

Jackson, Robert H. (1990) *Quasi-States: Sovereignty, International Relations and the Third World*. Cambridge Studies in International Relations no. 12. Cambridge: Cambridge University Press.

Jacobs, Susan. (1989) "Zimbabwe: State, Class, and Gendered Models of Land Resettlement," in Jane Parpart and Kathleen Staudt (eds.) *Women and the State in Africa*. Boulder, CO: Lynne Rienner.

James, C. L. R. (1986) *Every Cook Can Govern and What is Happening Every Day: 1985 Conversations*. Jan Hillegas (ed.). Jackson, MS: New Mississippi.

Jarman, Neil and Dominic Bryan. (1996) "Parade and Protest: A Discussion of Parading Disputes in Northern Ireland." Coleraine: Centre for the Study of Conflict, University of Ulster at Coleraine.

Jayawardena, Kumari. (1986) *Feminism and Nationalism in the Third World*. London: Zed Books.

Jeffords, Susan. (1989) *The Remasculinization of America: Gender and the Vietnam War*. Bloomington: Indiana University Press.

—— and Lauren Rabinovitz. (1994) "Seeing through Patriotism," in Susan Jeffords and Lauren Rabinovitz (eds.) *Seeing through the Media: The Persian Gulf War*. New Brunswick, NJ: Rutgers University Press.

Johnson, Allan G. (1997) *The Gender Knot: Unraveling our Patriarchal Legacy*. Philadelphia, PA: Temple University Press.

Johnson, Cheryl. (1986) "Class and Gender: A Consideration of Yoruba Women during the Colonial Period," in Claire Robertson and Iris Berger (eds.) *Women and Class in Africa*. New York: Africana Publishing.

Johnson, Harry G. (ed.). (1965) *Economic Nationalism in Old and New States*. London: Allen & Unwin.

Johnson, Kay Ann. (1983) *Women, the Family and Peasant Revolution in Rural China*. Chicago: University of Chicago Press.

Jones, Ann. (1994) *Next Time She'll Be Dead*. Boston, MA: Beacon.

Jones, David E. (1997) *Women Warriors: A History*. Washington & London: Brassney.

Jorgensen, Connie. (1994) "Women, Revolution, and Israel," in Mary Ann Tétreault (ed.) *Women and Revolution in Africa, Asia and the New World*. Columbia, SC: University of South Carolina Press.

Joseph, Suad (ed.). (2000) *Gender and Citizenship in the Middle East*. Syracuse, NY: Syracuse University Press.

Joshi, P. (ed.). (1988) *Gandhi on Women* (Collection of Mahatma Gandhi's Writings and Speeches on Women). Ahmedabad: Navjivan.

JT. (1995) (4) Supreme Court 331. Smt. Sarla Mudgal, President Kalyani and Ors. v. Union of India.

Kakkar, Sudhir. (1996) *The Colors of Violence: Cultural Identities, Religion and Conflict*. Chicago: University of Chicago Press.

Kandiyoti, Deniz. (1991a) "Introduction," in Deniz Kandiyoti (ed.) *Women, Islam and the State*. Philadelphia, PA: Temple University Press.

—— (1991b) "Identity and its Discontents: Women and the Nation." *Millennium*. 20: 3: 429–443.

Kanongo, Tabitha. (1987) *Squatters and the Roots of Mau Mau 1905–1963*. Nairobi: Heinemann.

Kaplan, Robert D. (1993) *Balkan Ghosts: A Journey through History*. New York: Vintage.

Kapur, Ratna and Brenda Cossman. (1995) "Communalizing Gender, Engendering Community: Women, Legal Discourse and the Saffron Agenda," in T. Sarkar and U. Butalia (eds.) *Women and the Hindu Right: A Collection of Essays*. New Delhi: Kali for Women.

Katrak, K. (1992) "Indian Nationalism, Gandhian 'Satyagraha,' and Representations of Female Sexuality," in Andrew Parker *et al.* (eds.) *Nationalisms and Sexualities*. New York: Routledge.

Keane, John. (1988) "Despotism and Democracy: The Origins and Development of the Distinction between Civil Society and the State 1750–1850," in John Keane (ed.) *Civil Society and the State*. London: Verso.

Kedourie, Elie. (1993) *Nationalism*. Oxford: Blackwell.

Keller, Evelyn Fox. (1985) *Reflections of Gender and Science*. New Haven, CT: Yale University Press.

Kerber, Linda K. (1995) "A Constitutional Right to be Treated Like American Ladies: Women and the Obligations of Citizenship," in Linda Kerber, Alice Kessler-Harris and Kathryn Kish Sklar (eds.) *US History as Women's History: New Feminist Essays*. Chapel Hill, NC: University of North Carolina Press.

Kesič, Obrad. (1994) "Women and Revolution in Yugoslavia, 1945–1989," in Mary Ann Tétreault (ed.) *Women and Revolution in Africa, Asia and the New World*. Columbia, SC: University of South Carolina Press.

Kimmerling, Baruch. (1984) "Making Conflict a Routine: Cumulative Effects of the Arab–Jewish Conflict upon Israeli Society," in Moshe Lissak (ed.) *Israeli Society and its Defense Establishment.* London: Frank Cass.

Kinzer, Stephen. (1993) "The War Memorial: To Embrace the Guilty, Too?" *New York Times.* November 15: A4.

—— (1995) "News Media in Belgrade Mute their Nationalism." *New York Times.* July 8: A5.

Kishwar, M. (1985a). "Gandhi on Women (Parts 1 & 2)." *Economic and Political Weekly.* 20: 40: 1691–1702.

—— (1985b). "Gandhi on Women (Part 3)." *Economic and Political Weekly.* 20: 41: 1753–1758.

—— (1995) "Stimulating Reform Not Forcing it: Uniform Versus Optional Civil Code." *Manushi.* 89: 5–14.

—— and R. Vanita. (1984) *In Search of Answers.* London: Zed Books.

Klug, Francesca. (1989) "'Oh To Be in England': The British Case Study," in Nira Yuval-Davis and Floya Anthias (eds.) *Woman–Nation–State.* London: Macmillan.

Kohli, Atul. (1990) *Democracy and Discontent: India's Growing Crisis of Governability.* Cambridge: Cambridge University Press.

Kohn, Hans. (1967) *The Idea of Nationalism*, 2nd edn. New York: Collier-Macmillan.

Kolodner, Eric. (1995) "The Political Economy of the Rise and Fall(?) of Hindu Nationalism." *Journal of Contemporary Asia.* 25: 2: 233–253.

Koonz, Claudia. (1987) *Mothers in the Fatherland: Women, the Family and Nazi Politics.* New York: St. Martin's Press.

Krause, Jill and Neil Renwick (eds.). (1996) *Identities in International Relations.* New York: St. Martin's Press.

Kretzmer, D. (1987) *The Legal Status of Arabs in Israel.* Tel Aviv: International Center for Peace in the Middle East.

Kriger, Norma J. (1988) "The Zimbabwean War of Liberation: Struggles within the Struggle." *Journal of Southern African Studies.* 14: 2: 304–322.

—— (1992) *Zimbabwe's Guerrilla War: Peasant Voices.* Cambridge: Cambridge University Press.

Kristeva, Julia. (1980) *Desire in Language: A Semiotic Approach to Literature and Art.* New York: Columbia University Press.

—— (1993) *Nations without Nationalism.* New York: Columbia University Press.

Kruks, Sonia, Rayna Rapp and Marilyn B. Young (eds.). (1989) *Promissory Notes: Women in the Transition to Socialism.* New York: Monthly Review Press.

Kurth, James. (1992) "The Post-Modern State." *National Interest.* 28 (Summer): 32.

Kuwait Ministry of Planning. (1992) *Annual Statistical Abstract.* Kuwait.

—— (1995) *Annual Statistical Abstract.* Kuwait.

Lan, David. (1985) *Guns and Rain.* Berkeley, CA: University of California Press.

Lapid, Yosef and Friedrich Kratochwil (eds.). (1996) *The Return of Culture and Identity in International Relations Theory.* Boulder, CO: Lynne Rienner Press.

Lazreg, Marnia. (1994) *The Eloquence of Silence: Algerian Women in Question.* London: Routledge.

Leavitt, Judith Walzer. (1986) "Under the Shadow of Maternity: American Women's Responses to Death and Debility Fears in Nineteenth Century Childbirth." *Feminist Studies.* 12: 129–154.

Lewin-Epstein, Noah and Moshe Semyanov. (1993) *The Arab Minority in Israel's Economy: Patterns of Ethnic Inequality.* Boulder, CO: Westview.

Lewis, Paul. (1993) "Stoked by Ethnic Conflict, Refugee Numbers Swell." *New York Times*. November 10: A6.

Lijphart, Arend. (1975) *The Politics of Accommodation: Pluralism and Democracy in the Netherlands*. Berkeley, CA: University of California Press.

Lindblom, Charles E. (1977) *Politics and Markets: The World's Political-Economic Systems*. New York: Basic Books.

Lipset, Seymour Marton. (1967) *The First New Nation: The United States in Historical and Comparative Perspectives*. Garden City, NY: Doubleday.

Lissak, Moshe. (1984) "Paradoxes of Israeli Civil–Military Relations: An Introduction," in Moshe Lissak (ed.) *Israeli Society and its Defense Establishment*. London: Frank Cass.

Liu, Lydia H. (1994) "The Female Body and Nationalist Discourse: Manchuria in Xiao Hong's *Field of Life and Death*," in Angela Zito and Tani E. Barlow (eds.) *Body, Subject and Power in China*. Chicago: University of Chicago Press.

Lloyd, Genevieve. (1984) *The Man of Reason: "Male" and "Female" in Western Philosophy*. Minneapolis: University of Minnesota Press.

Loftus, Belinda. (1990) *Mirrors: William III and Mother Ireland*. Dundrum, Co. Down, Northern Ireland: Picture Press.

Longva, Anh Nga. (1996) "Citizenship in the Gulf States: Conceptualisation and Practice." Paper presented to the Conference on Citizenship and the State in the Middle East. Oslo. November.

—— (1997) *Walls Built on Sand: Migration, Exclusion, and Society in Kuwait*. Boulder, CO: Westview.

Lorraine, Tamsin E. (1990) *Gender, Identity and the Production of Meaning*. Boulder, CO: Westview.

Love, Emily. (1994) "Equality and Political Asylum Law: For a Legislative Recognition of Gender Based Persecution." *Harvard Women's Law Journal*. 17: 133–156.

Lowi, Theodore J. (1969) *The End of Liberalism: Ideology, Policy, and the Crisis of Public Authority*. New York: W. W. Norton.

Ludden, David. (ed.). (1996a) *Contesting the Nation: Religion, Community and the Politics of Democracy in India*. Philadelphia: University of Pennsylvania Press.

—— (1996b) "Introduction. Ayodhya: A Window on the World," in David Ludden (ed.) *Contesting the Nation: Religion, Community and the Politics of Democracy in India*. Philadelphia: University of Pennsylvania Press.

McAuley, James W. (1994) *The Politics of Identity: A Loyalist Community in Belfast*. Aldershot: Avebury.

McClintock, Anne. (1991) "'No Longer in a Future Heaven': Women and Nationalism in South Africa." *Transition*. 51.

—— (1993) "Family Feuds: Gender, Nationalism, and the Family." *Feminist Review*. 44: 61–80.

—— (1995) *Imperial Leather: Race, Gender and Sexuality in the Colonial Contest*. New York: Routledge.

McGovern, Mark and Peter Shirlow. (1997) "Counter-Insurgency, Deindustrialization and the Political Economy of Ulster Loyalism," in Peter Shirlow and Mark McGovern (eds.) *Who are "the People"? Unionism, Protestantism and Loyalism in Northern Ireland*. London: Pluto Press.

MacKinnon, Catherine A. (1987) *Feminism Unmodified: Discourses on Life and Law*. Cambridge, MA: Harvard University Press.

—— (1989) *Toward a Feminist Theory of the State*. Cambridge, MA: Harvard University Press.

—— (1994) "Turning Rape into Pornography: Postmodern Genocide," in Alexandra Stiglmayer (ed.) *Mass Rape*. Lincoln: University of Nebraska Press.

McWilliams, Monica. (1995) "Struggling for Peace and Justice: Reflections on Women's Activism in Northern Ireland." *Journal of Women's History*. 6: 4/7: 1 (Winter/Spring): 13–39.

Mahmood, Tahir. (1977) *Muslim Personal Law: Role of State in Subcontinent*. Delhi: Vikas.

Malik, Yogendra K. and V. B. Singh. (1994) *Hindu Nationalists in India*. Boulder, CO: Westview.

Mandaza, Ibbo (ed.). (1986) *Zimbabwe: The Political Economy of Transition*. Harare: Codesria.

Mani, Lata (1990) "Contentious Tradition: The Debate on Sati in Colonial India," in Kumkum Sangari and Sudesh Vaid (eds.) *Recasting Women*. New Brunswick, NJ: Rutgers University Press.

Manicom, Linzi. (1992) "Ruling Relations: Rethinking the State and Gender in South African History." *Journal of African History*. 33: 441–465.

Manzo, Kathryn A. (1996) *Creating Boundaries: The Politics of Race and Nation*. Boulder, CO: Lynne Rienner.

Marchand, Marianne and Jane Parpart. (1995) "Exploding the Canon: an Introduction/Conclusion" in Marianne Marchand and Jane Parpart (eds.) *Feminism/Postmodernism/Development*. New York: Routledge.

Marr, David G. (1981) *Vietnamese Tradition on Trial, 1920–1945*. Berkeley, CA: University of California Press.

Marshall, Stuart. (1991) "The Contemporary Political Use of Gay History: The Third Reich," in Bad Object Choices (eds.) *How Do I Look? Queer Film and Video*. Seattle, WA: Bay Press.

Marshall, T. H. (1950) "Citizenship and Social Class," in T. H. Marshall, *Citizenship and Social Class and Other Essays*. Cambridge: Cambridge University Press.

Martin, Biddy. (1994) "Sexualities without Genders and other Queer Utopias," *diacritics* 24(2–3): 104–21.

Martin, David and Phyllis Johnson. (1981) *The Struggle for Zimbabwe*. New York: Monthly Review Press.

Mason, Mary Ann. (1994) *From Father's Property to Children's Rights: The History of Child Custody in the United States*. New York: Columbia University Press.

Mayall, James. (1990) *Nationalism and International Society*. Cambridge: Cambridge University Press.

Mayer, Ann Elizabeth. (1995) "Reform of Personal Status Laws in North Africa: A Problem of Islamic Law or of Mediterranean Laws?" *Middle East Journal*. 49: 3: 432–446.

Mayhall, Stacey. (1993) "Gendered Nationalism and 'New' Nation-States: Democratic Progress in Eastern Europe and the Former Soviet Union." *Fletcher Forum of World Affairs*. 17: 2: 91–99.

Memmi, A. (1965). *The Colonizer and the Colonized*. Boston, MA: Beacon.

Menon, Ritu and Kamala Bhasin. (1993) "Recovery, Rupture, Resistance: The State and Women during Partition." *Economic and Political Weekly* (Review of Women Studies). April.

Mernissi, Fatima. (1992) *Islam and Democracy: Fear of the Modern World*. Trans. Mary Jo Lakeland. Reading, MA: Addison-Wesley.

Mertus, Julie. (1993) "Women Warriors." *The Village Voice*. 32: 40 (October 5): 20.

Mill, John Stuart. (1929) *On the Subjection of Women*. New York: E. P. Dutton.

Miller, Laura. (1997) "Not Just Weapons of the Weak: Gender Harassment as a Form of Protest for Army Men." *Social Psychology Quarterly*. March: 32–51.

Miller, Robert Lee, Rick Wilford and Freda Donoghue. (1996) *Women and Political Participation in Northern Ireland*. Aldershot: Avebury.

Milosz, Czeslaw. (1993) "Swing Shift in the Baltics." *New York Review of Books*, 40: 18: 12–16.

Minh-ha, Trinh. (1989) *Woman, Native, Other*. Bloomington: Indiana University Press.

Mitchell, Juliet and Jacqueline Rose (eds.). (1983) *Feminine Sexuality: Jacques Lacan and the Ecole Freudienne*. New York: W. W. Norton.

Mittelman, James H. (ed.). (1996) *Globalization*. Boulder, CO: Lynne Rienner Press.

Moghadam, Valentine M. (ed.). (1992) *Privatization and Democratization in Central and Eastern Europe and the Soviet Union: The Gender Dimension*. Helsinki: World Institution for Development Economics Research of the United Nations University.

—— (1994a) *Identity Politics and Women: Cultural Reassertions and Feminism in International Perspective*. Boulder, CO: Westview.

—— (1994b) "Reform, Revolution and Reaction," in Valentine M. Moghadam (ed.) *Gender and National Identity*. London: Zed Books.

—— (1994c) "Introduction," in Valentine M. Moghadam (ed.) *Gender and National Identity*. London: Zed Books.

Mohanty, Chandra Talpade, Ann Russo and Lourdes Torres (eds.). (1991) *Third World Women and the Politics of Feminism*. Bloomington, IN: Indiana University Press.

Molyneux, Maxine. (1985) "Mobilization without Emancipation? Women's Interests, the State, and Revolution in Nicaragua." *Feminist Studies*. 11: 2: 227–254.

Moore, David. (1991) "The Ideological Formation of Zimbabwe's Ruling Class." *Journal of Southern African Studies*. 17: 473–495.

Morgan, Valerie and Grace Fraser. (1994) *The Company We Keep: Women, Community and Organizations*. Coleraine: Centre for the Study of Conflict and Centre for Research on Women, University of Ulster at Coleraine.

Moskos, Charles. (1990) "Army Women: A Look at the Life, the Sentiments, and the Aspirations – Including, for Some, Combat – of Women in the US Army." *The Atlantic*. August: 70–78.

—— (1993) "From Citizens' Army to Social Laboratory." *Wilson Quarterly*. 17: 83–94.

Mosse, George L. (1985) *Nationalism and Sexuality: Respectability and Abnormal Sexuality in Modern Europe*. New York: Howard Fertig.

Mostov, Julie. (1995) "Our Women? Their Women: Symbolic Boundaries, Territorial Markers, and Violence in the Balkans." *Peace and Change*. 20: 4: 515–529.

Motyl, Alexander J. (1992) "The Modernity of Nationalism: Nations, States and Nation-States in the Contemporary World." *Journal of International Affairs*. 45: 2: 307–323.

Moynihan, Daniel Patrick. (1993) *Pandemonium: Ethnicity in International Politics*. Oxford: Oxford University Press.

Muchena, Olivia. (1984) "Zimbabwe: It Can Only be Handled by Women," in Robin Morgan (ed.) *Sisterhood is Global*. New York: Anchor.

Mugabe, Robert. (1979) "Women's Liberation in the Zimbabwe Revolution." Opening address to the Zimbabwe African National Union (ZANU) Seminar. Xai-Xai-, Mozambique, May 21.

al-Mughni, Haya. (1993) *Women in Kuwait: The Politics of Gender*. London: Saqi Books.

—— (2000) "Women's Movements and the Autonomy of Civil Society in Kuwait," in Robin L. Teske and Mary Ann Tétreault (eds.) *Feminist Approaches to Social Movements, Community, and Power*. Vol. 1. *Conscious Acts and the Politics of Social Change*. Columbia, SC: University of South Carolina Press.

Mukhia, Harbans. (1996) "Communal Violence and the Transmutation of Identities," in Praful Bidwai *et al.* (eds.) *Religion, Religiosity and Communalism*. New Delhi: Manohar.

Murray, Charles and Richard Herrnstein. (1994) *The Bell Curve: Intelligence and Class Structure in America*. New York: Free Press.

Nairn, Tom. (1977) *The Break-up of Britain*. London: New Left Books.

Nandy, Ashish. (1990) "The Politics of Secularism and the Recovery of Religious Tolerance," in Veena Das (ed.) *Mirrors of Violence: Communities, Riots and Survivors in South Asia*. Delhi: Manohar.

Naples, Nancy A. (1997) "The 'New Consensus' on the Gendered 'Social Contract': The 1987–1988 US Congressional Hearings on Welfare Reform." *Signs*. 22: 1: 907–945.

al-Naqeeb, Khaldoun Hasan. (1990) *Society and State in the Gulf and Arab Peninsula: A Different Perspective*. Trans. L. M. Kenny. London: Routledge.

Natarajan, Nalini. (1994) "Woman, Nation, and Narration in Midnight's Children," in Inderpal Grewal and Caren Kaplan (eds.) *Scattered Hegemonies*. Minneapolis: University of Minnesota Press.

National Bank of Kuwait (NBK). (1997) "Special Topic: The Labor Force in Kuwait." *Economic and Financial Quarterly*. 3: 33–41.

Nauriya, Anil. (1996) "The Hindutva Judgements: A Warning Signal." *Economic and Political Weekly*. 31: 1: 10–13.

Ng, Roxana. (1993) "Racism, Sexism, and Nation Building in Canada," in Cameron McCarthy and Warren Crichlow (eds.) *Race, Identity, and Representation in Education*. New York: Routledge.

Nicholson, Linda J. (1990) "Introduction," in Linda J. Nicholson (ed.) *Feminism/Postmodernism*. London: Routledge.

O'Barr, Jean. (1976) "Pare Women: A Case of Political Involvement." *Rural Africana*. 29: 121–134.

O'Connor, Julia S. (1993) "Gender, Class and Citizenship in the Comparative Analysis of Welfare State Regimes: Theoretical and Methodological Issues." *British Journal of Sociology*. 44: 3: 501–518.

Okin, Susan Moller. (1979) *Women in Western Political Thought*. Princeton, NJ: Princeton University Press.

—— (1989) *Justice, Gender, and the Family*. New York: Basic Books.

Omvedt, G. (1980) *We Will Smash This Prison*. London: Zed Books.

Oron, Yisraela. (1995) "Women's Service in the IDF: Principles and Trends." The Israel Women's Network, *Women and IDF Service: Reality, Wish, and Vision – Proceedings*. 18–24.

Ortner, Sherry B. (1974) "Is Female to Male as Nature is to Culture?," in Michelle Zimbalist Rosaldo and Louise Lamphere (eds.) *Woman, Culture, and Society*. Stanford, CA: Stanford University Press.

Pandey, Gyanendra. (1990) *The Construction of Communalism in Colonial North India*. New Delhi: Viking.

—— (ed.). (1993) *Hindus and Others*. New Delhi: Viking.

Papić, Zarana. (1993) "Nationalism, Patriarchy and War." Paper delivered to the Network of East–West Women Public Policy Forum, Gender and Nationalism: The Impact of the Post-Communist Transition." Washington, DC. October 26–27.

—— (no date) "Nationalism, War and Gender: Ex-Femininity and Ex-Masculinity of Ex-Yugoslavian Ex-Citizens." Unpublished paper. Faculty of Philosophy, Department of Sociology, Belgrade.

Park, Kyung Ae. (1994) "Women and Revolution in China: The Sources of Constraints on Women's Emancipation," in Mary Ann Tétreault (ed.) *Women and Revolution in Africa, Asia and the New World*. Columbia, SC: University of South Carolina Press.

Parker, Andrew, Mary Russo, Doris Sommer and Patricia Yaeger (eds.). (1992a) *Nationalism and Sexualities*. New York: Routledge.

—— (1992b) "Introduction," in Andrew Parker *et al.* (eds.) *Nationalism and Sexualities*. New York: Routledge.

Patel, S. (1988) "Construction and Reconstruction of Women in Gandhi." *Economic and Political Weekly*. February 20: 377–387.

Pateman, Carole. (1988a) *The Sexual Contract*. Stanford, CA: Stanford University Press.

—— (1988b) "The Fraternal Social Contract." in John Keane (ed.) *Civil Society and the State*. London: Verso.

—— (1990) *The Disorder of Women: Women, Democracy, Feminism, and Social Theory*. Stanford, CA: Stanford University Press.

Pathak, Zakia and Rajeswari Sunder Rajan. (1989) "Shahbano." *Signs*. 14: 3: 558–571.

Patterson, Cynthia B. (1991) "Marriage and the Married Woman in Athenian Law," in Sarah B. Pomeroy (ed.) *Women's History and Ancient History*. Chapel Hill, NC: University of North Carolina Press.

Pendo, Elizabeth A. (1994) "Recognizing Violence against Women: Gender and the Hate Crime Statistics Act." *Harvard Women's Law Journal*. 17: 157–184.

Peri, Yoram. (1983) *Between Battles and Ballots: Israeli Military in Politics*. Cambridge: Cambridge University Press.

Peterson, V. Spike. (1988) "An Archeology of Domination: Historicizing Gender and Class in Early Western State Formation." PhD dissertation. The American University, Washington, DC.

—— (1992a). "Security and Sovereign States," in V. Spike Peterson (ed.) *Gendered States: Feminist (Re)visions of International Relations Theory*. Boulder, CO: Lynne Rienner Press.

—— (1992b) "Transgressing Boundaries: Theories of Knowledge, Gender, and International Relations." *Millennium*. 21: 2: 183–206.

—— (1993) "The Politics of Identity in International Relations." *Fletcher Forum of World Affairs*. 17: 2: 1–12

—— (1994) "Gendered Nationalisms." *Peace Review*. 6: 1: 77–83.

—— (1995a) "Reframing the Politics of Identity: Democracy, Globalization and Gender." *Political Expressions*. 1: 1: 1–16.

—— (1995b) "The Politics of Identity and Gendered Nationalism," in Laura

Neack, Patrick J. Haney and Jeane A. K. Hey (eds.) *Foreign Policy Analysis: Continuity and Change in Its Second Generation.* Englewood Cliffs, NJ: Prentice Hall.

—— (1996a) "Shifting Ground(s): Epistemological and Territorial Remapping in the Context of Globalization(s)," in Eleonore Kofman and Gillian Youngs (eds.) *Global Politics: Setting Agendas for the Year 2000.* London: Pinter Press.

—— (1996b) "The Politics of Identification in the Context of Globalization." *Women Studies International Forum.* 19: 1–2: 5–15.

—— (1997) "Whose Crisis? Early and Postmodern Masculinism," in Stephen Gill and James H. Mittelman (eds.) *Innovation and Transformation in International Studies.* Cambridge: Cambridge University Press.

—— (1998) "Making States, Making Sex." Paper presented to the Annual Meeting of the International Studies Association. Minneapolis, N. March.

—— and Larua Parisi. (1998) "Are Women Human? It's Not an Academic Question," in Tony Evans (ed.) *Human Rights Fifty Years On: A Radical Reappraisal.* Manchester: University of Manchester Press and New York: St. Martin's Press.

Pettman, Jan Jindy. (1992) "Women, Nationalism and the State: Towards an International Feminist Perspective." Occasional Paper no. 4 in Gender and Development Studies. Bangkok: Asian Institute of Technology.

—— (1996) *Worlding Women: A Feminist International Politics.* New York: Routledge.

Pfaff, William. (1993) *The Wrath of Nations.* New York: Simon & Schuster.

Phelps, Edith M. (ed.) (1912) *Selected Articles on Woman Suffrage.* Minneapolis: H. W. Wilson.

Phillips, Anne. (1991) *Engendering Democracy.* Philadelphia: Pennsylvania State University Press.

Pignone, Mary Margaret. (1992) "On Becoming a Global Citizen – Praxis in Identity Politics: A Participatory Development Education Project." PhD dissertation. The American University, Washington, DC.

Pine, Rachel and Julie Mertus. (1993) *Meeting the Health Needs of Women Survivors of the Balkan Conflict.* New York: Center for Reproductive Law and Policy.

Polanyi, Karl. (1944) *The Great Transformation.* New York: Farrar & Rinehart.

Porter, Bruce. (1993) "Can American Democracy Survive?" *Commentary.* 96: 5: 37–40.

Quindlen, Anna. (1994) "Barbie at 35," *New York Times.* September 10: A19.

al-Rahmani, Eqbal. (1996) "The Impact of Traditional Domestic Sexual Division of Labor on Women's Status: The Case of Kuwait." *Research in Human Capital and Development.* 9: 79–101.

Ranchod-Nilsson, Sita. (1992a) "'Educating Eve': The Women's Club Movement and Political Consciousness Among Rural African Women in Southern Rhodesia, 1950–1980," in Karen Tranberg Hansen (ed.) African Encounters with Domesticity. Rutgers, NJ: Rutgers University Press.

—— (1992b) "Gender Politics and National Liberation: Women's Participation in the Liberation of Zimbabwe." PhD dissertation, Northwestern University.

—— (1994) "'This, Too, is a Way of Fighting': Rural Women's Participation in Zimbabwe's Liberation War," in Mary Ann Tétreault (ed.) *Women in Revolution in Africa, Asia and the New World.* Columbia, SC: University of South Carolina Press.

—— (1997) "Zimbabwe: Women, Cultural Crisis, and the Reconfiguration of the One-Party State," in Leonardo Villalón and Philip Huxtable (eds.) *The African State at Critical Juncture: Between Disintegration and Reconfiguration.* Boulder, CO: Lynne Rienner.

Ranger, Terence. (1985) *Peasant Consciousness and Guerrilla War.* Berkeley, CA: University of California Press.

Ravia, Haim and Emanuel Rosen. (1987) *So You've Been Drafted! A Guide to New I.D.F. Inductees.* Jerusalem: Maxwell-Macmillan-Keter.

Reich, Wilhelm. (1970) *The Mass Psychology of Fascism.* New York: Farrar, Straus & Giroux.

Rejali, Darius M. (1996) "After Feminist Analyses of Bosnian Violence." *Peace Review.* 8: 3: 365–371.

Rolston, Bill. (1992) *Drawing Support: Murals of War and Peace.* Belfast: Beyond the Pale.

—— (1995) *Drawing Support II: Murals of War and Peace.* Belfast: Beyond the Pale.

Rooney, Eilish and Margaret Woods. (1995) *Women, Community and Politics in Northern Ireland: A Belfast Study.* Belfast: University of Ulster.

Rose, Jacqueline. (1993) *Why War?* Oxford: Blackwell.

Rosen, Leora N., Doris B. Durand, Paul D. Bliese, *et al.* (1996) "Cohesion and Readiness in Gender-Integrated Combat Service Support Units: The Impact of Acceptance of Women and Gender Ratio." *Armed Forces and Society: An Interdisciplinary Journal.* Fall.

Rosenberg, David and Harold Bloom. (1990) *The Book of J.* New York: Grove Weidenfeld.

Rosenberg, Justin. (1990) "A Non-Realist Theory of Sovereignty? Giddens' *The Nation-State and Violence.*" *Millennium.* 19: 2: 249–259.

Rowbotham, Sheila. (1992) *Women and Movement.* London: Routledge.

Roy, Kumkum. (1995) "Where Women are Worshipped, There the Gods Rejoice": The Mirage of the Ancestress of the Hindu Woman," in T. Sarkar and U. Butalia (eds.) *Women and the Hindu Right. A Collection of Essays.* New Delhi: Kali for Women.

Rubin, Gayle. (1975) "The Traffic in Women: Notes on the 'Political Economy' of Sex," in Rayna R. Reiter (ed.) *Toward an Anthropology of Women.* New York: Monthly Review Press.

—— (1984) "Thinking sex: Notes for a Radical Theory of the Politics of Sexuality," in Carole S. Vance (ed.) Pleasure and Danger: Exploring Female Sexuality. Boston, MA: Routledge.

Rudolph, L. I. and S. H. Rudolph (1967). *The Modernity of Modernity.* Chicago: University of Chicago Press.

Rudolph, S. H. (1961). "Consensus and Conflict in Indian Politics." *World Politics,* 13: 3.

—— and L. I. Rudolph (1983). *Gandhi, The Traditional Roots of Charisma.* Chicago: University of Chicago Press.

Ruggie, John Gerard. (1986) "Continuity and Transformation in the World Polity: Toward a Neorealist Synthesis," in Robert O. Keohane (ed.) *Neorealism and its Critics.* New York: Columbia University Press.

Rushdie, Salman. (1988) *The Satanic Verses.* Dover, DE: The Consortium.

Said, Edward (1978) *Orientalism.* New York: Vintage.

—— (1979, 1992) *The Question of Palestine.* New York: Vintage

—— (1986) *After the Last Sky.* London: Faber.

—— (1994) *Culture and Imperialism.* New York: Vintage.

Salecl, Renata. (1992) "Nationalism, Anti-Semitism, and Anti-Feminism in Eastern Europe." *New German Critique.* 57: (Fall): 54–59.

—— (1994) *The Spoils of Freedom*. New York: Routledge.

Sales, Rosemary. (1997) *Women Divided: Gender, Religion and Politics in Northern Ireland*. London: Routledge.

Sangari, Kumkum. (1995) "Politics of Diversity: Religious Communities and Multiple Patriarchies." *Economic and Political Weekly*. 30: 51: 3287–3310.

—— (1996) Part II, *Economic and Political* Weekly. 30: 52: 3381–3389.

Sarkar, Tanika. (1995) "Heroic Women, Mother Goddesses: Family and Organization in Hindutva Politics," In T. Sarkar and U. Butalia (eds.) *Women and the Hindu Right. A Collection of Essays*. New Delhi: Kali for Women.

—— and Urvashi Butalia (eds.). (1995) *Women and the Hindu Right: A Collection of Essays*. New Delhi: Kali for Women.

Sasser, Charles. (1992) "Women in Combat: One Grunt's Opinion." *Soldier of Fortune*. March: 40.

Savarkar, Vinayak Damodar. (1971) *The Six Glorious Epochs of Indian History*. Delhi: Rajdhani Granthagar.

—— (1989) *Hindutva: Who is a Hindu?* 6th edn. Delhi Bhartiya Sahitya Sadan.

SCC (India). (1992) Supreme Court Case 169, Manohar Joshi v. Nitin Bhaurao Patil

—— (1996) Supreme Court Case 130, Dr. Ramesh Yashwant Prabhoo v. Prabhakar Kunte

Schiff, Rebecca. (1992) "Civil–Military Relations Reconsidered: Israel as an 'Uncivil' State." *Security Studies*. 1: 4: 636–658.

Schmidt, Elizabeth. (1990) "Men, Women and the Law in Colonial Zimbabwe, 1890–1939." *Journal of South African Studies*. 16: 4: 622–648.

—— (1992) *Peasants, Traders, and Wives: Shona Women in the History of Zimbabwe, 1870–1939*. Portsmouth, NH: Heinemann.

Schmidt, Michael. (1993) *The New Reich: Violent Extremism in Unified Germany and Beyond*. New York: Pantheon.

Scholte, Jan Aart. (1997) "Global Capitalism and the State." *International Affairs*. 73: 3: 427–452.

Scott, J. W. (1988) "Deconstructing Equality – versus Difference: Or the Use of Poststructuralist Theory in Feminism." *Feminist Studies*. 14: 1: 33–50.

Sedghi, Hamideh. (1994) "Third World Feminist Perspectives on World Politics," in Peter R. Beckman and Francine D'Amico (eds.) *Women, Gender and World Politics*. Westport, CT: Bergin & Garvey.

Sedgwick, Eve Kosofsky. (1985) *Between Men: English Literature and Male Homosocial Desire*. New York: Columbia University Press.

—— (1990) *Epistemology of the Closet*. Berkeley, CA: University of California Press.

—— (1992) "Nationalisms and Sexualities in the Age of Wilde," in Andrew Parker *et al.* (eds.) *Nationalisms and Sexualities*. New York: Routledge.

—— (1993) *Tendencies*. Durham, NC: Duke University Press.

See, Katherine O'Sullivan. (1986) *First World Nationalisms: Class and Ethnic Politics in Northern Ireland and Quebec*. Chicago: University of Chicago Press.

Seidman, Gay. (1984) "Women in Zimbabwe: Postindependence Struggles." *Feminist Studies*. 10: 419–440.

Seifert, Ruth. (1994) "War and Rape: A Preliminary Analysis," in Alexandra Stiglmayer (ed.) *Mass Rape: The War against Women in Bosnia-Herzegovina*. Lincoln: University of Nebraska Press.

Sells, Michael A. (1996) *The Bridge Betrayed: Religion and Genocide in Bosnia*. Berkeley, CA: University of California Press.

Semyanov, M. and V. Kraus. (1993) "Gender, Ethnicity and Income Equality: The Israeli Experience" in Yael Azmon and Daphna Izraeli (eds.) *Women in Israel*. New Brunswick, NJ: Transaction.

Seton-Watson, Hugh. (1977) *Nations and States*. London: Methuen.

Shah, Nasra M. (1994) "Changing Roles of Kuwaiti Women in Kuwait: Implications for Fertility." Paper presented to the Conference on Women's Role in Cultural, Social, and Economic Development. Kuwait. April.

—— and Sulayman S. al-Qudsi. (1990) "Female Work Roles in a Traditional, Oil Economy." *Research in Human Capital and Development*. 6: 213–46

Shapiro, Michael. (1993) *Reading Adam Smith: Desire, History and Value*. Newbury Park, CA: Sage.

Sharabi, Hisham. (1988) *Neopatriarchy: A Theory of Distorted Change in Arab Society*. New York: Oxford University Press.

Sharoni, Simona. (1994) "Homefront as Battlefield: Military Occupation and Violence Against Women," in Tamar Mayer (ed.) *Women and the Occupation: The Politics of Change*. London: Routledge.

—— (1995) *Gender and the Israeli-Palestinian Conflict*. Syracuse, NY: Syracuse University Press.

Shirlow, Peter and Mark McGovern (eds.). (1997) *Who are "the People"? Unionism, Protestantism and Loyalism in Northern Ireland*. London: Pluto Press.

Shklar, Judith. (1991) *American Citizenship: The Quest for Inclusion*. Cambridge, MA: Harvard University Press.

Šiklová, J. (2000) "Women and the Charta 77 Movement in Czechoslovakia," in Robin Teske and Mary Ann Tétreault (eds.) *Feminist Approaches to Social Movements, Community, and Power*. Vol. 1. *Conscious Acts: The Politics of Social Change*. Columbia: University of South Carolina Press.

Skoçpol, Theda. (1992) *Protecting Soldiers and Mothers: The Political Origins of Social Policy in the United States*. Cambridge, MA: Harvard University Press.

Slobin, Greta N. (1992) "Revolution Must Come First: Reading V. Arsenov's Island of Crimea," in Andrew Parker *et al.* (eds.). New York: Routledge.

Smith, Annie Marie. (1994) *New Right Discourse on Race and Sexuality*. New York: Cambridge University Press.

Smith, Anthony. (1971) *Theories of Nationalism*, 2nd edn 1983. New York: Harper & Row.

—— (1973) "Nationalism: A Trend Report and Annotated Bibliography." *Current Sociology*. 21: 3. The Hague: Mouton.

—— (1976) *Nationalist Movements*. New York: St. Martin's Press.

—— (1979) *Nationalism in the Twentieth Century*. Oxford: Martin Robertson.

—— (1981) *The Ethnic Revival in the Modern World*. Cambridge: Cambridge University Press.

—— (1983) *State and Nation in the Third World*. Brighton: Harvester.

—— (1986) *The Ethnic Origins of Nations*. Oxford: Blackwell.

—— (1991a) *National Identity*. New York: Penguin.

—— (1991b) "The Nation: Invented, Imagined, Reconstituted?" *Millennium*. 20: 3: 353–368.

—— (1994) *Nationalism*, edited with John Hutchinson. Oxford: Oxford University Press.

—— (1995) *Nations and Nationalism in a Global Era.* Cambridge: Polity.

Smooha, Sammy. (1984) "Ethnicity and Army in Israel: Theses for Discussion and Research." *Nation State and International Research* (in Hebrew).

—— (1993) "Class, Ethnic and National Cleavages and Democracy in Israel," in Sprinzak and Larry Diamond (eds.) *Israeli Democracy under Stress.* Boulder, CO: Lynne Rienner.

—— and Vered Kraus. (1985) "Ethnicity as a Factor in Status Attainment in Israel." *Research in Social Stratification and Mobility.* 4: 151–175.

Snead, James. (1990) "European Pedigrees/African Contagions: Nationality, Narrative, and Communality in Tutuola, Achebe, and Reed," in Homi K. Bhabha (ed.) *Nation and Narration.* New York: Routledge.

Som, Reba. (1994) "Jawaharlal Nehru and the Hindu Code: A Victory of Symbol over Substance?" *Modern Asian Studies.* 28: 165–194.

Sommer, Doris (1991) *Foundational Fictions: The National Romances of Latin America.* Berkeley, CA: University of California Press.

Sophocles. (1982) *Three Theban Plays.* Trans. Robert Fagles. New York: Viking Penguin.

Soros, George. (1993) "Bosnia and Beyond." *New York Review of Books.* 40: 13: 15.

Spellberg, D. A. (1994) *Politics, Gender, and the Islamic Past: The Legacy of 'Aisha' Bint Abi Bakr.* New York: Columbia University Press.

Spelman, Elizabeth. (1988) *Inessential Woman: Problems of Exclusion in Feminist Thought.* Boston, MA: Beacon.

Spivak, Gayatri Chakravorty. (1993) *Outside the Teaching Machine.* New York: Routledge.

Springborg, Patricia. (1986). "Politics, Primordialism, and Orientalism: Marx, Aristotle, and the Myth of the Gemeinschaft." *American Political Science Review.* 80: 1: 185–211.

Srinivasan, A. (1987) "Women and Reform of Indian Tradition: Gandhian Alternative to Liberalism." *Economic and Political Weekly.* December 19: 2225–2228.

Stacey, Judith. (1983) *Patriarchy and Socialist Revolution in China.* Berkeley, CA: University of California Press.

Stanton, Elizabeth Cady. (1860/1996) "Address to the New York State Legislature," in Kenneth Dolbeare (ed.) *American Political Thought,* 3rd edn. Chatham, NJ: Chatham House.

—— Susan B. Anthony and Matilda Joslyn Gage (eds.). (1882) *History of Woman Suffrage.* Volume II. New York: Fowler & Wells.

Staunton, Irene (ed.). (1990) *Mothers of the Revolution.* Harare: Baobab.

Steans, Jill. (1998) *Gender and International Relations.* Cambridge: Polity Press.

Stevens, Jacqueline (1999) *Reproducing the State.* Princeton, NJ: Princeton University Press.

Stiehm, Judith. (1982) "The Protected, the Protector, the Defender." *Women's Studies International Forum.* 5: 3/4: 367–376.

Stiglmayer, Alexandra. (1994) "The Rapes in Bosnia-Herzegovina," in Alexandra Stiglmayer (ed.) *Mass Rape.* Lincoln: University of Nebraska Press.

Stone, Lawrence. (1979) *The Family, Sex and Marriage in England, 1500–1800.* New York: Harper Torchbooks.

Stoneman, Colin (ed.). (1988) *Zimbabwe's Prospects: Issues of Race, Class, State, and Capital in Southern Africa.* London: Macmillan.

Strom, Yale. (1993) *Uncertain Roads, Searching for the Gypsies.* New York: Four Winds Press.

Sulloway, Frank J. (1996) *Born to Rebel: Birth Order, Family Dynamics, and Creative Lives*. New York: Pantheon.

al-Sultan, Najat H. (1976) "The Professional Kuwaiti Woman Vis à Vis the Situation of Woman." Paper presented to the Association of Arab University Graduates. New York. October.

Swirski, Barbara and Marilyn P. Safir (eds.). (1991) *Calling the Equality Bluff: Women in Israel*. New York: Pergamon.

Sylvester, Christine. (1986) "Zimbabwe's 1985 Elections: A Search for National Mythology." *Journal of Modern African Studies*. 24: 427–443.

—— (1990) "Simultaneous Revolutions: The Zimbabwean Case." *Journal of Southern African Studies*. 16: 3: 452–475.

—— (1991) *Zimbabwe: The Terrain of Contradictory Development*. Boulder, CO: Westview.

Tal, Rami. (1995) "The Israeli Press." *Ariel*. 99–100: 128–142.

Taylor, Charles. (1992) *Multiculturalism and the Politics of Recognition*. Princeton, NJ: Princeton University Press.

Taylor, Peter. (1998) "The Modernity of Westphalia." Paper presented at the Annual Meeting of the International Studies Association, Minneapolis, March.

Tekiner, Roselle. (1994) "The Nonexistence of Israeli Nationality." *Contention*. 4: 1: 29–45.

Tétreault, Mary Ann. (1988) "Gender Belief Systems and the Integration of Women in the US Military." *Minerva Quarterly Report*. 6: 1: 44–71.

—— (1991) "Autonomy, Necessity, and the Small State: Ruling Kuwait in the Twentieth Century." *International Organization*. 45: 4: 565–591.

—— (1992) "Kuwait: The Morning After." *Current History*. January: 6–10.

—— (1993a) "Civil Society in Kuwait: Protected Spaces and Women's Rights." *Middle East Journal*. 47: 2: 275–291.

—— (1993b) "Independence, Sovereignty, and Vested Glory: Oil and Politics in the Second Gulf War." *Orient*. 34: 1: 87–103.

—— (ed.). (1994) *Women and Revolution in Africa, Asia, and the New World*. Columbia, SC: University of South Carolina Press.

—— (1995a) *The Kuwait Petroleum Corporation and the Economics of the New World Order*. Westport, CT: Quorum.

—— (1995b) "Patterns of Culture and Democratization in Kuwait." *Studies in Comparative International Development*, 30: 2: 26–45.

—— (1997a) "Accountability or Justice? Rape as a War Crime," in Laurel Richardson, Verta Taylor, and Nancy Whittier (eds.) *Feminist Frontiers IV*. New York: McGraw-Hill.

—— (1997b) "Designer Democracy in Kuwait." *Current History*. January: 36–39.

—— (1998a) "Formal Politics, Meta-Space, and the Construction of Civil Life," in Andrew Light and Jonathan M. Smith (eds.) *Philosophy and Geography II: The Production of Public Space*. Lanham, MD: Rowman and Littlefield.

—— (1998b) "Spheres of Liberty, Conflict, and Power: The Public Lives of Private Persons," *Citizenship Studies*. 2: 2: 273–289.

—— (2000) *Stories of Democracy: Politics and Society in Contemporary Kuwait*. New York: Columbia University Press.

—— and Haya al-Mughni. (1995) "Modernization and its Discontents: State and Gender in Kuwait." *Middle East Journal*. 49: 3: 403–417.

—— (2000) "Citizenship, Gender, and the Politics of Quasi-states," in Suad Joseph (ed.) *Gender and Citizenship in the Middle East*. Syracuse, NY: Syracuse University Press.

——, Tracey A. Johnstone, Jeffrey Ling and Lynette Hornung. (1997) "Final Report: Gender and International Relations, Part II: Effects of Gender on Publication Records of Scholars in International Studies." Report presented to the Governing Board of the International Studies Association. March.

Thapar, Romilla. (1975) *The Past and Prejudice*. New Delhi: National Book Trust.

—— (1989) "Imagined Religious Communities? Ancient History and the Modern Search for an Indian Identity." *Modern Asian Studies*. 23: 2: 209–231.

—— (1992a) *Interpreting Early India*. Delhi: Oxford University Press.

—— (1992b) "Ideology and the Interpretation of Early Indian History," in Romilla Thapar, *Interpreting Early* India. Delhi: Oxford University Press.

Theweleit, Klaus. (1987) *Male Fantasies*. Vol. 1. *Women, Floods, Bodies, History*. Trans. Stephen Conway with Erica Carter and Christ Turner. Minneapolis: University of Minnesota Press.

Tickner, J. Ann. (1992) *Gender in International Relations: Feminist Perspectives on Achieving Global Security*. New York: Columbia University Press.

—— (1996) "Identity in International Relations Theory: Feminist Perspectives," in Yosef Lapid and Friedrich Kratochwil (eds.) *The Return of Culture and Identity in IR Theory*. Boulder, CO: Lynne Rienner Press.

Tillion, Germaine. (1983) *The Republic of Cousins: Women's Oppression in Mediterranean Society*. London: Al Saqi Books

Tilly, Charles. (1975). *The Formation of National States in Western Europe*. Princeton, NJ: Princeton University Press.

—— (1992) "Futures of European States." *Social Research*. 59: 4: 705–717.

Tohidi, Nayereh. (1994) "Modernity, Islamization, and Women in Iran," in Valentine M. Moghadam (ed.) *Gender and National Identity*. London: Zed Books.

Tress, Madeleine. (1994) "Halakha, Zionism and Gender," in Valentine M. Moghadam (ed.) *Identity Politics and Women*. Boulder, CO: Westview.

True, Jacqui. (1993) "National Selves and Feminine Others." *Fletcher Forum of World Affairs*. 17: 2: 75–89.

—— (1996) "Fit Citizens for the British Empire?: Class-ifying Racial and Gendered Subjects in Godzone (New Zealand)," in Brackette F. Williams (ed.) *Women Out of Place*. New York: Routledge.

Truscott, Kate. (1985) "The Wedza Project: Its Impact on Farmer Households, Agricultural Production and Extension." Wedza Evaluation no. 10. Harare: Agritex.

Tuana, Nancy. (1993) *The Less Noble Sex: Scientific, Religious and Philosophical Conceptions of Woman's Nature*. Bloomington, IN: Indiana University Press.

Turner, Bryan S. (1996) "Islam, Civil Society and Citizenship: Some Reflections on the Sociology of Citizenship and Islamic Societies." Paper presented to the Conference on Citizenship and the State in the Middle East. Oslo. November.

Udovicki, Jasminka and James Ridgeway (eds.). (1995) *Yugoslavia's Ethnic Nightmare*. New York: Lawrence Hill.

United Nations High Commissioner for Refugees. (1993) *The State of the World's Refugees: The Challenge of Protection*. Harmondsworth: Penguin.

Urdang, Stephanie. (1979) *Fighting Two Colonialisms*. New York: Monthly Review Press.

—— (1989) *And Still They Dance: Women, War and the Struggle for Change in Mozambique*. London: Earthscan.

Vajpayee, Atal Behari. (1992a) "Secularism: the Indian Concept." Dr. Rajendra Prasad Lecture, organized by All India Radio, December 2 and 3.

—— (1992b) Speech on Ayodhya issue in *Lok Sabha*, December 17.

—— (1995) *Meri Ikyavan Kavitaye* (My Fifty-One Poems). New Delhi: Kitabghar.

Van Allen, Judith. (1974) "Memsahib, Militante and Femme Libre: Political and Apolitical Styles of Modern African Women," in Jane Jacquette (ed.) *Women and Politics*. New York: Wiley.

—— (1976) "'Aba Riots' or Igbo 'Women's War'? Ideology, Stratification, and the Invisibility of Women," in Nancy Hfkin and Edna Bay (eds.) *Women in Africa: Studies in Social and Economic Change*. Stanford, CA: Stanford University Press.

Vickers, Jill McCalla. (1990) "At His Mother's Knee: Sex/Gender and the Construction of National Identities," in Greta Hoffmann Nemiroff (ed.) *Women and Men: Interdisciplinary Readings on Gender*. Toronto: Fitzhenry & Whiteside.

Walby, Sylvia. (1992) "Woman and Nation." *International Journal of Comparative Sociology*. 33: 81–100 (January/April): 83.

Walker, Cherryl. (1982) *Women and Resistance in Southern Africa*. London: Onyx Press.

Wallerstein, Immanuel. (1991) "The Ideological Tensions of Capitalism: Universalism versus Racism and Sexism," in Etienne Balibar and Immanuel Wallerstein, *Race Nation, Class: Ambiguous Identities*. New York: Verso.

Waltz, Kenneth N. (1979) *Theory of International Politics*. Reading, MA: Addison-Wesley.

Walzer, Michael. (1970) *Obligations: Essays on Disobedience, War and Citizenship*. Cambridge, MA: Harvard University Press.

Warner, Marina. (1982) *Joan of Arc: The Image of Female Heroism*. New York: Vintage.

Warner, Michael (ed.) (1993) *Fear of a Queer Planet*. Minneapolis, MN: University of Minnesota Press.

Weber, Cynthia. (1995) *Simulating Sovereignty: Intervention, the State and Symbolic Exchange*. New York: Cambridge University Press.

Weiss, Ruth. (1986) *The Women of Zimbabwe*. London: Kesho.

Wells, Julia. (1991) "The Rise and Fall of Motherism as a Force in Black Women's Resistance Movements." Paper presented at the Conference on Gender in Southern Africa. University of Natal, Durban. 30 January – 2 February.

Werbner, Richard. (1991) *Tears of the Dead*. Harare: Baobab Books.

West, Lois. (ed.). (1997) *Feminist Nationalism*. New York: Routledge.

Whitney, Craig. (1993) "Germans Begin to Recognize Danger in Neo-Nazi Upsurge." *New York Times*. October 21: A1.

Wilford, Rick. (1996) "Representing Women," in *Democratic Dialogue Report no. 4*. Belfast: Democratic Dialogue.

—— Robert Miller, Yolanda Bell and Freda Donoghue. (1993) "In their Own Voices: Women Councillors in Northern Ireland." *Public Administration*. 71: 341–355.

Wipper, Audrey. (1975–76) "The Maendeleo ya Wanawake Organization: the Co-optation of Leadership." *African Studies Review*. 18: 99–119.

Wittig, Monique. (1980) "The Straight Mind." *Feminist Issues*. 1: 1: 103–111.

Wolf, Eric. (1982) *Europe and the People without History*. Berkeley, CA: University of California Press.

Wolkinson, Benjamin W. (1991) "Ethnic Discrimination in Employment: The Israeli Experience." *Journal of Ethnic Studies*. 19: 3.

Women and Citizenship Research Group. (1995) *Women and Citizenship: Power, Participation and Choice*. Belfast: Women and Citizenship Research Group.

Wood, Ellen Meiskins. (1994) *Democracy Against Capitalism: Renewing Historical Materialism*. Cambridge: Cambridge University Press.

Woolf, Virginia. (1938) *The Three Guineas*. London: Harcourt, Brace & Ward.

Yanagisako, Sylvia and Carol Delaney. (1995) "Naturalizing Power," in S. Yanagisako and C. Delaney (eds.) *Naturalizing Power: Essays in Feminist Cultural Analysis*. New York: Routledge.

Yeatmann, Anna. (1994) *Postmodern Revisionings of the Political*. New York: Routledge.

Yishai, Yael. (1997) *Between the Flag and the Banner: Women in Israeli Politics*. Albany, NY: State University of New York Press.

Young, C. (1976) *The Politics of Cultural Pluralism*. Madison, Wl: University of Wisconsin Press.

Yuval-Davis, Nira. (1985). "Front and Rear: The Sexual Division of Labour in the Israeli Army." *Feminist Studies*. 11: 3: 649–676.

—— (1997) *Gender and Nation*. London: Sage.

—— and Floya Anthias (eds.). (1989) *Woman–Nation–State*. London: Macmillan.

Zalewski, Marysia and Cynthia Enloe. (1995) "Questions about Identity in International Relations," in Ken Booth and Steve Smith (eds.) *International Relations Theory Today*. Oxford: Polity Press.

—— and Jane Parpart (eds.). (1998) *Feminism, Masculinity and Power in International Relations*. Boulder, CO: Westview,

—— and Jane Parpart (eds.). (1998) *The "Man" Question in International Relations*. Boulder, CO: Westview Press.

Index